DATE DUE

LEGAL RESEARCH AND WRITING

OTHER TITLES IN THE SERIES

Ransford C. Pyle, *Foundations of Law for Paralegals: Cases, Commentary, and Ethics,* 1992

Peggy N. Kerley, Paul A. Sukys, Joanne Banker Hames, *Civil Litigation for the Paralegal,* 1992.

Jonathan Lynton, Donna Masinter, Terri Mick Lyndall, *Law Office Management for Paralegals,* 1992.

Daniel Hall, *Criminal Law and Procedure,* 1992.

Daniel Hall, *Survey of Criminal Law,* 1992.

Jonathan Lynton, Terri Mick Lyndall, *Legal Ethics and Professional Responsibility,* 1994.

Michael Kearns, *The Law of Real Property,* 1994.

Angela Schneeman, *The Law of Corporations, Partnerships, and Sole Proprietorships,* 1993.

William Buckley, *Torts and Personal Injury Law,* 1993.

Gordon W. Brown, *Administration of Wills, Trusts, and Estates,* 1993.

Richard Stim, *Intellectual Property: Patients, Copyrights, and Trademarks,* 1994.

Ransford C. Pyle, *Family Law,* 1994.

Jack Handler, *Ballentine's Law Dictionary: Legal Assistant Edition,* 1994.

Jonathan Lynton, *Ballentine's Thesaurus for Legal Research & Writing,* 1994.

Daniel Hall, *Administrative Law,* 1994.

Angela Schneeman, *Paralegals in American Law,* 1994.

Eric M. Gansberg, *Paralegals in New York Law,* 1994.

Pamela Tepper, *The Law of Contracts and the Uniform Commercial Code,* 1995.

Jonathan Lynton, *Ballentine's Legal Dictionary and Thesaurus,* 1995.

Susan Covins, *Federal Taxation,* 1995.

C. B. Estrin, *Everything You Need to Know About Being a Legal Assistant, 1995.*

Karen Treffinger, *Life Outside the Law Firm: Non-Traditional Careers for Paralegals,* 1995.

Cathy Okrent, *Legal Terminology with Flash Cards,* 1995.

LEGAL RESEARCH AND WRITING

Carol M. Bast, Esq.

Lawyers Cooperative Publishing

Delmar Publishers
I(T)P An International Thomson Publishing Company

Albany • Bonn • Boston • Cincinnati • Detroit • London • Madrid • Melbourne
Mexico City • New York • Pacific Grove • Paris • San Francisco • Singapore • Tokyo
Toronto • Washington

NOTICE TO THE READER

ny of the products described herein or perform any independent analysis in connection
ed herein. Publisher does not assume, and expressly disclaims, any obligation to obtain
ided to it by the manufacturer.

and adopt all safety precautions that might be indicated by the activities herein and to
instructions contained herein, the reder willingly assumes all risks in connections with
such instructions.

The publisher makes no representation or warranties of any kind, including but not limited to, the warranties of fitness for particular purpose or merchantability, nor are any such representations implied with respect to the material set forth herein, and the publisher takes no responsibility with respect to such material. The publisher shall not be liable for any special consequential, or exemplary damages resulting, in whole or part, from the readers' use of, or reliance upon, this material.

Cover Photo Courtesy of: Michael Groll
Cover Design: Essinger Design

Delmar Staff:
Acquisitions Editor: Jay Whitney
Developmental Editor: Christopher Anzalone
Project Editor: Carolyn Ellis
Production Coordinator: Jennifer Gaines
Art & Design Coordinator: Douglas Hyldelund

Printed in the United States of America

For more information contact:

Delmar Publishers
3 Columbia Circle, Box 15015
Albany, New York 12212-5015

International Thomson Publishing Europe
Berkshsire House 168–173
High Holborn
London WC1V7AA
England

Thomas Nelson Australia
102 Dodds Street
South Melbourne, 3205
Victoria, Australia

Nelson Canada
1120 Birchmount Road
Scarborough, Ontario
Canada M1K 5G4

International Thomson Editores
Campos Eliseos 385, Piso 7
Col Palanco
11560 Mexico D F Mexico

International Thomson Publishing GmbH
Köigswinterer Strasse 418
53227 Bonn
Germany

International Thomson Publishing Asia
221 Henderson Road
#05-10 Henderson Building
Singapore 0315

International Thomson Publishing-Japan
Hirakawacho Kyowa Building, 3F
2-2-1 Hirakawacho
Chiyoda-ku, Tokyo 102
Japan

1 2 3 4 5 6 7 8 9 10 XXX 01 00 99 98 97 96 95

Library of Congress Cataloging-in-Publication Data

Bast, Carol M.
Legal research and writing/Carol M. Bast
p. cm.
Includes index.
ISBN 0-8273-6215-3
1. Legal research—United States. 2. Legal composition.
I. Title.
KF240.B27 1995
340'.072073—dc20

94-29908
CIP

CONTENTS

APPENDIXES

AM JUR LEGAL FORMS 2D: A COMPILATION OF BUSINESS AND LEGAL FORMS DEALING WITH A VARIETY OF SUBJECT MATTERS.

AM JUR PLEADING AND PRACTICE FORMS, REV: MODEL PRACTICE FORMS FOR EVERY STAGE OF A LEGAL PROCEEDING.

AM JUR PROOF OF FACTS: A SERIES OF ARTICLES THAT GUIDE THE READER IN DETERMINING WHICH FACTS ARE ESSENTIAL TO A CASE AND HOW TO PROVE THEM.

AM JUR TRIALS: A SERIES OF ARTICLES DISCUSSING EVERY ASPECT OF PARTICULAR SETTLEMENTS AND TRIALS WRITTEN BY 180 CONSULTING SPECIALISTS.

UNITED STATES CODE SERVICE: A COMPLETE AND AUTHORITATIVE ANNOTATED FEDERAL CODE THAT FOLLOWS THE EXACT LANGUAGE OF THE STATUTES AT LARGE AND DIRECTS YOU TO THE COURT AND AGENCY DECISIONS CONSTRUING EACH PROVISION.

ALR AND ALR FEDERAL: SERIES OF ANNOTATIONS PROVIDING IN-DEPTH ANALYSES OF ALL THE CASE LAW ON PARTICULAR LEGAL ISSUES.

U.S. SUPREME COURT REPORTS, L ED 2D: EVERY REPORTED U.S. SUPREME COURT DECISION PLUS IN-DEPTH DISCUSSIONS OF LEADING ISSUES.

FEDERAL PROCEDURE, L ED: A COMPREHENSIVE, A—Z TREATISE ON FEDERAL PROCEDURE—CIVIL, CRIMINAL, AND ADMINISTRATIVE.

FEDERAL PROCEDURAL FORMS, L ED: STEP-BY-STEP GUIDANCE FOR DRAFTING FORMS FOR FEDERAL COURT OR FEDERAL AGENCY PROCEEDINGS.

FEDERAL RULES SERVICE, 2D AND 3D: REPORTS DECISIONS FROM ALL LEVELS OF THE FEDERAL SYSTEM INTERPRETING THE FEDERAL RULES OF CIVIL PROCEDURE AND THE FEDERAL RULES OF APPELLATE PROCEDURE.

FEDERAL RULES DIGEST, 3D: ORGANIZES HEADNOTES FOR THE DECISIONS REPORTED IN FEDERAL RULES SERVICE ACCORDING TO THE NUMBERING SYSTEMS OF THE FEDERAL RULES OF CIVIL PROCEDURE AND THE FEDERAL RULES OF APPELLATE PROCEDURE.

FEDERAL RULES OF EVIDENCE SERVICE: REPORTS DECISIONS FROM ALL LEVELS OF THE FEDERAL SYSTEM INTERPRETING THE FEDERAL RULES OF EVIDENCE.

FEDERAL RULES OF EVIDENCE NEWS

FEDERAL PROCEDURE RULES SERVICE

FEDERAL TRIAL HANDBOOK, 2D

FORM DRAFTING CHECKLISTS: AM JUR PRACTICE GUIDE

GOVERNMENT CONTRACTS: PROCEDURES AND FORMS

HOW TO GO DIRECTLY INTO YOUR OWN COMPUTERIZED SOLO PRACTICE WITHOUT MISSING A MEAL (OR A BYTE)

JONES ON EVIDENCE, CIVIL AND CRIMINAL, 7TH

LITIGATION CHECKISTS: AM JUR PRACTICE GUIDE

MEDICAL LIBRARY, LAWYERS EDITION

MEDICAL MALPRACTICE — ALR CASES AND ANNOTATIONS

MODERN APPELLATE PRACTICE: FEDERAL AND STATE CIVIL APPEALS

MODERN CONSTITUTIONAL LAW

NEGOTIATION AND SETTLEMENT

PATTERN DEPOSITION CHECKLISTS, 2D

QUALITY OF LIFE DAMAGES: CRITICAL ISSUES AND PROOFS

SHEPARD'S CITATIONS FOR ALR

SUCCESSFUL TECHNIQUES FOR CIVIL TRIALS, 2D

STORIES ET CETERA — A COUNTRY LAWYER LOOKS AT LIFE AND THE LAW

SUMMARY OF AMERICAN LAW

THE TRIAL LAWYER'S BOOK: PREPARING AND WINNING CASES

TRIAL PRACTICE CHECKLISTS

2000 CLASSIC LEGAL QUOTATIONS

WILLISTON ON CONTRACTS, 3D AND 4TH

FEDERAL RULES OF EVIDENCE DIGEST: ORGANIZES HEADNOTES FOR THE DECISIONS REPORTED IN FEDERAL RULES OF EVIDENCE SERVICE ACCORDING TO THE NUMBERING SYSTEM OF THE FEDERAL RULES OF EVIDENCE.

ADMINISTRATIVE LAW: PRACTICE AND PROCEDURE

AGE DISCRIMINATION: CRITICAL ISSUES AND PROOFS

ALR CRITICAL ISSUES: DRUNK DRIVING PROSECUTIONS

ALR CRITICAL ISSUES: FREEDOM OF INFORMATION ACTS

ALR CRITICAL ISSUES: TRADEMARKS

ALR CRITICAL ISSUES: WRONGFUL DEATH

AMERICANS WITH DISABILITIES: PRACTICE AND COMPLIANCE MANUAL

ATTORNEYS' FEES

BALLENTINE'S LAW DICTIONARY

CONSTITUTIONAL LAW DESKBOOK

CONSUMER AND BORROWER PROTECTION: AM JUR PRACTICE GUIDE

CONSUMER CREDIT: ALR ANNOTATIONS

DAMAGES: ALR ANNOTATIONS

EMPLOYEE DISMISSAL: CRITICAL ISSUES AND PROOFS

ENVIRONMENTAL LAW: ALR ANNOTATIONS

EXPERT WITNESS CHECKLISTS

EXPERT WITNESSES IN CIVIL TRIALS

FORFEITURES: ALR ANNOTATIONS

FEDERAL LOCAL COURT RULES

FEDERAL LOCAL COURT FORMS

FEDERAL CRIMINAL LAW AND PROCEDURE: ALR ANNOTATIONS

FEDERAL EVIDENCE

FEDERAL LITIGATION DESK SET: FORMS AND ANALYSIS

PREFACE

When I first started teaching legal research and legal writing, I was unable to discover a single text able to deliver the coverage I felt my students needed. I was looking for a text that would combine:

- a clear explanation of basic information; and
- plenty of exercises to give the student the necessary practice in researching and writing.

The ideal text would also be user-friendly and readable, while balancing the need for detail. Visual tools such as charts, tables, and flowcharts would be used for information that is hard to follow in narrative form. Sample pages from legal sources would be included so students could see the format of the particular legal source and the professor would not have to supplement the text. Each chapter would cover a manageable amount of material for someone who had not previously been exposed to the law.

This book attempts to fill that need for paralegal and legal studies students and instructors. It is divided into two parts. The objectives of Part I, Legal Research, are to teach the student:

1. To understand the fundamentals of legal research;
2. To competently perform legal research in the law library and on the computer; and
3. To use correct citation form.

The objectives of Part II, Legal Writing, are:

1. To explain the fundamentals of legal analysis and writing;
2. To teach the student how to communicate clearly; and
3. To explain how to eliminate mechanical errors.

Organization of the Text

- The legal research portion of the book includes sample pages from the legal sources discussed in the text and contains basic citation rules and research exercises. To facilitate student participation, Part I emphasizes the process of finding and using primary sources and gives the student hands-on experience through completing legal research exercises. Chapter 1 gives an important overview of the legal system and legal reasoning. Chapters 2 through 6 introduce legal encyclopedias, digests, American Law Reports, cases, constitutions, statutes, court rules, administrative law, and shepardizing. The chapters also contain lengthy research assignments, allowing the professor to assign certain of the exercises one term and a different set of exercises another term. Chapter 7 gives an overview of the research process and explains how the various legal sources studied relate to each other.

Primary and secondary sources are covered in separate chapters in this text. This organization allows the instructor the freedom to choose which type of source to cover first.

- The sequence chosen for these chapters tracks the order in which a researcher who is unfamiliar with a particular area of the law commences a research assignment. Unless the legal researcher has somehow already found a primary source on point, the researcher will most likely begin research by referring to a secondary source first.
- The legal writing portion of the book explains how to write legal documents and includes samples of various types of legal documents. Chapters 8 and 9 give an introduction to legal writing and legal writing fundamentals. Chapters 10 through 15 are each devoted to a different type of legal document, starting with the transmittal letter and the client opinion letter and continuing through the contract, pleadings and motions, the law office memo, the memorandum of law, and the appellate brief. The chapter on contracts covers material rarely discussed in a legal writing class.

  The various types of legal documents are explained in separate chapters, again to allow the instructor to choose which chapters are to be covered, time permitting. A professor who does not usually cover a particular type of document may enjoy the challenge of teaching something a little different. In addition, the book is a good reference for the student who is later asked to write a type of legal document not studied in legal writing class.
- The appendixes contain material that could be profitably used in either legal research or legal writing. They provide students with an explanation of and necessary practice in eliminating mechanical errors, quoting correctly, and writing short and long form citations correctly. The rules for quotations and short form citations are not covered in other texts but are something the student should master. Appendix G contains four fact patterns. These patterns can serve first as the subject of a legal research assignment and then, later, as the subject of a client opinion letter, law office memo, memorandum of law, or appellate brief.

Making the Book User-Friendly by Including a Search-and-Seizure Problem

My challenge was to write a book that would spark student interest and involve the student in the research and writing process; students learn more if they are involved in a practical exercise. I found that students are keenly interested in search and seizure because the topic is current, easy to picture, and easy to understand. Therefore, I decided to use this topic to make the book student-friendly.

The text entices the student to participate in the learning process by including interesting and relevant examples of primary sources and documents relating to the search and seizure topic. Many of the sources deal with Sheriff Vogel of Volusia County, Florida. Sheriff Vogel, at the time of writing of this text, had, under the auspices of the Florida Contraband Forfeiture Act, seized large amounts of cash from motorists without making arrests. The search and seizure materials are fairly easy to understand, contain interesting and easy-to-grasp facts, and can be a basis for a number of class discussions. Students can be asked to determine whether their state has similar civil forfeiture statutes and to investigate whether the state has its own "Sheriff Vogel."

Appendix A introduces students to two brothers who have a legal problem. The Williams brothers were driving through Florida when law enforcement officers stopped their car and seized $35,000 in cash from the brothers. The brothers decide to consult an attorney to see if they could get their money back. Repeated references throughout the book to the search and seizure topic involve the students in the course materials and provide continuity. The topic also lends itself to some great class discussions. Where the search and seizure topic is not used, other topics appear several times in the text and in the exercises.

In addition to the search-and-seizure problem, Appendix A contains examples of primary sources used in researching the issue. Moreover, the appendix includes an explanation of law on search and seizure, a flowchart of the issues involved in the search and seizure problem and a suggested outline for a law office memo to be written after researching the search and seizure problem. By using this important topic, students will learn legal research and writing and some substantive law at the same time.

Appendix A is designed to be a vital part of the text, but the material was gathered together in a separate appendix rather than in a single chapter so the instructor could assign the entire appendix or portions of it at any time during the course. The whole appendix might be overwhelming to the novice researcher if it were assigned at the beginning of the course. The research problem and the newspaper articles could be assigned immediately, with the rest of the materials assigned as applicable chapters in Part I are covered. An alternative is to assign Appendix A after the student knows enough about legai research to pull the Appendix A materials together. A third alternative is to assign the problem at the beginning of the course and ask students to glance over the rest of the material. After reading a particular chapter, students could be required to explain how Appendix A illustrates the chapter material.

Preparation Time

Legal research and legal writing are typically the most time-consuming courses in a paralegal/legal studies curriculum. Many instructors shy away from teaching these courses because of the out-of-classroom commitment. Just keeping up with grading assignments leaves very little time for outside preparation of material.

The first few semesters I taught legal research and writing, I spent hours preparing additional student-friendly materials to supplement available texts. I also used several different texts and the *Bluebook* those first few semesters because I could not find one text that contained all the information I knew my students needed to know. From this experience, I knew that an instructor-friendly book would be self-contained and would eliminate the need for a great deal of self-prepared materials.

This book is designed to be the only one the student and the instructor need for legal research and legal writing. Basic citation rules are included, eliminating the need for the *Bluebook,* although some professors may require students to purchase a *Bluebook* for reference. The citation rules are consistent with *Bluebook* form so that the advanced student can later refer to the *Bluebook* when necessary. As explained previously, the legal research portion of the book contains sample pages from the various authorities and research exercises. The legal writing portion of the book contains sample documents, heavily annotated to offer the student guidance on the writing process.

The Instructor's Guide is designed to further reduce preparation time. The Guide contains the following instructor-friendly materials:

1. Legal research exams and answer keys;
2. Keys to the research and writing exercises presented in the book;
3. Sample syllabi;
4. Sample student-written client opinion letters, law office memos, and memoranda of law;
5. Classroom-tested pedagogical techniques, including:
   a. student preparation of a research and writing journal;
   b. use of group work;
   c. use of the overhead projector;
   d. use of peer critiques; and
   e. grading sheets;
6. A list of legal research and writing organizations and journals.

ACKNOWLEDGMENTS

I could not have written this book without the help of a number of people I would like to acknowledge here. Some of them provided me with valuable ideas along the way and others gave me the emotional support I needed.

I would first like to recognize those persons whose contribution was both informational and inspirational: my colleagues at the University of Central Florida, Dr. Ransford Pyle, Dr. Daniel Hall, and Dr. Bernard McCarthy; my editor, Jay Whitney; and all of my students over the years. Three special people who also fit in this category are my students, Renee Hicks, Jean Slizyk, and Kathy Patterson. Cathleen Mestre provided me with ideas early in the writing process, as did Kathleen Bell later on. Emotionally, I could not have written the book without Betsey Clarke, Jan Messervey, and Amelia Sherouse.

Special thanks go to three important people in my life: my husband, Buddy, and my children, Christopher and Kathryn Elizabeth.

Early drafts and the final manuscript were read by the following reviewers:

Wendy B. Edson, Hilbert College, New York

Nancy Hart, Midland College, Texas

Frances M. McClean, Dyke College, Ohio

Brian McCully, Fresno City College, California

Christopher Sadler, Denver Paralegal Institute, Colorado

C.M.B.

PART I
Legal Research

CHAPTER 1
Law and Sources of Law

OUTLINE

Introduction
The American System of Law
Sources of Law

INTRODUCTION

The information in this chapter provides a framework into which you can fit the pieces of the legal research puzzle. The chapter first explains how law relates to our tripartite system of government; the second part of the chapter discusses sources of law. You may find yourself referring back to this chapter as you learn to perform legal research. You will be amazed at how much better you understand it after you have covered a few more chapters.

THE AMERICAN SYSTEM OF LAW

The federal and state governments are each divided into three branches: **legislative**, **judicial**, and **executive**. Each of the branches has a role in making law, and there is an important interplay among the three branches of each government. The charts in Figures 1-1 and 1-2 show these three branches for the federal and state governments. Figure 1-1 gives the names of the various entities within those branches and the reference materials containing the law made by each entity. You may want to add state-specific references to Figure 1-2 as a quick and handy guide for your state's law.

LEGAL TERMS

legislative branch
1. With the judicial branch and the executive branch, one of the three divisions into which the Constitution separates the government of the United States. These branches of government are also referred to as *departments of government*. The legislative branch is primarily responsible for enacting the laws. 2. A similar division in state government.

FEDERAL GOVERNMENT		
Judicial Branch	**Legislative Branch**	**Executive Branch**
United States Supreme Court (9 Justices) *slip opinions* *loose-leaf service* United States Law Week *reporters* United States Reports Supreme Court Reporter United States Supreme Court Reports, Lawyers Edition	**Senate** **House of Representatives** *slip laws* *session laws* United States Statutes at Large *code* United States Code *annotated codes* United States Code Annotated United States Code Service	**President** *Presidential Documents*
United States Circuit Courts of Appeal *reporter* Federal Reporter		**Administrative Agencies** Federal Register *code* Code of Federal Regulations
United States District Courts *reporter* Federal Supplement		

FIGURE 1-1 The three branches of the federal government are the legislative, the executive, and the judicial.

The Judicial Branch

The judicial branch comprises the various levels of courts. As shown in Figure 1-3, the federal trial-level court is the United States District Court. Each state contains one or more districts. At the trial level, questions of fact are determined by the jury (**jury trial**) or by the court (**bench trial**). Issues of law are decided by the trial judge.

The losing party may appeal. An appeal ordinarily goes to the intermediate appellate court. Generally, review by the intermediate appellate court is mandatory. This means that if a case is appealed to the intermediate appellate court, the court must hear the appeal. The federal intermediate appellate court is one of the United States Circuit Courts of Appeals. The United States is divided into 13 circuits, as shown in Figure 1-4.

LEGAL TERMS

judicial branch
1. With the legislative branch and the executive branch, one of the three divisions into which the Constitution separates the government of the United States. . . . The judicial branch is primarily responsible for interpreting the laws. 2. A similar division in state government.

executive branch
1. With the legislative branch and the judicial branch, one of the three divisions into which the Constitution separates the government of the United States. . . . The executive branch is primarily responsible for enforcing the laws. 2. A similar division in state government.

STATE GOVERNMENT		
Judicial Branch	**Legislative Branch**	**Executive Branch**
court of last resort	state legislature	**Governor**
slip opinion	slip laws	**Administrative Agencies**
advance sheets	session laws	*daily or weekly publications*
reporters	code	
intermediate appellate court	annotated codes	*code*
advance sheets		
reporter		
trial level courts		
reporters		

FIGURE 1-2 State governments, like the federal government, have three co-equal branches.

At the intermediate appellate level, three judges are empaneled to decide an appeal. The appellate decision is made based on appellate briefs and other documents submitted to the court. Often the attorneys are also allowed to present their arguments orally to the appellate panel, with the judges having the opportunity to question the attorneys. The appellate court may **affirm, reverse**, or **remand** the lower court's decision.

The judges at the intermediate appellate level may decide to hear or rehear a case ***en banc***. This means that all the members of the court sit to hear the case, rather than the case being heard by a three-judge panel. For example, if the Eleventh Circuit Court of Appeals decides to hear a case en banc, and there are 11 judges who are members of the Eleventh Circuit, all 11 judges would hear the case. Because very few cases are heard en banc, and cases heard en banc deal with important legal issues, special attention should be paid to en banc decisions.

A case from the United States Circuit Court would go to the United States Supreme Court by appeal or by petition for certiorari, as set forth in federal statutes. Review by the United States Supreme Court is discretionary for most cases. This means that it is within the discretion of the United States Supreme Court whether it will hear and decide a case. Only a very small percentage of the cases that go up to the United States Supreme Court are heard.

jury trial
A trial in which the jurors are the judges of the facts and the court is the judge of the law. Trial by jury is guaranteed in all criminal cases by the Sixth Amendment, and in most civil cases by the Seventh Amendment.

bench trial
A trial before a judge without a jury; a nonjury trial.

affirm
In the case of an appellate court, to uphold the decision or judgment of the lower court after an appeal.

reverse
To turn around or in an opposite direction. . . . A term used in appellate court opinions to indicate that the court has set aside the judgment of the trial court.

remand
To return or send back. . . . The return of a case by an appellate court to the trial court for further proceedings, for new trial, or for entry of judgment in accordance with an order of the appellate court.

en banc
Means "on the bench." A court, particularly an appellate court, with all the judges sitting together (*sitting en banc*) in a case.

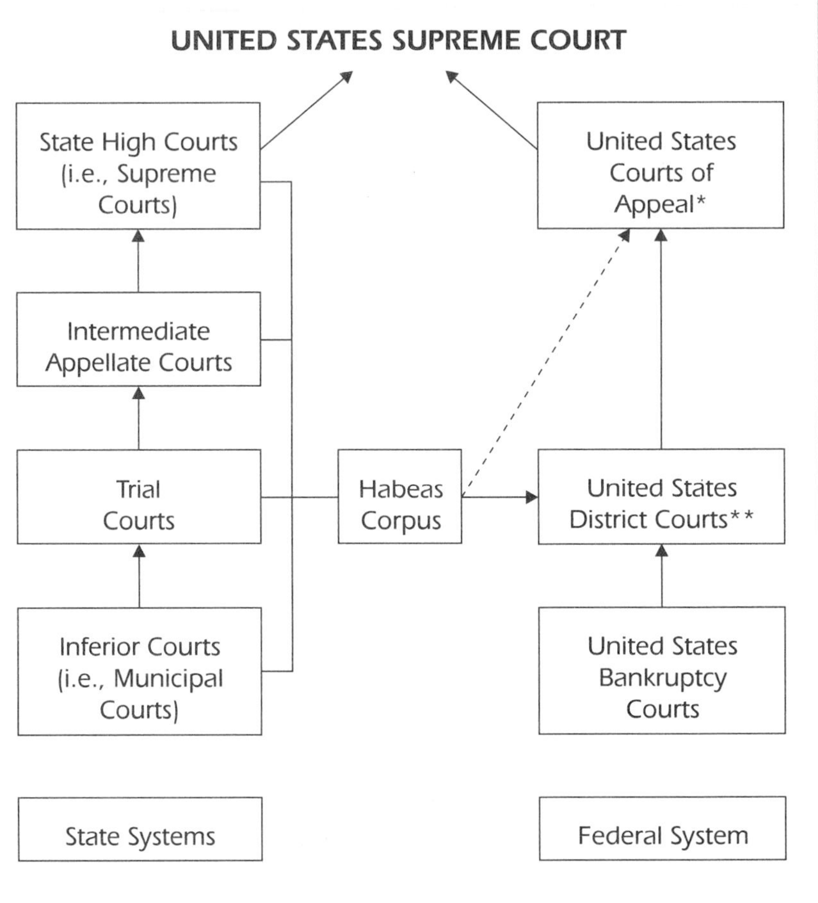

FIGURE 1-3 State and federal court structures. (From Hall, *Criminal Law and Procedure,* copyright 1992. Courtesy of Delmar Publishers.)

LEGAL TERMS

slip opinion
A single judicial decision published shortly after it has been issued by the court and well before it is incorporated into a reporter.

advance sheets
Printed copies of judicial opinions published in loose-leaf form shortly after the opinions are issued. These published opinions are later collected and published in bound form with the other reported cases which are issued over a longer period of time.

reporters
Court reports, as well as official, published reports of cases decided by administrative agencies.

common law
Law found in the decisions of the courts rather than in statutes; judge-made law.

Published court opinions usually come out first as **slip opinions**. They are then published in **advance sheets**, and finally they are printed in **reporters**. Very recent cases may be available from a *loose-leaf service* after the opinions are announced and before they are published in advance sheets. The law contained in court opinions is called **common law**, *case law,* or *judge-made law.*

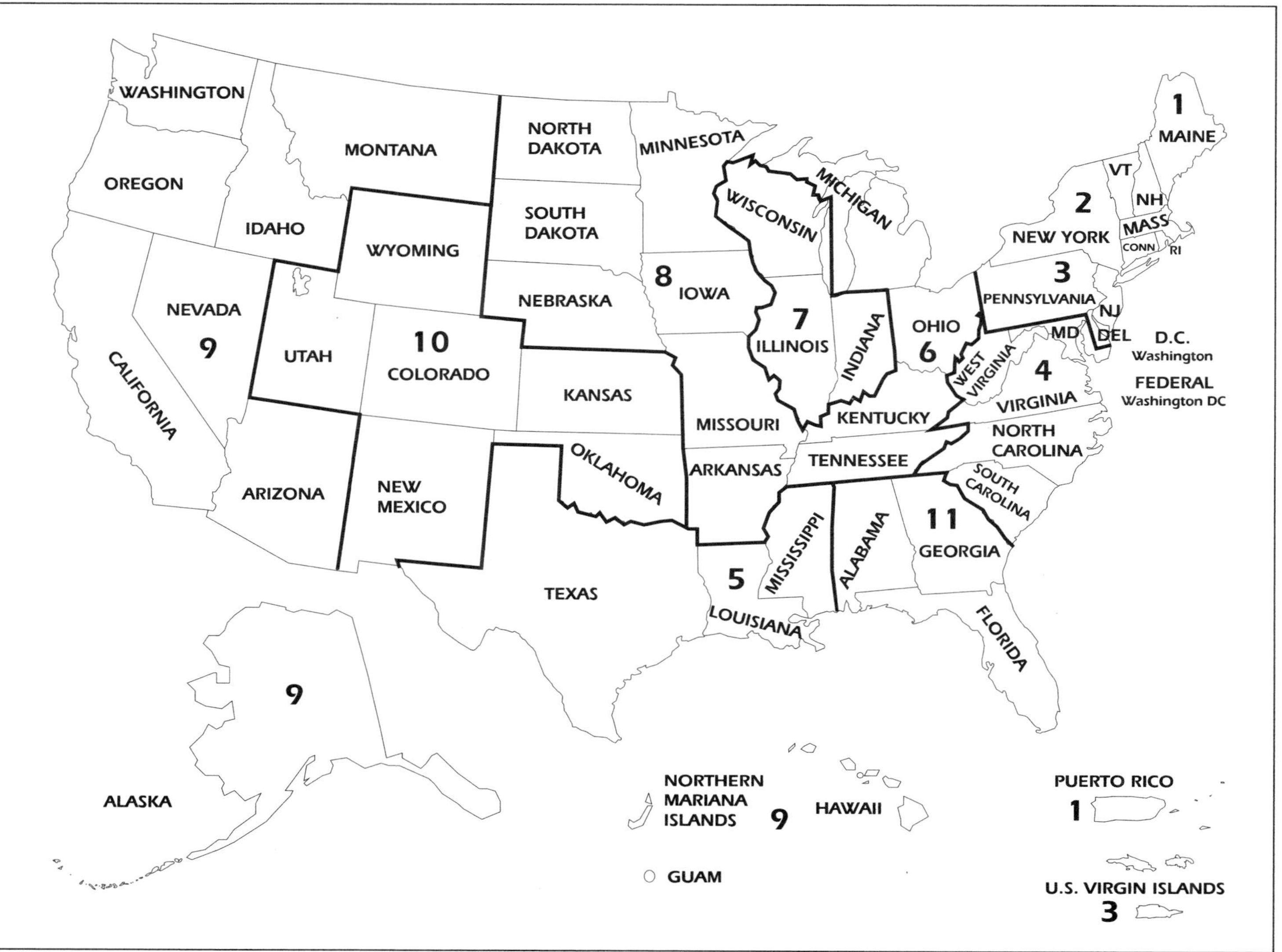

FIGURE 1-4 The 13 federal judicial circuits. (From Hall, *Criminal Law and Procedure*, copyright 1992. Courtesy of Delmar Publishers.)

The Legislative Branch

The legislative branch, composed of bodies of elected representatives, passes **statutes**. Statutes are first published as slip laws, then as **session laws**. They are then codified. *Slip laws* are similar to slip opinions, in that each statute passed is printed separately on the number of pieces of paper necessary to contain the statute. Session laws are compilations that contain recently passed statutes arranged chronologically. A statute appearing in session laws is usually numbered to identify the session of Congress in which it was passed and the order in which it was passed in relation to other statutes passed that year. For example, the fourth statute passed in the 103d session of Congress would be designated as Public Law No. 103-4.

To *codify* statutes means to arrange them by topic. The United States Code, the official codified version of federal statutes, is divided into 50 titles, each dealing with a particular topic. The United States Code Service and The United States Code Annotated are annotated versions of the United States Code that contain the same statutes found in the United States Code, but also provide **annotations** relating to the subject matter of each statute. An *annotation* is a short summary of an important legal principle from a case or other document; it usually ends with a citation to that case or document.

LEGAL TERMS

statute
A law enacted by a legislature; an act.

session laws
The collected statutes enacted during a session of a legislature.

annotation
1. A notation, appended to any written work, which explains or comments upon its meaning. 2. A commentary that appears immediately following a printed statute and describes the application of the statute in actual cases. Such annotations, with the statutes on which they comment, are published in volumes known as annotated statutes or annotated codes. 3. A notation that follows an opinion of court printed in a court report, explaining the court's action in detail.

The Executive Branch and Administrative Agencies

Administrative agencies are an important source of law. Although some consider these agencies a "fourth branch" of government, Figure 1-1 places them under the executive branch because the heads of administrative agencies may be nominated by the chief executive (president or governor). Like the executive, administrative agencies are charged with enforcing the law. Another similarity is that the executive and administrative agencies have the power to make rules and regulations. Several of the president's official roles, including that of commander in chief, give the president this power. Administrative agencies are given their power by statute. The president issues proclamations and executive orders, whereas the administrative agencies promulgate administrative rules and regulations. These documents have the force of law, just like case law or statutory law. Presidential proclamations and executive orders and administrative regulations are printed chronologically in the *Federal Register*. Later these documents are codified in the Code of Federal Regulations (C.F.R.).

Interplay among Governmental Branches in Lawmaking

The founders of the American legal system chose to adopt the common law system as the basis of our country's law. Historically, **case law** was emphasized over legislation, but this has changed with the rapid growth and importance of legislation. Today, some areas of the law, such as defamation, continue to be governed almost exclusively by case law; some areas are governed by statutes (as interpreted by the courts and administrative agencies); and other areas are governed partly by case law and partly by statutes.

Let's look first at the interplay between the legislative and judicial branches. The legislature can change the common law by passing statutes that supersede the common law. One reason to change common law is because the legislature recognizes a need to systematically regulate activity previously governed by case law. An example of this is the **Uniform Commercial Code**, a portion of which, in some form, has been adopted by all 50 states. Another reason to change the prior common law is to reverse or legislatively overrule unpopular court decisions. Several years ago, when the United States Supreme Court ruled that burning the United States flag was constitutionally protected as a mode of free speech, several federal representatives and senators proposed amending the United States Constitution to outlaw flag-burning. Because it generally takes a long time to amend the Constitution, they suggested passing a federal statute prohibiting flag-burning in the meantime. That proposed statute might have been enforced until challenged in court.

A traditional common law system emphasizes case law or common law over legislation. The other approach is the civil law system, which traditionally emphasizes a comprehensive statutory code over case law. Because of its French heritage, Louisiana is the only state whose law is based on both the common and civil law systems.

Once enacted, constitutions, statutes, and regulations are then interpreted by the courts. In applying constitutions, statutes, and regulations to a particular case, a court in effect explains what a legislative provision means. The court's interpretative role is such a significant one that constitutions, statutes, and regulations must be read in light of case law applications of them. Sometimes a court is asked to determine the constitutionality of a statute or regulation. For example, in *Roe v. Wade,* 410 U.S. 113 (1973), the United States Supreme Court based its decision on an implied constitutional right to privacy. Although this right is not explicitly stated in the Constitution, the Court interpreted the Bill of Rights to require the existence of this right under the theory that other enumerated rights, such as the right against unreasonable search and seizure, would be meaningless without an implied right to privacy. The Court thus struck down Texas anti-abortion statutes because they conflicted with the constitutional right to privacy.

The executive branch affects the other two branches in a number of ways. The chief executive may veto legislation. Vetoed legislation can be enacted only if the legislature has sufficient votes to override the executive veto. The chief executive also greatly influences enforcement of legislation, in part through funding and publicity. Usually there is insufficient money and personnel to enforce all legislation, so the executive may direct that special attention be paid to certain laws. A priority in recent years has been the enforcement of criminal statutes prohibiting the illegal drug trade. The most lasting effect a president has may be from the constitutional mandate to nominate federal judges. Once confirmed by the Senate, such an appointment is for life, unless the judge resigns or is impeached.

Administrative agencies promulgate administrative rules and regulations that have the force of law. Theses rules and regulations are in effect an interpretation of statutes passed by the legislature. Further, the agencies'

case law
The law as laid down in the decisions of the courts in similar cases that have previously been decided.

Uniform Commercial Code
One of the Uniform Laws, which has been adopted in much the same form in every state. It governs most aspects of commercial transactions, including sales, leases, negotiable instruments, deposits and collections, letters of credit, bulk sales, warehouse receipts, bills of lading and other documents of title, investment securities, and secured transactions.

priorities in regulation and enforcement influence both the legislative and the judicial branches.

Supremacy Clause: Relationship Between Federal and State Law

Article VI of the United States Constitution states, in part: "This Constitution, and the Laws of the United States . . . shall be the supreme Law of the Land; and the Judges in every State shall be bound thereby, any Thing in the Constitution or Laws of any State to the contrary notwithstanding." Because of this provision, known as the **supremacy clause**, no federal statute, state constitution, or state statute may conflict with the federal Constitution. A constitutional or statutory provision found by a court to be in conflict would be held unconstitutional, and thus ineffective.

The United States Constitution grants certain powers to the federal government. Some of the powers are given exclusively to the federal government; other powers may be exercised by both state and federal governments. No state constitutional provision or statute may govern an area belonging exclusively to the federal government. For example, only the federal government may coin money and negotiate treaties with foreign countries. In contrast, the power to tax is exercised concurrently by both the federal and the state governments.

When there is a conflict between a federal and a state statute in an area governed concurrently by both federal and state governments, the federal statute will control. For example, the Fair Labor Standards Act, a federal act, requires most employers to pay employees at least a specified minimum wage and prohibits employment of children under 14 years of age. A state statute that allowed employers to pay less than the federal specified minimum wage, or to employ 12- or 13-year-olds, would be in direct conflict with the federal act. A court would hold the state statute unconstitutional and unenforceable.

Powers not given to the federal government are reserved to the states. The areas of family law, real property law, and tort law are governed mainly by state statutes and case law.

Another piece to fit into the research puzzle is local law. Counties, townships, municipalities, and other local governmental entities have laws governing matters such as zoning, occupational licenses, and construction permits, considered to be "local" in nature. Local laws include charters and ordinances (sometimes referred to as *resolutions*). A charter is similar to federal and state constitutions in that a charter is the fundamental document setting up the local government. Once formed, the local government passes ordinances to implement the power given it under its charter. Just as state statutes are grouped by subject matter into a state code, ordinances may be compiled into a code. If not available at the public library, a copy of the local government's charter and ordinances or code usually may be purchased from the local governmental entity.

Now that you know something about the law produced by the three branches of our government, you need to know where to look to find it. The second part of this chapter discusses primary sources, secondary sources, and finding tools and describes some of the common legal sources. The chapter then gives some basic information on computer-assisted legal research.

SOURCES OF LAW

Your first trip through the law library may seem overwhelming. The law library contains all kinds of sources you need to consult when researching a legal question. By the end of your legal research class, you will be familiar with many of these sources. Primary sources, secondary sources, and finding tools are all sources of law, but they are used in different ways. Their use depends on the information they contain and how authoritative they are. *Primary sources* contain the law itself, *secondary sources* contain commentary on the law, and *finding tools,* as the name implies, are used to find primary and secondary sources. Primary sources are given the most weight, but secondary sources may be used if no primary sources are available. Finding tools are not authoritative and may not be quoted or cited. Nevertheless, finding tools are an important part of legal research. You may be able to locate relevant primary and secondary sources only by using finding tools.

Primary and Secondary Sources

The difference between primary sources and secondary sources is critical when working with the law. Table 1-1 lists common and frequently used primary and secondary sources and finding tools. These sources are covered in greater depth in later chapters.

Primary sources contain the actual law. Constitutions, cases, statutes, and administrative regulations are all examples of primary sources. Secondary sources are everything else, including treatises, legal periodicals, law review articles, legal encyclopedias, American Law Reports annotations, law dictionaries, legal thesauruses, continuing legal education publications, Restatements, and hornbooks. Finding tools are reference publications used to find primary and secondary sources. They include American Law Reports annotations, legal encyclopedias, digests, Shepard's Citators, and the *Index to Legal Periodicals.* You may have noticed that American Law Reports annotations and legal encyclopedias are listed as both secondary sources and finding tools in Table 1-1. American Law Reports annotations and legal encyclopedias are secondary sources, because of their commentary on law, but they are also used to find primary and secondary authority. Loose-leaf services are listed as a primary source, a secondary source, and a finding tool because they may contain the text of primary sources and commentaries on the law, as well as features used to find primary sources.

LEGAL TERMS

supremacy clause
The provision in Article VI of the Constitution that "this Constitution and the laws of the United States . . . shall be the supreme law of the land, and the judges in every state shall be bound thereby."

Primary Sources	Secondary Sources	Finding Tools
constitutions‡	treatises*	American Law Reports*
statutes‡	law review articles*	legal encyclopedias*
court rulings‡	legal periodicals*	digests*
administrative regulations‡	law dictionaries*	Shepard's Citators‡‡
reporters**	legal thesaurus*	loose-leaf services*
loose-leaf services*	continuing legal education publications*	*Index to Legal Periodicals**
	Restatements*	
	hornbooks*	
	American Law Reports annotations*	
	legal encyclopedias*	
	loose-leaf services*	

Table 1-1 Legal Sources and finding tools.

* See Chapter 3
** See Chapter 4
‡ See Chapter 5
‡‡ See Chapter 6

A major goal in legal research is to locate the primary sources relevant to the problem you are researching. Secondary sources are often used to find primary sources. Another reason for consulting a secondary source is to gain a basic understanding of the subject matter being researched.

In legal writing, always **cite** the relevant primary source. Determining which primary sources are relevant, and then deciding which of those sources to cite requires an understanding of legal reasoning and performance of legal analysis. (Legal reasoning and legal analysis are discussed in Chapter 2.) If you have found few or no relevant primary sources, you may cite certain types of secondary sources. The preferred secondary sources are treatises, legal periodicals, law review articles, law dictionaries, legal thesauruses, Restatements, and continuing legal education publications. Digests should never be cited. Although you may cite legal encyclopedias and American Law Reports annotations, they are not preferred citation sources, and you should do so with caution. It is always better to find ("pull") the primary authority referred to in the legal encyclopedia or annotation and cite that primary authority rather than the secondary source.

Secondary sources include *treatises* which are books covering a particular subject matter written by an expert in the field. *Legal periodicals* are legal journals and magazines containing articles usually written by attorneys and judges. National, state, and local bar associations publish legal periodicals, and other periodicals are published by commercial publishers. *Law review articles* are articles contained in law reviews or journals published by law schools. Although law reviews and journals are put together by second- and third-year law school students, these publications are highly respected. It is a great honor for a law school student to be selected to be on the staff of a law review.

Computer-Assisted Legal Research

Computer-assisted legal research (CALR) uses on-line services, such as the WESTLAW (provided by West Publishing Company of St. Paul, Minnesota) and LEXIS (provided by Mead Data Central, Inc., of Dayton, Ohio), services contained on CD-ROM (Compact Disc-Read Only Memory), and services accessible through Internet, the worldwide computer network. This section provides basic information on CALR, and Chapters 3 through 6 each contain a note on computer-assisted legal research. Each of these notes gives you CALR information concerning the sources discussed in the chapter. The on-line services and CD-ROM services (depending on the particular CD being used) contain some of the same primary and secondary sources and allow similar key word searches; however they differ greatly in the commands used to perform research. Only a general description of CALR is possible in this book because of the differences in detailed operation among the various services and the focus of this book.

CALR assists the researcher in several different ways. The various CALR services are usually accompanied by an information manual, and may have tutorials available to help the researcher learn how to use the service. The on-line services may offer a number of hours of free training time to new subscribers. Attorneys on staff with the various publishers are usually available by telephone to answer questions.

On-Line Services Generally

With on-line services such as WESTLAW and LEXIS, the researcher is connected with the main computer by modem. The on-line service generally charges a subscription fee, to give the researcher access to the service, and also charges for the amount of computer time used during research.

The Internet, often referred to as the "information superhighway," allows the user to access information and communicate with others worldwide. On the Internet, the legal researcher can access countless sources, from library holding catalogs to government agency information to legal bulletin boards to law-related mailing lists. Users may log on to the Internet free through many universities, or can pay for access through on-line commercial service providers.

CD-ROM stands for Compact Disc-Read Only Memory. The disc resembles the audio CD but contains information in an interactive format. *Interactive* means that the legal researcher can search for relevant information and then print or download information. One disc can hold the equivalent of 260,000 pages of printed text. CD-ROM legal research requires access to a late-model personal computer with a CD-ROM reader (also known as a CD-ROM drive). The CD-ROM reader is either built into the personal computer or is added as a separate peripheral.

A researcher using a CD-ROM usually pays a fixed cost for the base CD-ROM and any updates during a given period of time. The CD-ROM allows unlimited research time without having to pay for on-line time. The CD-ROM is updated periodically by the publisher, which sends the researcher a replacement CD. The new CD contains all the information on the old CD plus any information available since publication of the last CD.

Now let's look at the CALR services in a little more detail.

WESTLAW and LEXIS

WESTLAW and LEXIS, each more than 20 years old, are similar in that they contain the full text of federal and state primary sources, as well as secondary and other related sources. Data on WESTLAW and LEXIS is found within "libraries." There are libraries for federal case law, state case law, federal statutes, state statutes, and so on. Some of the libraries overlap, so you may be able to access a primary source through more than one library. Compare the primary sources named in this chapter with the libraries on WESTLAW or LEXIS and determine which library you should be looking in to find each primary source. Then select a particular library and try to pull up the authority by inputting its citation.

New features and databases are continually being added to WESTLAW and LEXIS. Both allow similar search strategies (see Chapter 4; both allow the legal researcher to shepardize online (see Chapter 7); both allow access to nonlegal sources such as newspapers, business and corporate information, and medical journals.

CD-ROMs

Various CD-ROMs contain different primary and secondary sources. Some "bundle" (package together) a number of sources. For example, one CD may contain a particular state's court cases, statutes, court rules, constitution, and administrative code.

The type of data on a CD depends on the particular CD. You would not find the text of cases on an American Law Reports CD, but you could find a citation to a relevant case. The ALR CD only contains the text of the ALR annotations. Once you have a case citation, you can find (and print hard copy of) the case. If you have another CD containing the correct reporter, you may be able to access the case from that CD. See Figure 1-5 for a representative list of available CD-ROMs currently being used for legal research.

A wide range of resources are available in CD-ROM. West Publishing Company, Lawyers Cooperative Publishing Company, Commerce Clearing House, Matthew Bender & Company, and Michie Company all have entered the CD-ROM market. The *Directory of Law-Related CD-ROMS 1994,* published by Infosources Publishing and compiled and edited by Arlene L. Eis, provides information on more than 400 CD-ROM products and contains a 12-page publisher/distributor index.

CD-ROMS	
Courts and Legal System	**Source**
A.L.R. LawDesk	LCP
U.S.C.S. LawDesk	LCP
C.F.R.	LCP
Federal Appeals on Disc	HyperLaw
United States Code on Disc	HyperLaw
Supreme Court on Disc	HyperLaw
Federal Practice	Matthew Bender
U.S.C.A.	West Publishing
Supreme Court Reporter	West Publishing
Federal Reporter	West Publishing
DocsFinder	Auto-Graphics
Shepard's Federal Citations	Shepard's/McGraw-Hill

Figure 1-5 There are a variety of CD-ROM products that can be used to help in legal research.

The Internet

Many books about the Internet have been published, including several that could be useful for the legal researcher. Three that were recommended in the April 1994 issue of the newsletter *Legal Information Alert* are *Legal Researcher's Internet Directory (Legal Research of New York 1993); Internet Primer for Information Professionals: A Basic Guide to Internet Working Technology* (Meckler 1993) and *The Internet Guide for New Users* (McGraw-Hill 1995). *Legal Information Alert* is published 10 times a year by Alert Publications.

Advantages and Disadvantages of On-Line CALR

There are both advantages and disadvantages to using CALR. Perhaps the biggest advantage of CALR is that it is more timely than the hard-copy version of the same source in your law library. Recent cases and legislation may often be accessed within a day or so after after the cases are announced or the legislation is passed. With CALR, the researcher can either "download" (transfer information from the source to a computer disk) or

Advantages of online CALR:

1. Information available quickly
2. Takes up less space than books
3. Less upkeep with CALR
4. Information can be printed
5. Available whenever computer is accessible
6. No indexes or digests needed
7. Some types of searches possible that are nearly impossible in books

Disadvantages on online CALR:

1. Costly
2. Harder to read from computer screen
3. Computer printout harder to read

print information off-line (without being charged the expensive on-line rate) to save information. Law libraries are very expensive to maintain, and they may be accessible only at certain hours. CALR is often less expensive than purchasing the hard copy of the sources needed by the researcher, and CALR is accessible whenever the researcher has access to the computer terminal. CALR also eliminates the need for indexes and digests. Because the CALR user searches with the exact words of the authority, rather than using terms under which the authority is indexed, CALR may turn up authority nearly impossible to find through more traditional printed sources.

The big disadvantage of CALR is that the researcher is generally charged a hefty amount for use of computer time. The cost-conscious researcher will decide which library to search in, and have a query formulated, before starting CALR. Another cost-saving trick is to print information off-line to read later rather than run up on-line charges by reading information from the computer screen. Another disadvantage of CALR is that it is much more difficult and time-consuming to read from a computer screen or a computer printout than it is to read from a law book. The computer screen allows the researcher to read only one-third to one-half of a page at a time. In contrast, the hard copy allows the researcher to scan two pages at a time. The computer printout is usually much lighter in color and of poorer print quality than the hard-copy version.

SUMMARY

- Federal and state governments are each made up of three branches: legislative, judicial, and executive.
- The judicial branch (the courts) produces what is called common law, case law, or judge-made law.
- The legislative branch (elected representatives) passes statutes.
- Administrative agencies (often considered part of the executive branch) promulgate administrative rules and regulations.
- The chief executive (the president or governor) issues proclamations and executive orders.
- Federal and state laws are a product of an important interplay among the three branches of government.
  - The legislature can pass statutes that supersede the common law.
  - The courts interpret and apply constitutions, statutes, and administrative regulations.
  - The chief executive may veto legislation, set priorities in law enforcement, and appoint judges.
- The supremacy clause of the United States Constitution makes the federal Constitution the supreme law of the land. No federal statute or state constitution or state may conflict with it.
- In the law library, primary sources contain the law itself, whereas secondary sources and finding tools are used to locate relevant primary sources.

- In addition to books from the law library, many legal researchers use computers to assist them. Computer-assisted legal research may use on-line services, services contained on CD-ROM, and the Internet.

EXERCISES

1. Fill in the state government chart in Figure 1-2 with the appropriate information from your state.
2. Visit the law library you will be using and identify the federal and state primary sources, secondary sources, and finding tools you will be using in your research. Compare the list in Table 1-1 with the books available in your law library.
3. Find out what types of computer-assisted research are available to you.

CHAPTER 2
Legal Reasoning and Analysis

OUTLINE

INTRODUCTION

When you research a legal problem, you are looking for primary sources applicable to your problem. You must use legal reasoning and analysis to determine whether a source is in fact applicable. Because we have a common law system, cases are central to legal reasoning and analysis. As explained in Chapter 1, some areas of the law are governed solely by case law. Even if you find a constitutional or statutory provision that seems to apply, you must research the provision to see how it has been interpreted by the courts. This chapter first discusses a number of terms central to understanding cases and then explains legal analysis.

DOCTRINE OF STARE DECISIS

The doctrine of **stare decisis** states that when a court has set forth a legal principle, that court and all lower courts under it will apply that principle in future cases in which the facts are substantially the same. Let's illustrate this abstract doctrine with an example.

LEGAL TERMS

stare decisis
Means "standing by the decision." Stare decisis is the doctrine that judicial decisions stand as precedents for cases arising in the future. It is a fundamental policy of our law that, except in unusual circumstances, a court's determination on a point of law will be followed by courts of the same or lower rank in later cases presenting the same legal issue, even though different parties are involved and many years have elapsed.

Griswold v. Connecticut, 381 U.S. 479 (1965) was a **landmark case** in which the United States Supreme Court first recognized an implied right to privacy under the United States Constitution. *Griswold* involved a Connecticut statute that banned the use of contraceptives. The constitutionality of the statute was first challenged in the Connecticut state courts. After the Supreme Court of Errors of Connecticut (the highest state court) affirmed the lower state court's enforcement of the state statute, the United States Supreme Court reviewed the case.

The Court found that "specific guarantees in the Bill of Rights have **penumbras**, formed by emanations from those guarantees that help give them life and substance. . . . Various guarantees create zones of privacy." The Court then determined that the Connecticut ban on the use of contraceptives "concerns a relationship lying within the zone of privacy created by several fundamental constitutional guarantees" and held the Connecticut statute unconstitutional (see Figure 2-1).

Applying this definition of the doctrine of stare decisis to *Griswold,* "that court" is the United States Supreme Court. The "legal principle" is that there is a constitutionally protected right to an abortion, although the right is not absolute. "Lower courts" to the United States Supreme Court are all federal courts and all levels of state courts in all 50 states. Because the Court has established this principle, it and all lower courts should reach the same decision in future cases, but they need to do so only if "the facts are substantially the same."

Legal reasoning involves determining what the legal principle is and when the facts of the present case are "substantially the same" as the prior case, so that the prior case can be used as **precedent**. *Griswold* itself was binding only on the parties to the case, but the doctrine of stare decisis makes the legal principle set forth in *Griswold* applicable to future cases. Although no two cases have material facts that are exactly the same, the facts of two cases may be similar.

ROE V. WADE AND STARE DECISIS

The United States Supreme Court decided *Roe v. Wade,* 410 U.S. 113 (1973), eight years after *Griswold. Roe v. Wade* was brought by a pregnant

Enumerated or Listed Constitutional Right	Penumbra or Expanded Constitutional Protection
The Fourth Amendment of the Bill of Rights protects people and property "against unreasonable searches and seizure."	Right to privacy
	Right to use birth control
	Abortion rights

FIGURE 2-1 Constitutional rights generated by the Fourth Amendment.

woman ("Jane Roe" was a pseudonym) to challenge the constitutionality of Texas abortion laws. The laws made abortion a crime, except to save the mother's life. Before the case reached the United States Supreme Court, the federal district court had held the laws unconstitutional.

The right to privacy identified in *Griswold* was applied in *Roe* to allow abortion.

In *Roe,* the issue before the United States Supreme Court was whether the Texas laws were constitutional. Roe argued that a "woman's right [to an abortion] is absolute and that she is entitled to terminate her pregnancy at whatever time, in whatever way and for whatever reason she alone chooses." Texas argued that "life begins at conception and is present throughout pregnancy, and that therefore the State has a compelling interest in protecting that life from and after conception."

In deciding *Roe,* the United States Supreme Court was bound by the doctrine of stare decisis to use *Griswold* as precedent if the facts in *Griswold* were "substantially the same" as the facts in *Roe.* The Court decided that the facts in *Griswold* and *Roe* were similar and found that the "right of privacy . . . is broad enough to encompass a woman's decision whether or not to terminate her pregnancy." The Court held that "the right of personal privacy includes the abortion decision, but that this right is not unqualified and must be considered against important state interests in regulation." The Court also held that the Texas statute was unconstitutional, but that the state could regulate the right to an abortion during the second trimester and prohibit it during the third trimester.

Application of Roe v. Wade to Later Cases

Would a state abortion statute requiring a 24-hour wait and spousal consent be constitutional? That was the issue in *Planned Parenthood v. Casey,* 112 S. Ct. 2791 (1992), after the Pennsylvania abortion statute containing these provisions was challenged in federal court.

The attorney for the plaintiffs who challenged the statute might have characterized *Roe* by saying that it was **on point** with *Casey.* The plaintiffs' attorney probably urged the court to apply the doctrine of stare decisis and hold the Pennsylvania statute unconstitutional. The attorney would have argued that the facts in *Casey* were substantially the same as those in *Roe,* because the waiting period and consent requirements effectively denied the right to an abortion to a woman who could not obtain her spouse's consent or who could not afford to travel a great distance.

In *Casey,* the attorney for the defendant—the state of Pennsylvania—might have argued that the facts in *Casey* were different from the facts in *Roe.* The state might have pointed out that the Pennsylvania statute did not criminalize almost all abortions, as did the statute in *Roe,* and would have argued that the waiting period and consent requirements made sure that women did not make hasty or ill-informed decisions. The state would thus be **distinguishing** *Casey* from *Roe* on the facts. The state might then have argued that, because the two statutes were not substantially the same, holding the statute constitutional would not violate the doctrine of stare decisis.

LEGAL TERMS

landmark case (leading case)
A court decision of great significance in establishing an important legal precedent.

penumbra doctrine
The doctrine of constitutional law that the rights specifically guaranteed in the Bill of Rights have "penumbras" creating other rights that are not specifically enumerated.

precedent
Prior decisions of the same court, or a higher court, which a judge must follow in deciding a subsequent case presenting similar facts and the same legal problem, even though different parties are involved and many years have elapsed.

on point
Refers to a judicial opinion that, with respect to the facts involved and the applicable law, is similar to but not on all fours with another case.

distinguish
To explain why a particular case is not precedent or authority with respect to the matter in controversy.

The United States Supreme Court ruled that the 24-hour wait was constitutional but that the spousal consent requirement was unconstitutional. The decision was a plurality opinion. Justices O'Connor, Kennedy, and Souter announced the judgment of the Court. Justices Stevens, Blackmun, and Scalia, and Chief Justice Rehnquist, each wrote separate opinions concurring in part and dissenting in part. Justices White, Scalia, and Thomas joined in the separate opinion by Chief Justice Rehnquist, and Justices White and Thomas and Chief Justice Rehnquist joined in the separate opinion by Justice Scalia.

In deciding *Casey,* the Court explicitly reaffirmed *Roe* and restated *Roe*'s holding:

> It must be stated at the outset and with clarity that *Roe*'s essential holding, the holding we reaffirm, has three parts. First is the recognition of the right of the woman to choose to have an abortion before viability and to obtain it without undue interference from the State. Before viability, the State's interests are not strong enough to support a prohibition of abortion or the imposition of a substantial obstacle to the woman's effective right to elect the procedure. Second is a confirmation of the State's power to restrict abortion after fetal viability, if the law contains exceptions for pregnancies which endanger a woman's life or health. And third is the principle that the State has legitimate interests from the outset of the pregnancy in protecting the health of the woman and the life of the fetus that may become a child. These principles do not contradict one another; and we adhere to each.

AT LEAST TWO SIDES TO EVERY PROBLEM

In *Casey,* the state and the plaintiffs' attorney reached opposite conclusions about the applicability of *Roe.* The state urged the court to hold the Pennsylvania statute constitutional, while the plaintiffs' attorney urged the court to hold the statute unconstitutional. They were pressing opposite decisions because their legal analyses of the effect of *Roe* on *Casey* was different. The state emphasized the differences between *Roe* and *Casey,* whereas the plaintiffs' attorney emphasized the similarity between *Roe* and *Casey.*

Every legal problem has at least two sides. The job of each attorney team is to represent the client's best interest. An attorney represents the client's best interest by explaining to the court which primary sources apply to the problem, why certain primary sources apply, and what decision the court should reach based on those applicable primary sources. Assuming that both legal teams have competently performed their legal research on a problem, they both have the same primary sources on which to base their arguments. Although the attorneys are relying on the same primary sources, their answers will be much different because of the way they have applied the primary sources to the problem. Each attorney will argue that the primary authority favorable to the client's case is substantially similar to the problem and should control. In contrast, each attorney will argue that primary authority unfavorable to the client's case is readily distinguishable from the problem or that the court should change the law.

In *Casey,* the United States Supreme Court reaffirmed that *Roe* was still good law and applied the holding of *Roe* to *Casey.*

The doctrine of stare decisis has worked well over the centuries because it gives case law relative stability and predictability while at the same time allowing for gradual change. There is stability and predictability because courts are bound to look to prior cases before deciding present cases. Much of what an attorney does is to research the law to find cases on point and then predict how a court will decide—or try to convince the court to decide—based on those prior cases. Although the United States Supreme Court and the highest courts of each state have the power to **overrule** prior decisions, they hesitate to do so. A chronic practice of overruling prior decisions undermines the stability and predictability of the legal system.

Courts rarely state explicitly that they are overruling a prior case. Decades may pass between a precedent-setting case and a later case that overrules it. In *Plessy v. Ferguson,* 163 U.S. 537 (1896), the United States Supreme Court held that separate but equal accommodations for black and white railway passengers were constitutional. Over the years, *Plessy* was used to justify separate but equal public schools. It was not until half a century later that the Court overruled *Plessy.* In *Brown v. Board of Education,* 347 U.S. 483 (1954), the Court held that separate but equal public school accommodations violated the equal protection clause found in the Fourteenth amendment to the United States Constitution.

Instead of explicitly overruling a prior case, courts may **limit** its effect. The effect of a landmark case like *Roe* is unclear until the United States Supreme Court applies it in later cases. Many have argued that *Roe* was not the correct interpretation of the Constitution. In *Casey,* the Court was under great pressure to overrule or greatly curtail the implications of *Roe.* The Court ruled only that the states may place certain limits, such as a 24-hour waiting period, on the abortion right.

The *Casey* plurality opinion contained some interesting comments on the Court's apparent struggle to decide whether *Roe* should be overturned and how it applied to *Casey*:

> [I]t is common wisdom that the rule of *stare decisis* is not an "inexorable command," and certainly it is not such in every constitutional case . . . . Rather, when this Court reexamines a prior holding, its judgment is customarily informed by a series of prudential and pragmatic considerations designed to test the consistency of overruling a prior decision with the ideal of the rule of law, and to gauge the respective costs of reaffirming and overruling a prior case. Thus, for example, we may ask whether the rule has proved to be intolerable simply in defying practical workability . . . ; whether the rule is subject to a kind of reliance that would lend a special hardship to the consequences of overruling and add inequity to the cost of repudiation . . . ; whether related principles of law have so far developed as to have left the old

LEGAL TERMS

overrule
To disallow; to override; to reverse; to veto; to annul; to nullify. The overruling of precedent is the nullification of a prior decision as precedent; it occurs when the same court, or a higher court in a later case, establishes a different rule on the same point of law involved in the earlier case. When a decision is overruled, it is said to be "reversed."

limit
To restrain; to restrict; to impose a limitation.

> rule no more than a remnant of abandoned doctrine . . . ; or whether facts have so changed or come to be seen so differently, as to have robbed the old rule of significant application or justification . . . .
>
> * * *
>
> Within the bounds of normal *stare decisis* analysis, then, and subject to the considerations on which it customarily turns, the stronger argument is for affirming *Roe*'s central holding, with whatever degree of personal reluctance any of us may have, not for overruling it.

JUDICIAL OPINIONS

The type of opinion (majority, plurality, concurring, dissenting, per curiam, or en banc opinion) in a case is important. A **majority opinion** is an opinion agreed upon by at least a majority of the judges deciding the case. Usually one judge writes the opinion and other judges who agree with the opinion join in it. A **plurality opinion** is agreed upon by more judges than any other opinion, although less than a majority of the court. *Casey* is an example of a plurality opinion. In *Casey,* only three Justices agreed upon the opinion. The only courts issuing plurality opinions are the United States Supreme Court, the highest court of each state, and intermediate appellate courts sitting en banc, because they are the only courts with enough members to have a plurality opinion. A **concurring opinion** is one agreeing with the result reached in the majority opinion, but for different reasons. In *Casey,* a number of Justices agreed with (concurred in) the results, but wrote separate concurring opinions to explain how their reasoning differed from the reasoning of the plurality opinion. A **dissenting opinion** is written by a judge who disagrees with the result reached by the majority opinion; it expresses the judge's reasons for the disagreement. One or more judges may join in a concurring or dissenting opinion. A judge may join in any part of any decision. For example, a judge may join in part in the majority opinion, write his or her own concurring opinion as to another part of the question, and join in part of another judge's dissenting opinion. A **per curiam opinion** is written by the whole court rather than by one particular judge. Usually you will see a per curiam opinion in a relatively unimportant case. In contrast, as discussed earlier, an **en banc opinion** is usually reserved for the most important or controversial cases, decided by the entire membership of the intermediate appellate court rather than by a three-judge panel.

Except for en banc decisions, intermediate appellate courts sit in panels to decide cases. The panels are made up of three judges selected at random from the membership of the intermediate appellate court. Sometimes one of the judges on the panel may be a lower court judge specially designated to hear an intermediate appellate case. After the three judges review the appellate briefs and hear any oral argument, they meet to decide the case. One of the two or three judges agreeing on how the case should be decided is assigned to write the majority opinion. Any judge disagreeing may choose to write a concurring or dissenting opinion. Before the opinion is announced,

LEGAL TERMS

majority opinion
An opinion issued by an appellate court that represents the view of a majority of the members of the court.

plurality opinion
An appellate court opinion joined in by less than a majority of the justices, but by more justices than the number joining any other concurring opinion.

concurring opinion
An opinion issued by one or more judges which agrees with the result reached by the majority opinion rendered by the court, but reaches that result for different reasons.

dissenting opinion
A written opinion filed by a judge of an appellate court who disagrees with the decision of the majority of judges in a case, giving the reasons for his or her differing view. Often a dissenting opinion is written by one judge on behalf of one or more other dissenting judges.

per curiam opinion
An opinion, usually of an appellate court, in which the judges are all of one view and the legal question is sufficiently clear that a full written opinion is not required and a one- or two-paragraph opinion suffices.

it is circulated to the other judges. A judge disagreeing with the opinion may either negotiate with the judge who wrote the opinion, to attempt to change certain language, or may decide not to join in the opinion after all. A judge who originally was going to concur or dissent may decide to join in the majority opinion instead.

Types of opinions:
majority dissenting
plurality per curiam
concurring en banc

The entire membership of the United States Supreme Court and the highest state court in the state usually sit to decide a case. Each member of the United States Supreme Court is referred to as a "Justice" rather than a "judge," with the leader of the Court called the "Chief Justice." The members of the highest court in your state may also be referred to as "Justices." A Justice may be excused from hearing a case because of illness or because the Justice **recuses** himself or herself. The procedure for deciding a case in the United States Supreme Court or in the highest court of a state is similar to that described previously for the intermediate appellate courts. Decisions of the United States Supreme Court and the highest state courts, sometimes referred to as **courts of last resort,** are not called en banc decisions, though, because the standard procedure is for the entire membership of the court to hear cases.

Most opinions you will use in research are published opinions of appellate courts, but not all opinions are published. If you learn of an unpublished opinion you would like to use as authority, you may obtain a copy of it from the clerk of the court that issued the opinion, usually for a nominal fee. You very rarely see published opinions of trial courts when researching state case law of certain states. Perhaps it is customary not to publish them because they are only persuasive authority for other courts.

en banc
Means "on the bench." A court, particularly an appellate court, with all the judges sitting together (*sitting en banc*) in a case.

recuse
To disqualify oneself from sitting as a judge in a case, either on the motion of a party or on the judge's own motion, usually because of bias or some interest in the outcome of the litigation.

court of last resort (highest court)
The highest court of a state; the Supreme Court of the United States; a court whose decisions are not subject to review by a higher court.

MANDATORY AND PERSUASIVE AUTHORITY

A **mandatory authority** is a case that must be followed as precedent under the doctrine of stare decisis. A **persuasive authority**, just as the term implies, is a case that may be only persuasive and is not required to be followed. More precisely, the part of the case that is mandatory authority and therefore binding on other courts is the **holding** of the majority opinion.

Brown v. Board of Education is mandatory authority from the United States Supreme Court, unless the Court overrules it, for all lower courts. This means that *Brown* must be followed; it is binding on all federal and all state courts because it is the most current interpretation of the United States Constitution.

A decision of a United States Circuit Court is binding on that circuit and all federal district courts within that circuit. The decision of a United States Circuit Court is not mandatory authority for another circuit because all circuits are on the same level. For example, the United States Eleventh Circuit Court of Appeals covers Alabama, Georgia, and Florida. The United States Fifth Circuit Court of Appeals covers Texas, Louisiana, and Mississippi. A decision of one three-judge panel of the Eleventh Circuit would be

binding (mandatory) authority
Previous decisions of a higher court or statutes that a judge must follow in reaching a decision in a case.

persuasive authority
Authority that is neither binding authority nor precedent, but which a court may use to support its decision if it chooses.

holding
The proposition of law for which a case stands; the "bottom line" of a judicial decision.

mandatory authority for any future Eleventh Circuit case and any federal district courts in Alabama, Georgia, and Florida. That decision would only be persuasive authority, however, for the Fifth Circuit Court of Appeals and federal district courts within Texas, Louisiana, and Mississippi. Interestingly enough, a decision of a United States district or circuit court is considered persuasive rather than mandatory authority for state courts, even state courts geographically located within the district or circuit. This is because a case that is appealed through the various state courts to the highest court in the state would go up to the United States Supreme Court rather than to a United States circuit or district court. In practice, though, a state court may give great weight to decisions of United States district and circuit courts covering the same geographic area when the federal court decisions deal with constitutional issues.

Plurality, concurring, and dissenting opinions are considered persuasive authority, as are all secondary sources. A decision of a court in one state is persuasive authority on the courts of another state. Although not binding, persuasive authority may be cited if there is no mandatory authority on point, or it may be cited to back up one's argument that the court should change the law by overruling a precedent.

Before becoming a United States Supreme Court Justice, Thurgood Marshall was one of the attorneys who argued *Brown* before the Court, claiming that *Plessy v. Ferguson* should be overruled. Marshall had only persuasive authority to rely on in his argument, because the only way the Court could rule in favor of his client was to overrule *Plessy v. Ferguson.* The Court accepted his argument that the law should be changed and did overrule *Plessy.*

A decision of the highest court in a state is binding on all courts within that state. A decision of an intermediate appellate court is binding on the trial-level courts within the geographic area covered by that intermediate appellate court. If the intermediate appellate court in your state is divided into districts or circuits, it would be interesting for you to do some research to determine whether the decision of one district or circuit is mandatory or persuasive authority for other districts or circuits. You will very likely find that the relationship between different intermediate appellate courts in your state is that of "sister courts," with the decision of one intermediate appellate court considered persuasive rather than mandatory. The United States Circuit Courts have this same relationship.

Another question is what effect a decision of an intermediate appellate court has on the trial-level court geographically located outside the area covered by the intermediate appellate court. The decision of the intermediate appellate court could be considered either mandatory or persuasive authority.

Let's examine examples of mandatory and persuasive authority. In *Johnson v. Davis,* 480 So. 2d 625 (Fla. 1985), the Florida Supreme Court held that "where the seller of a home knows of facts materially affecting the value of the property which are not readily observable and are not known to the buyer, the seller is under a duty to disclose them to the buyer." In *Johnson,* the homeowner knew that the roof leaked but failed to disclose this to the buyer. The court ruled that the seller's "fraudulent concealment" entitled the buyer to return of the deposit plus interest, costs, and attorney fees.

Johnson was a landmark case because the law in Florida had previously been that the doctrine of *caveat emptor,* which states "let the buyer beware," applied to home sales. The *Johnson* court cited decisions in California, Illinois, Nebraska, West Virginia, Louisiana, New Jersey, and Colorado in its decision announcing that the doctrine of caveat emptor would no longer apply to the sale of homes in Florida. These other state decisions acted as persuasive authority for the Florida court. A court of another state can now cite to *Johnson* as persuasive authority. After *Johnson,* a Florida trial court considering a similar case would have to follow *Johnson* and hold the home seller liable for fraud if the home seller knew the home had a leaky roof but failed to disclose it to the buyer. This could then become mandatory authority.

LEGAL ANALYSIS

Legal analysis is a sequential process (see Figure 2-2). First, one must read all authority relevant to the problem and synthesize the main point. The facts in each case will be different from the facts in every other case, but from them you can formulate a rule of law. *Synthesizing* cases means extracting from the different fact patterns and holdings a rule of law. Once you know the rule of law, you can apply it to a present case to predict the outcome. If a statute controls, one must synthesize the statute with case law interpretations of it and extract the rule of law. Similarly, if a constitutional provision controls, one must synthesize the constitutional provision with case law interpretations of it and extract the rule of law. Sometimes the meaning of a statute (or constitutional provision) which appears quite clear on its

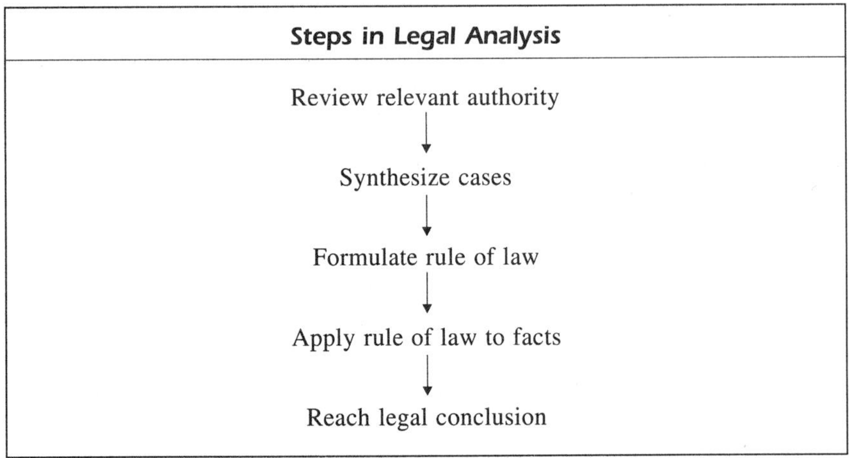

Steps in Legal Analysis
Review relevant authority
Synthesize cases
Formulate rule of law
Apply rule of law to facts
Reach legal conclusion

FIGURE 2-2 The sequential process of legal analysis begins with reviewing relevant legal authority.

face has been greatly changed by case law interpretation. Case law may have created exceptions to the statute (or constitutional provision) that leave very little of the statute.

For example, in 1982, Anthony Paul Inciarrano shot and killed Earvin Herman Trimble in Trimble's office. Unbeknownst to Inciarrano, Trimble was tape-recording what happened in the office. A tape found by the police after the murder contained Trimble's last conversation with Inciarrano, the gunshots, Trimble moaning, and Inciarrano leaving Trimble's office.

At his murder trial, Inciarrano moved to suppress the recording because it had been made without his consent. The Florida Supreme Court found that Inciarrano had no reasonable expectation of privacy in Trimble's office because Inciarrano had gone there intending to kill Trimble. The court held that the tape recording should not be excluded from evidence. *State v. Inciarrano,* 473 So. 2d 1272 (Fla. 1985). Thus, the *Inciarrano* ruling created an exception to the statute excluding tape recordings of intercepted communications. The exception allowed Trimble's recording to be admitted into evidence at Inciarrano's murder trial.

The next step in legal analysis is to apply the rule of law to the facts of the problem. Application of law to facts requires one to determine how the rule of law and the authority backing it up are similar to or different from the facts in the present problem. If the facts in prior cases are substantially the same, then the result in the problem should be the same as the result in the prior cases. If there is a controlling statute, the result in the problem should be as dictated by that statute and cases interpreting it. Application of the law to the facts of the problem is the most important part of legal analysis, but it is the step most often overlooked when students perform legal analysis. Students tend to carefully explain the rule of law and then skip directly from the rule of law to the conclusion. Instead, the reasoning followed must be explained. Written legal analysis should lead step by step from the rule of law, through the application of the rule of law to the facts in the problem, to the conclusion.

The last step is to reach a conclusion by tying the rule of law and the application of law to facts together. The conclusion is the solution to the problem, and it must be thoroughly backed up by the rule of law and the reasoning applying the rule of law to the facts in the problem. The conclusion is also a prediction of what a court will do based on relevant authority.

SUMMARY

- The doctrine of stare decisis states that when a court has set forth a legal principle, that court and all lower courts under it will apply that principle in future cases in which the facts are substantially the same.
- *Roe v. Wade* illustrates the doctrine of stare decisis:
  - In *Roe v. Wade* the United States Supreme Court held that a Texas statute making abortion a crime was unconstitutional but that the

  state could regulate the right to an abortion during the second trimester and prohibit it during the third trimester.
  - Applying the doctrine of stare decisis, *Roe v. Wade* is used as precedent in later cases in which the facts are substantially the same.
  - If the facts in a later abortion case in which a state abortion statute is challenged are substantially the same as the facts in *Roe v. Wade*, then the court in the later case should hold the challenged abortion statute unconstitutional. However, if the challenged abortion statute in the later case is distinguishable from the *Roe* statute, a court may uphold the constitutionality of the challenged statute.
- The doctrine of stare decisis gives case law predictability while allowing gradual change.
- There are at least two sides to every problem, and the attorney represents the client's best interest by arguing that authority favorable to the client's case should be applied and that unfavorable authority is distinguishable.
- When reading a court decision, note what type of opinion it is: majority, plurality, concurring, dissenting, per curiam, or en banc.
- A case may be mandatory authority, which must be followed under the doctrine of stare decisis, or persuasive authority, which may, but is not required, to be followed.
- Legal analysis involves three steps:
  - Reading and synthesizing all relevant authority to extract a rule of law
  - Applying the rule of law to the facts of the problem
  - Reaching a conclusion.

EXERCISES

1. What was the holding (the central decision) of *Griswold v. Connecticut*?
2. What were the arguments of the two attorneys in *Roe v. Wade*?
3. Was *Griswold* used as precedent in *Roe*?
4. What was the issue (legal question before the court) in *Planned Parenthood v. Casey*?
5. What were the arguments of the two attorneys in *Casey*?
6. Was *Roe* used as precedent in *Casey*?
7. What are the differences among majority, plurality, concurring, dissenting, per curiam, and en banc court decisions?
8. What is a court of last resort?
9. Give an example of mandatory authority for federal courts and for the courts of your state.
10. Give an example of persuasive authority for federal courts and for the courts of your state.

CHAPTER 3

Secondary Sources and Finding Tools

OUTLINE

COMMON LEGAL SOURCES AND FINDING TOOLS

Note: Sources used in this chapter are indicated by boldface type.

Primary Sources	Secondary Sources	Finding Tools
reporters	**treatises**	**American Law Reports**
constitutions	**law review articles**	**legal encyclopedias**
statutes	**legal periodicals**	**digests**
administrative regulations	**law dictionaries**	Shepard's Citators
court rules	**legal thesauruses**	**Index to Legal Periodicals**
loose-leaf services	**continuing legal education publications**	loose-leaf services
	Restatements	
	American Law Reports	
	legal encyclopedias	
	loose-leaf services	

This chapter introduces secondary sources and finding tools. It includes detailed explanations of legal encyclopedias, American Law Reports, and digests. As explained in Chapter 2, digests are *never* cited, and it is preferable to cite to the primary authorities found throughout the legal encyclopedias and American Law Reports rather than citing to the legal encyclopedias and American Law Reports themselves.

LEGAL ENCYCLOPEDIAS

Legal encyclopedias are organized like the multivolume encyclopedias found in schools and public libraries. Information in a legal encyclopedia is divided into topics, with the topics arranged in alphabetical order. Each topic gives a textual explanation of the law relating to that topic. Index volumes are located at the end of the set; to find information, you can either go directly to a topic or use the index to locate a topic.

The two most widely used national legal encyclopedias are *Corpus Juris Secundum* (C.J.S.), published by West Publishing Company, and *American Jurisprudence 2d* (Am. Jur. 2d), published by Lawyers Cooperative Publishing Company. Both contain explanations of federal and state law. Separate legal encyclopedias are published for some states. For example, Florida law is covered in *Florida Jurisprudence 2d* (Fla. Jur. 2d), published by Lawyers Cooperative Publishing. If you were researching Florida law, *Florida Jurisprudence* would be your first choice. If your research did not locate any primary sources from Florida, you could consult the national encyclopedias to find authority from other states. You could use this authority as persuasive authority to answer your legal question.

Legal encyclopedias divide each topic into sections. An outline of section numbers and subjects appears at the beginning of the legal encyclopedia topic. For example, Figure 3-1 shows a partial table of contents for the "Forfeitures and Penalties" topic from 36 Am. Jur. 2d. This topic is divided into 110 sections. Once you locate a relevant topic in the legal encyclopedia, it is a good idea to glance over the table of contents for the topic to determine which sections might answer your questions. If you had questions on the trial of a forfeiture case, you could start your research by reading §§ 103 to 109 in "Forfeitures and Penalties." The index volumes usually refer you to a topic and section number so that you can go directly to that section.

Special Features of Legal Encyclopedias

Legal encyclopedias differ from other encyclopedias in several important ways. Basic background information on a topic is heavily footnoted, with the footnotes containing citations to primary sources. The footnotes in the sample page in Figure 3-1 are quite extensive compared to the text portion.

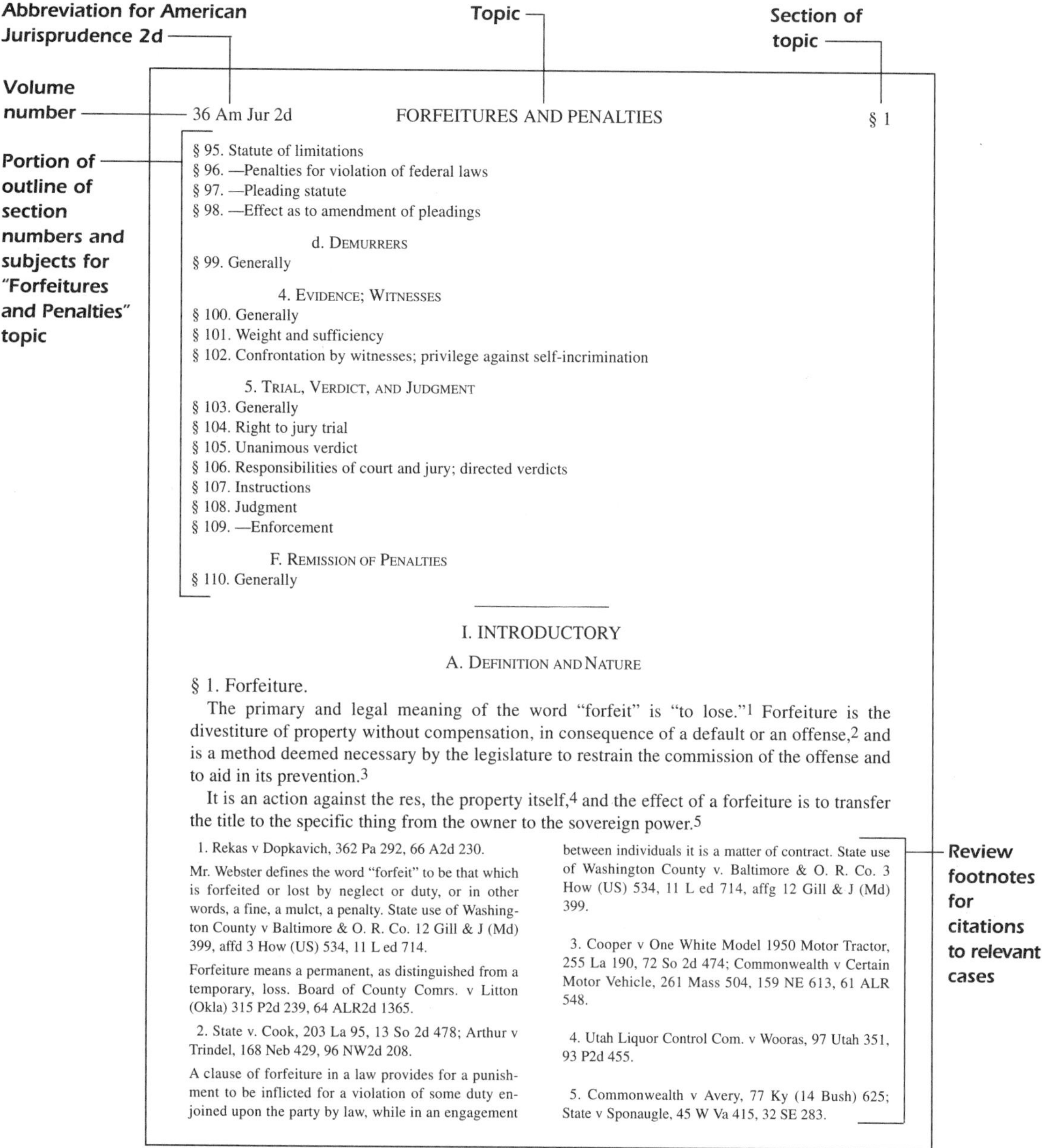

Abbreviation for American Jurisprudence 2d
Topic
Section of topic
Volume number
Portion of outline of section numbers and subjects for "Forfeitures and Penalties" topic
Review footnotes for citations to relevant cases
36 Am Jur 2d
FORFEITURES AND PENALTIES
§ 1
§ 95. Statute of limitations
§ 96. —Penalties for violation of federal laws
§ 97. —Pleading statute
§ 98. —Effect as to amendment of pleadings
d. DEMURRERS
§ 99. Generally
4. EVIDENCE; WITNESSES
§ 100. Generally
§ 101. Weight and sufficiency
§ 102. Confrontation by witnesses; privilege against self-incrimination
5. TRIAL, VERDICT, AND JUDGMENT
§ 103. Generally
§ 104. Right to jury trial
§ 105. Unanimous verdict
§ 106. Responsibilities of court and jury; directed verdicts
§ 107. Instructions
§ 108. Judgment
§ 109. —Enforcement
F. REMISSION OF PENALTIES
§ 110. Generally
I. INTRODUCTORY
A. DEFINITION AND NATURE
§ 1. Forfeiture.
The primary and legal meaning of the word "forfeit" is "to lose."1 Forfeiture is the divestiture of property without compensation, in consequence of a default or an offense,2 and is a method deemed necessary by the legislature to restrain the commission of the offense and to aid in its prevention.3
It is an action against the res, the property itself,4 and the effect of a forfeiture is to transfer the title to the specific thing from the owner to the sovereign power.5
1. Rekas v Dopkavich, 362 Pa 292, 66 A2d 230.
Mr. Webster defines the word "forfeit" to be that which is forfeited or lost by neglect or duty, or in other words, a fine, a mulct, a penalty. State use of Washington County v Baltimore & O. R. Co. 12 Gill & J (Md) 399, affd 3 How (US) 534, 11 L ed 714.
Forfeiture means a permanent, as distinguished from a temporary, loss. Board of County Comrs. v Litton (Okla) 315 P2d 239, 64 ALR2d 1365.
2. State v. Cook, 203 La 95, 13 So 2d 478; Arthur v Trindel, 168 Neb 429, 96 NW2d 208.
A clause of forfeiture in a law provides for a punishment to be inflicted for a violation of some duty enjoined upon the party by law, while in an engagement between individuals it is a matter of contract. State use of Washington County v. Baltimore & O. R. Co. 3 How (US) 534, 11 L ed 714, affg 12 Gill & J (Md) 399.
3. Cooper v One White Model 1950 Motor Tractor, 255 La 190, 72 So 2d 474; Commonwealth v Certain Motor Vehicle, 261 Mass 504, 159 NE 613, 61 ALR 548.
4. Utah Liquor Control Com. v Wooras, 97 Utah 351, 93 P2d 455.
5. Commonwealth v Avery, 77 Ky (14 Bush) 625; State v Sponaugle, 45 W Va 415, 32 SE 283.

FIGURE 3-1 A partial table of contents of a topic in *American Jurisprudence,* a legal encyclopedia. (From 36 Am. Jur. 2d. Courtesy of Lawyers Cooperative Publishing.)

Footnote 1 on the sample page contains citations to cases from Pennsylvania, Maryland, and Oklahoma. Legal encyclopedias emphasize case law rather than statutory law.

Legal encyclopedias, like many other law books, are updated by pocket parts. A *pocket part* is a paperbound booklet containing recent legal information, so called because the back cover of the pocket part is inserted into a "pocket" inside the back cover of the hardbound volume. When you are doing research, it is essential to check the pocket part for updated material. Pocket parts are usually reprinted at least annually and contain more recent information than the hardbound volume. When you are doing research, note the copyright date of the hardbound volume and then the date on the front of the pocket part. Also note the date of coverage for the pocket part (this *currency date* tells on what date research and update for that pocket part was cut off). This information is found in the first few pages of the pocket part. Because of its inherent datedness, a pocket part dated May 1993 may only cover material through December of the preceding year. Every so often the publisher reprints a volume. The reprinted volume contains whatever is still correct from the old hardbound volume and incorporates new material previously published in the pocket parts. There may be no pocket part published in the year in which the reprinted volume is published, because the material in the hardbound volume is current without it.

Use of Legal Encyclopedias

Use legal encyclopedias while keeping in mind their limitations. The text provides a short summary of the law, without detail, which gives some background but is not usually specific enough to answer the legal question. You must look up the cases cited in the legal encyclopedia. Do not rely on what the legal encyclopedia says about a case, because it may not be completely accurate. Researchers generally do not quote from legal encyclopedias. Because a legal encyclopedia only contains a publisher's interpretation of the law at the time it was written, it is preferable to use the primary source itself. Do not omit statutory research. Legal encyclopedias emphasize case law rather than statutory law and may not reference applicable statutes. See Figure 3-2 for a summary of ways to use legal encyclopedias.

Currency in legal research is the key to answering a legal question correctly. Although the legal encyclopedias may be updated annually by pocket parts, the last cases cited may be several years old. The textual explanation may be dated or inapplicable if new cases or statutes has changed the law since the text was written. Most legal encyclopedias cite representative cases relevant to a particular legal point rather than citing all decided cases on point. Start with the latest cases found in the legal encyclopedia and then find later cases on point by using digests and shepardizing. The use of digests is discussed later in this chapter and the use of Shepard's Citators is discussed in Chapter 6.

In summary, legal encyclopedias are best used:

1. To find primary authority; and
2. To give the researcher general background information.

TIPS ON USING LEGAL ENCYCLOPEDIAS	
Do	**Do not**
1. Use footnotes to locate relevant primary authority.	1. Rely on a legal encyclopedia alone as an accurate statement of the law.
2. Pull and read primary authority.	2. Generally cite to a legal encyclopedia.
3. Check pocket parts for recent information.	
4. Update information found.	

FIGURE 3-2 Do's and don'ts of using legal encyclopedias.

For information on how to make legal encyclopedias a part of your research strategy, see Chapter 7.

Citation to Legal Encyclopedias

Although legal encyclopedias are not usually cited in documents submitted to the court or opposing counsel, you will need to cite legal encyclopedias for assignments and more informal documents such as office memos. (See Chapter 13 for an explanation of the purpose and use of office memos.)

Figure 3-3 is the citation for § 1 of the *American Jurisprudence 2d* "Forfeitures and Penalties" topic. The number "36" is the volume in which § 1 is located; "1968" is the copyright year of the volume; "1993" is the year of the pocket part supplement. The ampersand ("&") indicates that the material you are referring to was found in both the hardbound volume and the pocket part supplement. The citation should be revised to show only "1968" in the parentheses if the material to which you are referring was found only in the hardbound volume. Similarly, the parentheses should contain only "Supp. 1993" if the material to which you are referring was found only in the pocket part supplement. A citation to *Corpus Juris Secundum*

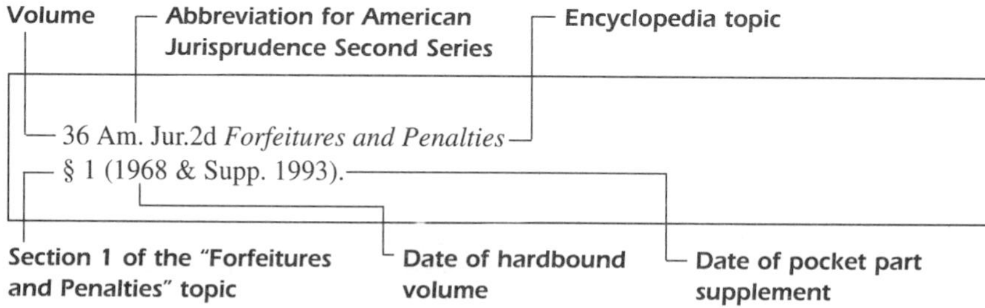

FIGURE 3-3 *American Jurisprudence* 2d citation.

or a state legal encyclopedia would be in similar form, except you would substitute the abbreviation for that legal encyclopedia for "Am. Jur. 2d" as shown in Figure 3-4.

DIGESTS

Digests contain summaries of cases and references to other research materials. The case summaries are arranged by topic and subtopic to allow you to find cases related to a particular legal principle. Figure 3-5 is from Federal Practice Digest Fourth Series, which contains summaries of federal cases. Federal Practice Digest Fourth Series uses the West Publishing Company's key number system. This key number system is universal in West publications.

West Key Number System

The West key number system divides the law into more than 400 topics and numerous subtopics within those topics (see Figure 3-6 for topics). Each subtopic is assigned a key number. For example, if you were researching a search and seizure problem and wanted to know the permissible scope of a search, you might look under key number 147 of "Searches and Seizures." Notice from the sample page in Figure 3-5 that that key number is entitled "Scope of search." To refer back to the same key number later, or to give an answer on a research assignment, you need to note both the topic and the key number. There is a "key number 147" in hundreds of different topics. If you write down just "147," you may not remember that you looked at key number 147 of "Searches and Seizures"; if you write down just "Searches and Seizures" you may not remember that you looked under key number 147. The topics comprising the West key number system are printed inside the cover each West digest. A table of contents containing the key numbers and titles of subtopics appears at the beginning of each topic of the digest.

Lawyers Cooperative Publishing Company publishes digests to accompany reporters such as *United States Supreme Court Reports, Lawyers Edition,* published by Lawyers Cooperative. The Lawyers Cooperative publications use similar topics and subtopics, even though they are not referred to as key numbers.

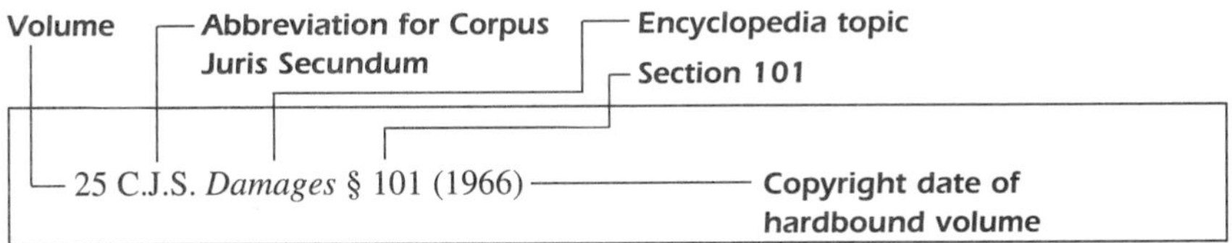

FIGURE 3-4 *Corpus Juris Secundum* citation.

Volume 85 Federal Practice Digest 4th, page 19

1991 United States Supreme Court case originally from Florida

85 F P D 4th—19 SEARCHES & SEIZURES ⚷147

For references to other topics, see Descriptive-Word Index

It was not necessary for FBI agent to have warrant in hand prior to executing nighttime search, but even if his failure to have warrant in hand was a violation of rule, suppression was not required in absence of evidence that search would not have occurred, or would not have been so abrasive, in absence of violation. Fed.Rules Cr.Proc.Rule 41(d), 18 U.S.C.A.; U.S.C.A. Const.Amend. 4.

U.S. v. Pryor, 652 F.Supp. 1353.

1984 United States District Court case from the district of Maine

D.C.Me. 1984. U.S. v. Rule, 594 F.Supp. 1223, vacated U.S. v. Streifel, 781 F.2d 953, on remand 633 F.Supp. 535, reversed 815 F.2d 153.

E.D.N.Y. 1988. Probable cause existed for issuance of nighttime warrant to search premises of businesses operated by mail fraud defendants where it appeared that defendants had attempted over period of past week to either steal or destroy evidence pertinent to investigation. U.S.C.A. Const.Amend. 4.

U.S. v. Turoff, 701 F.Supp. 981.

S.D.N.Y. 1987. Government acted within constitutional boundaries when it obtained warrants to search defendants' briefcases the day after it had probable cause to believe that the briefcases contained evidence pertaining to illegal arms sales, and searched the briefcases within the time constraints expressly imposed by the warrants.

U.S. v. Evans, 667 F.Supp. 974.

W.D.Pa. 1991. Officer was not liable to homeowner injured during nighttime search of erroneous residence; there was no allegation that injury was intentional and, as a matter of law, nighttime entry by force with little warning was not constitutionally unreasonable. U.S.C.A. Const.Amend. 4.

Reed v. Marker, 762 F.Supp. 652.

D.R.I. 1988. Under federal law, state officers who executed search warrant for house at approximately 9:30 p.m. were not required to have "good cause" to execute warrant at night; federal law defines daytime as hours between 6:00 a.m. and 10:00 p.m., so no showing of exceptional cause was necessary. Fed.Rules Cr.Proc.Rule 41(h), 18 U.S.C.A.

U.S. v. One Parcel of Real Property with Bldgs., Appurtenances, and Improvements, Known as 147 Div. Street, Located in City of Woonsocket, R.I., 696 F.Supp. 783, affirmed 873 F.2d 7, certiorari denied Latraverse v. U.S., 110 S.Ct. 236, 493 U.S. 891, 107 L.Ed.2d 187.

Key number 147

⚷147. Scope of search.

Library references

C.J.S. Searches and Seizures § 83.

U.S.Fla. 1991. Scope of search is generally defined by its expressed object. U.S.C.A. Const.Amend. 4.

Florida v. Jimeno, 111 S.Ct. 1801, 114 L.Ed.2d 297, on remand 588 So.2d 233.

Same wording as headnote 4 from Jimeno (Jimeno included in Appendix A)

Citation to Jimeno

U.S.Md. 1987. Validity of search of one of two apartments on third floor of building pursuant to overbroad warrant authorizing search of entire third floor, based on mistaken belief that other apartment was the only one on third floor, depended on whether officers' failure to realize overbreadth of warrant was objectively understandable and reasonable, and since objective facts available to officers at the time suggested no distinction between suspect's apartment and third-floor premises, search by mistake of other apartment occupied by party not mentioned in warrant was valid; moreover, even if warrant was interpreted as authorizing search limited to suspect's apartment rather than entire third floor, search was valid because prior to officers' discovery of mistake, they perceived suspect's apartment and third-floor premises as one and the same, and their execution of warrant reasonably included entire third floor.

Maryland v. Garrison, 107 S.Ct. 1013, 480 U.S. 79, 94 L.Ed.2d 72.

1991 United States Ninth Circuit Court of Appeals case originally from California

C.A.9 (Cal.) 1991. Officer, pursuant to search warrant, determines what is seized. U.S.C.A.Const.Amend. 4.

In re Grand Jury Subpoenas Dated Dec. 10, 1987, 926 F.2d 847.

C.A.9 (Cal.) 1988. While supporting affidavit of Office of Export Enforcement officer was not specifically incorporated by reference in her search warrant, affidavit did serve to limit warrant's lack of particularity and avoided suppression of incriminating evidence discovered during execution where officer who executed warrant read affidavit, instructed other officers about warrant's breadth, and officers seized only evidence related to discussion in affidavit. U.S.C.A. Const.Amend. 4.

U.S. v. Luk, 859 F.2d 667.

C.A.8 (Minn.) 1991. Even if officers had been told that necklace named in search warrant was located in jewelry box, their search under bed and coat pocket was consistent with Fourth Amendment so that gun and cocaine found under bed and in coat pocket were properly seized under plain view doctrine; officers were not required to accept word of witness regarding necklace's location. U.S.C.A. Const.Amend. 4.

U.S. v. Hughes, 940 F.2d 1125, certiorari denied 112 S.Ct. 267, 116 L.Ed.2d 220.

C.A.9 (Or.) 1987. Search warrant which permitted Immigration and Naturalization Service officers to enter factory to conduct "factory sweep" operation in search of illegal aliens

For cited U.S.C.A. sections and legislative history, see United States Code Annotated

For more information on this topic, see section 83 of the legal encyclopedia Corpus Juris Secundum.

FIGURE 3-5 Sample page from Federal Practice Digest 4th. (Reprinted with permission from Federal Practice Digest 4th, copyright © by West Publishing Company.)

DIGEST TOPICS

See, also, Outline of the Law by Seven Main Divisions of Law, Page VII

The topic numbers shown below may be used in WESTLAW searches for cases within the topic and within specified key numbers.

1 Abandoned and Lost Property
2 Abatement and Revival
3 Abduction
4 Abortion and Birth Control
5 Absentees
6 Abstracts of Title
7 Accession
8 Accord and Satisfaction
9 Account
10 Account, Action on
11 Account Stated
11A Accountants
12 Acknowledgment
13 Action
14 Action on the Case
15 Adjoining Landowners
15A Administrative Law and Procedure
16 Admiralty
17 Adoption
18 Adulteration
19 Adultery
20 Adverse Possession
21 Affidavits
22 Affray
23 Agriculture
24 Aliens
25 Alteration of Instruments
26 Ambassadors and Consuls
27 Amicus Curiae
28 Animals
29 Annuities
30 Appeal and Error
31 Appearance
33 Arbitration
34 Armed Services
35 Arrest
36 Arson
37 Assault and Battery
38 Assignments
40 Assistance, Writ of
41 Associations
42 Assumpsit, Action of
43 Asylums
44 Attachment
45 Attorney and Client
46 Attorney General
47 Auctions and Auctioneers
48 Audita Querela
48A Automobiles
48B Aviation
49 Bail
50 Bailment
51 Bankruptcy
52 Banks and Banking
54 Beneficial Associations
55 Bigamy
56 Bills and Notes
57 Blasphemy
58 Bonds
59 Boundaries
60 Bounties
61 Breach of Marriage Promise
62 Breach of the Peace
63 Bribery
64 Bridges
65 Brokers
66 Building and Loan Associations
67 Burglary
68 Canals
69 Cancellation of Instruments
70 Carriers
71 Cemeteries
72 Census
73 Certiorari
74 Champerty and Maintenance
75 Charities
76 Chattel Mortgages
76A Chemical Dependents
76H Children Out-Of-Wedlock
77 Citizens
78 Civil Rights
79 Clerk of Courts
80 Clubs
81 Colleges and Universities
82 Collision
83 Commerce
83H Commodity Futures Trading Regulation
84 Common Lands
85 Common Law
86 Common Scold
88 Compounding Offenses
89 Compromise and Settlement
89A Condominium
90 Confusion of Goods
91 Conspiracy
92 Constitutional Law
92B Consumer Credit
92H Consumer Protection
93 Contempt
95 Contracts
96 Contribution
97 Conversion
98 Convicts
99 Copyrights and Intellectual Property
100 Coroners
101 Corporations
102 Costs
103 Counterfeiting
104 Counties
105 Court Commissioners
106 Courts
107 Covenant, Action of
108 Covenants
108A Credit Reporting Agencies
110 Criminal Law
111 Crops
113 Customs and Usages
114 Customs Duties

FIGURE 3-6 Topics and subtopics in the West key number system.

Relationship Between Reporters and Digests

To better understand digests, let's look at how the digest material is generated. Before a case such as *Florida v. Jimeno* is reprinted by a publisher, it is read by an editor. The editor writes a **syllabus** (a summary) of the case. This syllabus may be in addition to the syllabus prepared by the official reporter. This is the reason some cases may be preceded by two syllabi.

115	Damages
116	Dead Bodies
117	Death
117G	Debt, Action of
117T	Debtor and Creditor
118A	Declatory Judgment
119	Dedication
120	Deeds
122a	Deposits and Escrows
123	Deposits in Court
124	Descent and Distribution
125	Detectives
126	Detinue
129	Disorderly Conduct
130	Disorderly House
131	District and Prosecuting Attorneys
132	District of Columbia
133	Disturbance of Public Assemblage
134	Divorce
135	Domicile
136	Dower and Curtesy
137	Drains
138	Drugs and Narcotics
140	Dueling
141	Easements
142	Ejectment
143	Election of Remedies
144	Elections
145	Electricity
146	Embezzlement
147	Embracery
148	Eminent Domain
148A	Employers' Liability
149	Entry, Writ of
150	Equity
151	Escape
152	Escheat
154	Estates in Property
156	Estoppel
157	Evidence
158	Exceptions, Bill of
159	Exchange of Property
160	Exchanges
161	Execution
162	Executors and Administrators
163	Exemptions
164	Explosives
165	Extortion and Threats
166	Extradition and Detainers
167	Factors
168	False Imprisonment
169	False Personation
170	False Pretenses
170A	Federal Civil Procedure
170B	Federal Courts
171	Fences
172	Ferries
174	Fines
175	Fires
176	Fish
177	Fixtures
178	Food
179	Forcible Entry and Detainer
180	Forfeitures
181	Forgery
182	Fornication
183	Franchises
184	Fraud
185	Frauds, Statue of
186	Fraudulent Conveyances
187	Game
188	Gaming
189	Garnishment
190	Gas
191	Gifts
192	Good Will
193	Grand Jury
195	Guaranty
196	Guardian and Ward
197	Habeas Corpus
198	Hawkers and Peddlers
199	Health and Environment
200	Highways
201	Holidays
202	Homestead
203	Homicide
204	Hospitals
205	Husband and Wife
205H	Implied and Constructive Contracts
206	Improvements
207	Incest
208	Indemnity
209	Indians
210	Indictments and Information
211	Infants
212	Injunction
213	Innkeepers
216	Inspection
217	Insurance
218	Insurrection and Sedition
219	Interest
220	Internal Revenue
221	International Law
222	Interpleader
223	Intoxicating Liquors
224	Joint Adventures
225	Joint-Stock Companies and Business Trusts
226	Joint Tenancy
227	Judges
228	Judgment
229	Judicial Sales
230	Jury
231	Justices of the Peace
232	Kidnapping
232A	Labor Relations
233	Landlord and Tenant
234	Larceny
235	Levees and Flood Control
236	Lewdness
237	Libel and Slander
238	Licenses
239	Liens
240	Life Estates
241	Limitations of Actions
242	Lis Pendens
245	Logs and Logging
246	Lost Instruments
247	Lotteries
248	Malicious Mischief
249	Malicious Prosecution
250	Mandamus
251	Manufactures
252	Maritime Liens
253	Marriage
255	Master and Servant
256	Mayhem
257	Mechanics Liens
257A	Mental Health
258A	Military Justice
259	Militia
260	Mines and Minerals
261	Miscegenation
265	Monopolies
266	Mortgages
267	Motions
268	Municipal Corporations
269	Names
270	Navigable Waters
271	Ne Exeat

FIGURE 3-6 *(Continued)*

The editor also writes paragraphs called **headnotes** summarizing the important principles contained in the case. Each headnote contains one legal principle. After completing the annotations, the editor assigns each one to one or more topics and key numbers. All six headnotes to *Jimeno* are under "Searches and Seizures," key numbers 23, 53, 147, and 186. See the sample digest page in Figure 3-5, which demonstrates how a case headnote is

A copy of *Florida v. Jimeno* from Supreme Court Reporter appears in Appendix A. The first few pages of the case also appear in Chapter 4.

LEGAL TERMS

syllabus
1. The headnote of a reported case. 2. A summary outline of a course of study.

headnote
A summary statement that appears at the beginning of a reported case to indicate the points decided by the case.

272	Negligence	319	Quo Warranto	365	Submission of Controversy
273	Neutrality Laws	320	Railroads	366	Subrogation
274	Newspapers	321	Rape	367	Subscriptions
275	New Trial	322	Real Actions	368	Suicide
276	Notaries	323	Receivers	369	Sunday
277	Notice	324	Receiving Stolen Goods	370	Supersedeas
278	Novation	325	Recognizances	371	Taxation
279	Nuisance	326	Records	372	Telecommunications
280	Oath	327	Reference	373	Tenancy in Common
281	Obscenity	328	Reformation of Instruments	374	Tender
282	Obstructing Justice	330	Registers of Deeds	375	Territories
283	Officers and Public Employees	331	Release	376	Theaters and Shows
284	Pardon and Parole	332	Religious Societies	378	Time
285	Parent and Child	333	Remainders	379	Torts
286	Parliamentary Law	334	Removal of Cases	380	Towage
287	Parties	335	Replevin	381	Towns
288	Partition	336	Reports	382	Trade Regulation
289	Partnership	337	Rescue	384	Treason
290	Party Walls	338	Reversions	385	Treaties
291	Patents	339	Review	386	Trespass
292	Paupers	340	Rewards	387	Trespass to Try Title
294	Payment	341	Riot	388	Trial
295	Penalties	342	Robbery	389	Trover and Conversion
296	Pensions	343	Sales	390	Trusts
297	Perjury	344	Salvage	391	Turnpikes and Toll Roads
298	Perpetuities	345	Schools	392	Undertakings
299	Physicians and Surgeons	346	Scire Facias	393	United States
300	Pilots	347	Seals	394	United States Magistrates
301	Piracy	348	Seaman	395	United States Marshals
302	Pleading	349	Searches and Seizures	396	Unlawful Assembly
303	Pledges	349A	Secured Transactions	396A	Urban Railroads
304	Poisons	349B	Securities Regulation	398	Usury
305	Possessory Warrant	350	Seduction	399	Vagrancy
306	Post Office	351	Sequestration	400	Vendor and Purchaser
307	Powers	352	Set-Off and Counterclaim	401	Venue
307A	Pretrial Procedure	353	Sheriffs and Constables	402	War and National Emergency
308	Principal and Agent	354	Shipping	403	Warehousemen
309	Principal and Surety	355	Signatures	404	Waste
310	Prisons	356	Slaves	405	Waters and Water Courses
311	Private Roads	356A	Social Security and Public Welfare	406	Weapons
312	Prize Fighting	357	Sodomy	407	Weights and Measures
313	Process	358	Specific Performance	408	Wharves
313A	Products Liability	359	Spendthrifts	409	Wills
314	Prohibition	360	States	410	Witnesses
315	Property	361	Statutes	411	Woods and Forests
316	Prostitution	362	Steam	413	Workers' Compensation
316A	Public Contracts	363	Stipulations	414	Zoning and Planning
317	Public Lands				
317A	Public Utilities				
318	Quieting Title				

FIGURE 3-6 *(Continued)*

reproduced as a digest paragraph under the relevant topic. The words "Scope of search is generally defined by its expressed object. U.S.C.A. const. Amend. 4." appear three times in the digest: once under key number 53, once under key number 147, and once under key number 186 of "Searches and Seizures." Notice that those words appear under key number 147 of the sample digest page.

Digest Page Format

Examine the format for digest paragraphs using the sample page in Figure 3-5. Under key number 147, you first see a library reference, which cites to *Corpus Juris Secundum* under Searches and Seizures § 83. Numerous case summary paragraphs follow the library reference. Case summaries from the highest court come first; then case summaries from other courts are arranged in descending order. Also notice that the summaries of cases of a particular court are arranged with the most current one first (reverse chronological order). The abbreviation in bold type at the beginning of the case summary identifies the court and the year of the decision. For example, "**U.S.Fla. 1991**" identifies a 1991 United States Supreme Court case originally from Florida (Jimeno), and "**C.A.9 (Cal.) 1991**" identifies a 1991 United States Ninth Circuit Court of Appeals case and adds the information that the case was originally from California. The material in bold is followed by the case summary, and the case summary is then followed by the case citation.

Types of Digests

The Federal Practice Digest sampled in Figure 3-5 is just one of many digests published. A list of digests and their coverage appears in Figure 3-7. When choosing which digest to use, pick the one that will give you results the quickest. The West American Digest System (comprised of the Century Digest, Decennial Digests, and the General Digest) is the most comprehensive digest, covering state and federal cases since 1658.

United States Supreme Court Digest, Lawyers Edition covers United States Supreme Court cases. A note on *United States Supreme Court Digest, Lawyers Edition* (L. Ed): Because this digest is published by Lawyers Cooperative Publishing Company, it does not use the West key number system. It does use a similar classification system with topics and subtopics, as seen in Figure 3-8. The case summaries in the digest are reprints of the headnotes from Lawyers Edition.

The Federal Practice Digest (now in its fourth series) covers federal cases. Southern Digest is an example of a regional digest. It covers state court cases from Louisiana, Mississippi, Alabama, and Florida.

West's Florida Digest is an example of a state digest. It covers Florida cases.

Finding Relevant Material in Digests

How would you choose which digest to consult? Let's look at a few examples. If you wanted to find a United States Supreme Court opinion, you could consult the West American Digest System, Federal Practice Digest, or *United States Supreme Court Digest, Lawyers' Edition*. The Federal Practice Digest or *Lawyers Edition* would be your preferred choices because these digests are considerably less massive than the West American Digest

Digests

West's American Digest System—state and federal courts
  Century Digest
  Decennial Digests (each covers a five- to ten-year period)
  General Digest (updates the latest Decennial Digest)

Digests for United States Supreme Court cases
  United States Supreme Court Digest (West)
  United States Supreme Court Digest, Lawyers Edition (Lawyers Cooperative Publishing Co.)

Federal Courts (United States Supreme Court, circuit courts, and district courts) (West)
  Federal Digest (through 1939)
  Modern Federal Practice Digest (1940–1960)
  Federal Practice Digest 2d (1961–1975)
  Federal Practice Digest 3d (1975–1989)
  Federal Practice Digest 4th (1989–present)

Regional Digests (West)
  Atlantic Digest
  North Western Digest
  South Eastern Digest
  Pacific Digest
  Southern Digest

State Digests
  [West publishes for most states]

FIGURE 3-7 The coverage of various digests.

System. If you wanted to find a United States circuit court opinion, you could consult the West American Digest System or Federal Practice Digest. Your choice would be Federal Practice Digest rather than the West American Digest System because Federal Practice Digest contains only federal court case summaries. If you wanted to find a Florida Supreme Court opinion, you could consult the West American Digest System, Southern Digest, or Florida Digest. Your choice would be Florida Digest rather than the West American Digest System or Southern Digest, because Florida Digest contains only Florida case summaries.

There are several ways to find digest material. One way is to use the descriptive word index for the digest. The index supplies a topic and key number when you look up key words. If you have the name of a case on point without the citation, you can find the citation by consulting the case name volumes. Once you find the case on point, determine from the case which topics and key numbers are relevant to your search. Then look at the topics and key numbers in the digests. Cases concerning the same legal

First Page of Florida v. Jimeno as printed in L. Ed. 2d.

FLORIDA, Petitioner
v
ENIO JIMENO et al

500 US—, 114 L Ed 2d 297, 111 S Ct—
[No. 90-622]

Argued March 25, 1991. Decided May 23, 1991.

Decision: Police officer's opening of a closed paper bag found on floor of suspect's car during search of car for narcotics held not to violate Fourth Amendment where suspect had consented to search of car.

SUMMARY

A county police officer in Florida—having overheard a suspect arranging what appeared to be a drug transaction over a public telephone, and having observed the suspect commit a traffic infraction—stopped the suspect's car to issue a traffic citation. The officer told the suspect that the officer had reason to believe that the suspect was carrying narcotics in his car, and the officer asked to search the car. The suspect said that he had nothing to hide and gave the officer permission to conduct the search. The officer opened a door on the passenger side and saw a folded, brown paper bag on the floorboard. The officer picked up the bag, opened it, and found a kilogram of cocaine inside. The suspect was charged with possession with intent to distribute cocaine in violation of Florida law. Before the trial in Circuit Court of Dade County, Florida, the suspect moved to suppress the cocaine found in the bag on the ground that his consent to a search of the car did not extend to the opening of the bag. The trial court, agreeing with the suspect's argument, granted the motion. The District Court of Appeal of Florida, Third District, affirming, expressed the view that consent to a general search for narcotics does not extend to sealed containers within the general area agreed to by the suspect (550 S02d 1176). The Supreme Court of Florida, approving the District Court of Appeals decision, held that the consent to search a vehicle does not extend to a closed container found inside a vehicle (564 So2d 1083).

On certiorari, the United States Supreme Court reversed and remanded. In an opinion by REHNQUIST, Ch. J., joined by WHITE, BLACKMUN, O'CONNER,

FIGURE 3-8 *Florida v. Jimeno* as printed in *Lawyers Edition.*

principle are grouped together under the same topic and key number. If you know a topic relevant to your problem, look at the table of contents at the beginning of the topic. From the titles of the subtopics, you can identify relevant key numbers to research. If a particular term is important to your research, you can look up the term in the Words and Phrases index located at the end of the digest. This index will give you citations to cases defining that term.

SCALIA, KENNEDY, and SOUTER, JJ., it was held that (1) a criminal suspect's right, under the Federal Constitution's Fourth Amendment, to be free from unreasonable searches is not violated where (a) after the suspect gives a police officer permission to search the suspect's automobile, the officer opens a closed container, found within the automobile, that might reasonably hold the object of the search, and (b) under the circumstances, it is objectively reasonable for the officer to believe that the scope of the suspect's consent permitted the officer to open that particular container; and (2) the officer did not violate the suspect's Fourth Amendment rights in the case at hand, given that (a) a reasonable person may be expected to know that narcotics are generally carried in some form of container, and thus (b) it was objectively reasonable, under the circumstances presented, for the officer to conclude that the general consent to search the suspect's car included consent to search containers within the car which might bear drugs.

MARSHALL, J., joined by STEVENS, J., dissenting, expressed the view that an individual's consent to a search of the interior of a car should not be understood to authorize a search of closed containers inside the car, given that an individual's expectation of privacy in a container is distinct from, and greater than, the expectation of privacy in the interior of a car.

FIGURE 3-8 *(Continued)*

Currency is important in using digests. Digests are published in series. Each hardbound volume in the series is updated by an annual pocket part. Paperbound supplementary pamphlets update the pocket parts. The pamphlets are updated by digest paragraphs found in any later hardbound volumes or advance sheets of the applicable reporter. Start your digest research with the most recent series. If there are no case summmaries printed for the digest subtopic you are researching, look in the prior series. For example, if you are looking for a search and seizure case from a United States circuit court, you would start with Federal Practice Digest Fourth Series. Review the "Searches and Seizures" topic in the hardbound volume, the pocket part to that volume, any available supplement pamphlet, and any later hardbound volumes or advance sheets of the applicable reporter. For summaries of earlier cases, consult a prior series of the digest.

Use of Digests

The only appropriate use of digests is to find primary authority. See Figure 3-9 for tips on using digests. For information on how to make legal encyclopedias and digests part of your research strategy, see Chapter 7.

FLORIDA v JIMENO

(1991) 114 L ed 2d 297 — As printed in

HEADNOTES

Classified to U. S. Supreme Court Digest, Lawyers' Edition.

Search and Seizure §§ 10. 14 — consent — scope of search — closed container found within car

1a, 1b. A criminal suspect's right, under the Federal Constitution's Fourth Amendment, to be free from unreasonable searches is not violated where (1) after the suspect gives a police officer permission to search the suspect's automobile, the officer opens a closed container, found within the automobile, that might reasonably hold the object of the search, and (2) under the circumstances, it is objectively reasonable for the officer to believe that the scope of the suspect's consent permitted the officer to open that particular container; although a suspect is permitted to delimit the scope of the search to which the suspect consents, the Fourth Amendment does not require the officer to request a more explicit authorization to search a particular closed container within an automobile if the suspect's con-

Reprinted in digest for Lawyers Edition

TOTAL CLIENT-SERVICE LIBRARY® REFERENCES

68 Am Jur 2d, Searches and Seizures §§ 16, 53, 100, 101
8 Federal Procedure L Ed, Criminal Procedure § 22:156; 12A Federal Procedure L Ed, Evidence §§ 33:615, 33:635
7 Federal Procedural Forms, L Ed, Criminal Procedure § 20:618
8 Am Jur Pl & Pr Forms (Rev), Criminal Procedure, Form 254
5 Am Jur Trials 331, Excluding Illegally Obtained Evidence USCS, Constitution, Amendment 4
L Ed Digest, Search and Seizure §§ 10, 14
L Ed Index, Automobile and Highway Traffic; Search and Seizure
Index to Annotations, Automobiles and Highway Traffic; Search and Seizure
Auto-Cite©: Cases and annotations referred to herein can be further researched through the Auto-Cite© computer-assisted research service. Use Auto-Cite to check citations for form, parallel references, prior and later history, and annotation references.

ANNOTATION REFERENCES

Validity, under Federal Constitution, of warrantless search of motor vehicle—Supreme Court Cases. 89 L Ed 2d 939.

Validity, under Federal Constitution, of consent to search—Supreme Court cases. 36 L Ed 2d 1143.

FIGURE 3-8 *(Continued)*

AMERICAN LAW REPORTS

American Law Reports (ALR), published by Lawyers Cooperative Publishing, combines both case reporter and legal encyclopedia features. This reference series is like reporters in that it contains cases, and the full text of selected cases is included. A case is selected to be published in American

sent would reasonably be understood to extend to that container. (Marshall and Stevens, JJ., dissented from this holding.)

Search and Seizure §§ 10, 14 — consent — scope of narcotics search — closed paper bag inside car

2a-2d. A police officer does not violate a suspect's right under the Federal Constitution's Fourth Amendment, to be free from unreasonable searches, where (1) the officer has reason to believe that narcotics are being carried in the suspect's automobile, (2) the officer informs the suspect of this belief and asks permission to search the automobile, (3) the suspect permits the officer to search the automobile and does place not any explicit limitation on the scope of the search, and (4) the officer finds a closed paper bag on the automobile's floor and opens the bag; in such a case the authorization to search extends beyond the surface of the automobile's interior to the paper bag, because (1) a reasonable person may be expected to know that narcotics are generally carried in some form of container, (2) it is objectively reasonable for the officer to conclude that the general consent to search the automobile includes consent to search containers within that automobile which might bear drugs, and (3) although it is likely unreasonable to think that a suspect, by consenting to the search of the trunk of his automobile, has agreed to to the breaking open of a locked briefcase within the trunk, it is otherwise with respect to a closed paper bag. (Marshall and Stevens, JJ., dissented from this holding.)

Reprinted in digest for Lawyers Edition

Search and Seizure § 5 — constitutional guarantee

3. Not all state-initiated searches and seizures are proscribed by the Federal Constitution's Fourth Amendment; the Fourth Amendment merely proscribes those searches and seizures which are unreasonable.

Search and Seizure § 14 — scope of consent

4. Under the Federal Constitution's Fourth Amendment, the standard for measuring the scope of a suspect's consent to a search is that of objective reasonableness—that is, what the typical reasonable person would have understood by the exchange between the police officer and the suspect.

Search and Seizure § 8 — scope

5. The scope of a search is generally defined by the search's expressed object.

SYLLABUS BY REPORTER OF DECISIONS

Having stopped respondent Enio Jimeno's car for a traffic infraction, police officer Trujillo, who had been following the car after overhearing Jimeno arranging what appeared to be a drug transaction, declared that he had reason to believe that Jimeno was carrying narcotics in the car, and asked permission to search it. Jimeno consented, and Trujillo found cocaine inside a folded paper bag on the car's floorboard. Jimeno and a passenger, respondent Luz Jimeno, were charged with possession with intent to distribute cocaine in violation of Florida law, but the state trial court granted their motion to suppress the cocaine on the ground that Jimeno's consent to search the car did not carry with it specific

FIGURE 3-8 *(Continued)*

FLORIDA v JIMENO

(1991) 114 L Ed 2d 297

consent to open the bag and examine its contents. The Florida District Court of Appeal and Supreme Court affirmed.

Held: A criminal suspect's Fourth Amendment right to be free from unreasonable searches is not violated when, after he gives police permission to search the car, they open a closed container found within the car that might reasonably hold the object of the search. The Amendment is satisfied when, under the circumstances, it is objectively reasonable for the police to believe that the scope of the suspect's consent permitted them to open the particular container. Here, the authorization to search extended beyond the car's interior surfaces to the bag, since Jimeno did not place any explicit limitation on the scope of the search and was aware that Trujillo would be looking for narcotics in the car, and since a reasonable person may be expected to know that narcotics are generally carried in some form of container. There is not basis for adding to the Fourth Amendment's basic test of objective reasonableness a requirement that, if police wish to search closed containers within a car, they must separately request permission to search each container.

564 So 2d, reversed and remanded.

Rehnquist, C. J., delivered the opinion of the court, in which White, Blackmun, O'Conner, Scalia, Kennedy and Souter, JJ., joined. Marshall, J., filed a dissenting opinion, in which Stevens, J., joined.

APPEARANCES OF COUNSEL

Michael J. Neimand argued the cause for petitioner.

John G. Roberts, Jr. argued the cause for the United States, as amicus curiae, supporting petitioner, by special leave of court.

Jeffrey S. Weiner argued the cause for respondents.

OPINION OF THE COURT

Chief Justice Rehnquist delivered the opinion of the court.

[1a, 2a] In this case we decide whether a criminal suspect's Fourth Amendment right to be free from unreasonable searches is violated when, after he gives a police officer permission to search his automobile, the officer opens a closed container found within the car that might reasonably hold the object of the search. We find that it is not. The Fourth Amendment is satisfied when, under the circumstances, it is objectively reasonable for the officer to believe that the scope of the suspect's consent permitted him to open a particular container within the automobile.

This case began when a Dade County police officer, Frank Trujillo, overheard respondent, Enio Jimeno, arranging what appeared to be a drug transaction over a public telephone. Believing that Jimeno might be involved in illegal drug trafficking, Officer Trujillo followed his car. The officer observed respondents make a right turn at a red light without stopping. He then pulled Jimeno over to the side of the road in order to issue him a traffic citation. Officer Trujillo told Jimeno that he had been stopped for com-

FIGURE 3-8 *(Continued)*

TIPS ON USING DIGESTS	
Do	**Do not**
1. Use citations to locate relevant primary authority.	1. Rely on a digest entry as an accurate summary of a case.
2. Pull and read primary authority.	2. Cite to or quote from digests.
3. Check pocket parts for recent information.	
4. Update information found.	

FIGURE 3-9 Do's and don'ts of using digests.

Law Reports because it contains an important, novel, or interesting legal issue. American Law Reports are also similar to legal encyclopedias in that they contain textual explanations (called **annotations**) of the law with lengthy footnotes to relevant cases. A case selected for publication in American Law Reports illustrates a legal issue covered in the annotation.

Sample American Law Reports Annotation

The sample pages in Figure 3-10 show the organization and content of a typical recent ALR annotation. An outline of the material covered in the annotation precedes the text. Also preceding the text are an index to terms used in the annotation and a "Jurisdictional Table of Cited Statutes and Cases" (indicating where in the annotation you would look to find the law from a particular jurisdiction). Section 1[a] of the annotation text defines the scope of the annotation (what it covers) and § 1[b] gives a list of related annotations. Related annotations are useful in showing whether you have found the most relevant annotation to the problem you are researching. The format and organization of the ALR annotations may vary slightly from series to series.

Unlike the topical arrangement of legal encyclopedias, annotations are published in the order they are written. The legal issues covered by annotations grow with developing case law. Extensive changes in case law may require a new, "superseding" annotation. Annotations from one of the earlier series may be consulted for topics that have undergone little change.

Finding and Updating American Law Reports

Figure 3-11 shows the American Law Reports published, the time period covered, and the method of updating the particular series. Prior to

LEGAL TERMS

annotation
1. A notation, appended to any written work, which explains or comments upon its meaning. 2. A commentary that appears immediately following a printed statute and describes the application of the statute in actual cases. Such annotations, with the statutes on which they comment, are published in volumes known as *annotated statutes* or *annotated codes*. 3. A notation that follows an opinion of court printed in a court report, explaining the court's action in detail.

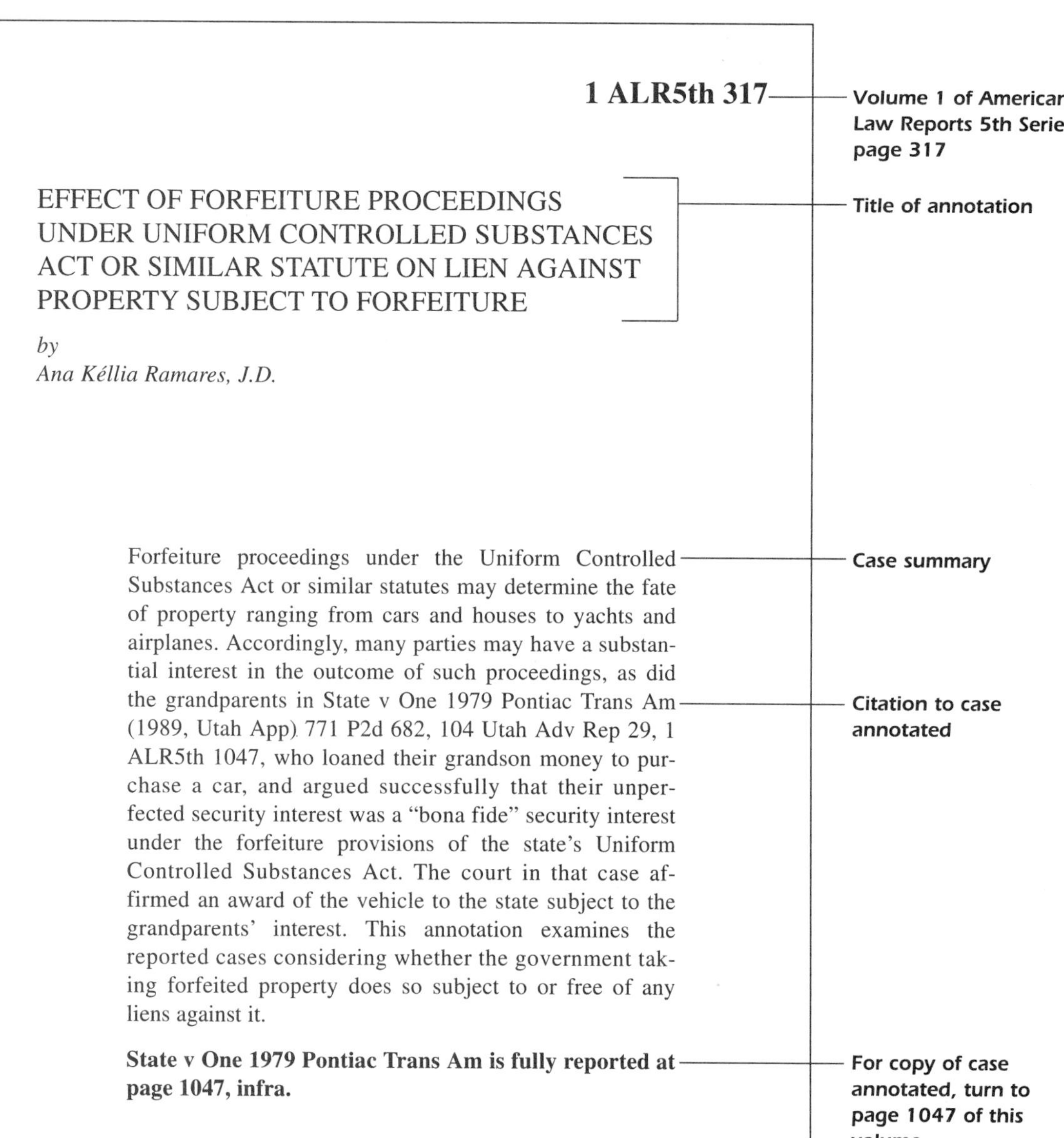
1 ALR5th 317

EFFECT OF FORFEITURE PROCEEDINGS UNDER UNIFORM CONTROLLED SUBSTANCES ACT OR SIMILAR STATUTE ON LIEN AGAINST PROPERTY SUBJECT TO FORFEITURE

by
Ana Kéllia Ramares, J.D.

Forfeiture proceedings under the Uniform Controlled Substances Act or similar statutes may determine the fate of property ranging from cars and houses to yachts and airplanes. Accordingly, many parties may have a substantial interest in the outcome of such proceedings, as did the grandparents in State v One 1979 Pontiac Trans Am (1989, Utah App) 771 P2d 682, 104 Utah Adv Rep 29, 1 ALR5th 1047, who loaned their grandson money to purchase a car, and argued successfully that their unperfected security interest was a "bona fide" security interest under the forfeiture provisions of the state's Uniform Controlled Substances Act. The court in that case affirmed an award of the vehicle to the state subject to the grandparents' interest. This annotation examines the reported cases considering whether the government taking forfeited property does so subject to or free of any liens against it.

State v One 1979 Pontiac Trans Am is fully reported at page 1047, infra.

FIGURE 3-10 Sample American Law Reports annotation. (From 1 A.L.R.5th 317–326. Courtesy of Lawyers Cooperative Publishing.)

1969, the first through third series of American Law Reports had covered both federal and state material. Since 1969, federal material has been covered in American Law Reports Federal. For state material since 1969, you would consult the third through the fifth series of American Law Reports.

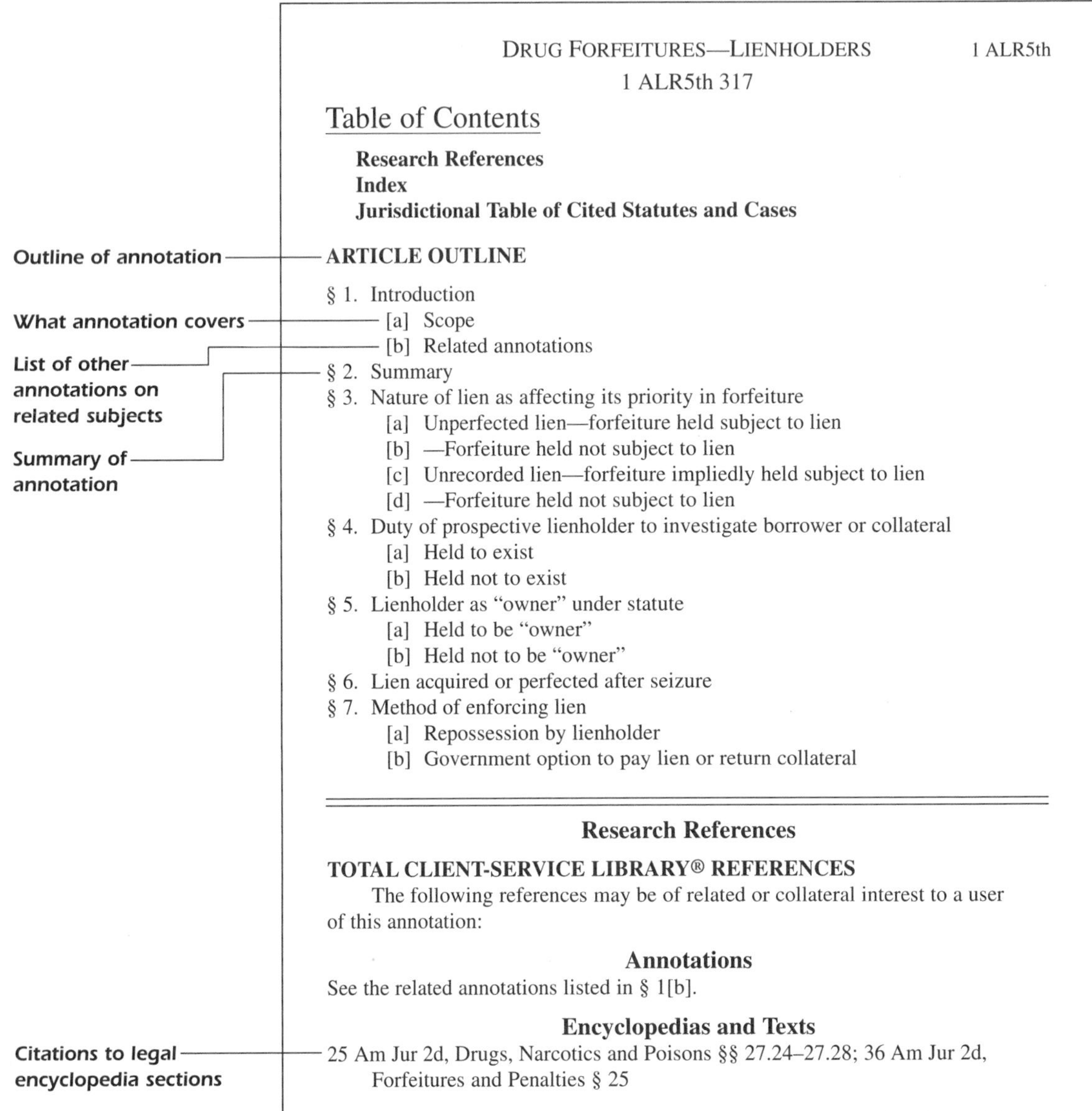

DRUG FORFEITURES—LIENHOLDERS 1 ALR5th

1 ALR5th 317

Table of Contents

Research References
Index
Jurisdictional Table of Cited Statutes and Cases

ARTICLE OUTLINE

§ 1. Introduction
[a] Scope
[b] Related annotations
§ 2. Summary
§ 3. Nature of lien as affecting its priority in forfeiture
[a] Unperfected lien—forfeiture held subject to lien
[b] —Forfeiture held not subject to lien
[c] Unrecorded lien—forfeiture impliedly held subject to lien
[d] —Forfeiture held not subject to lien
§ 4. Duty of prospective lienholder to investigate borrower or collateral
[a] Held to exist
[b] Held not to exist
§ 5. Lienholder as "owner" under statute
[a] Held to be "owner"
[b] Held not to be "owner"
§ 6. Lien acquired or perfected after seizure
§ 7. Method of enforcing lien
[a] Repossession by lienholder
[b] Government option to pay lien or return collateral

Research References

TOTAL CLIENT-SERVICE LIBRARY® REFERENCES

The following references may be of related or collateral interest to a user of this annotation:

Annotations

See the related annotations listed in § 1[b].

Encyclopedias and Texts

25 Am Jur 2d, Drugs, Narcotics and Poisons §§ 27.24–27.28; 36 Am Jur 2d, Forfeitures and Penalties § 25

FIGURE 3-10 *(Continued)*

Use the index and digest volumes of American Law Reports to find relevant annotations. Updates to the index and digest volumes are contained in pocket parts. The index also contains an "Annotation History Table," which tells you if an annotation has been supplemented or superseded. An annotation that supplements an earlier annotation should be read together with the earlier annotation. When an annotation supersedes an earlier annotation, only the later annotation should be read.

1 ALR5th DRUG FORFEITURES—LIENHOLDERS
1 ALR5th 317

5 Federal Procedure, L Ed, Bonds, Civil fines, and Forfeitures §§ 10:14–10:30, 10:51–10:65

Practice Aids

7 Federal Procedural Forms, L Ed, Criminal Procedure § 20:1063
12 Am Jur Pl & Pr Forms (Rev), Forfeitures and Penalties, Forms 2, 6, 21, 25
8 Am Jur Legal Forms 2d, Forfeitures and Penalties §§ 123:4–123:8
13 Am Jur Proof of Facts 391, Criminal Drug Addiction and Possession
8 Am Jr Trials 573, Defense of Narcotic Cases

Federal Statutes

21 USCS §§ 848(a), 881, 883, 885(c) — Citations to federal forfeiture statutes

Digests and Indexes

ALR Digests, Drugs and Druggists §§ 7–13; §§ 1–4
Index to Annotation, Drugs and Narcotics; Fines, Forfeitures and Penalties; Liens and Encumbrances; Secured Transactions; Uniform Controlled Substances Act

Auto-Cite®

Cases and annotations referred to herein can be further researched through the Auto-Cite® computer-assisted research service. Use Auto-Cite to check citations for form, parallel references, prior and later history, and annotation references.

RESEARCH SOURCES

The following are the research sources that were found to be helpful in compiling this annotation:

Texts

La Fave, Search and Seizure 2d § 7.3(b).
Herman, Search and Seizure Checklist.
Hall, Search and Seizure §§ 9:29, 9:31, 25:2.
9 ULA § 505 n 33.

Citations to treatises

Encyclopedias

25 Am Jur 2d, Drugs, Narcotics, and Poisons §§ 27.24–27.28
36 Am Jur 2d, Forfeitures and Penalties § 25.
28 CJS Supplement, Drugs and Narcotics §§ 139–148.

Electronic Search Query

Suggested wording for computer-assisted legal research search

lien or (secure or security) w/2 interest and (drugs or narcotics) and forfeit! date aft 1969.

FIGURE 3-10 *(Continued)*

Figure 3-11 also shows how the various American Law Reports are updated. Update third through fifth series and ALR Federal annotations by consulting pocket parts. Update ALR 2d by consulting the ALR Later Case Service volumes and the pocket parts to those volumes. Update the first series by consulting the ALR Bluebook of Supplemental Decisions.

Index to this annotation

Warning that statutes cited may not be only ones dealing with subject

DRUG FORFEITURES—LIENHOLDERS

1 ALR5th 317

1 ALR5th

West Digest Key Numbers

Drugs and Narcotics 190, 191, 192, 193, 194, 195, 196, 197, 198
Forfeitures 3, 4, 5, 6, 7, 8

INDEX

Jurisdictional Table of Cited Statutes and Cases*

UNITED STATES

Calero-Toledo v Pearson Yacht Leasing Co. (1974) 416 US 663, 40 L Ed 2d 452, 94 S Ct 2080—§§ 2, 5[b]

*Statutes, rules, regulations and constitutional provisions bearing on the subject of the annotation are included in this table only to the extent, and in the form, that they are reflected in the court opinions discussed in this annotation. The reader should consult the appropriate statutory or regulatory compilations to ascertain the current status, rules, regulations, and constitutional provisions.

For federal cases involving state law, see state headings.

FIGURE 3-10 *(Continued)*

Use of American Law Reports

The same cautions given about legal encyclopedias apply to American Law Reports. An annotation is a summary of the law and may not contain enough detail for your research. Be sure to review the cases cited in the

1 ALR5th DRUG FORFEITURES—LIENHOLDERS
1 ALR5th 317

ALABAMA

Ala Code § 20-2-93 (1975) See § 4[a, b]
Ala Code § 20-2-93(a)(4)(c) (1975). See § 4[b]
Ala Code § 20-2-93(h) (1975). See § 4[b]
Ala Code § 20-2-93(4)c (1975). See § 4[a]

Air Shipping International v State (1981, Ala) 392 So 2d 828—§ 4[a]
Singleton v State (1981 Ala) 396 So 2d 1050—§ 4[b]
State v Johnston (1990, Ala App) 565 So 2d 262—§ 4[b]

FLORIDA

Florida Rules of Civil Procedure, Rule 1.540(b). See § 3[b]
Florida Stat Ann §§ 932.701-932.704. See §§ 3[b], 6

Forfeiture of 1979 Chevrolet Corvette, Re, (1988, Fla App D4) 526 So 2d 708, 13 FLW 1114—§ 6
Forfeiture of One 1975 35' Cigarette Boat, Re (1986, Fla App D3) 498 So 2d 960, 11 FLW 1977, 12 FLW 140—§ 3[b]

GEORGIA

Ga Code ch 68-4a. See § 3[c]
Ga Code Ann § 79A-828. See § 3[c]

Hallman v State (1977) 141 Ga App 527, 233 SE2d 839—§ 3[c]

IDAHO

Idaho Code § 37-2744. See §§ 4[a], 6

Rooney, State ex rel., v One 1974 Green Targa Porsche Auto. (1986) 112 Idaho 432, 732 P2d 670—§§ 4[a], 6

IOWA

Iowa Code ch 127 (1981). See § 6
Iowa Code Ann ch 127. See § 4[b]

State v One Certain Conveyance, etc. (1973, Iowa) 207 NW2d 547—§ 4[b]
State v One Certain Conveyance 1978 Dodge Magnum, etc. (1983, Iowa) 334 NW2d 724—§ 6

FIGURE 3-10 *(Continued)*

annotation rather than relying on the annotation. The emphasis in the annotations is on case law, so do not omit statutory research. Never assume that the cases cited in the annotation—even in the pocket part to the annotation—are the most recent ones available. Use the cases cited in the annotation as a starting point and shepardize to locate more recent ones (see Chapter 6).

Do not rely on the annotation as an accurate explanation of the law. The law may have changed since the annotation was written.

Explains what annotation covers

DRUG FORFEITURES—LIENHOLDERS 1 ALR5th
1 ALR5th 317

§ 1. Introduction

[a]Scope

This annotation collects and analyzes decisions discussing or determining whether the government, in taking property[1] under the Uniform Controlled Substances Act (Uniform Act)[2] or similar statutes,[3] does so subject to or free of a lien.[4]

The issue of whether a valid lien exists is discussed only insofar as the question of validity relates to the issue of forfeitability. The issue of whether the terms of a contract, promissory note, or other document created a lien is not germane to this annotation. Cases involving sales on contract or conditional vendors in which the seller keeps title to the property until the full purchase price has been paid are included herein.

However, the method of calculating the dollar value of the lien is also not within the scope of this annotation.

There is no attempt to make an exhaustive collection of the various versions of the Uniform Act enacted by the states, and they are discussed in this annotation, and included in the Table of Statutes Construed, only to the extent that they are reflected in the reported cases and rulings within the scope of this annotation. Furthermore, in 1990, the National Conference of Commissioners on Uniform State Laws approved a new Uniform Controlled Substances Act intended to supersede the 1970 Act. To ascertain the current state of such laws, the reader should examine the legislation in the jurisdiction of interest.

---

1. Both real and personal property are within the scope of this annotation.

2. For a list of the jurisdictions that have adopted the uniform laws, see Am Jur 2d Desk Book, Document 124.

3. This annotation excludes cases decided prior to 1970, the date of the earliest enactment of the Uniform Act. However, this annotation includes cases involving statutes that were enacted prior to 1970 if the statutes contained provisions similar to those of the Uniform Act and if the cases were decided in 1970 or later. Cases involving criminal as well as civil drug forfeiture statutes are within the scope of this annotation.

4. For the purposes of this annotation, a lien is a charge on property for the payment of a debt. The lien may be secured or unsecured, perfected or unperfected. However, tax liens are excluded from this annotation. The annotation assumes that the purported lienholder had actual or constructive notice of the forfeiture proceedings and came forward to present a claim to the property; thus notice issues are excluded.

Section 505 of the Uniform Controlled Substances Act, pertaining to liens, provides as follows: (4) (iii) a forfeiture of a conveyance encumbered by a bona fide security interest is subject to the interest of the secured party if he neither had knowledge of nor consented to the act or omission [that subjected the conveyance to forfeiture].

FIGURE 3-10 *(Continued)*

Generally, in legal writing, you would not quote from or refer to an ALR annotation because ALR annotations are not the law. They contain only the publisher's interpretation of the law. It is preferable to refer to the primary source itself.

1 ALR5th DRUG FORFEITURES—LIENHOLDERS § 1[b]
1 ALR5th 317

[b] Related annotations

Forfeitability of property, under Uniform Controlled Substances Act or similar statute, where property or evidence supporting forfeiture was illegally seized. 1 ALR5th 346.

Timeliness of institution of proceedings for forfeiture under Uniform Controlled Substances Act or similar statute. 90 ALR4th 493.

Real property as subject of forfeiture under Uniform Controlled Substances Act or similar statutes. 86 ALR4th 995.

Validity and construction of provisions of Uniform Controlled Substances Act providing for forfeiture hearing before law enforcement officer. 84 ALR4th 515.

Forfeitability of property held in marital estate under Uniform Controlled Substances Act or similar statute. 84 ALR4th 620.

Necessity of conviction of offense associated with property seized in order to support forfeiture of property to state or local authorities. 38 ALR4th 515.

Forfeiture of money to state or local authorities based on its association with or proximity to other contraband. 38 ALR4th 496.

Right of accused to be present at suppression hearing or at other hearing or conference between court and attorneys concerning evidentiary questions. 23 ALR4th 955.

Admissibility of evidence discovered in search of defendant's property or residence authorized by defendant's spouse (resident or non-resident)—state cases. 1 ALR4th 673.

Lease provisions allowing termination or forfeiture for violation of law. 92 ALR3d 967.

Relief to owner of motor vehicle subject to state forfeiture for use in violation of narcotics laws. 50 ALR3d 172.

Lawfulness of seizure of property used in violation of law as prerequisite to forfeiture action or proceeding. 8 ALR3d 473.

Validity, construction, and application of criminal forfeiture provisions of Comprehensive Drug Abuse Prevention and Control Act of 1970 (21 USCS § 853). 88 ALR Fed 189.

Availability of defense of duress or coercion in prosecution for violation of federal narcotics laws. 75 ALR Fed 722.

Delay between seizure of personal property by Federal Government and institution of proceedings for forfeiture thereof as violation of Fifth Amendment due process requirements. 69 ALR Fed 373.

Construction and application of provision of Organized Crime Control Act of 1970 (18 USCS § 1963(a)) that whoever violated 18 USCS § 1962 shall forfeit to United States any interest in unlawful enterprise. 61 ALR Fed 879.

Forfeiture of personal property used in illegal manufacture, processing, or sale of controlled substances under § 511 of Comprehensive Drug Abuse Prevention and Control Act of 1970 (21 USCS § 881). 59 ALR Fed 765.

Federal criminal liability of licensed physician for unlawfully prescribing or

Lists other American Law Reports annotations to consult

FIGURE 3-10 *(Continued)*

In summary, American Law Reports are best used:

1. To find primary authority; and
2. To give the researcher general background information.

§ 1[b] DRUG FORFEITURES—LIENHOLDERS 1 ALR5th
1 ALR5th 317

trolled substance" or drug in violation of the Controlled Substances Act (21 USCS §§ 801 et seq.). 33 ALR Fed 220.

Supreme Court's views as to due process requirements of forfeitures. 76 L Ed 2d 852.

§ 2. Summary

Summary of annotation

In Calero-Toledo v Pearson Yacht Leasing Co. (1974) 416 US 663, 40 L Ed 2d 452, 94 S Ct 2080, reh den 417 US 977, 41 L Ed 2d 1148, 94 S Ct 3187, the United States Supreme Court outlined the history of forfeiture jurisprudence, noting that "[C]ontemporary federal and state forfeiture statutes reach virtually any type of property that might be used in the conduct of a criminal enterprise. Despite this proliferation of forfeiture enactments, the innocence of the owner of the property subject to forfeiture has almost uniformly been rejected as a defense. Judicial inquiry into the guilt or innocence of the owner could be dispensed with because state lawmakers, in the exercise of the police power, were free to determine that certain uses of property were undesirable and then establish a secondary defense against a forbidden use.

In Calero, the ownership interest of a yacht leasing company in a yacht was forfeited after Puerto Rican authorities discovered marijuana on board the yacht and charged one of the lessees with violation of the Controlled Substances Act of Puerto Rico. It was conceded that the leasing company was in no way involved in the criminal enterprise of the lessee and had no knowledge that its property was being used in connection with a violation of the drug law. Nonetheless, the Supreme Court upheld the constitutionality of the forfeiture provisions of the Puerto Rican Controlled Substances Act, even though it failed to provide an "innocent owner" defense.[5] The Supreme Court held that to the extent that forfeiture provisions are applied to lessors, bailors, or secured creditors who are innocent of any wrongdoing, confiscation may have the desirable effect of inducing them to exercise greater care in transferring possession of their property.

Thus, although the Uniform Controlled Substances Act contains a provision protecting innocent encumbrancers of conveyance from forfeiture,[6] the extent of the protection offered to lienholders is wholly the creature of the adopting jurisdiction. Although one court held that the provision of the act exempting innocent owners from forfeiture applied to innocent conditional vendors (§ 5[a]), it has been held not to be a violation of constitutional rights to fail to include lienholders in an "innocent owner" provision (§ 5[b]).

Also, some courts have held that a prospective lienholder has the duty to investigate the borrower or collateral to ascertain whether the property would possibly be used to

5. The typical "innocent owner" defense preserves from forfeiture the property interest of an owner who can prove that he or she neither knew of nor consented to the act which subjected the property to forfeiture.

6. For the text of the relevant provision of the Uniform Act, see § 1[a].

FIGURE 3-10 *(Continued)*

Figure 3-12 provides useful tips on utilizing American Law Reports. For information on how to make American Law Reports a part of your research strategy, see Chapter 7.

AMERICAN LAW REPORTS		
Title	**Coverage**	**Supplemented by**
American Law Reports	(1919–1948)	ALR Bluebook of Supplemental Decisions
American Law Reports 2d	(1948–1965)	ALR Later Case Service volumes and pocket parts
American Law Reports 3d	(1965–1980)	pocket parts
American Law Reports 4th	(1980–1992)	pocket parts
American Law Reports 5th	(1992–present)	pocket parts
American Law Reports Federal	(1992–present)	pocket parts

FIGURE 3-11 American Law Reports editions and updates.

Citation to American Law Reports

Figure 3-13 is the proper citation for the annotation entitled "Effect of Forfeiture Proceedings under the Uniform Controlled Substances Act or Similar Statute on Lien against Property Subject to Forfeiture" beginning on page 317 of the first volume of American Law Reports Fifth Series, copyright 1992. The title of the annotation is fairly descriptive of the scope of the annotation. The case published in American Law Reports, which

TIPS ON USING AMERICAN LAW REPORTS	
Do	**Do not**
1. Use footnotes to locate relevant primary authority.	1. Rely on American Law Reports alone as an accurate statement of the law.
2. Pull and read primary authority.	2. Generally cite to American Law Reports.
3. Check pocket parts, Later Case Sevice, or ALR Bluebook for recent information.	
4. Update information found.	

FIGURE 3-12 Do's and don'ts of using American Law Reports.

serves as the basis for the annotation, is *State v. One 1979 Pontiac Trans Am*, 771 P.2d 682 (Utah Ct. App. 1989).

The citation to an annotation from American Law Reports Federal would be similar in form except for substituting "A.L.R. Fed." for "A.L.R.5th."

OTHER SECONDARY SOURCES

Other secondary sources you might consult include treatises, law review articles, legal periodicals, law dictionaries, legal thesauruses, continuing education publications, and Restatements. You can find these secondary sources in your library by consulting the card catalog or the *Index to Legal Periodicals*. You may also see these sources cited in primary authority, American Law Reports, legal encyclopedias, digests, and annotated statutory codes.

A **treatise** is a book that discusses, in depth, important principles in some area of the law. Often treatises are written by noted legal scholars and may be published in multivolume sets.

Law review articles are articles by law professors and other authorities with respect to legal issues of current interest published in academic journals called **law reviews**. An article advocating a change in the law is a respected source to cite if you are arguing that present law should be changed. The law reviews also include summaries of significant recent cases, written by law students. Almost every law school has a law review staffed by second- and third-year law students. Law students are generally selected for the law review staff based on their grades and writing ability.

Many *legal periodicals* are published by state and local bar associations and commercial publishers. Articles in legal periodicals often review a new development in the law or a legal issue of current interest. A recent article on an issue being researched can be very helpful to the researcher. By reading the article, the researcher gets a capsule summary of the issue and citations to a number of primary authorities which the researcher can consult.

Legal or *Law dictionaries* are used to find definitions of legal terms. They may also give you a citation to a case in which the term was discussed. A *legal thesaurus* gives you synonyms and antonyms of legal terms. As

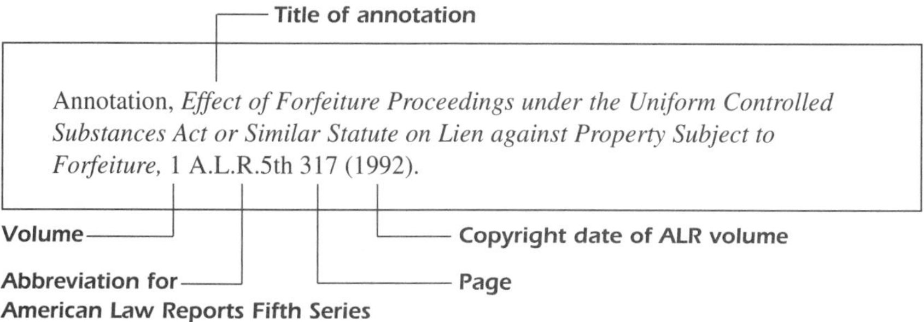

FIGURE 3-13 American Law Reports citation.

explained in Chapter 7, one of the first steps in research is to identify key terms to search. You may want to consult a legal thesaurus at that point to expand your list of key terms.

Many state bar associations offer continuing legal education seminars to their members, and may require attorneys to attend seminars to maintain their membership. The associations regularly publish *continuing legal education materials* to be used in the seminars or as a handy in-office reference for the attorney. Like treatises, each publication offers an explanation of a particular area of the law. The difference is that continuing legal education publications focus on the law of a particular state.

The American Law Institute publishes the **Restatements of the Law**. This is a series of volumes written by legal scholars; each volume or set of volumes covers a major field of the law (for example, torts, property, contracts, agency, etc.). Each of the Restatements is, among other things, a statement of the law as it is generally interpreted and applied by the courts concerning particular legal principles (for example, attractive nuisance, fraud, bilateral contracts, etc.). A researcher who finds that no reported state decision has dealt with a particular legal principle may consult and cite to a Restatement to explain the legal principle.

NOTE ON COMPUTER-ASSISTED RESEARCH

Some of the secondary sources and finding tools discussed in this chapter are accessible using computer-assisted legal research (CALR). Because CALR is such a rapidly changing field, by the time you read this, other sources discussed in this chapter may be available to you in CALR. At the date of this writing, though, only the tax portion of *Corpus Juris Secundum* is available on WESTLAW (West Publishing Company publishes both C.J.S. and WESTLAW), and none of *American Jurisprudence* is available on LEXIS (most Lawyers Cooperative publications are found on LEXIS). Some of the state legal encyclopedias are included on LEXIS. Legal encyclopedias are not currently available on CD-ROM, but probably will be in the future.

Digest research using the information available in the hard copy of the digests is possible on WESTLAW but not on LEXIS. On WESTLAW you can research using the West key number system, just as you would with hard-copy digests. WESTLAW includes all the headnotes and West key numbers as do printed West publications. There is no comparable key number search mechanism on LEXIS. However, you could in effect create your own digest by searching for key words. The key word search is explained in the Note on Computer-Assisted Legal Research of Chapter 4.

The full text of American Law Reports annotations is available on LEXIS and on CD-ROM. The researcher can find information in ALR either by using a known citation to an ALR annotation or by performing a key word search. With LEXIS, the researcher can also find information by performing a "plain English" search. Key word and plain English searches are explained in the Note on Computer-Assisted Legal Research in chapter 4.

LEGAL TERMS

treatise
A book that discusses, in depth, important principles in some area of human activity or interest, [such as] law or medicine.

law review
A publication containing articles by law professors and other authorities, with respect to legal issues of current interest, and summaries of significant recent cases, written by law students. Another name for a law review is *law journal* or *legal periodical*.

Restatement of the Law
A series of volumes published by the American Law Institute, written by legal scholars, each volume or set of volumes covering a major field of the law. Each of the Restatements is, among other things, a statement of the law as it is generally interpreted and applied by the courts with respect to particular legal principles.

SUMMARY

- Legal encyclopedias can be used as secondary authority and as finding tools.
- *Corpus Juris Secundum* and *American Jurisprudence 2d* are the two most widely used national encyclopedias. There may also be a legal encyclopedia for the law of your state.
- Legal encyclopedias contain a textual explanation of hundreds of legal topics, with the explanations heavily footnoted with citations to relevant primary authority.
- Legal encyclopedias are best used to find primary authority and to give the researcher general background information.
- Digests are finding tools that contain case summaries and references to other research materials.
- Digests serve as indexes to cases and allow the researcher to locate relevant cases.
- When using digests, try to use the digest set that is most specific to the type of case you are trying to find: a United States Supreme Court digest for cases from that court, a federal digest for cases from any of the federal courts, your state's digest for cases from your state, and so on.
- Legal encyclopedias, digests, and other law books are updated by annual pocket parts and by paperbound supplementary pamphlets.
- American Law Reports contain selected cases, accompanied by a textual explanation (called an annotation) of the law, with lengthy footnotes to relevant cases.
- American Law Reports are best used to find primary authority and to give the researcher general background information.
- Other secondary sources include treatises, law review articles, legal periodicals, legal dictionaries, legal thesauruses, continuing education publications, and Restatements.
- Many secondary sources are also accessible using computer-assisted legal research.

RESEARCH ASSIGNMENTS

Legal Research Assignment—Legal Encyclopedias

1. Answer the following questions concerning legal encyclopedias:
   a. What are the names of the two most widely used national legal encyclopedias?
   b. What are the common abbreviations for those names?
   c. What is the legal encyclopedia for your state?
   d. What is the common abbreviation for the name of that encyclopedia?
   e. What type of authority is a legal encyclopedia?
   f. Is it proper to cite to a legal encyclopedia in legal writing? Why or why not?

2. Use the legal encyclopedia for your state:
   a. Is a nondivorced parent obligated to pay for his or her child's post-secondary education?
   b. What is the citation for the case or statute supporting your answer?
   c. Where did you find your answer in the legal encyclopedia for your state?
3. Use *Corpus Juris Secundum* or *American Jurisprudence*:
   a. What is the definition of eminent domain?
   b. Where did you find your answer?
4. Use *Corpus Juris Secundum* or *American Jurisprudence*:
   a. What are the two elements of entrapment?
   b. Where did you find your answer?
5. Use *Corpus Juris Secundum* or *American Jurisprudence*:
   a. What capacity does one need to make a will?
   b. Where did you find your answer?
6. Use *Corpus Juris Secundum* or *American Jurisprudence*:
   a. How must consent be given for someone to waive his or her constitutional right against unreasonable search and seizure?
   b. Where did you find your answer?
7. Use *Corpus Juris Secundum* or *American Jurisprudence*:
   a. What is the difference between contributory negligence and comparative negligence?
   b. Where did you find your answer?
8. Use *Corpus Juris Secundum* or *American Jurisprudence*:
   a. What is the term of a mechanical patent?
   b. Where did you find your answer?
9. Use *Corpus Juris Secundum* or American Jurisprudence:
   a. What is the effective date of the Copyright Act of 1976, which made copyright matters governed exclusively by federal law, rather than by both federal and state law?
   b. Where did you find your answer?
10. Use *Corpus Juris Secundum* or *American Jurisprudence*:
    a. What is another name for exemplary damages?
    b. What is the purpose of awarding exemplary damages?
    c. What type of conduct is required as a basis for exemplary damages?
    d. Where did you find your answer?
11. Use *Corpus Juris Secundum* or *American Jurisprudence*:
    a. What are liquidated damages?
    b. Where did you find your answer?
12. Use *American Jurisprudence*:
    a. What does "consumer product" mean in the Consumer Product Safety Act?
    b. Where did you find your answer?

13. Use *American Jurisprudence,* under Pennsylvania law:
    a. Is a nondivorced parent obligated to pay for his or her child's post-secondary school education?
    b. What factors must be considered?
    c. Where did you find your answer in *American Jurisprudence*?

Legal Research Assignment—Digests

For questions 2–21, use West's Federal Practice Digest 4th.

Note: Because proper case citation form is not covered until Chapter 4, when a question calls for a citation, just write down the citation as you find it in the digest.

1. Answer the following questions concerning digests:
    a. What is the name of the most current West Publishing Company digest you would use to research cases from federal courts?
    b. What is the name of the most current digest you would use to research cases from state courts of your state?
2. If you were looking for cases addressing whether, in a products liability action, a manufacturer could be held liable for damages caused by a heating appliance, what topic and key number would you look under?
    a. If you were looking for cases addressing whether, in a products liability action, a manufacturer would be liable for injuries caused by a butane cigarette lighter, what topic and key number would you look under?
    b. If you were looking for cases addressing whether, in a products liability action, a manufacturer would be liable for injuries caused by cooking equipment, what topic and key number would you look under?
    c. If you were looking for cases addressing whether, in a products liability action, a toy manufacturer would be liable for injuries caused by the toy, what topic and key number would you look under?
3. a. Give the *citation* to the 1990 District of Nebraska case in which the federal court found that a space heater was an unreasonably dangerous product (because there was no warning attached to the heater itself that the heater should not be plugged into an extension cord).
    b. Give the *citation* to the 1991 case from the Eastern District of Tennessee in which the federal court held that a disposable butane cigarette lighter (which a three-year-old used to set a two-year-old child's diaper on fire) was not unreasonably dangerous even though it was not designed to be child-resistant.
    c. Give the *citation* to the 1989 case from the Western District of Oklahoma in which the federal court held that a slow cooker was not defective even though, when the cooker tipped, the lid came off and spilled hot food on a child.
    d. Give the *citation* to the 1986 case from the Seventh Circuit Court of Appeals in which the federal court held the manufacturer of lawn

darts not liable, when the danger of not properly handling a dart was obvious to an eight-year-old who threw a dart and hit another child.

4. If you were looking for cases addressing what evidence was necessary to convict someone of attempted robbery, what topic and key number would you look under?
5. a. Give the *citation* to the 1988 federal case involving a defendant being tried for attempted bank robbery who was arrested with a ski mask, overalls, and gloves in a car on the way to a planned robbery.
   b. Give the *citation* to the 1992 federal bank robbery case in which the evidence showed that (1) the stolen car was found near the robbery site with a bag in it from a ski shop that had sold the defendant a distinctive scarf; (2) a man seen leaving the car resembled the defendant; and (3) the defendant had used the scarf in the bank robbery.
6. If you were looking for cases addressing the amount of damages awardable in an assault and battery action, what topic and key number would you look under?
7. a. Give the *citation* for the 1987 District of Connecticut case in which the federal court found that the evidence supported $347,046.95 in damages for lost boxing wages, lost wages as a store detective, medical expenses, pain and suffering, and other injuries which the plaintiff received when he was shot by a police officer trying to arrest the plaintiff.
   b. Give the *citation* for the 1990 United States Second Circuit Court of Appeals case in which the plaintiff in an assault and battery case was awarded $150,000 in damages because the plaintiff was left with earaches, lockjaw, temporomandibular joint syndrome, and atypical anxiety disorder from being falsely imprisoned and battered by store security personnel.
   c. Give the *citation* to the 1992 United States Circuit Court for the District of Columbia case in which the plaintiff's left ring finger was injured but because the plaintiff had no lost wages, loss of earning capacity, or substantial emotional distress, the court held that the $200,000 damages award was too high.
8. a. Give the *citation* to the 1991 Fifth Circuit Court of Appeals case in which the defendant was convicted of burglary of a habitation after his fingerprints were found on two silver trays which had been stored inside a buffet in the victim's home.
   b. Give the *citation* to the 1984 United States Court of Appeals case in which the defendant was convicted of burglary after police officers, responding to a burglary alarm, found the defendant sitting near a desk whose drawers had been emptied and the contents scattered on the floor.
9. a. If you were looking for cases addressing how similar allegedly counterfeit currency had to be to support a conviction under statutes prohibiting counterfeiting United States currency, what topic and key number would you look under?

b. If you were looking for cases addressing when the alteration of a check or other obligation could be considered counterfeiting, what topic and key number would you look under?
c. If you were looking for cases addressing what evidence was sufficient to convict a defendant for counterfeiting, what topic and key number would you look under?

10. a. Give the *citation* to the United States Fourth Circuit Court of Appeals case in which the court held that the defendant could not be convicted of counterfeiting for obtaining change from a coin change machine by inserting a black-and-white photocopy of a one-dollar bill (because the photocopy would not have fooled anyone into believing it was a genuine one-dollar bill).
b. Give the *citation* of the United States Eleventh Circuit Court of Appeals case in which a $5 cashier's check which had been altered to appear to be a check for $35,000 was found to be counterfeit.
c. Give the *citation* of the United States Eleventh Circuit Court of Appeals case in which a defendant was convicted of passing counterfeit currency at a number of stores (the defendant was identified by several store clerks as the one who had passed the counterfeit currency and paid $100 bills for low-cost items).

11. a. Give the *citation* of the 1988 Southern District of Florida case in which the federal court ruled that, even though the trial court refused to delay the trial, which began on Yom Kippur, the jury pool was not defective for not including any Jews.
b. Give the *citation* of the 1991 United States Supreme Court case in which the Court held that prospective jurors may not be excluded on the basis of race.

12. a. Give the *citation* to the 1992 Eastern District of Virginia case in which the federal court held that an article investigating a project to send holiday packages to service people participating in Operation Desert Shield was not defamatory, even though the plaintiff claimed the article was defamatory because it implied that the project was "profiteering or gouging" and that surpluses existed based on the difference between wholesale and retail prices.
b. Give the *citation* to the 1992 Sixth Circuit Court of Appeals case in which an official of a company manufacturing automobile trim stated that some employees had quit after they were told they could refuse to take drug tests; the plaintiff claimed that the statement was defamatory, because it meant that those employees refusing to take the test were illegal drug users, but the court held that the statement was not defamatory.
c. Give the *citation* to the 1990 District of New Hampshire case in which a former employee's leaflet said the employer had been "indicted," even though the National Labor Relations Board had determined only that there was probable cause to issue a complaint against the

employer for an unfair labor practice; the federal court held that the leaflet was defamatory.

d. Give the *citation* to the 1991 Western District of New York case in which the federal court held that a school superintendent's saying that teachers had participated in making "a film which is not of the type that we believe should be produced for a school" did not defame the teachers.

13. If you were looking for cases addressing whether a judge should recuse himself or herself because of the judge's relationship to a party in a case being heard by the judge, what topic and key number would you look under?

14. a. Give the *citation* to the 1991 United States Ninth Circuit Court of Appeals case in which the judge was not required to recuse himself from an antitrust case involving a manufacturer who had employed the judge's son for the past 15 years.

    b. Give the *citation* to the 1991 United States Fourth Circuit Court of Appeals case in which the judge was not required to recuse himself from a case brought by parents of a school-age child to challenge the board's program for the child, even though the judge had been a member of the school board when the parents had first applied for certain services for their child.

    c. Give the *citation* for the 1991 Southern District of Indiana case in which the federal court decided that the judge should recuse himself from a case in which a witness, who had a monetary interest in the case and whose testimony was likely to be crucial, was a personal friend of the judge.

15. Give the *citation* to the 1990 District for the District of Columbia case in which the federal court held that the person claiming title to a parcel of real property by adverse possession had not established adverse possession, because the property had been occupied with the consent of the owner between 1957 to as late as 1972, and from that date on the title had been in litigation.

16. If you were looking for cases addressing what evidence would support a conviction for attempted arson, what topic and key number would you look under?

17. Give the *citation* to the 1989 United States Ninth Circuit Court of Appeals case in which the court determined that the acts of driving by a store, parking, and then driving away from the store with gasoline bottles in the trunk of the car were not a "substantial step" toward arson.

18. If you were looking for cases addressing the admissibility of evidence in the trial of someone who had been accused of illegally accepting or receiving bribes, what topic and key number would you look under?

19. Give the *citation* for the 1990 United States Seventh Circuit case in which the court held that, in the bribery trial of a defendant accused of illegally receiving bribes, a witness could testify that the witness, who claimed to

have paid the defendant large bribes, saw the defendant take a shoe box with $31,500 cash from the defendant's office to open two bank accounts.

20. Give the *citation* to a 1985 United States Tenth Circuit Court of Appeals case in which the court held that Utah's statute prohibiting plural marriage was constitutional.

21. a. Give the *citation* to the 1989 Eleventh Circuit Court of Appeals case in which the court ruled that the student government of the University of Alabama could constitutionally limit election activities by allowing distribution of campaign literature to three days prior to the election (but not on election day) and allowing campaign debates or open forums only during election week.
    b. Give the *citation* to the 1988 United States Fourth Circuit case in which the court held that a Virginia university could constitutionally enforce its policy prohibiting any structures on the lawn on the south side of the university rotunda (a historical architectural area), even though the policy would require removal of "symbolic shanties" placed on the lawn to protest the university's investment in South African corporations.
    c. Give the *citation* to the 1988 Middle District of Alabama case in which the federal court ruled that a university could constitutionally prohibit a proposed week-long campout on university property to limit disruption of university activities.

22. Using the Table of Cases volumes from the digest for United States Supreme Court cases, look up the following cases and give the citations to them:
    a. The 1973 United States Supreme Court decision *Roe v. Wade.*
    b. The 1963 United States Supreme Court decision *Gideon v. Wainright.*
    c. The 1968 United States Supreme Court decision *Terry v. Ohio.*
    d. The 1966 United States Supreme Court decision *Miranda v. Arizona.*
    e. The 1991 United States Supreme Court decision *California v. Acevedo.*

23. Using the Table of Cases volumes from the appropriate series of the Federal Practice Digest, look up the following cases and give the citations to them:
    a. The 1989 United States Circuit Court decision *Melear v. Spears.*
    b. The 1986 United States Circuit Court decision *United States v. $41,305.00 in Currency & Traveler's Checks.*
    c. The 1991 United States District Court decision *United States v. $14,500.00 in United States Currency.*
    d. The 1991 United States District Court decision *United States v. Borromeo.*

24. Using the Table of Cases volumes from West's Florida Digest 2d, look up the following cases and give the citations to them:
    a. The 1992 Florida state court decision *In re Forfeiture of 1985 Ford Ranger Pickup Truck.*

b. The 1987 Florida state court decision *In re Forfeiture of $6,003.00 in U.S. Currency.*
c. The 1992 Florida state court decision *Brown v. State.*

25. a. Using the Words and Phrases index in Federal Practice Digest 4th, give the citation of the case defining eminent domain and give the definition of *eminent domain* stated in the case.
b. Using the Words and Phrases index in Federal Practice Digest 4th, give the citation to the case defining *slander* and give the definition of *slander* stated in the case.
c. Using the Words and Phrases index in Federal Practice Digest 4th, give the citation to the case defining *attractive nuisance doctrine* and give the definition of *attractive nuisance doctrine* stated in the case.

Legal Research Assignment—American Law Reports

1. a. What is the title of the annotation located at 62 A.L.R.4th 16?
b. Using the annotation from question a, what is the citation to a related annotation discussing employer liability?
c. Using the annotation from question a, what is the common law rule concerning a social host's liability for furnishing alcohol?
2. a. What is the title of the annotation located at 81 A.L.R. Fed. 549?
b. Using the annotation from question a, what is the citation to a related annotation discussing whether the good faith of an officer is a defense?
3. a. What is the title of the annotation located at 51 A.L.R. Fed. 285?
b. For the purpose of this annotation, what does *vicarious liability* mean?
4. What is the citation of the A.L.R. Fed. annotation discussing liability of superiors for training officers who allegedly violated a person's civil rights?
5. a. What is the citation to the annotation discussing the obligation of a nondivorced parent to pay for a child's college education?
b. Using the annotation from question a, what is the citation to a related annotation discussing the obligation of a divorced noncustodial parent to pay for a child's college education?
6. a. What is the citation to the annotation discussing whether a judge may forbid a newspaper from publishing the names of jurors in a criminal case?
b. Using the annotation from question a, what are the citations to the two United States Supreme Court cases discussing judicial restraints?
7. a. What is the citation to the annotation discussing when an entire law firm should be disqualified from representing a client based on the action of one of attorneys in the firm?
b. Using the annotation from question a, what is the citation to the case on which the annotation was based?

c. Using the case from question b, why was the law firm disqualified from representing the plaintiff?

8. a. What is the citation to the annotation discussing whether a church may be liable for the sexual misconduct of its clergy?
   b. At common law, what was the reason a church could not be held liable?
   c. Using the annotation from question a, what are various legal theories under which a church has been sued?

9. a. What is the citation to the annotation discussing whether plaintiffs claiming that they were exposed to toxic substances may recover for their emotional distress?
   b. What is the scope of the annotation?

10. a. What is the citation to the annotation discussing whether a defendant can be liable for slander when the defendant claims that the statement was only made as a joke?
    b. Using the annotation from question a, what is the citation to a related annotation discussing whether someone can be held liable for criticizing a restaurant's food?
    c. What is the citation to the 1967 Ohio case in which the court held that the defendant could not be liable even if the defendant claimed that the statement was made as a joke?

11. a. What is the citation to the annotation discussing whether a defendant can be held liable for allegedly giving the plaintiff a venereal disease?
    b. Using the annotation from question a, what is the citation to a related annotation discussing whether a doctor may be held liable when a plaintiff allegedly caught a contagious disease from the doctor's patient?

12. a. What is the citation to the annotation discussing whether a private swimming pool owner is liable when someone drowns in the pool?
    b. Using the annotation from question a, what is the citation to the 1982 Indiana case stating that a swimming pool owner had a duty to control the conduct of guests at a pool party?

13. a. What is the citation to the annotation discussing whether parents can recover damages for the cost of raising a child born after a failed sterilization?
    b. What is the citation to the 1991 New Mexico case allowing recovery?

14. a. What is the citation to the annotation discussing whether a plaintiff can recover punitive damages from a drunk driver?
    b. Using the annotation from question a, what is the citation to the 1981 Florida case allowing punitive damages?

CHAPTER 4
Primary Sources: Cases

OUTLINE

Reading Cases
Briefing a Case
Locating Cases
Citing Cases
Note on Computer-Assisted Research

COMMON LEGAL SOURCES AND FINDING TOOLS

Note: Sources used in this chapter are indicated by boldface type.

Primary Sources	Secondary Sources	Finding Tools
constitutions statutes administrative regulations court rules **reporters** **loose-leaf services**	treatises law review articles legal periodicals law dictionaries legal thesauruses continuing legal education publications Restatements American Law Reports legal encyclopedias loose-leaf services	American Law Reports legal encyclopedias digests Shepard's Citators *Index to Legal Periodicals* loose-leaf services

In this chapter you will learn how to read a case, brief a case, locate cases in the law library, and cite to cases.

READING CASES*

Reported judicial decisions have a style and format all their own. The following discussion is designed to acquaint readers with the form and the nature of judicial decisions. Although judges have considerable freedom in how they write opinions, some uniformity of pattern comes from the similarity of purpose for decisions, especially decisions of appellate courts, which frequently serve as authority for later cases. Similarity is also a product of custom. The influence of West Publishing Company, which publishes the regional reporter series as well as many of the federal reporters, has been great.

For Whom Are Judicial Opinions Written?

In evaluating any written material, the reader should assess the audience the writer is addressing and the writer's goals. Judges write decisions for two reasons. The first is to inform the parties to the dispute who won and who lost, giving the rules and reasoning the judge applied to the facts. The second is to inform the legal profession—attorneys and judges—of the rules applied to a given set of facts and the reasons for the decision.

Very few laypersons ever enter a law library to find and read cases. The people found in the county law library are usually lawyers, paralegals, and judges. Cases are rarely intended to be entertaining, and judges are not motivated to make their cases "reader-friendly." Their tasks are quite specific. Because any case may serve as precedent, or at least form a basis for subsequent legal arguments, judges are especially concerned with conveying a precise meaning by carefully framing the rules and providing the reasoning behind them. The higher the court, the greater this concern will be. Imagine writing an opinion for a highly skilled, highly intelligent readership that critically analyzes every word and phrase, an opinion that may very well affect important rights of citizens in the future.

Judicial writing is different from most other kinds of writing, in that its goal is neither simply to pass on information nor to persuade the reader of the author's point of view. The time for persuasion is past; the judge is stating the law and making a final judgment, but must do so with caution so that the statements are not misinterpreted or misused. An appreciation of the judge's dilemma is essential to critical evaluation of cases.

---

* Grateful thanks to Ransford C. Pyle, Ph.D., J.D., who authored this portion of the chapter. Reproduced by permission. *Foundations of Law for Paralegals: Cases, Commentary, and Ethics,* by Ransford C. Pyle. Delmar Publishers, Inc., Albany, New York; Copyright © 1992.

The Effect of Setting Precedent

The cost of litigation is great, and appeal of a decision incurs significant additional cost. It makes sense to appeal if the losing party legitimately concludes that the lower court was incorrect in its application of the law. It would be quite foolish to spend large sums of money to go to the higher court if the chances of winning were slim and the stakes were small. This means that the cases we read from appellate courts, and especially from the highest courts, generally involve questions that have strong arguments on both sides. The judges in these cases are faced with difficult decisions and must respect the reasonable arguments of both sides in deciding which side prevails.

The Format of a Reported Decision

The cases found in the reporters generally follow a uniform format with which researchers must become familiar. The first part of the case has no official authority. Authoritative statements begin with the actual text of the opinion.

Material Preceding the Opinion

West Publishing Company, publisher of the regional reporters and many of the federal reporters, has established a quite uniform format. Lawyers Cooperative Publishing, publisher of *United States Supreme Court Reports, Lawyers Edition* and other important law books, uses a similar format. All the elements of the West Publishing Company format appear in the first three pages of *Florida v. Jimeno*, 111 S. Ct. 1801 (1991), shown in Figure 4-1. As you read the following explanation, it would be helpful for you to refer to Figure 4-1, or you may want to refer to Appendix A for the full text of the opinion. After you understand the West Publishing Company format, look up *Jimeno,* starting on page 297 of volume 114 of United States Supreme Court Reports, Lawyers Edition Second Series. You will notice that the text of the opinion itself is exactly the same. However, the material prepared by the publisher, which precedes the opinion, is different in format and longer than the West Publishing Company-prepared material preceding the same case in the Supreme Court Reporter.

The Citation

The heading of the page (Figure 4-1) indicates the citation "FLORIDA v. JIMENO" and "Cite as 111 S.Ct. 1801 (1991)." This is the name of the case and where it can be found, namely on page 1801 in volume 111 of the Supreme Court Reporter. Cases from some courts are printed in more than one reporter, with one of the reporters being designated as the "official reporter" because it is published by the government. Opinions of the United

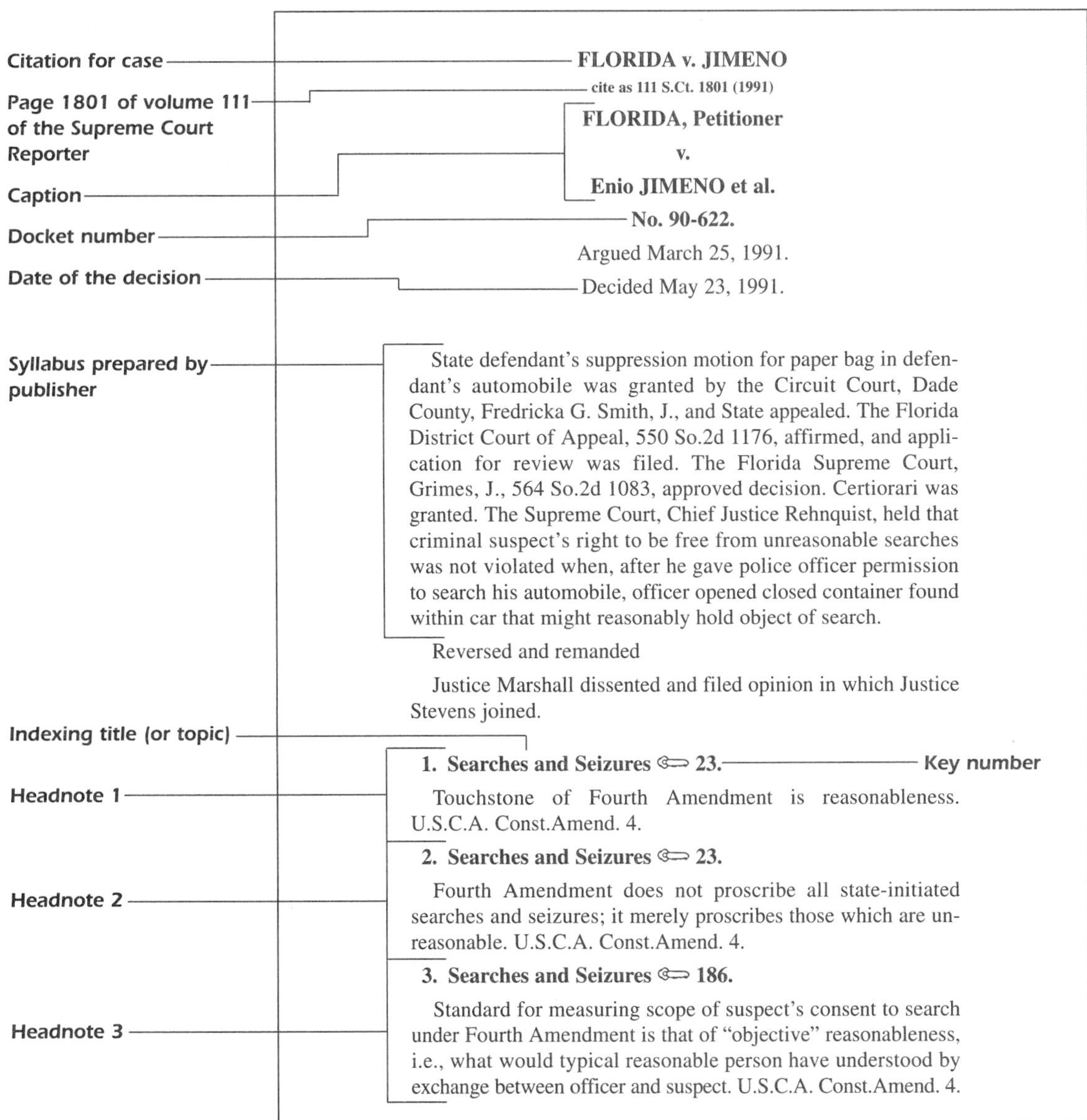
Citation for case
FLORIDA v. JIMENO
cite as 111 S.Ct. 1801 (1991)
Page 1801 of volume 111 of the Supreme Court Reporter
FLORIDA, Petitioner
v.
Enio JIMENO et al.
Caption
Docket number
No. 90-622.
Argued March 25, 1991.
Date of the decision
Decided May 23, 1991.
Syllabus prepared by publisher
State defendant's suppression motion for paper bag in defendant's automobile was granted by the Circuit Court, Dade County, Fredricka G. Smith, J., and State appealed. The Florida District Court of Appeal, 550 So.2d 1176, affirmed, and application for review was filed. The Florida Supreme Court, Grimes, J., 564 So.2d 1083, approved decision. Certiorari was granted. The Supreme Court, Chief Justice Rehnquist, held that criminal suspect's right to be free from unreasonable searches was not violated when, after he gave police officer permission to search his automobile, officer opened closed container found within car that might reasonably hold object of search.
Reversed and remanded
Justice Marshall dissented and filed opinion in which Justice Stevens joined.
Indexing title (or topic)
1. Searches and Seizures ⚷ 23.
Key number
Headnote 1
Touchstone of Fourth Amendment is reasonableness. U.S.C.A. Const.Amend. 4.
2. Searches and Seizures ⚷ 23.
Headnote 2
Fourth Amendment does not proscribe all state-initiated searches and seizures; it merely proscribes those which are unreasonable. U.S.C.A. Const.Amend. 4.
3. Searches and Seizures ⚷ 186.
Headnote 3
Standard for measuring scope of suspect's consent to search under Fourth Amendment is that of "objective" reasonableness, i.e., what would typical reasonable person have understood by exchange between officer and suspect. U.S.C.A. Const.Amend. 4.

FIGURE 4-1 Part of *Florida v. Jimeno.* (Reprinted with permission from 111 Supreme Court Reporter, copyright © by West Publishing Company.)

States Supreme Court are printed in United States Reports (abbreviated "U.S."), the official reporter, and in the Supreme Court Reporter and United States Supreme Court Reports, Lawyers Edition. Although the official citation would be to the United States Reports, at this date it is impossible to use that citation. Because the publication of United States Reports by the United States government lags considerably behind the other two reporters,

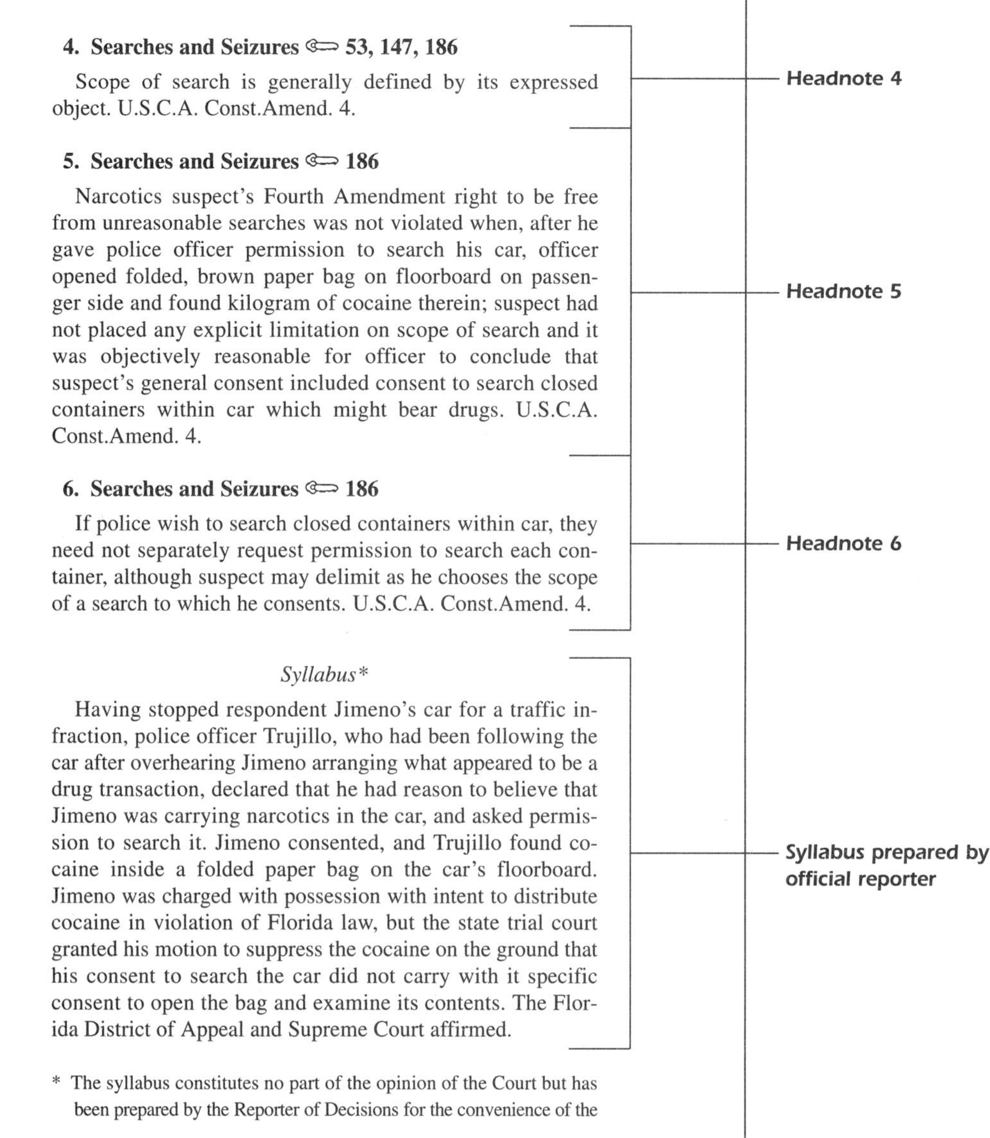

4. Searches and Seizures ⚿ 53, 147, 186

Scope of search is generally defined by its expressed object. U.S.C.A. Const.Amend. 4.

5. Searches and Seizures ⚿ 186

Narcotics suspect's Fourth Amendment right to be free from unreasonable searches was not violated when, after he gave police officer permission to search his car, officer opened folded, brown paper bag on floorboard on passenger side and found kilogram of cocaine therein; suspect had not placed any explicit limitation on scope of search and it was objectively reasonable for officer to conclude that suspect's general consent included consent to search closed containers within car which might bear drugs. U.S.C.A. Const.Amend. 4.

6. Searches and Seizures ⚿ 186

If police wish to search closed containers within car, they need not separately request permission to search each container, although suspect may delimit as he chooses the scope of a search to which he consents. U.S.C.A. Const.Amend. 4.

*Syllabus**

Having stopped respondent Jimeno's car for a traffic infraction, police officer Trujillo, who had been following the car after overhearing Jimeno arranging what appeared to be a drug transaction, declared that he had reason to believe that Jimeno was carrying narcotics in the car, and asked permission to search it. Jimeno consented, and Trujillo found cocaine inside a folded paper bag on the car's floorboard. Jimeno was charged with possession with intent to distribute cocaine in violation of Florida law, but the state trial court granted his motion to suppress the cocaine on the ground that his consent to search the car did not carry with it specific consent to open the bag and examine its contents. The Florida District of Appeal and Supreme Court affirmed.

* The syllabus constitutes no part of the opinion of the Court but has been prepared by the Reporter of Decisions for the convenience of the

FIGURE 4-1 *(Continued)*

it is known that *Jimeno* will be printed in volume 500 of United States Reports, but the page has not yet been determined.

The Caption

The caption of the case (see Figure 4-2) shows the parties as "FLORIDA, Petitioner v. Enio JIMENO et al." Note that the citation names only one

Syllabus prepared by official reporter

Held: A criminal suspect's Fourth Amendment right to be free from unreasonable searches is not violated when, after he gives police permission to search his car, they opened a closed container found within the car that might reasonably hold the object of the search. The Amendment is satisfied when, under the circumstances, it is objectively reasonable for the police to believe that the scope of the suspect's consent permitted them to open the particular container. Here, the authorization to search extended beyond the car's interior surfaces to the bag, since Jimeno did not place any explicit limitations on the scope of the search and was aware that Trujillo would be looking for narcotics in the car, and since a reasonable person may be expected to know that narcotics are generally carried in some form of container. There is no basis for adding to the Fourth Amendment's basic test of objective reasonableness a requirement that, if police wish to search closed containers within a car, they must separately request permission to search each container. Pp. 1803–1804.

564 So.2d 1083 (Fla. 1990), reversed and remanded.

Justices joining in majority opinion

REHNQUIST, C.J., delivered the opinion of the Court, in which WHITE, BLACKMUN, O'CONNOR, SCALIA, KENNEDY, and SOUTER, JJ., joined.

Justices joining in dissenting opinion

MARSHALL, J., filed a dissenting opinion, in which STEVENS, J., joined.

Attorney for State of Florida

Michael J. Neimand, Miami, Fla., for petitioner.

John G. Roberts, Jr., Washington, D.C., for the U.S., as amicus curiae, supporting the petitioner, by special leave of Court.

Attorney for Jimeno

Jeffrey S. Weiner, Miami, Fla., for respondent.

reader. See United States v. Detroit Lumber Co., 200 U.S. 321, 337, 26 S.Ct. 282, 287, 50 L.Ed. 499.

FLORIDA v. JIMENO

Cite as 111 S.Ct. 1801 (1991)

Opinion begins

Chief Justice REHNQUIST delivered the opinion of the Court.

inside of the car. The trial court granted the motion. It found that although respon-

FIGURE 4-1 *(Continued)*

party for each side and uses only the individual's surname, whereas the caption gives the respondent's first name ("Enio") and indicates that there was more than one respondent by the use of "et al.," meaning "and others." The caption also indicates the status of Florida as "Petitioner." We can surmise from this that Florida lost in the lower court and filed a petition for certiorari for the case to be heard by the United States Supreme Court.

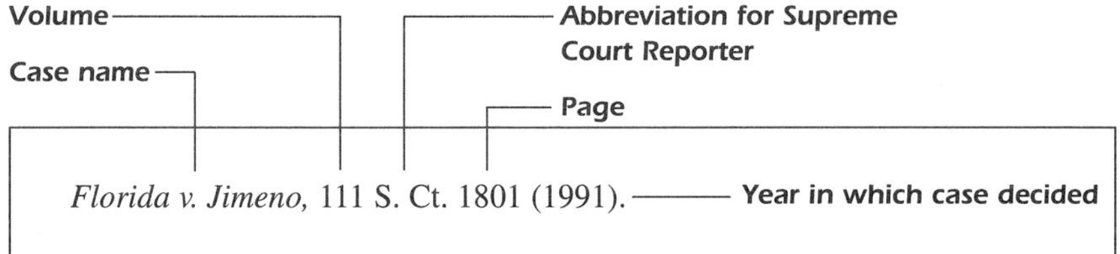

FIGURE 4-2 Caption of case for *Florida v. Jimeno.*

Even though not stated, we know that Jimeno is the "respondent," because that is the name given by the Court to the party who won below.

Because the caption does not indicate, the reader must discover from the text who was the **plaintiff** and who was the **defendant** originally. It is important to note who is the respondent because the opinion refers to Jimeno by that term.

Below the parties we find "No. 90-622," the docket number, which is a number assigned to the case upon initial filing with the clerk of the court and by which the case is identified before it is published with a volume and page number in the reporter series. Docket numbers are important when attempting to research cases prior to their official publication. Below the docket number is the date of oral argument and the date of the decision.

The Syllabus

Following the caption is a brief summary of the case, called the **syllabus**. There is another, more detailed syllabus on the second page of the opinion. In regional reporters, the Federal Supplement, and the Federal Reporter, cases usually include the first syllabus, prepared by West Publishing Company, but not the second. Although the syllabi are sometimes written by the court or a reporter appointed by the court, as indicated by the note on the bottom of the second page, a syllabus is a narrow condensation of the court's ruling and cannot be relied upon as the precise holding of the court. The syllabus can be useful in obtaining a quick idea of what the case concerns—a summary of the issue and the holding of the court. Legal researchers frequently follow leads to cases that, upon reading, prove to be unrelated to the issue of the research. Reading the syllabus may make reading the entire opinion unnecessary. However, if the syllabus suggests that the case may be important, a careful reading of the entire text of the opinion is usually necessary.

Headnotes

There are six headnotes in *Jimeno,* located on the first and second pages of the case and numbered consecutively one through six. The **headnotes** are statements of the major points of law discussed in the case. With limited editing, the headnotes tend to be nearly verbatim statements lifted from the

LEGAL TERMS

plaintiff
A person who brings a lawsuit.

defendant
The person against whom an action is brought.

syllabus
1. The headnote of a reported case. 2. A summary outline of a course of study.

headnote
A summary statement that appears at the beginning of a reported case to indicate the points decided by the case.

opinion. The headnotes are listed in numerical order, starting at the beginning of the opinion, so that the reader may look quickly for the context of a point expressed by a headnote. For example, the part of the text that deals with a particular point made in the headnote will have the number of the headnote in brackets, e.g., [4], at the beginning of the paragraph or section in which that point is discussed. This is very helpful when researching lengthy cases in which only one issue is of concern to the researcher.

To the right of the headnote number is a generic heading, such as "Searches and Seizures" and a key number. Because this reporter is published by West Publishing Company, it uses an indexing title and number that can be found through the many West indexes, reporters, and encyclopedias. Lawyers Cooperative Publishing uses a similar indexing title and number that can be found through the many Lawyers Cooperative publications.

Attorneys for the Parties

The end of the syllabus on the third page of the reported case identifies the Justice who wrote the majority opinion, the Justices who joined in the majority opinion, the Justice who dissented, and the Justice who joined in the dissenting opinion. This was a seven-to-two decision. Chief Justice Rehnquist wrote the majority opinion, which was joined by Justices White, Blackmun, O'Connor, Scalia, Kennedy, and Souter. Justice Marshall wrote the dissenting opinion, which was joined in by Justice Stevens. The attorneys for the parties are listed just above the beginning of the opinion. The petitioner had one attorney, the respondent had one attorney, and there was an attorney for the United States as ***amicus curiae***. *Amicus curiae* means "friend of the court." This is a person who, although not a party to the case, is granted permission to file a brief in the case. Usually the person wants to present to the court a point of view that otherwise might not be represented in the case.

Format of the Opinion

Following the names of the attorneys, the formal opinion (that is, the official discussion of the case) begins. In *Jimeno,* the opinion states "Chief Justice REHNQUIST delivered the opinion of the Court." In cases other than United Supreme Court opinions, the opinion may simply start with the name of the judge writing the opinion, rather than specifically explaining which judge delivered the opinion. The author of the opinion has considerable freedom in presentation. Some opinions are written mechanically, but a few are almost poetic. The peculiarities of any particular case may dictate a special logical order for the decision. Nevertheless, the majority of opinions follow a standard format. When this format is followed, reading and understanding are simplified, but no judge is required to make an opinion easy reading. The following format is the one most frequently used.

As far as opinions of the United States Supreme Court are concerned, *Jimeno* is brief, well organized, and easy to understand. Compare *Jimeno* with *United States v. Sokolow,* 490 U.S. 1 (1989) (*Sokolow* is one of the cases in your reading cases assignment at the end of this chapter). *Sokolow* is twice as long and much more difficult to understand.

The Facts

Most of the text of an opinion in an appellate decision is concerned with a discussion of the law, but because a case revolves around a dispute concerning events that occurred between the parties, no opinion is complete without some discussion of the events that led to the trial. Trials generally explore these events in great detail so that the judge or jury may decide on the facts; appellate opinions, however, usually narrow the fact statement to the most relevant facts. In an interesting case, the reader is often left wanting to know more about what happened, but the judge is not writing a story. The important element in the opinion concerns the application of law.

Procedure

Near or at the beginning of the opinion is a reference to the outcome of the trial in the lower court and the basis for appeal. In the third paragraph of *Jimeno*, for example, the opinion states that Jimeno was charged with possession with intent to distribute cocaine and that his motion to suppress the cocaine was granted by the trial court. The Florida District Court of Appeal (the Florida intermediate appellate court) affirmed, as did the Florida Supreme Court. The United States Supreme Court granted certiorari.

Often the remarks about procedure are brief and confusing, especially if the reader is not familiar with the procedural rules. An understanding of the relevant state or federal court system and jurisdiction will help unravel the procedural steps leading to the appellate decision. If the procedure is important to the opinion, a more elaborate discussion is usually found in the body of the opinion. Many things in the opinion become clear only upon further reading, and many opinions must be read at least twice for full understanding. An opinion is like a jigsaw puzzle—the reader must put the parts together to see the full picture.

The Issue

Many writers describe the questions of law that must be decided either at the beginning of the opinion or following the relevant facts. In *Jimeno*, Rehnquist states the issue very clearly in the first sentence. "In this case we decide whether a criminal suspect's Fourth Amendment right to be free from unreasonable searches is violated when, after he gives a police officer

LEGAL TERMS

amicus curiae (*Latin*) "Friend of the court." A person who is interested in the outcome of the case, but who is not a party, whom the court permits to file a brief for the purpose of providing the court with a position or a point of view which it might not otherwise have. An *amicus curiae* is often referred to simply as an *amicus*.

permission to search his automobile, the officer opens a closed container found within the car that might reasonably hold the object of the search."

Unfortunately, few writers pinpoint the issues in this fashion, so the reader must search the opinion text for the issue. At this point it is appropriate to introduce a favorite term used by attorneys: *caveat*. This means "warning" or, literally, "Let him beware."

Caveat: The issue is the most important element in an opinion. If the issue is not understood, the significance of the rule laid down by the court can easily be misunderstood. This point cannot be emphasized too strongly. Law students study cases for three years with one primary goal: "Identify the issues." Anyone can fill out forms, but a competently trained person can go right to the heart of a case and recognize its strengths and weaknesses.

The Discussion

The main body of the text of an opinion, often 90 percent of it, discusses the meaning of the issue(s) and offers a line of reasoning that leads to a disposition of the case and explains why a certain rule or rules must apply to the dispute. This part of the opinion is the most difficult to follow. The writer has a goal, but the goal is often not clear to the reader until the end. For this reason, it is usually helpful to look at the final paragraph in the case to see whether the appellate court affirmed (agreed with the lower court) or reversed (disagreed with the lower court). The final paragraph of the *Jimeno* majority opinion states that the Court reversed and remanded the case. Many judges seem to like to hold the reader in suspense, but there is no reason the reader has to play this game. By knowing the outcome of the decision, the reader can see how the writer of the opinion is building the conclusion. By recognizing the issue and knowing the rule applied, the reader can see the structure of the argument. The discussion section is the writer's justification of the holding.

The Holding

The holding states the rule of the case, that is, the rule the court applied to conclude whether or not the lower court was correct. The rule is *the law,* meaning that it determines the rights of the parties until reversed by a higher court. It binds lower courts faced with a similar dispute in future cases. It is best to think of the holding as an answer to the issue.

In the first paragraph of *Jimeno,* Rehnquist answers the issue with "no" and then goes beyond the simple answer and clarifies it. "The Fourth Amendment is satisfied when, under the circumstances, it is objectively reasonable for the officer to believe that the scope of the suspect's consent permitted him to open a particular container within the automobile." The negative answer and the clarification, taken together, comprise the holding of the case.

Finding the Law

Research of cases is done for a number of reasons. The principles that apply to a dispute may be unknown, unfamiliar, or forgotten. With experience, legal professionals come to develop a knack for guessing how a dispute will be decided and can even predict what rules will be applied. Once the issues of a case are recognized, a reasonable prediction of a fair outcome can be made. This is, however, merely tentative; the researchers must check their knowledge and memory against definitive statements of the law. In some instances, a statute will clearly define the rights and duties that pertain to the case at hand; in others, the elaboration of the law in the cases will leave little room for doubt. Frequently, however, the issue in a client's case will be complex or unique, and no case can be found that is directly **on point.** Ideally, research will result in your finding a case that contains a fact situation so similar to that of your client that an assumption can be made that the same rule will apply.

Evaluating Cases

Once the purpose, style, and structure of appellate decisions are grasped, mastering the content is a matter of concentration and experience. Researching cases generally has one or more of the following three goals:

1. Finding the statements of the law.
2. Assessing the law in relation to the client's case.
3. Building an argument.

These three goals can be illustrated using the Williams search and seizure problem found in Appendix A. A researcher might look for cases stating what the law is concerning police officers opening a closed container found in a car. *Jimeno* appears to be a good case to evaluate because it deals with this issue.

Now the researcher would assess *Jimeno* in relation to the Williams situation. Although the facts are not identical, *Jimeno* and *Williams* are on point on the issue of whether a suspect's Fourth Amendment rights are violated when an officer opens a closed container found in the suspect's car.

What argument can be built in the Williamses' favor? In some instances, the facts of a dispute are used to **distinguish** that case from similar cases. For example, although *Jimeno* and *Williams* are on point on the issue of whether opening a closed container violates the suspect's rights, the facts evidencing consent to the search may be distinguished. In *Jimeno,* the officer asked permission to search and explained that Jimeno did not have to consent. Jimeno verbally gave the officer permission to search. The Williamses were asked whether the officer could search and then the officer proceeded with the search without giving the Williamses a chance to respond. The Williamses can argue that the officer needed their consent to search the car and that silence should not be interpreted as consent. The

LEGAL TERMS

on point
Refers to a judicial opinion that, with respect to the facts involved and the applicable law, is similar to but not on all fours with another case.

distinguish
To explain why a particular case is not precedent or authority with respect to the matter in controversy.

officer took them by surprise and did not give the brothers a chance to respond before opening the car door.

Only experience and knowledge of the law will develop the keen sense it takes to separate cases that are on point from those that are distinguishable. It is often the advocate's job to persuade on the basis of a path threaded through a host of seemingly conflicting cases.

BRIEFING A CASE

Briefing a case means taking notes of the most important parts of a case so that you can later refer to your "case brief" to quickly refresh your memory, rather than having to read the case over again. When you write out a case brief, you engage in active learning as you write a summary in your own words. This leads to better understanding of the case than underlining or rereading. Professors may require you to brief cases, with class time spent discussing the cases and synthesizing them. *Synthesizing* involves analyzing how cases deal with a particular subject matter and extracting a rule of law from them.

A second reason to brief cases is as a research and writing tool. When researching a problem, you should brief the cases found, synthesize them to determine the rule of law, and apply the rule of law to the current problem.

Although some professors may require you to turn in your first few case briefs when you are learning how to brief a case, case briefs are generally read only by you. The format described here is a fairly standard one, but there is no one right way to brief a case. You may find yourself developing your own format for case briefs you know you will not be required to turn in. If a professor asks you to brief cases, it may be a good idea to ask if he or she prefers a particular format.

As the name suggests, a case brief should be fairly concise. If your case brief is as long as or longer than the case, you might just as well reread the entire case rather than refer to the brief. For most cases, a good length is a page or less.

Case Brief Format

A standard format for briefing a case is the following:

Correct case citation—Your professor will probably ask you to cite cases as in the examples provided in this book or by the citation rules for your state.

Facts—This section should contain only the significant facts in light of the legal question asked, but may state what facts are not known if the absence of facts is significant.

History—State briefly what happened at trial and at each level before the case reached the court whose opinion you are briefing.

Question(s)—State the question or questions considered by the court. Each question should be one sentence in length, and the questions should be numbered if there are more than one. A question is easier to understand if it is stated in the form of a question, rather than beginning with the word "whether," and it should end with a question mark.

Holding(s)—Generally you will have the same number of holdings as you do questions, with each holding containing the answer to the corresponding question. Sometimes you may have one question and more than one answer if the question is a broad one and there is more than one answer to it. Each holding should be one sentence. Even if the court does not explicitly state the holding or give a simple "yes" or "no" answer to a question, reread the case until you can write a one-sentence holding.

Reasoning—State the court's reasoning for reaching the holding from the question considered.

Result—State what the court did with the lower court's decision: affirmed, reversed, vacated, and so on.

When attorneys refer to a "brief," they may be referring to a case brief, but more likely than not they are referring to an appellate brief. An *appellate brief* is the document containing the arguments of a party to a case, which is usually prepared by the party's attorney and submitted to the appellate court when a case is appealed.

Jimeno Case Brief

The following is a suggested case brief for *Jimeno*. It would be good practice for you to try to brief *Jimeno* yourself and compare your case brief with this one.

***Florida v. Jimeno,* 111 S. Ct. 1801 (1991).**

Facts: An officer followed Jimeno's car after overhearing Jimeno make what the officer believed was a drug transaction. When Jimeno failed to stop when turning right on red, the officer pulled Jimeno over. The officer stated that he believed Jimeno was carrying drugs. When the officer requested permission to search the car, Jimeno consented. The officer discovered a kilogram of cocaine in a folded brown paper bag on the car floorboard.

History: Jimeno was charged with possession with intent to distribute cocaine and the trial court granted his motion to suppress the cocaine. The Florida District Court of Appeal and the Florida Supreme Court affirmed. The United States Supreme Court granted certiorari.

Question: Is "a criminal suspect's Fourth Amendment right to be free from unreasonable searches . . . violated when, after he gives a police officer permission to search his automobile, the officer opens a closed container found within the car that might reasonably hold the object of the search"?

Holding: The criminal suspect's Fourth Amendment right is not violated "when, under the circumstances, it is objectively reasonable for the officer to believe that the scope of the suspect's consent permitted him to open a particular container within the automobile."

Reasoning: An officer does not need a search warrant if the officer has the suspect's consent to search a car, but the scope of the search is limited to what a reasonable person would believe Jimeno had consented to. Because the officer had told Jimeno that the officer thought Jimeno was carrying drugs, the officer could search the paper bag, as drugs might be contained in it. Note: the court states in *obiter dictum* that Jimeno's rights probably would have been violated if the drugs had been in a locked briefcase and the officer pried open the briefcase without asking Jimeno's permission to search the briefcase.

Results: Reversed and remanded.

LOCATING CASES

Cases are generally found in the law library in loose-leaf publications, **advance sheets**, or **reporters**. Libraries designated as government depositories may also have cases in **slip opinion** form. For the names of the loose-leaf publications and reporters for federal court cases, refer to the chart in Figure 4-3. You will need to obtain the names of the loose-leaf publication (if any) and reporters for your state's cases from your professor or from your own research. You would use the loose-leaf service's publication to read recently announced cases that are not yet contained in the advance sheets or reporters. Once a case is available in the advance sheets or the reporters, you would cite to the reporter rather than the loose-leaf publication. Cases in loose-leaf publications, advance sheets, and reporters are organized chronologically.

Reporters and Loose-Leaf Services

Federal

United States Supreme Court
- United States Law Week (loose-leaf)
- United States Reports (official)
- Supreme Court Reporter (unofficial—West)
- United States Supreme Court Reports, Lawyers Edition (unofficial—Lawyers Cooperative Publishing)

United States Circuit Courts of Appeal
- Federal Reporter (unofficial—West)

United States District Courts
- Federal Supplement (unofficial—West)

State (fill in for your state)

Court of last resort

Intermediate appellate court

Trial court(s)

FIGURE 4-3 Publications and reporters for federal court cases.

Cases from a particular court may be printed in more than one reporter. For example, United States Supreme Court opinions are printed in three different reporters: the United States Reports, the Supreme Court Reporter, and United States Supreme Court Reports, Lawyers Edition. The text of the court opinion is identical in each of the three reporters, but the material preceding the case, which is prepared by the publisher, is different. The reporter prepared by the government or under authority of the government is referred to as the *official reporter.* The official reporter for United States Supreme Court opinions is United States Reports. Although United States Reports is considered the official reporter, many law libraries may only have one of the other two reporters. Because United States Reports is a government publication, it lags considerably behind the other two reporters in publication date and does not contain the headnotes and other materials prepared by the commercial publishers of the other two reporters.

West Publishing Company publishes seven different *regional reporters* (see Figure 4-4). A particular regional reporter will contain state cases from court in a particular region of the country. For example, Southern Reporter contains cases from Louisiana, Mississippi, Alabama, and Florida. With the wide availability of the regional reporters, many states that used to have official reporters in addition to the regional reporters no longer publish official reporters.

There are three important pieces of information you need to find a case. First, you need to know what series of what reporter it is in. You will find that many law books with multiple volumes are published in *series.* When the volume numbers for a reporter are so large that they become unmanageable,

The West Publishing Company regional reporters and the states covered are:

Atlantic Reporter Connecticut, Delaware, District of Columbia, Maine, New Hampshire, New Jersey, Rhode Island, Vermont

North Eastern Reporter Illinois, Indiana, Massachusetts, New York, Ohio

North Western Reporter Iowa, Michigan, Minnesota, Nebraska, North Dakota, South Dakota, Wisconsin

Pacific Reporter Alaska, Arizona, California, Colorado, Hawaii, Idaho, Kansas, Montana, Nevada, New Mexico, Oklahoma, Oregon, Utah, Washington, Wyoming

South Eastern Reporter Georgia, North Carolina, South Carolina, Virginia, West Virginia

Southern Reporter Alabama, Florida, Louisiana, Mississippi

South Western Reporter Arkansas, Kentucky, Missouri, Tennessee, Texas

FIGURE 4-4 West Publishing Company's regional reporters and their coverage.

Parallel Citations: A case may be published in more than one reporter. *Parallel citations* are citations to the various reporters containing the authority being cited. For state court decisions, you need to include parallel citations only when you are in the state in which the decision was rendered, with the citation to the official reporter coming before the citation to the unofficial reporter. Otherwise, you can give the citation only to the regional reporter containing the case.

LEGAL TERMS

advance sheets
Printed copies of judicial opinions published in loose-leaf form shortly after the opinions are issued. These published opinions are later collected and published in bound form with the other reported cases which are issued over a longer period of time.

reporters
Court reports, as well as official, published reports of cases decided by administrative agencies.

slip opinion
A single judicial decision published shortly after it has been issued by the court and well before it is incorporated into a reporter.

the publisher will start a new series of reporter beginning with volume 1. The series are designated by ordinal numbers, with the highest series number containing the most recent information. For example, the most recent United States Supreme Court opinions are published in United States Supreme Court Reports, Lawyers Edition Second Series, abbreviated "L. Ed. 2d." Assume you wanted to find *Brown v. Board of Education* and you know the citation in Lawyers Edition is "98 L. Ed. 873." First of all, "L. Ed." tells you you would need to look in the first series rather than the second series of the reporter. (See Figure 4-5.) Each time you write a citation or pull a case, make sure you have the correct series.

The second and third things you need to know are the volume number and the page on which the case begins. In a citation, the volume number precedes the abbreviation for the reporter and the page number follows it. In the citation for *Brown,* "98" is the volume number and "873" is the first page of the case.

Citation tip on case names. In a reporter, a case begins with the full name of the case, with a portion of the name appearing in all capital letters. Unless your reader requires Bluebook form for case names, use the portion of the case name that appears in all capitals (with the further modifications explained here) as the case name in your citation. You will have a very close approximation of Bluebook form without having to master a very complicated Bluebook rule. For case names, individuals are referred to only by their surnames. When the United States of America is a party to the case, the citation should show "United States" rather than "United States of America" or "U.S." If a state is a party to the case and the case is being decided by a court of that state, the citation should contain only "State," "Commonwealth," or "People." If a state is a party to the case but the case is being decided by a court other than a court of that state, then the citation should contain only the name of the state (for example, "Minnesota").

CITING CASES

A **citation** is an abbreviation used to refer to a legal authority which allows the reader to find the legal authority in the law library. When you answer a research question or perform legal analysis, it is expected that your answer or analysis will be backed up by a citation to your legal authority. It is important for you to learn correct citation form, because that form allows legal professionals to speak the same language. Correct usage is a sign of excellence.

For years *The Bluebook: A Uniform System of Citation,* compiled by several prominent law reviews and published by the Harvard Law Review Association, has been the standard for citation. The *Bluebook* has been rightly criticized for being too detailed and hard to learn. Perhaps because of this criticism, many have argued that citation form should be simplified and less emphasis placed on form. An attempt in this direction is *The University of Chicago Manual of Legal Citation,* referred to as the "Maroon Book" because of the color of its cover. A number of states have their own citation rules, which may be found in state statutes or court rules. Most law reviews and other scholarly publications will probably continue to use the *Bluebook*, however.

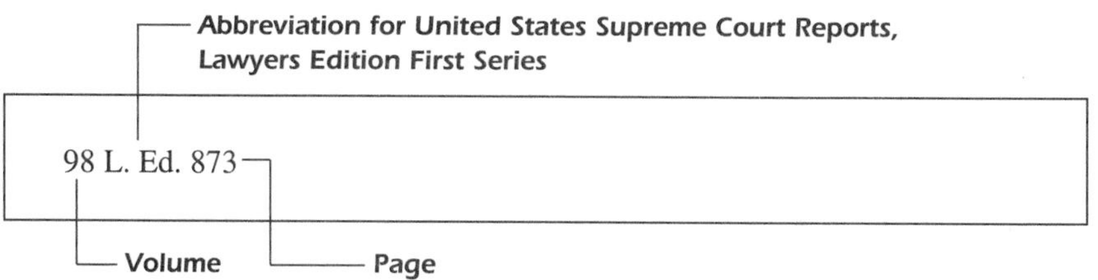

FIGURE 4-5 Citation to Lawyers Edition

Sample citation forms and explanations of how to cite particular types of legal authority are included in the chapters of this book in which each legal authority is introduced. The sample citation forms approximate *Bluebook* form. The suggestion is to either learn citation forms from this book or learn the citation forms contained in your state's citation rule. Your professor can tell you which he or she prefers. Those citation forms will be the only ones you will need much of the time. If the form for something you need to cite is not in this book or in your state's citation rule, you can refer to the *Bluebook.* The following sections explain the basics of citation form for cases and then give you sample citations for federal cases.

Citation tip on ordinal numbers. In legal citations the ordinal number "second" and "third" are abbreviated to "2d" and "3d." For all other ordinal numbers, use the standard abbreviations.

Citation tip on subsequent history. Connect subsequent history to the end of the citation of the lower court decision by explaining what the higher court did, underlining the explanation, and setting it off by commas. "Certiorari denied" should be abbreviated to "*cert. denied,*" "affirmed" should be abbreviated to "*aff'd,*" and "reversed" should be abbreviated to "*rev'd.*" Otherwise the explanation should be written out (for example, "*vacated*" or "*dismissed*").

Basic Citation Form

There is a certain framework for case citations which is fairly consistent for cases from all courts. Let's look at the typical citation in Figure 4-6 and analyze its components.

The name of the case comes first, is underlined, and is followed by a comma. Only the name of the first party on each side is given, with "v." (for versus) in between. The United States of America is the plaintiff-appellant. "Walker" is the last name of the defendant-appellee. The number "933" is the volume number, "F.2d" is the abbreviation for Federal Reporter Second Series, and "812" is the page on which the case begins. If needed, the first information within the parentheses identifies the court deciding the case. *Walker* was decided by the United States Tenth Circuit Court of Appeals, but only the number of the circuit is stated in the citation. You know it is a United States court of appeals case because the Federal Reporters contain only United States court of appeals cases. The year within the parentheses is the year in which the case was decided. Make sure you put the year of the decision in your citation, rather than the year in which the case was argued.

Subsequent History

After the United States Tenth Circuit Court of Appeals decided *Walker,* the United States petitioned for a rehearing. The petition was denied in a

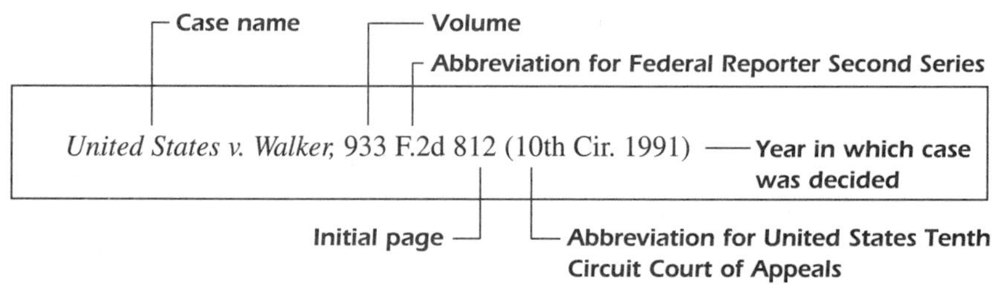

FIGURE 4-6 Components of a case citation.

LEGAL TERMS

citation
Reference to authority (a case, article, or other text) on a point of law, by name, volume, and page or section of the court report or other book in which it appears.

four-page order. *United States v. Walker,* 941 F.2d 1086 (10th Cir. 1991). The United States then petitioned for writ of certiorari to the United States Supreme Court. In *United States v. Walker,* 112 S. Ct. 1168 (1992), the petition was denied. The denial of the rehearing and the denial of the petition for writ of certiorari are called *subsequent history* because they happened subsequent to or after the Tenth Circuit's decision in *Walker.*

When citing to a case, you must give your reader all subsequent history *except for* denial of a rehearing or history on remand. The reason you would not give the citation for the denial of a rehearing is that many parties routinely petition for rehearings and rehearing is routinely denied. A denial of a rehearing is different from a court denying review or the United States Supreme Court denying a petition for certiorari. A rehearing is denied by the same court that has already rendered a decision. In contrast, only a higher court can deny review or deny a petition for certiorari. Therefore, a denial of review or a denial of a petition for certiorari is important enough to be given as subsequent history, whereas denial of rehearing is not. When an appellate court remands a case, it sends it back to the lower court to redo something the lower court did incorrectly before. The appellate decision in which the appellate court lays down the rule of law to be followed by the lower court on remand, and not the lower court decision in which the rule of law is carried out, is more important for its precedential value. For that reason, history on remand is not usually cited in subsequent history.

The full citation of *Walker,* including subsequent history, is shown in Figure 4-7. Notice that you place a comma after the first set of parentheses; underline the explanation of what happened in subsequent history ("*cert. denied*" explains that certiorari was denied); add a comma; identify the volume, reporter, and page at which certiorari was denied; and give the year of the denial. As explained earlier, the citation to subsequent history includes the citation to where the United States Supreme Court denied the petition for certiorari, but not the citation to where the Tenth Circuit Court of Appeals denied the petition for rehearing.

Page Numbers

When you are referring to specific information from a case or you are quoting from a case, you should give a *pinpoint* or *locus* page reference to

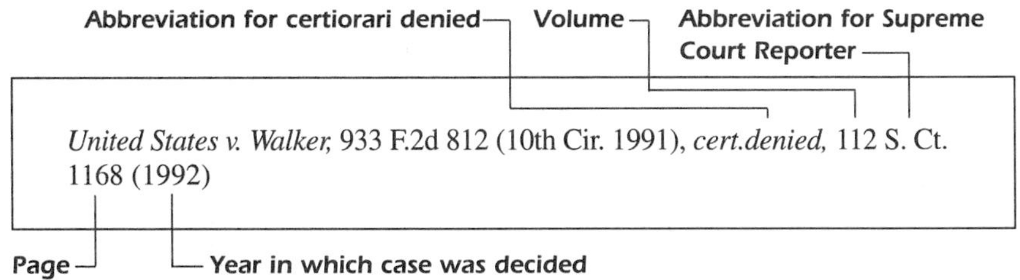

FIGURE 4-7 Full citation of *United States v. Walker.*

the page or pages on which that material was found. Page references to material within a case can be made part of your full citation as shown in Figure 4-8.

The page numbers in this citation mean that 812 is the first page of the case and the material you are referring to is found on pages 813 through 814 and on page 816. If you wanted to refer to material on the first page of the opinion, you would repeat the number of the first page and separate the numbers by a comma. Notice that when you refer to inclusive pages, such as pages 813 through 814, you join the page numbers by an en dash or a hyphen and retain only the last two digits of the second number.

United States Supreme Court Cases

The following is an example of a citation for a case found in United States Law Week, but which has not yet been published in the reporters:

> *Lee v. International Society for Krishna Consciousness, Inc.,* 60 U.S.L.W. 4761 (U.S. 1992).

If the case has been printed in a reporter, you should give the citation to a reporter rather than to the advance sheets. Although the *Bluebook* does not require **parallel citations** to United States Supreme Court cases, you may give parallel citations to those cases, as shown in Figure 4-9; they are often helpful to readers with more limited library resources.

Figure 4-9 shows a blank in the citation to the United States Reports because that reporter has not yet published the case, so the page number of the case in that reporter is not yet known. If you are citing to only one

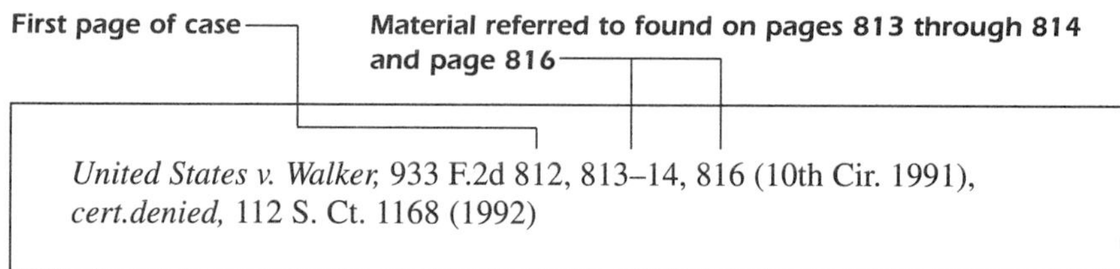

FIGURE 4-8 Page reference within the *Walker* case.

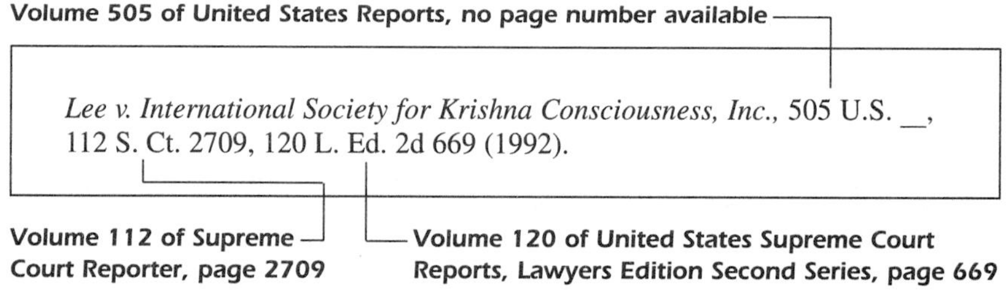

FIGURE 4-9 Parallel citations (with one reporter that has yet to publish the case).

LEGAL TERMS

parallel citation
A citation to a court opinion or decision that is printed in two or more reporters.

reporter, cite to the United States Reports, if the case is contained in it, or to the Supreme Court Reporter.

United States Circuit Courts of Appeal

The following is an example of a citation to a case in the United States Tenth Circuit Court of Appeal:

> *United States v. Walker,* 933 F.2d 812 (10th Cir. 1991), *cert. denied,* 112 S. Ct. 1168 (1992).

United States District Courts

The following is an example of a citation to a case in the United States District Court for the Northern District of Texas:

> *Sexton v. Gibbs,* 327 F. Supp. 134 (N.D. Tex. 1970), *aff'd,* 446 F.2d 904 (5th Cir. 1971), *cert. denied,* 404 U.S. 1062 (1972).

Notice that "Northern District of Texas" has been abbreviated to "N.D. Tex." You know from this citation that Texas has more than one district. Some of the less populous or smaller states, such as New Jersey, have only one United States district court to cover the whole state. The abbreviation for the United States District Court for the District of New Jersey would be "D.N.J." After the *Sexton* case was decided by the United States District Court for the Northern District of Texas in 1970, it was affirmed by the United States Fifth Circuit Court of Appeals in 1971 and certiorari was denied by the United States Supreme Court in 1972.

NOTE ON COMPUTER-ASSISTED RESEARCH

If you have access to computer-assisted legal research (CALR), you have the following alternatives:

1. Perform the research exercises in this book on the computer
2. Use the computer for some exercises and hard-copy law books for other exercises
3. Use the computer and law books together.

A researcher can access known primary sources by typing in the applicable citation. If you do not know the citation, search for relevant authority using information or key words related to the problem. This section first discusses on-line CALR and then examines CALR using CD-ROMs.

WESTLAW and LEXIS both offer the researcher three search methods:

1. Key word search
2. "Plain English" search
3. Search using a menu.

A *key word search* is the traditional search method for on-line searching. In a key word search, the researcher formulates a query using words that the researcher might expect to find to answer a particular question. For example, to locate cases concerning the search and seizure problem, a researcher might use the words "search," "seizure," "forfeiture," "drug courier profile," "highway," or "interstate." If the researcher wants to find a case containing several of these key words, the key words could be joined by connectors. For example, if you wanted to find a case containing "search," "forfeiture," and "highway," your query would contain those three words and the appropriate connectors telling the computer that you are looking for cases containing all three of those words.

Citation tip on spacing in abbreviations. If every letter in the abbreviation but the series is upper case, spell the abbreviation solid: N.E.2d; D.D.C.; P.2d; N.C.; F.2d; U.S.

If the abbreviation uses both upper- and lower-case letters, put a space between the parts: W. Va.; F. Supp.; S. Ct.; So. 2d; D.C. Cir.

Formulating queries using key words can be fairly complex. A researcher can expand the search by using synonyms, universal characters, and root expanders in a query. Because the computer searches only for the key words used in the query, a researcher may miss important cases if synonyms are not part of the query. A query including "highway" would not turn up cases using "interstate" instead of "highway." Specifying that the search should find cases using either of the synonyms "highway" or "interstate" would increase the number of cases found.

The researcher can also include universal characters and root expanders in a query to find words with variant spelling or endings. A *universal character* is like a "wild card" which can be used in the middle or at the end of a word. It tells the computer that there should be something in place of the universal character, but does not specify what that something should be. A root expander is similar except that it can be used only at the end of a word and is not limited in the number of characters it picks up. (With universal characters, the ending is limited to the number of universal characters included in the search.) If the researcher wanted to find cases containing "forfeit" and "forfeiture," the query could contain "forfeit" with a root expander or three universal characters tacked onto the end of "forfeit." Use of the root expander or three universal characters broadens the search to pick up cases containing either or both of the two words.

A search can be limited in any number of ways: by date, judge, attorney, court, citation, and case name. Certain of the limitations, such as judge and attorney, make it possible to retrieve cases impossible to locate without CALR. These limitations are useful if the researcher wants to know all of the cases decided by a particular judge or all the cases argued by a particular attorney. A search could also be limited by selecting a more specific library, such as tax or securities. Generally, the more specific the library the researcher is searching, the smaller the number of documents retrieved.

WESTLAW and LEXIS recently added "plain English" as a search method. The plain English search method may be more comfortable for the less experienced researcher. Instead of formulating a query using key words and connectors, the researcher would input a description of the question being researched. The description may be in the form of a statement, a question, or a phrase. For example, a researcher researching the Williams problem might search using the phrase "constitutionality of highway stop made on drug courier profile." The search under that description would find the documents most relevant to the description.

In a Boolean search or a plain English search, the computer searches for certain key words and brings up the documents containing the key words. The difference between a Boolean search and a plain English search is in the way the search is made. If you wanted to find cases in which an officer stopped a car on an interstate highway, searched it, and confiscated money, you would have to first formulate a search query. Let's look at the difference between a Boolean serch and a plain English search.

In a Boolean search, you would have to determine key words that will yield relevant cases. Searching for "search" would give you all the thousands of cases containing "search," many of which would not concern a car stop and search for money. To narrow the search, you might ask for cases containing "search," "seizure," "money,"and "highway." The cases found would contain those four words but would not find a case that used the word "interstate" instead of "highway." You might want to reformulate the search to look for "search," "seizure," "money," *and* "highway" *or* "interstate." The reformulated search would turn up the same cases as in the prior search, as well as cases containing "search," "seizure," and "money" as well as "interstate."

In a plain English search, your query would be a phrase such as "constitutionality of highway stop made on drug courier profile." The computer will identify significant words and match the significant words with the words in a document in the data base. The search results give the researcher a list of the documents containing the significant words, with the documents ordered by the number of significant word found (the document with the highest number of significant words is listed first).

The novice researcher may be most comfortable with a search using menus. Such a search can be performed on both WESTLAW and LEXIS. Instead of formulating a query or inputting a plain English description, a researcher can be guided by, and can select options from, a series of menus.

The research methods available with a particular CD-ROM depend on the capabilities of the particular CD. The researcher can perform a key word search on a CD-ROM and may be able to perform a plain English search and a menu search as well.

SUMMARY

- Cases are easier to read and understand once you are familiar with typical case style and format.
- The syllabus (case summary) and the headnotes (summaries of important legal principles contained in the case) preceding the opinion are prepared by the publisher and have no official authority.

- The main parts of a typical opinion are the facts, the procedural history of the case before it reached the court writing the opinion, the issue(s) (legal question(s) considered by the court), the holding(s) (the rule(s) of the case), and the court's explanation of why it reached the particular holding.
- "Briefing a case" means taking notes of the most important parts of a case so that you can later refer to your case brief to quickly refresh your memory.
- A standard format for briefing a case contains:
  - Correct case citation
  - Facts
  - History
  - Question(s)
  - Holding(s)
  - Reasoning
  - Result.
- Cases are organized chronologically in loose-leaf publications, advance sheets, and reporters.
- A reporter contains cases from a particular court or courts; the reporters are published in series (1st, 2d, 3d, etc.).
- It is important for you to learn correct citation form to allow you to communicate with other legal professionals.
- Case citations contain the case name, the volume, the name and series of the reporter, and the first page of the case, as well as information identifying the court writing the decision.
- A full case citation should contain the page number(s) on which the cited material is located and any subsequent history of the case.
- Computer-assisted legal research allows you to find relevant cases by searching for words that you might expect to find in the answer to a particular question.

RESEARCH ASSIGNMENTS

Legal Research Assignment—Reading Cases

1. Answer the following questions regarding *United States of America v. Timothy Andrew Smith* (starting at page 704 of volume 799 of Federal Reporter Second Series):
   a. What is the correct citation of the case?
   b. Who was the plaintiff in the lower court?
   c. Who were the defendants in the lower court?
   d. Who were the attorneys who represented the appellants?
   e. Who were the attorneys who represented the appellee?
   f. Who wrote the opinion?
   g. How many judges participated in the decision?

h. Who was the trial judge?
i. What was the docket number of the case at the trial level?
j. What was the name of the trial court?
k. How many headnotes are there?
l. What are the key numbers?
m. What are the important facts?
n. What was the result in the trial court?
o. What was the issue on appeal?
p. What did the court hold?
q. Why did the court reject the two possible reasons for the stop?
r. What result did the appellate court reach?

2. Answer the following questions regarding *Florida v. Enio Jimeno* (this case is included in Appendix A):
   a. What is the correct citation of the case?
   b. On what page does the court's decision begin?
   c. Is it proper to quote anything prior to this page?
   d. Which Justice wrote the opinion?
   e. Which Justice(s) joined in that opinion?
   f. Which Justice wrote the dissenting opinion?
   g. Which Justice(s) joined in the dissenting opinion?
   h. Is this a per curiam, majority, or plurality opinion?
   i. What are the important facts?
   j. Who won at the trial level?
   k. Where did the case go after it left the trial court and before it reached the United States Supreme Court?
   l. What was the issue before the United States Supreme Court?
   m. What did the Court hold?
   n. What was the Court's reasoning for reaching this holding?
   o. What was the result?
   p. Why did the dissent reason that the result should have been different?

3. Answer the following questions regarding *United States v. Sokolow* (a 1989 United States Supreme Court case):
   a. What is the correct citation of this case?
   b. How many Justices joined in the opinion (including the Justice who wrote the opinion), and how many Justices joined in the dissenting opinion (including the Justice who wrote the opinion)?
   c. What are the important facts?
   d. Who won at the trial level?
   e. Where did the case go after it left the trial court and before it reached the United States Supreme Court?
   f. What was the issue before the United States Supreme Court?
   g. What did the Court hold?
   h. What was the Court's reasoning for reaching this holding?
   i. What was the result?
   j. Why did the dissent reason that the result should have been different?

Legal Research Assignment—Case Law

1. What are the names of the three reporters containing current decisions of the United States Supreme Court?
2. What is the name of the advance sheet containing current decisions of the United States Supreme Court?
3. What is the name of the reporter containing current decisions of the United States circuit courts of appeal?
4. What is the name of the reporter containing current decisions of the United States district courts?
5. What is the name of the highest court in your state and what is the name of the reporter containing current decisions of that court? (If there is more than one reporter, give the names of all reporters containing decisions from the court.)
6. What is the name of the intermediate appellate court in your state and what is the name of the reporter containing current decisions of that court? (If there is more than one reporter, give the names of all reporters containing decisions from the court.)
7. What is the name of the advance sheet containing decisions of the courts of your state?
8. Give the name of the trial-level court in your state and the name, if any, of the reporter containing current decisions of that court. (If there is more than one trial-level court in your state, give the names of all trial level courts. If there is more than one reporter, give the names of all reporters containing decisions from the court or courts.)
9. Answer the following questions regarding the case found at 98 F. Supp. 797:
   a. What is the correct citation for this case?
   b. What does this decision deal with?
10. Answer the following questions regarding the case found at 347 U.S. 483, 74 S. Ct. 686, 98 L. Ed. 873:
    a. What is the correct citation for this case?
    b. What does the Court hold?
11. Answer the following questions regarding *Lee v. International Society for Krishna Consciousness,* 505 U.S. ____, 112 S. Ct. 2709, 120 L. Ed. 2d 669 (1992):
    a. Did the Court allow or not allow distribution of literature by the Hare Krishnas?
    b. How many Justices agreed with the decision (by joining in or concurring or both)
    c. How many Justices dissented (including the Justice who wrote the dissenting opinion)?
    d. Who wrote the dissenting opinion?
    e. Is this a per curiam, majority, or plurality opinion?

f. This case is a companion case to another case between the same parties in which the Court upheld a ban on another Hare Krishna activity. Read the dissenting opinion in *Lee* and state what other activity the Court did not allow.

12. Answer the following questions regarding *Lindsey v. Prive Corp.*, 987 F.2d 324 (5th Cir. 1993):
    a. What federal act did Ann Marie Lindsey sue under?
    b. What reason did the manager give for not promoting Ms. Lindsey?
    c. What were the necessary qualifications for the promotion?
    d. What was the decision of the lower court?
    e. What did the Fifth Circuit decide?
    f. Why?
13. Answer the following questions regarding *Cippollone v. Liggett Group, Inc.*, ______ U.S. ______, 112 S. Ct. 2608, 120 L. Ed. 2d 407 (1992):
    a. What is the name of the federal act that the tobacco company claimed protected it against liability?
    b. What did the federal act preempt and what did it not preempt?
    c. Based on *Cippollone,* state what "preempt" means in your own words.
14. Answer the following questions regarding the case found at 112 S. Ct. 2649, 120 L. Ed. 2d 467:
    a. What is the proper citation for this case?
    b. Who were Daniel Weisman and Robert E. Lee?
    c. What did Mr. Lee do that Mr. Weisman objected to?
    d. What is the question the Court has to decide?
    e. Based on this decision, what is a public school prohibited from doing?
15. Answer the following questions regarding the case found at 112 S. Ct. 1535, 118 L. Ed. 2d 174:
    a. What is the proper citation for this case?
    b. What was Mr. Jacobson charged with?
    c. What did Mr. Jacobson claim was his defense?
    d. How did the trial court explain Mr. Jacobson's defense in the jury instructions?
    e. What did the United States Supreme Court do with the Eighth Circuit Court of Appeal's decision and why?
16. Answer the following questions regarding the case found at 113 S. Ct. 853, 122 L. Ed. 2d 203:
    a. What is the proper citation for this case?
    b. What was Mr. Herrera convicted of?
    c. What did Mr. Herrera claim in his second federal habeas corpus petition and why?
    d. Who did Mr. Herrera claim had committed the murder?
    e. What would Mr. Herrera have to show, in addition to evidence supporting his innocence, for his habeas corpus petition to be granted?
    f. What can Mr. Herrera do, since his petition was turned down?

17. Answer the following questions regarding *United States v. $144,600.00, United States Currency,* 757 F. Supp. 1342 (M.D. Fla. 1991):
    a. What type of action was involved and what statute was this case brought under?
    b. What did the government have to show before the money could be forfeited?
    c. What evidence did the government use to make this showing?
    d. Once the government presented this evidence, what are two arguments Mr. Gordon could have used to support his claim that the money should not be forfeited?
    e. What evidence did Mr. Gordon present in support of this claim?
    f. Why didn't the court decide whether there was a violation of Mr. Gordon's right against unreasonable search and seizure?
18. Answer the following questions regarding the case found at 933 F.2d 812:
    a. What is the correct citation for the case?
    b. Why was Mr. Walker stopped?
    c. After the officer checked Mr. Walker's driver's license and car registration, what level of proof did the officer need to continue questioning Mr. Walker?
    d. What is the citation for the lower court's opinion?
    e. Why did the lower court grant Mr. Walker's motion to suppress?
    f. What is the circuit court instructing the lower court to do on remand?
    g. What effect will the "fruit of the poisonous tree doctrine" have on the lower court's decision on remand?
19. Answer the following questions regarding *Sexton v. Gibbs,* 327 F. Supp. 134 (N.D. Tex. 1970):
    a. What two of his constitutional rights did Bruce Sexton claim had been violated?
    b. Who were Bruce Gibbs and Terry Stephens?
    c. What did the court hold concerning Mr. Sexton's arrest?
    d. What does the court state are two permissible grounds for a warrantless search of an automobile?
    e. What does the court hold concerning the search?
    f. Why does the court reject good faith as a valid defense?
20. Answer the following questions regarding *Medious v. Department of Highway Safety & Motor Vehicles,* 534 So. 2d 729 (Fla Dist. Ct. App. 1988):
    a. What items did the lower court order be forfeited?
    b. What reasons did the district court of appeals give for reversing the lower court's finding of probable cause?
    c. With respect to what item did the district court of appeals agree with the lower court?
    d. Why?

21. Answer the following questions concerning the case found at 613 So. 2d 554:
    a. What is the correct citation for the case?
    b. Why did the defendants claim that their motion to suppress should have been granted?
    c. Assuming that the defendants did consent to be searched, how does the court determine the limits of the consent?
    d. What will happen on remand?
22. Answer the following questions concerning the case found at 480 So. 2d 625:
    a. What is the correct citation for the case?
    b. What legal duty is imposed upon the seller by this decision?
    c. What legal doctrine was in effect prior to this decision?
23. Answer the following questions concerning the case found at 473 So. 2d 1272:
    a. What is the correct citation for the case?
    b. What is the correct citation for the lower court (district court of appeals) decision that was appealed to the Florida Supreme Court?
    c. What statutes does the Florida Supreme Court decision deal with?
    d. How does the Florida Supreme Court interpret these statutes?

CHAPTER 5

Primary Sources: Constitutions, Statutes, Court Rules, and Administrative Law

OUTLINE

Constitutions
Statutes
Court Rules
Administrative Law
Note on Computer-Assisted Legal Research

COMMON LEGAL SOURCES AND FINDING TOOLS

Note: Sources used in this chapter are indicated by boldface type.

Primary Sources	Secondary Sources	Finding Tools
reporters	treatises	American Law Reports
constitutions	law review articles	legal encyclopedias
statutes	legal periodicals	digests
administrative regulations	law dictionaries	Index to Legal Periodicals
court rules	legal thesauruses	loose-leaf services
loose-leaf services	continuing legal education publications	Shepard's Citators
	Restatements	
	American Law Reports	
	legal encyclopedias	
	loose-leaf services	

This chapter introduces and explains the correct citation forms for four primary sources: constitutions, statutes, court rules, and administrative law.

CONSTITUTIONS

Because there is a United States Constitution (the federal Constitution) and each state has its own constitution, constitutional law research may be done at the federal and the state level. As explained in Chapter 1, Article VI of the United States Constitution contains the **supremacy clause**. The supremacy clause makes the Constitution prevail over any federal statute, state constitutional provision, or state statute in conflict with the Constitution. Congress is given certain **enumerated powers** in Article I, § 8 of the Constitution. Sections 9 and 10 of Article I prohibit the federal and state governments from taking certain actions (for example, passing any **ex post facto law**). The tenth amendment to the Constitution reserves all other powers to the states.

A written constitution is the document setting forth the fundamental principles of governance. For example, Article I of the United States Constitution deals with the legislative branch, Article II deals with the executive branch, and Article III deals with the judicial branch of the federal government. A state constitution sets forth the basic framework of state government in a similar fashion.

Some people differentiate between the written and the "living" constitution. The written United States Constitution, including all amendments, is less than 20 pages in length. The living constitution includes those pages and all case law interpretations of the Constitution. If printed, the living constitution would require numerous volumes. Scholars and laypersons alike have hotly debated constitutional interpretation. Some believe that any interpretation should be based on the plain language of the Constitution and should not stray far from it. Others believe that the broad language of the Constitution should be interpreted as needed to deal with legal questions never dreamed of when the Constitution was first enacted.

The language of the United States Constitution is very broad, setting up a framework of government, often without much detail. For example, Article III of the Constitution established the United States Supreme Court, but left the establishment of other federal courts to Congress. State constitutions may be much longer than the United States Constitution and may include many subjects that are dealt with on the federal level by statute. The only limits on state constitutions is that they may not conflict with the United States Constitution or any federal statute concerning a matter given exclusively to the federal government.

Constitutions generally follow the same basic format. A constitution usually begins with a **preamble**, a paragraph or clause explaining the reason for enactment of the constitution and the object or objects it seeks to accomplish. The body of the document is divided into various parts (called *articles* in the United States Constitution and many state constitutions) corresponding to the various subjects dealt with in the constitution; the parts are in turn divided into subparts (called *sections* and *clauses* in the United States Constitution). Near the end of the constitution is a provision describing the procedure for amending it. Any amendments to a constitution are either printed at the end of the constitution (the procedure followed for the United States Constitution), or the new language is simply incorporated into the body of the document (the procedure followed for the Florida Constitution and the constitutions of many states).

The United States Constitution is unique in that it was adopted in 1787 and has been the fundamental document of American government ever since. There are 26 amendments to it, the first 10 amendments of which are known as the **Bill of Rights**. The fourteenth amendment, adopted in 1868, has been interpreted to make most of the provisions of the Bill of Rights applicable to the states. In contrast, many states have been governed under more than one constitution. For example, the present Constitution of the State of Florida is dated 1968 and is a revision of the constitution of 1885. The Florida Constitution has been amended a number of times since 1968.

Locating Constitutions

The actual text of a constitution may be found in many reference books in the law library. If you just want to read the United States Constitution, you could read it from a constitutional law textbook or other source. (Even many dictionaries contain a copy of the United States Constitution.) The text of your state's constitution may be printed in the set of books containing the official version of your state's statutory code.

An annotated version of the federal Constitution is found in the sets of books containing the annotated United States Code. If you want to know how the first amendment to the United States Constitution has been interpreted concerning restrictions on prayer in public schools, you would look at the case summaries of cases interpreting the first amendment. The case summaries are found in United States Code Service or United States Code Annotated following the text of the first amendment. You would follow a similar procedure to research your state's constitution. Often codes and annotated codes contain a separate index located at the end of a constitution. The index is designed to help you locate a particular provision within the constitution.

Don't forget to update your research. Hardbound volumes of the annotated codes are updated by pocket parts. The pocket parts are updated by quarterly supplements. Because of the lag time between the announcement of an important United States Supreme Court decision interpreting the Constitution and the printing of the annual pocket part to the annotated code, the annotated code may be as much as two years behind current case

LEGAL TERMS

supremacy clause
The provision in Article VI of the Constitution that "this Constitution and the laws of the United States . . . shall be the supreme law of the land, and the judges in every state shall be bound thereby."

enumerated powers
Powers specifically granted by the Constitution to one of the three branches of government. Another term for enumerated powers is *express powers*.

ex post facto law
A law making a person criminally liable for an act that was not criminal at the time it was committed. The Constitution prohibits both Congress and the states from enacting such laws.

preamble
A paragraph or clause at the beginning of a constitution, statute, or ordinance explaining the reasons for its enactment and the object or objects it seeks to accomplish.

Bill of Rights
The first 10 amendments to the United States Constitution. The Bill of Rights is the portion of the Constitution that sets forth the rights which are the fundamental principles of the United States and the foundation of American citizenship.

law. Update your research by shepardizing and using computer-assisted legal research.

When researching, you may find it helpful to consult one or more of the various treatises dealing with constitutional law, in addition to reading the annotations in the annotated codes.

Citations for Constitutions

The clause prohibiting ex post facto laws and § 1 of the fourteenth amendment to the Constitution may be cited as follows:

U.S. Const. art. I, § 9, cl. 3. (abbreviation for United States Constitution, Article I, section 9, clause 3)

U.S. Const. amend. XIV, § 1. (abbreviation for United States Constitution, fourteenth amendment, section 1)

Give the section number when the Constitution specifically identifies a portion of an article as a section. When a section such as § 9 of article I is long and contains a number of paragraphs, you can reference a particular paragraph as a "clause." Some copies of the United States Constitution identify the amendments as "articles" instead of "amendments." This is because the amendments are technically articles in amendment of the Constitution. To avoid confusion, cite the amendments to the Constitution as "amendments" rather than as "articles." State constitutions can be cited using the same citation form as set forth here or the form in your state's citation rules.

Capitalize a state constitution only when naming it in full. Capitalize the United States Constitution and any reference to it. Do not capitalize the name of any portion of a constitution except for the Bill of Rights.

STATUTES

As explained in Chapter 1, the federal and state legislatures pass statutes. A statute first appears as a slip law; then a number of statutes are printed chronologically as session laws; later the statutes are codified. Once passed, a statute may be amended, repealed, or held to be unconstitutional. Commercial publishers publish annotated versions of statutory codes. To research case law interpretations of the United States Code, consult United States Code Service or United States Code Annotated. Look in your law library and identify the session law, codified, and annotated code versions of your state's statutes. Then fill in that information on the chart in Table 1-1 (in Chapter 1 of this book) so you have a record of it.

Statutory Codes

When statutes are codified, they are grouped by subject matter. The United States Code is divided into 50 broad subject categories called *titles*. For example, the federal forfeiture statute, 21 U.S.C. § 881, is part of title 21, which deals with food and drugs. The federal forfeiture statute is in title 21 because the purpose of the statute is to discourage the possession or use of illegal drugs by allowing the forfeiture of money or other property connected with the illegal drug trade.

Federal statutes are further grouped by subject matter within each title of the United States Code. Notice in the United States Code that a number of statutes will appear numbered consecutively and then there may be a break in numbering before the next group of statutes. The break in numbering allows new statutes to be inserted in the middle of a title without having to renumber existing statutes. Often a group of consecutively numbered statutes will be preceded by a table of contents to the statutes. These tables of contents are helpful because they allow you to get an overview of a series of statutes and to tell at a glance the general scope of those statutes.

Look at your state's statutory code and determine the major subject groupings and what these groupings are called. For example, Florida Statutes are divided into more than 900 *chapters,* instead of into titles as is the United States Code, with the chapters further divided into sections. Florida Statutes are cited by decimal numbers, with the numbers to the left of the decimal point identifying the chapter number and the numbers following the decimal point identifying the section number. For example, the Florida Contraband Forfeiture Act is located at Fla. Stat. §§ 932.701–932.707 (1991 & Supp. 1992). If you had the citation to the Act and wanted to read it, you would look at sections 701 through 707 of chapter 932.

Florida Statutes are recodified in every odd-numbered year. A supplement containing only the new statutory material passed during the even-numbered years is published at the end of those years. The material inside the parentheses at the end of the preceding citation tells the reader that part of the Act is located in Florida Statutes 1991 and part is in the Florida Statutes Supplement 1992. Even though this book is being written during 1993–94, the citation is to the 1991 recodification and the 1992 supplement. This is because the 1993 recodification will not be published until late 1993 or early 1994. To be current during 1993, you must consult Florida Statutes 1991, Florida Statutes Supplement 1992, and West's Florida Session Law Service for 1993. If you are doing your research in Florida Statutes Annotated instead of Florida Statutes, you need to check the hardbound volume and the pocket part. You may still have to check session laws if the pocket part does not contain statutes from the most current legislative session. The first few pages of the pocket part will tell the latest legislation covered in the pocket part. If the session laws are more current, you will need to check them as well as Florida Statutes Annotated.

Statutes Passed as "Acts"

A legislature may pass statutes either singly or as part of an "act." Single statutes are passed when the legislative provision is short. When the new statute is codified, it will be inserted into the statutory code with statutes concerning the same or related subject matter. When the new statutory language is longer, and particularly when it concerns matters not previously dealt with by statute, the legislature may pass an **act** comprised of several consecutively numbered statutes.

An act often is identified by a name given it by the legislature, and for easy reference is often referred to by that name. This *short title* or *popular name* is usually found in one of the first sections of an act; at the beginning of a table of contents preceding the act; or, in annotated codes, in the historical references following each provision of the act. For example, 42 U.S.C. § 1983, which prohibits the states from depriving persons of their constitutional rights, was passed as part of the Civil Rights Act of 1871.

Other common provisions in an act are a preamble, which identifies the objective or objectives of the act, and a definitions section, which defines terms used in the act. A section describing the effective date or dates of the act frequently appears at the end.

Statutory Research

The first step in statutory research is to read the statute carefully and read any other statute or material cross-referenced in the first statute. Generally, statutes are drafted in broad language to set forth a legal principle rather than to deal with a specific problem. Great care must be taken in drafting statutory language so that the language is neither underinclusive nor overinclusive. A statute that is underinclusive may leave loopholes, allowing practices that the statute was intended to preclude. A statute that sweeps too broadly may be held unconstitutionally vague.

A court faced with statutory interpretation will look first to the language of the statute itself and its context. A statute that is part of an act should be interpreted by the way it fits into the scheme of the act. Another tool for statutory interpretation is **legislative history**. Committee reports and other legislative documents may shed light on the meaning of a statute. A source of congressional legislative history available in many law libraries is *United States Code Congressional and Administrative News.* This publication contains the text of federal acts and selected committee reports. A court will also look to prior case law interpretation of the statute. An interpretation by the same or a higher court would be mandatory authority, whereas an interpretation by a lower court or the courts of another jurisdiction would be persuasive.

Don't forget to update your research. Hardbound volumes of the annotated codes are updated by pocket parts. The pocket parts of United States

Code Service and United States Code Annotated are updated by quarterly supplements. You can further update your research by shepardizing and using computer-assisted legal research. If you are researching state statutes, update the annotated code by researching session laws.

Sample Pages of Statutes

Subsection (d) of 21 U.S.C.S. § 881 (Law. Co-op. Supp. 1992) tells one to apply customs statutes in determining the procedure for civil forfeiture. After an item is seized under 21 U.S.C. § 881, a determination must be made about whether the item will be forfeited to the government. This determination is made either by a "customs officer" under 19 U.S.C.S. §§ 1607, 1609 (Law. Co-op. 1993) or by a court under 19 U.S.C.S. §§ 1608, 1610, 1615 (Law. Co-op. 1993). The first type of forfeiture is called an *administrative forfeiture* because the forfeiture determination is made by an executive agency. The second type of forfeiture is called a *judicial forfeiture* because a court makes the determination. Administrative forfeiture is used when the value of the item is $500,000 or less and the forfeiture is uncontested. A judicial forfeiture is used when the value of the item is more than $500,000 or the forfeiture is contested. Following are copies of 19 U.S.C.S. §§ 1607–1610 and 1615 (Figure 5-1). Read through those statutes and 21 U.S.C.S. § 881 (reprinted in Appendix A) and see if you can follow the forfeiture procedure.

United States Code Service contains the text of the statutes and various research tools, including annotations. Because of page constraints, you have been given only the research tools following 19 U.S.C.S. § 1609. Turn to the beginning of that statute and we'll walk through it and the research tools. The text of the statute is divided into parts (a) and (b). The material on the next six lines is legislative history. The statute was first passed in 1930 and was subsequently amended several times. If you wanted to look up the text of the statute as originally passed and the text of the amendments, you could use the information in parentheses to look up the information in **Statutes at Large.** More references to legislative history are contained in the section entitled "HISTORY; ANCILLARY LAWS AND DIRECTIVES."

After legislative history, the material following the statute cross-references to administrative law, other federal statutes, and other Lawyers Cooperative publications, including *American Jurisprudence.* Attorneys commonly refer to "INTERPRETIVE NOTES AND DECISIONS" as annotations. Numbered items 1 through 5 comprise a short table of contents for the annotations to § 1609. Similar to digest annotations, annotations to statutes give a summary of a legal principle contained in a case interpreting § 1607 and the citation to the case. If you would like to know how § 1609 has been interpreted, you can read through the annotations and use the citation therein to pull the case for further research. Although the citations are usually to cases, sometimes they can be to other legal authority.

LEGAL TERMS

act
A statute; a bill that has been enacted by the legislature.

legislative history
Recorded events that provide a basis for determining the legislative intent underlying a statute enacted by a legislature. The records of legislative committee hearings and of debates on the floor of the legislature are among the sources for legislative history.

Statutes at Large
An official publication of the federal government, issued after each session of Congress, which includes all statutes enacted by the Congress and all congressional resolutions and treaties, as well as presidential proclamations and proposed or ratified amendments to the Constitution.

This statute (19 U.S.C.S. § 1607) was originally part of the "Tariff Act of 1930"

Section 1607 of title 19 United States Code Service

TARIFF ACT OF 1930 **19 USCS § 1607**

§ 1607. Seizure; value $500,000 or less, prohibited articles, transporting conveyances, monetary instruments

Includes cash

(a) Notice of seizure. If—

(1) the value of such seized vessel, vehicle, aircraft, merchandise, or baggage does not exceed $500,000;

(2) such seized merchandise is merchandise the importation of which is prohibited;

(3) such seized vessel, vehicle, or aircraft was used to import, export, transport, or store any controlled substance; or

(4) such seized merchandise is any monetary instrument within the meaning of section 5312(a)(3) of title 31 of the United States Code;

Notice

Publication of notice

Written notice also sent

the appropriate customs officer shall cause a notice of the seizure of such articles and the intention to forfeit and sell or otherwise dispose of the same according to law to be published for at least three successive weeks in such manner as the Secretary of the Treasury may direct. Written notice of seizure together with information on the applicable procedures shall be sent to each party who appears to have an interest in the seized article.

(b) Definition of "controlled substance". As used in this section, the term "controlled substance" has the meaning given that term in section 102 of the Controlled Substances Act [21 USCS § 802].

(c) Report to Congress. The Commissioner of Customs shall submit to the Congress, by no later than February 1 of each fiscal year, a report on the total dollar value of uncontested seizures of monetary instruments having a value of over $100,000 which, or the proceeds of which, have not been deposited into the Customs Forfeiture Fund under section 613A [19 USCS § 1613b] within 120 days of seizure, as of the end of the previous fiscal year.

FIGURE 5-1 Federal statutes outlining the procedure for forfeiture. (From 19 United States Code Service. Courtesy of Lawyers Cooperative Publishing. Reprinted by permission.)

When you are researching statutes, don't forget to check the pocket part for later annotations. Also, do not assume that an annotated code contains the most recent cases interpreting a statute. Use the cases you find from the annotations to find more recent cases through the digests (see Chapter 3) or through shepardizing (see Chapter 6).

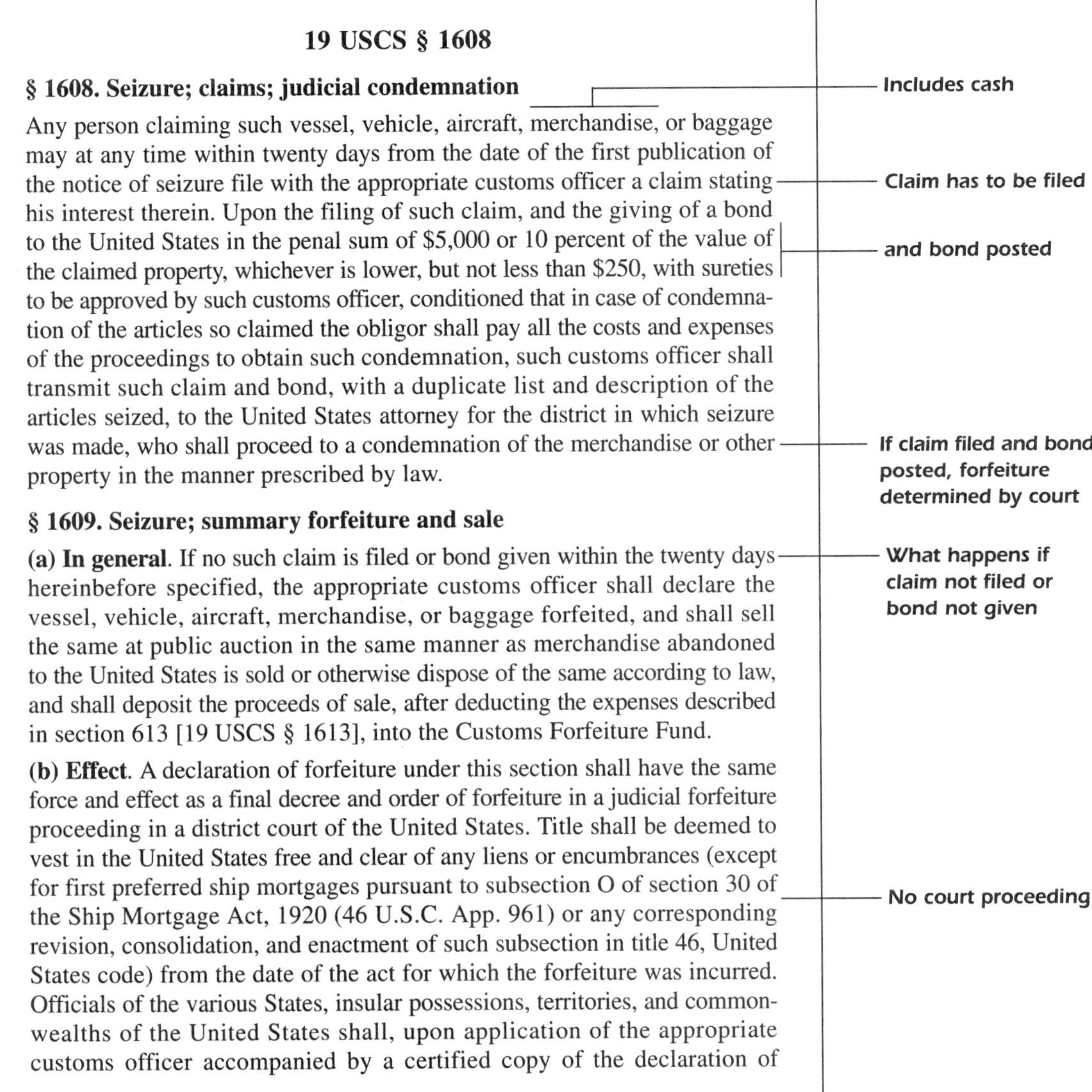

19 USCS § 1608

§ 1608. Seizure; claims; judicial condemnation

Any person claiming such vessel, vehicle, aircraft, merchandise, or baggage may at any time within twenty days from the date of the first publication of the notice of seizure file with the appropriate customs officer a claim stating his interest therein. Upon the filing of such claim, and the giving of a bond to the United States in the penal sum of $5,000 or 10 percent of the value of the claimed property, whichever is lower, but not less than $250, with sureties to be approved by such customs officer, conditioned that in case of condemnation of the articles so claimed the obligor shall pay all the costs and expenses of the proceedings to obtain such condemnation, such customs officer shall transmit such claim and bond, with a duplicate list and description of the articles seized, to the United States attorney for the district in which seizure was made, who shall proceed to a condemnation of the merchandise or other property in the manner prescribed by law.

§ 1609. Seizure; summary forfeiture and sale

(a) In general. If no such claim is filed or bond given within the twenty days hereinbefore specified, the appropriate customs officer shall declare the vessel, vehicle, aircraft, merchandise, or baggage forfeited, and shall sell the same at public auction in the same manner as merchandise abandoned to the United States is sold or otherwise dispose of the same according to law, and shall deposit the proceeds of sale, after deducting the expenses described in section 613 [19 USCS § 1613], into the Customs Forfeiture Fund.

(b) Effect. A declaration of forfeiture under this section shall have the same force and effect as a final decree and order of forfeiture in a judicial forfeiture proceeding in a district court of the United States. Title shall be deemed to vest in the United States free and clear of any liens or encumbrances (except for first preferred ship mortgages pursuant to subsection O of section 30 of the Ship Mortgage Act, 1920 (46 U.S.C. App. 961) or any corresponding revision, consolidation, and enactment of such subsection in title 46, United States code) from the date of the act for which the forfeiture was incurred. Officials of the various States, insular possessions, territories, and commonwealths of the United States shall, upon application of the appropriate customs officer accompanied by a certified copy of the declaration of

FIGURE 5-1 *(Continued)*

Citations for Statutes

Subsection (b)(4) of the federal forfeiture statute may be cited as follows:

21 U.S.C. § 881(b)(4) (1988) (abbreviation for volume 21 of United States Code, subsection (b)(4) of section 881; 1988 is the date of the latest version of the Code containing the statute)

Legislative history

Explanation of legislative history

Prior wording of statute

TARIFF ACT OF 1930 **19 USCS § 1609**

forfeiture, remove any recorded liens or encumbrances which apply to such property and issue or reissue the necessary certificates of title, registration certificates, or similar documents to the United States or to any transferee of the United States.

(June 17, 1930, ch 497, Title IV, Part V, § 609, 46 Stat. 755; June 25, 1938, ch 679 § 28(b), 52 Stat. 1089; June 2, 1970, P. L. 91-271, Title III, § 301(b), 84 Stat. 287; Oct. 12, 1984, P. L. 98-473, Title II, ch III, Part D, §§ 313, 321, 98 Stat. 2054, 2056; Oct. 30, 1984, P. L. 98-573, Title II, Subtitle A, § 213(a)(6), 98 Stat. 2985; Nov. 18, 1988, P. L. 100-690, Title VII, Subtitle K, § 7367(b), 102 Stat. 4479.)

HISTORY; ANCILLARY LAWS AND DIRECTIVES

Explanatory notes:

Provisions similar to those of this section were contained in Act Sept. 21, 1922, ch 356, Title IV, § 609, 42 Stat. 985. That section was superseded by § 609 of the Tariff Act of 1930, comprising this section, and was repealed by § 651(a)(1) of the 1930 Act.

Provisions for sale of the property by the collector if no claim should be filed or bond given were contained in R.S. § 3077, which was repealed by Act Sept. 21, 1922, ch 356, Title IV, § 642, 42 Stat. 989.

For full classification of the above Acts, consult USCS Tables volumes.

Effective date of section:

Act June 17, 1930, ch 497, Title IV, § 653, 46 Stat. 763, which appears as 19 USCS § 1653, provides that this section shall take effect on the day following the date of its enactment on June 17, 1930.

Amendments:

1938. Act June 25, 1938 (effective on the 30th day following enactment on 6/25/38, as provided by § 37 of such Act, which appears as 19 USCS § 1401 note), inserted "or otherwise dispose of the same according to law."

1970. Act June 2, 1970, substituted "appropriate customs officer" for "collector".

1984. Act Oct. 12, 1984 purported to insert "aircraft," following "vehicle", but such amendment could not be executed because the word "vehicle" only appears in the section followed by a comma, and substituted "after deducting expenses enumerated in section 613 of this Act into the Customs Forfeiture Fund" for "after deducting the actual expenses of seizure, publication, and sale in the Treasury of the United States."

Act. Oct. 30, 1984 (effective 10/15/84, as provided by § 214(e) of such Act, which appears as 19 USCS § 1304 note) designated the existing provisions as subsec. (a) and, in subsec. (a) as so designated, inserted "aircraft," following "vehicle," and inserted "(except as provided in subsection (b) of this section)"; and added subsec. (b).

1988. Act Nov. 18, 1988 substituted this section for one which read:

"(a) If no such claim is filed or bond given within the twenty days herein before specified, the appropriate customs officer shall declare the vessel, vehicle, aircraft, merchandise, or baggage forfeited, and shall sell the same at public auction in the same manner as merchandise abandoned to the United States is sold, or otherwise

FIGURE 5-1 *(Continued)*

A citation to the United States Code is preferred because the United States Code is the official code. Many law libraries do not have the United States Code, though, so you may use the following citations to either United States Code Service or United States Code Annotated:

19 USCS § 1609 CUSTOMS DUTIES

dispose of the same according to law and (except as provided in subsection (b) of this section) shall deposit the proceeds of sale, after deducting expenses enumerated in section 613 of this Act into the Customs Forfeiture Fund.

"(b) During the period beginning on the date of the enactment of this subsection and ending on September 30, 1987, the appropriate customs officer shall deposit the proceeds of sale (after deducting such expenses) in the Customs Forfeiture Fund".

Other provisions:

Application of amendment made by Act June 2, 1970. Act June 2, 1970, P. L. 91-271, Title II, § 203, 84 Stat. 283, which appears as 19 USCS § 1500 note, provided that the amendment made to this section by such Act is effective with respect to articles entered, or withdrawn from warehouse for consumption, on or after Oct. 1, 1970, and such other articles entered or withdrawn from warehouse for consumption prior to such date, the appraisement of which has not become final before Oct. 1, 1970, and for which an appeal for reappraisement has not been timely filed with the Bureau of Customs before Oct. 1, 1970, or with respect to which a protest has not been disallowed in whole or in part before Oct. 1, 1970.

CODE OF FEDERAL REGULATIONS

Recordkeeping, inspection, search, and seizure, 19 CFR Part 162.

Reference to administrative regulations

CROSS REFERENCES

Destruction of forfeited vessels, 19 USCS § 1705.
This section is referred to in 19 USCS § 1600.

RESEARCH GUIDE

Federal Procedure L. Ed:
5A Fed Proc L Ed, Bonds, Civil Fines, and Forfeitures § 10:125.
12 Fed Proc L Ed, Evidence § 33:11.
14 Fed Proc L Ed, Foreign Trade and Commerce § 37:113.
18A Fed Proc L Ed, Immigration, Naturalization, and Nationality § 45:1568.

Am Jur:
3A Am Jur 2d, Aliens and Citizens § 1940.
21A Am Jur 2d, Customs Duties and Import Regulations § 131.

References to legal encyclopedias

INTERPRETIVE NOTES AND DECISIONS

Table of contents of case summaries

1. Generally
2. Filing of claim and bond
3. Summary sale
4. Remedies of claimant, generally
5. —Right to bid at sale

1. Generally

Forfeiture statute takes effect immediately upon commission of illegal act; at that moment right to property vests in United States, and when forfeiture is sought, condemnation, when obtained, relates back to that time and avoids all intermediate sales and alienations, even as to purchasers in good faith. Simons v United States (1976, CA9 Ariz) 541 F2d 1351.

Customs authorities may adopt seizure of automobile made by state police and turned over to federal prohibition department and forfeit vehicle under 19 USCS §§ 1607–1609. Re Commercial Inv. Trust Corp. (1927, DC NY) 31 F2d 494.

Delay of government in enforcing forfeiture of

FIGURE 5-1 *(Continued)*

21 U.S.C.S. § 881(b)(4) (Law. Coop. 1984 & Supp. 1993).

(United States Code Service is published by Lawyers Cooperative Publishing Company; part of the cited statute is in the 1984 hardbound volume and part is in the 1993 pocket part)

TARIFF ACT OF 1930 **19 USCS § 1610**

vessel seized for violation of customs laws did not work abandonment of claim for forfeiture; and intervention of government in ineffective attachment suit against vessel which had been seized by customs officers conferred jurisdiction on court to dispose of case according to law. The Whippoorwill (1931, DC Md) 52 F2d 985.

2. Filing of claim and bond

Owner of automobile that is seized for transporting contraband in violation of 21 USCS § 881 must file claim to property and post penal bond of $250 within 20 days after government has posted notice of intention to forfeit, otherwise, there is summary forfeiture of vehicle to government; but this does not transform forfeiture proceedings into criminal actions requiring establishment beyond reasonable doubt that crime was committed. Bramble v Richardson (1974, CA10 Colo) 498 F2d, 968, cert den (1974) 419 US 1069, 42 L Ed 2d 665, 95 S Ct 656.

Seized property owner's late filing, prior to execution of process, of unverified claim with Drug Enforcement Administration rather than in district court does not fulfill claim requirements so as to convert administrative summary forfeiture proceeding to judicial forfeiture proceeding. United States v United States Currency in Amount of $2,857.00 (1985, CA7 Ind) 754 F2d 208.

In proceeding under 19 USCS § 1609, no action on part of United States Attorney is necessary, and it is immaterial whether or not criminal prosecution is instituted; but owner may file claim and cost bond under 19 USCS § 1608 and thus bring matter before court. Re C.I.T. Corp. (1928, DC NY) 28 F2d 50.

3. Summary sale

Sale of automobile under 19 USCS § 1609 is sale under judicial decree of condemnation. Re Commercial Inv. Trust Corp. (1927, DC NY) 31 F2d 494.

Sale of seized property in accordance with 19 USCS §§ 1606–1609 is in legal effect and operation equivalent to sale under judicial decree of condemnation. McGuire v Winslow (1886, CC NY) 26 F 304; The Motor Boat No. L-7869 (1927, CA3 NJ) 21 F2d 594.

Smuggled goods seized may be sold by collector of customs although protected by patents. 21 Op Atty Gen No. 72.

4. Remedies of claimant, generally

Claimant of seized automobile must pursue available remedies given by 19 USCS § 1609 and cannot sue government in court of claims for unpaid balance due him. Hord v United States (1929) 67 Ct Cl 582.

5. —Right to bid at sale

There being no effort on part of owner of property sold for customs duties to defraud government of its duties, and no conspiracy entered into for that purpose, there is no law denying owner right to bid in property at sale. Ney v Ladd (1902, Tex Civ App) 68 SW 1014.

§ 1610. Seizure; summary forfeiture and sale

Procedure for property not listed in § 1610

If any vessel, vehicle, aircraft, merchandise, or baggage is not subject to section 607 [19 USCS § 1607], the appropriate customs officer shall transmit a report of the case, with the names of available witnesses, to the United States attorney for the district in which the seizure was made for the institution of the proper proceedings for the condemnation of such property. (June 17, 1930, ch 497, Title IV, Part V, § 610, 46 Stat. 755; Sept. 1, 1954, ch 1213, Title V, § 506, 68 Stat. 1141; June 2, 1970, P. L. 91–271, Title III, § 301(ee), 84 Stat. 291; Oct. 3, 1978, P. L. 95–410, Title I, § 111(b), 92 Stat. 898; Oct. 12, 1984, P. L. 98–473, Title II, §314, 98 Stat. 2054; Oct. 30, 1984, P. L. 98-573, Title II, Subtitle A, § 213(a)(7)(B), 98 Stat. 2985; Nov. 18, 1988, P. L. 100–690, title VII, Subtitle K, § 7367(c)(3), 102 Stat. 4480.)

HISTORY; ANCILLARY LAWS AND DIRECTIVES

Explanatory notes:

Provisions similar to those of this section were contained in Act Sept. 21, 1922, ch 356, Title IV, § 610, 42 Stat. 985. That section was superseded by § 610 of the Tariff Act of 1930, comprising this section, and was repealed by § 651(a)(1) of the 1930 Act. For full classification of the above Acts, consult USCS Tables volumes.

FIGURE 5-1 *(Continued)*

21 U.S.C.A. § 881(b)(4) (West 1981 & Supp. 1993)	(United States Code Annotated is published by West Publishing Company; part of the cited statute is in the 1981 hardbound volume and part is in the 1993 pocket part)

TARIFF ACT OF 1930 **19 USCS § 1615**

1615. Burden of proof in forfeiture proceedings

In all suits or actions (other than those arising under section 592 of this Act [19 USCS § 1592] brought for the forfeiture of any vessel, vehicle, aircraft, merchandise, or baggage seized under the provisions of any law relating to the collection of duties on imports or tonnage, where the property is claimed by any person, the burden of proof shall lie upon such claimant; and in all suits or actions brought for the recovery of the value of any vessel, vehicle, aircraft, merchandise, or baggage, because of violation of any such law, the burden of proof shall be upon the defendant: Provided, That probable cause shall be first shown for the institution of such suit or action, to be judged of by the court, subject to the following rules of proof:

(1) The testimony or deposition of the officer of the customs who has boarded or required to come to a stop or seized a vessel, vehicle, or aircraft, or has arrested a person, shall be prima facie evidence of the place where the act in question occurred.

(2) Marks, labels, brands, or stamps, indicative of foreign origin, upon or accompanying merchandise [merchandise] or containers of merchandise, shall be prima facie evidence of the foreign origin of such merchandise.

(3) The fact that a vessel of any description is found, or discovered to have been, in the vicinity of any hovering vessel and under any circumstances indicating contact or communication therewith, whether by proceeding to or from such vessel, or by coming to in the vicinity of such vessel, or by delivering to or receiving from such vessel any merchandise, person, or communication, or by any other means effecting contact or communication therewith, shall be prima facie evidence that the vessel in question has visited such hovering vessel.

Burden of proof on claimant

Government must show probable cause first

FIGURE 5-1 *(Continued)*

If you are referring to a portion of the statute rather than to the entire statute, pinpoint the portion by subsection. If you do give the subsection in your citation, be sure the subsection is designated just as it is in the statute, including whether letters are lower or upper case, whether numbers are arabic or roman, and whether numbers and letters are enclosed in parentheses or not. For example, the preceding citation refers to sub-subsection (4) of subsection (b) of section 881 of title 21 of the United States Code.

The parentheses at the end of the citation contain an abbreviation of the commercial publisher's name and the location of the statute. In the two preceding citations, "Law. Co-op" is an abbreviation for "Lawyers Cooperative Publishing" and "West" is an abbreviation for "West Publishing Company." At the time this chapter was written, the hardbound volume of United States Code Service containing the statutes was copyrighted 1984 and the pocket part supplement was dated 1993. Similarly, the hardbound volume of United States Code Annotated was copyrighted 1981 and the pocket part supplement was dated 1993. Include as much parenthetical information as needed to locate the statutory language. In the preceding citations, information was given for the hardbound volume and the pocket part supplement. If the statutory language is found entirely in the hardbound volume, you need only include information on the hardbound volume in the parentheses. Conversely, if the statutory language is found entirely in the pocket part supplement, you need only include information on the pocket part supplement in the parentheses.

COURT RULES

Court rules govern litigation procedure. The rules cover such mundane matters as the size of paper on which documents are to be submitted to the courts and the format for appellate briefs. They also set forth important time limitations, such as the time period within which the defendant must answer a complaint and the time period within which a party may appeal a decision. Depending on the jurisdiction, court rules may be created by the legislature, or by the judicial branch, or by the legislative and judicial branches together. In many jurisdictions, the judicial branch promulgates court rules under the statutory authority given to it by the legislative branch.

There is a separate sets of rules for each different court, with the trial-level court rules being separated into one set of court rules for civil cases and one set of rules for criminal cases. A special set of rules determines what material may be admitted into evidence at trial. For federal courts, the basic court rules used at the trial level are the Federal Rules of Civil Procedure, the Federal Rules of Criminal Procedure, and the Federal Rules of Evidence. At the appellate level, the Federal Rules of Appellate Procedure are used in the United States Circuit Courts, and the Revised Rules of the Supreme Court of the United States are used in the United States Supreme Court. In addition, each of the United States District Courts has its own set of local rules, as do each of the United States Circuit Courts.

Your state probably has similar sets of rules and may have sets of rules for **courts of limited jurisdiction** such as traffic court and small claims court. You will become familiar with some of your state's court rules by completing the legal research assignment on court rules.

Sample Pages of Court Rules

Figure 5-2 contains Rule 23 of the Federal Rules of Civil Procedure. This rule contains the basic requirements for maintaining a lawsuit as a class action in a federal district court. In addition to complying with Rule 23, you would also have to comply with any requirements of the local rules of the district court in which the lawsuit was filed.

FEDERAL RULES OF CIVIL PROCEDURE

FOR THE

UNITED STATES DISTRICT COURTS

Rule 23. Class Actions

(a) Prerequisites to a Class Action. One or more members of a class may sue or be sued as representative parties on behalf of all only if (1) the class is so numerous that joinder of all members is impracticable, (2) there are questions of law or fact common to the class, (3) the claims or defenses of the representative parties are typical of the claims or defenses of the class, and (4) the representative parties will fairly and adequately protect the interests of the class.

(b) Class Actions Maintainable. An action may be maintained as a class action if the prerequisites of subdivision (a) are satisfied, and in addition:

(1) the prosecution of separate actions by or against individual members of the class would create a risk of

(A) inconsistent or varying adjudications with respect to individual members of the class which would establish incompatible standards of conduct for the party opposing the class, or

(B) adjudications with respect to individual members of the class which would as a practical matter be dispositive of the interests of the other members not parties to the adjudications or substantially impair or impede their ability to protect their interests; or

(2) the party opposing the class has acted or refused to act on grounds generally applicable to the class, thereby making appropriate final injunctive relief or corresponding declaratory relief with respect to the class as a whole; or

(3) the court finds that the questions of law or fact common to the members of the class predominate over any questions affecting only individual members, and that a class action is superior to other available methods for the fair and efficient adjudication of the controversy. The matters pertinent to the findings include: (A) the interest of members of the class in individually controlling the prosecution or defense of separate actions; (B) the extent and nature of any litigation concerning the controversy already commenced by or against members of the class; (C) the desirability or undesirability of concentrating the litigation of the claims in the particular forum; (D) the difficulties likely to be encountered in the management of a class action.

(c) Determination by Order Whether Class Actions to be Maintained; Notice; Judgement; Actions Conducted Partially as Class Actions. (1) As soon as practicable after the commencement of an action brought as a class action, the court shall determine by order whether it is to be so maintained. An order under this subdivision may be conditional, and may be altered or amended before the decision on the merits.

FIGURE 5-2 Federal rule of civil procedure governing class actions. (Courtesy of Lawyers Cooperative Publishing. Reprinted by permission.)

Locating Court Rules

All the federal rules identified earlier, except for the local rules of the United States District Courts, may be found in United States Code

LEGAL TERMS

court of limited jurisdiction
A court whose jurisdiction is limited to civil cases of a certain type or which involve a limited amount of money, or whose jurisdiction in criminal cases is confined to petty offenses and preliminary hearings. A court of limited jurisdiction is sometimes called a *court of special jurisdiction*.

(2) In any class action maintained under subdivision (b)(3), the court shall direct to the members of the class the best notice practicable under the circumstances, including individual notice to all members who can be identified through reasonable effort. The notice shall advise each member that (A) the court will exclude the member from the class if the member so requests by a specified date; (B) the judgment, whether favorable or not, will include all members who do not request exclusion, and (C) any member who does not request exclusion may, if the member desires, enter an appearance through counsel.

(3) The judgment in an action maintained as a class action under subdivision (b)(1) or (b)(2), whether or not favorable to the class, shall include and describe those whom the court finds to be members of the class. The judgment in an action maintained as a class action under subdivision (b)(3), whether or not favorable to the class, shall include and specify or describe those to whom the notice provided in subdivision (c)(2) was directed, and who have not requested exclusion, and whom the court finds to be members of the class.

(4)When appropriate (A) an action may be brought or maintained as a class action with respect to particular issues, or (B) a class may be divided into subclasses and each subclass treated as a class, and the provisions of this rule shall then be construed and applied accordingly.

(d) Orders in Conduct of Actions. In the conduct of actions to which this rule applies, the court may make appropriate orders: (1) determining the course of proceedings or prescribing measures to prevent undue repetition or complication in the presentation of evidence or argument; (2) requiring, for the protection of the members of the class or otherwise for the fair conduct of the action, that notice be given in such manner as the court may direct to some or all of the members of any step in the action or of the proposed extent of the judgment, or of the opportunity of members to signify whether they consider the representation fair and adequate, to intervene and present claims or defenses, or otherwise to come into the action; (3) imposing conditions on the representative parties or on intervenors; (4) requiring that the pleadings be amended to eliminate therefrom allegations as to representation of absent persons, and that the action proceed accordingly; (5) dealing with similar procedural matters. The orders may be combined with an order under Rule 16, and may be altered or amended as may be desirable from time to time.

(e) Dismissal or Compromise. A class action shall not be dismissed or compromised without the approval of the court, and notice of the proposed dismissal or compromise shall be given to all members of the class in such manner as the court directs.

FIGURE 5-2 *(Continued)*

Service or in United States Code Annotated. West Publishing Company publishes paperbound volumes of certain of the federal court rules, including certain of the United States District Court local rules, and the court rules for certain states. The paperbound volumes, which are printed annually, have the virtue of being fairly inexpensive and easily transportable, and contain an index following each set of rules. The paperbound volumes are not annotated, however. Be sure you are researching in the most current version available.

Besides being printed in a publication containing just court rules, you may find your state's court rules in volumes of the publication containing your state's annotated code. Court rules may be in separate volumes, or, if enacted by the legislature, may be part of the statutory code. For example, the Florida Rules of Evidence are chapter 90 of the Florida Statutes, whereas the rest of the state's court rules are printed in volumes at the end of Florida Statutes Annotated.

Citations for Court Rules

The following are sample citations to the most important types of court rules:

Fed. R. Civ. P. 23.	(Rule 23 of the Federal Rules of Civil Procedure)
Fed. R. Crim. P. 1.	(Rule 1 of the Federal Rules of Criminal Procedure)
Fed. R. App. P. 5.	(Rule 5 of the Federal Rules of Appellate Procedure)
Fed. R. Evid. 610.	(Rule 610 of the Federal Rules of Evidence)
Sup. Ct. R. 1.	(Rule 1 of the Rules of the United States Supreme Court)

ADMINISTRATIVE LAW

As explained in Chapter 1, administrative agencies promulgate administrative regulations pursuant to a legislative grant of authority. Administrative regulations usually go through a notice and hearing procedure before being adopted. After they are adopted, administrative regulations have the force of law.

Administrative regulations are published chronologically as they are adopted, and they are later codified. Federal administrative regulations are published chronologically in the *Federal Register* and are codified in the Code of Federal Regulations. The *Federal Register* is published each business day. The Code of Federal Regulations is divided into 50 titles, with the regulations contained within most of the titles roughly related to the same subject matter as contained in the same number title within the United States Code. For example, title 26 of both the United States Code and the Code of Federal Regulations concerns the Internal Revenue Service. The regulations within a particular title are arranged by the agencies responsible for them, rather than by subject matter. Regulations governing a particular topic are grouped in the same *part,* with the parts divided into sections. As in the United States Code, in which each section is considered a separate statute, one section of the Code of Federal Regulations contains one administrative regulation.

The Code of Federal Regulations is printed in hundreds of colorful paperbound volumes, with one-fourth of the Code titles reissued quarterly and each year's reissue bound in a different color from that of the preceding year. The spine of each volume gives you the year of publication. Look at the front cover of the volume to determine the effective date within the year.

If you are looking for a regulation covering a particular subject matter, look in the index to the Code. Once you have located the regulation in the Code, note the effective date of the volume containing the regulation. The regulation must be updated with any amendments to the regulation contained in the *Federal Register.* The first step in updating is to check "LSA: List of CFR Section Affected," published monthly. Because the LSA is cumulative, you need only check the latest LSA. When you check the LSA, note the end of the period covered by the LSA. For the period between the latest date covered by the LSA and the latest *Federal Register,* check the last issue of the *Federal Register* for each month since the LSA. Each issue of the *Federal Register* contains a "List of CFR Parts Affected in [the name of the month of the particular Federal Register]." To find case law interpretations of administrative regulations, check *Shepard's Code of Federal Regulations Citations.*

Sample Pages of Administrative Law

Figure 5-3 contains a portion of the table of contents for 21 C.F.R. part 1316 (1992) and the text of 21 C.F.R. §§ 1316.71–1316.81 (1992). These regulations cover the same subject matter as 19 U.S.C.S. §§ 1607–1610, 1615 (1993) but in more detail and in a little more readable form. Read through the following regulations and compare them with the statutes on forfeiture procedure.

Sample Pages of LSA and Federal Register

Figure 5-4 shows how you would update 21 C.F.R. §§ 1316.71–1316.81 (1992). You would first look at the latest LSA. The latest LSA available when this book was being written was January 1994. The January 1994 issue of the LSA shows that there have been no changes to 21 C.F.R. §§ 1316.71–1316.81 (1992). The latest *Federal Register* available was April 22, 1994. Because the tables in the back of the *Federal Register* are cumulative for the month, you would only need to check the table in the March 31, 1994 and the April 22, 1994 issues of the *Federal Register.* The tables from those two issues show that there has been no change in 21 C.F.R. §§ 1316.71–1316.81 (1992).

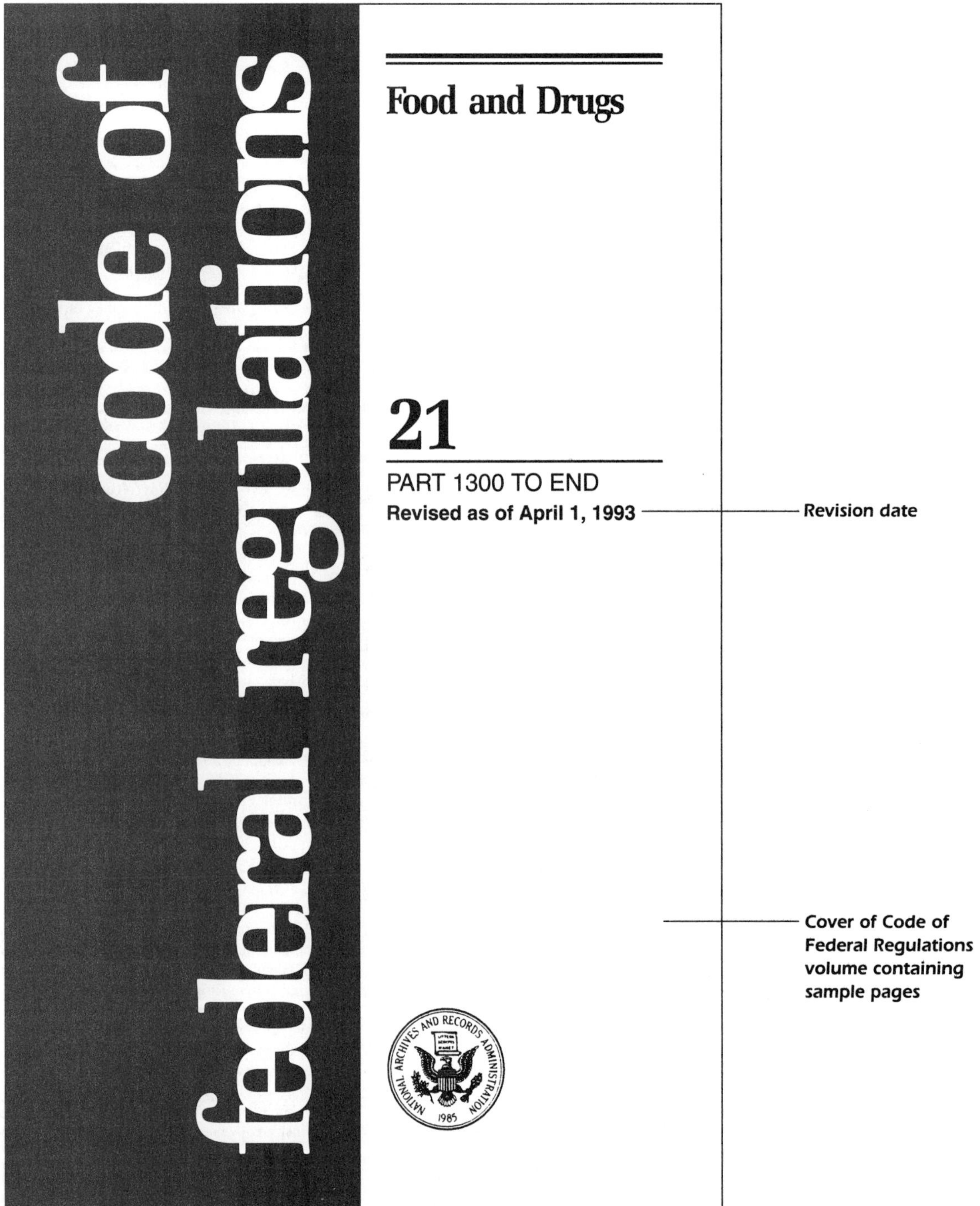

code of federal regulations
Food and Drugs
21
PART 1300 TO END
Revised as of April 1, 1993
Revision date
Cover of Code of Federal Regulations volume containing sample pages
NATIONAL ARCHIVES AND RECORDS ADMINISTRATION
1985

FIGURE 5-3 Administrative regulations governing forfeiture procedure as published in C.F.R.

Table of contents for part 1316

Relevant administrative regulations

21 CFR Ch. II (4-1-92 Edition) | Drug Enforcement Administration, Justice

PARTS 1314–1315—[RESERVED]

PART 1316—ADMINISTRATIVE FUNCTIONS, PRACTICES, AND PROCEDURES

Subpart A—Administrative Inspections

Subpart B—Protection of Researchers and Research Subjects

Subpart C—Enforcement Proceedings

Subpart D—Administrative Hearings

Subpart E—Seizure, Forfeiture, and Disposition of Property

Subpart F—Expedited Forfeiture Proceedings for Certain Property

FIGURE 5-3 *(Continued)*

§ 1316.71 21 CFR Ch. II (4-1-92 Edition)

§ 1316.71 Definitions.

As used in this subpart, the following terms shall have the meanings specified:

(a) The term *Act* means the Controlled Substances Act (84 Stat. 1242; 21 U.S.C. 801) and/or the Controlled Substances Import and Export Act (84 Stat. 1285; 21 U.S.C. 951).

(b) The term *custodian* means the officer required under § 1316.72 to take custody of particular property which has been seized pursuant to the Act.

(c) The term *property* means a controlled substance, raw material, product, container, equipment, money or other asset, vessel, vehicle, or aircraft within the scope of the Act.

(d) The terms *seizing officer, officer seizing,* etc. means any officer, authorized and designated by § 1316.72 to carry out the provisions of the Act, who initially seizes property or adopts a seizure initially made by any other officer or by a private person.

(e) The term *Special Agents-in-Charge* means Drug Enforcement Administration Special Agents-in-Charge or Resident Agents in Charge and Federal Bureau of Investigation Special Agents-in-Charge.

(f) Any term not defined in this section shall have the definition set forth in sections 102 and 1001 of the Act (21 U.S.C. 802 and 951) and in § 1301.02 of this chapter.

[36 FR 7820, Apr. 24, 1971. Redesignated at 38 FR 26609, Sept. 24, 1973, and amended at 45 FR 20096, Mar. 27, 1980; 47 FR 43370, Oct. 1, 1982; 49 FR 28701, July 16, 1984]

1316.72 Officers who will make seizures.

For the purpose of carrying out the provisions of the Act, all special agents of the Drug Enforcement Administration and the Federal Bureau of Investigation are authorized and designated to seize such property as may be subject to seizure.

[47 FR 43370, Oct. 1, 1982]

1316.73 Custody and other duties.

An officer seizing property under the Act shall store the property in a location designated by the custodian, generally in the judicial district of seizure. The Special Agents-in-Charge are designated as custodians to receive and maintain in storage all property seized pursuant to the Act, are authorized to dispose of any property pursuant to the Act and any other applicable statutes or regulations relative to disposal, and to perform such other duties regarding such seized property as are appropriate, including the impound release of property pursuant to 38 CFR 0.101(c).

[47 FR 43370, Oct. 1, 1982]

§ 1316.74 Appraisement.

The custodian shall appraise the property to determine the domestic value at the time and place of seizure. The domestic value shall be considered the price at which such or similar property is freely offered for sale. If there is no market for the property at the place of seizure, the domestic value shall be considered the value in the principal market nearest the place of seizure.

(Sec 606, 46 Stat. 754 (19 U.S.C. 1606))

[36 FR 7820, Apr. 24, 1971. Redesignated at 38 FR 26609, Sep. 24, 1973, and amended at 52 FR 41418, Oct. 28, 1987]

§ 1316.75 Advertisement.

(a) If the appraised value does not exceed the monetary amount set forth in title 19, United States Code, Section 1607; the seized merchandise is any monetary instrument within the meaning of section 5312(a)(3) of title 31 of the United States Code; or if a conveyance used to import, export or otherwise transport or store any controlled substance is involved, the custodian or DEA Asset Forfeiture Section shall cause a notice of the seizure and of the intention to forfeit and sell or otherwise dispose of the property to be published once a week for at least 3 successive weeks in a newspaper of general circulation in the judicial district in which the processing for forfeiture is brought.

(b) The notice shall; (1) Describe the property seized and show the motor and serial numbers, if any; (2) state the time, cause, and place of seizure; and (3) state that any person desiring to claim the property may, within 20 days from the date of first publication of the notice, file with the custodian or DEA Asset Forfeiture Section a claim to the property and a bond

"Property" includes cash

History of regulation

Notice and required publication

Contents of notice

FIGURE 5-3 *(Continued)*

with satisfactory sureties in the sum of $5,000 or ten percent of the value of the claimed property whichever is lower, but not less than $250.

(Sec. 607, 46 Stat. 754, as amended (19 U.S.C. 1607); Pub. L. 98–473, Pub. L. 98–573) [36 FR 7820, Apr. 24, 1971. Redesignated at 38 FR 26609, Sept. 24, 1973 and amended at 44 FR 56324, Oct. 1, 1979; 49 FR 1178, Jan. 10, 1984; 49 FR 50643, Dec. 31, 1984; 52 FR 24446, July 1, 1987; 56 FR 8686, Mar. 1, 1991]

§ 1316.76 Requirements as to claim and bond.

Explanation of bond requirement

(a) The bond shall be rendered to the United States, with sureties to be approved by the custodian or DEA Asset Forfeiture Section, conditioned that in the case of condemnation of the property the obligor shall pay all costs and expenses of the proceedings to obtain such condemnation. When the claim and bond are received by the custodian or DEA Asset Forfeiture Section, he shall, after finding the documents in proper form and the sureties satisfactory, transmit the documents, together with a description of the property and a complete statement of the facts and circumstances surrounding the seizure, to the United States Attorney for the judicial district in which the proceeding for forfeiture is brought. If the documents are not in satisfactory condition when first received, a reasonable time for correction may be allowed. If correction is not made within a reasonable time the documents may be treated as nugatory, and the case shall proceed as though they had not been tendered.

If claim filed and bond posted, proceeding turned over to a court; claimant does not get money back at this point

(b)The filing of the claim and the posting of the bond does not entitle the claimant to possession of the property, however, it does stop the administrative forfeiture proceedings. The bond posted to cover costs may be in cash, certified check, or satisfactory sureties. The costs and expenses secured by the bond are such as are incurred after the filing of the bond including storage cost, safeguarding, court fees, marshal's costs, etc.

(Sec. 608, 46 Stat. 755 (19 U.S.C. 1608); Pub. L.98–473, Pub. L. 98–573)

[36 FR 7820, Apr. 24, 1971. Redesignated at 38 FR 26609, Sept. 24, 1973 and amended at 49 FR 1178, Jan. 10, 1984; 49 FR 50643. Dec. 31, 1984; 56 FR 8686, Mar. 1, 1991]

§ 1316.77 Administrative forfeiture.

(a) For property seized by officers of the Drug Enforcement Administration, if the appraised value does not exceed the jurisdictional limits in § 1316.75(a), and a claim and bond are not filed within the 20 days hereinbefore mentioned, the DEA Special Agent-in-Charge or DEA Asset Forfeiture Section shall declare the property forfeited. The DEA Special Agent-in-Charge or DEA Asset Forfeiture Section shall prepare the Declaration of Forfeiture and forward it to the Administrator of the Administration as notification of the action he has taken. Thereafter, the property shall be retained in the district of the DEA Special Agent-in-Charge or DEA Asset Forfeiture Section or delivered elsewhere for official use, or otherwise disposed of, in accordance with official instructions received by the DEA Special Agent-in-Charge or DEA Asset Forfeiture Section.

(b)For property seized by officers of the Federal Bureau of Investigation, if the appraised value does not exceed the jurisdictional limits in § 1316.75(a), and a claim and bond are not filed within the 20 days hereinbefore mentioned, the FBI Property Management Officer shall declare the property forfeited. The FBI Property Management Officer shall prepare the Declaration of Forfeiture. Thereafter, the property shall be retained in the field office or delivered elsewhere for official use, or otherwise disposed of, in accordance with the official instructions of the FBI Property Management Officer.

(28 U.S.C. 509 and 510; 21 U.S.C. 871 and 881(d); Pub. L. 98–473, Pub. L. 98–573)

[48 FR 35087, Aug. 3, 1983, as amended at 49 FR 1178, Jan. 10, 1984; 49 FR 50643, Dec. 31, 1984; 56 FR 8686, Mar. 1, 1991]

1316.78 Judicial forfeiture.

Proceeding is handled by court

If the appraised value is greater than the jurisdictional limits in § 1316.75(a) or a claim and satisfactory bond have been received for property the jurisdictional limits in § 1316.76,

FIGURE 5-3 *(Continued)*

§ 1316.79 **21 CFR Ch. II (4-1-92 Edition)**

the custodian or DEA Asset Forfeiture Section shall transmit a description of the property and a complete statement of the facts and circumstances surrounding the seizure to the U.S. Attorney for the judicial district in which the proceeding for forfeiture is sought for the purpose of instituting condemnation proceedings. The U.S. Attorney shall also be furnished the newspaper advertisements required by § 1316.75. The Forfeiture Counsel of DEA shall make applications to the U.S. District Courts to place property in official DEA use.

(Sec. 610, 46 Stat. 755 (19 U.S.C. 1610); Pub. L. 98–473, Pub. L. 98–573)

[36 FR 7820, Apr. 24, 1971. Redesignated at 38 FR 26609, Sept. 24, 1973 and amended at 44 FR 56324, Oct. 1, 1979; 49 FR 1178, Jan. 10, 1984; 49 FR 32174, Aug. 13, 1984; 49 FR 50643, Dec 31, 1984; 56 FR 8686, Mar. 1, 1991]

1316.79 Petitions for remission or mitigation of forfeiture.

(a) Any person interested in any property which has been seized, or forfeited either administratively or by court proceedings, may file a petition for remission or mitigation of the forfeiture. Such petition shall be filed in triplicate with the DEA Asset Forfeiture Section or Special Agent-in-Charge of the DEA or FBI, depending upon which agency seized the property, for the judicial district in which the proceeding for forfeiture is brought. It shall be addressed to the Director of the FBI or the Administrator of the DEA, depending upon which agency seized the property, if the property is subject to administrative forfeiture pursuant to § 1316.77, and addressed to the Attorney General if the property is subject to judicial forfeiture pursuant to § 1316.78. The petition must be executed and sworn to be the person alleging interest in the property.

(b) The petition shall include the following: (1) A complete description of the property, including motor and serial numbers, if any, and the date and place of seizure; (2) the petitioner's interest in the property, which shall be supported by bills of sale, contracts, mortgages, or other satisfactory documentary evidence; and, (3) the facts and circumstances, to be established by satisfactory proof, relied upon by the petitioner to justify remission or mitigation.

(c) Where the petition is for restoration of the proceeds of sale, or for value of the property placed in official use, it must be supported by satisfactory proof that the petitioner did not know of the seizure prior to the declaration of condemnation of forfeiture and was in such circumstances as prevented him from knowing of the same.

(Secs. 613, 618, 46 Stat. 758, 757, as amended (19 U.S.C. 1613, 1618; 28 U.S.C. 509 and 510; 21 U.S.C. 871 and 881(d)); Pub. L. 98–473, Pub. L. 98–573)

[36 FR 7820, Apr. 24, 1971. Redesignated at 38 FR 26609, Sept. 24, 1973, and amended at 48 FR 35088, Aug. 3, 1983; 49 FR 1178, Jan. 10, 1984; 49 FR 50643, Dec. 31, 1984; 56 FR 8686, Mar. 1, 1991]

§ 1316.80 Time for filing petitions.

(a) In order to be considered as seasonably filed, a petition for remission or mitigation of forfeiture should be filed within 30 days of the receipt of the notice of seizure. If a petition for remission or mitigation of forfeiture has not been received within 30 days of the notice of seizure, the property will either be placed in official service or sold as soon as it is forfeited. Once property is placed in official use, or is sold, a petition for remission or mitigation of forfeiture can no longer be accepted.

(b) A petition for restoration of proceeds of sale, or for the value of property placed in official use, must be filed within 90 days of the sale of the property, or within 90 days of the date the property is placed in official use.

(Secs. 613, 618, 46 Stat. 756, 757, as amended (19 U.S.C. 1613, 1618); Pub. L. 98–473, Pub. L. 98–573)

[36 FR 7820, Apr. 24, 1971. Redesignated at 38 FR 26609, Sept. 24, 1973, and amended at 49 FR 50643, Dec. 31, 1984]

1316.81 Handling of petitions.

Upon receipt of a petition, the custodian or DEA Asset Forfeiture System shall request an appropriate investigation. The petition and the report of investigation shall be forwarded to the Director of the FBI or to the Administrator of the DEA, depending upon which agency seized the property. If the petition involves a case which has been referred to the U.S. Attorney for the institution of court proceedings, the custodian or DEA Asset Forfeiture System shall tansmit the petition to the U.S. Attorney for the judicial district in which the proceeding for forfeiture is brought. He shall notify the petitioner of this action.

FIGURE 5-3 *(Continued)*

code of federal regulations

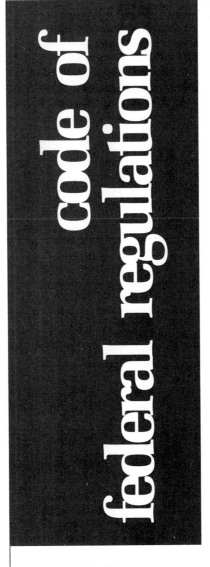

LSA

List of CFR Sections Affected

February 1994

United States
Government
Printing Office
SUPERINTENDENT
OF DOCUMENTS
Washington, DC 20402

OFFICIAL BUSINESS
Penalty for Private Use

SECOND CLASS NEWSPAPER
Postage and Fees Paid
U.S. Government Printing Office
(ISSN 0097–6326)

Cover of latest LSA available to author

FIGURE 5-4 This LSA shows no changes or proposed changes to part 1316 of 21 C.F.R.

code of federal regulations

LSA

List of CFR Sections Affected

February 1994

Title 1–16
Changes January 3, 1994
through February 28, 1994

Title 17–27
Changes April 1, 1993
through February 28, 1994

Title 28–41
Changes July 1, 1993
through February 28, 1994

Title 42–50
Changes February 1, 1993
through February 28, 1994

Covers from effective date of Code of Federal Regulations volume

Inside page of LSA showing time period covered

FIGURE 5-4 *(Continued)*

42 **LSA—LIST OF CFR SECTIONS AFFECTED**

CHANGES APRIL 1, 1993 THROUGH FEBRUARY 28, 1994

TITLE 21 Chapter 1—Con.

Page

821.20 (b)(1) table and (c) table amended **43455**
864.5680 (b) revised; (c) removed **51571**
874.4490 Revised **29534**
878 Authority citation revised **57558**
878.5030 Added **57558**
890.3450 Removed **29535**
900 (Subchapter I) Added; interim **67562**
900.2 (f) corrected 6899
900.10—900.14 (Subpart B) Added; interim **67570**
900.12 (d)(1) corrected 6899
1020 Authority citation revised **26396**
1020.30 Revised; eff. in part 5-3-94 .... **26396**
1020.31 Revised; eff. in part 50-3-94 .... **26401**
(c)(2) corrected **31067**
1020.32 Revised; eff. in part 5-3-94 .... **26404**
1220.40 (a) revised **64137**
1270 Added; interim **65520**

Chapter II—Drug Enforcement Administration, Department of Justice (Parts 1300—1399)

1301 Technical correction **31907**
1301.13 (a) and (b) revised 8859
1301.22 (b)(6) revised **31175**
1301.24 (b) and (c) introductory text revised **31175**
1304 Technical correction **31907**
1304.02 (f) through (i) redesignated as (g) through (j); new (f) added **31175**
1304.03 (e) through (g) redesignated as (f) through (h); new (e) added; new (h) revised **31175**
1308.11 Regulation at 57 FR 18824 eff. date extended to 11-1-93 .... **25934**
(b)(4) revised **43796**
Regulation at 57 FR 43401 eff. date extended to 3-21-94 .... **44611**
(g)(3) removed; (f)(3), (4), (5), (g)(4) and (5) redesignated as (f)(4), (5), (6), (g)(3) and (4); new (f)(3) added **53406**
(g)(5) added 673
1308.12 (c)(11) through (25) redesignated as (c)(12) through (26); new (c) (11) added **43796**
1308.24 (i) table revised **17107**
1308.34 Table ammeded; interim **34708**
Regulation at 58 FR 16772 confirmed **34709**

No listing for part 1316 means that there have been no changes

Page

Regulation at 58 FR 34708 confirmed **49924**

Chapter III—Office of National Drug Control Policy (Parts 1400—1499)

1403 Appendix A corrected **26185**

Title 21—Proposed Rules:

1—1299 (Ch. I) **33690, 34389, 40393, 43579, 45080, 59695, 59697**
.... 3040, 3042, 3043, 6934
1 .... **29716, 67444**
5 .... **52719, 65139**
17 .... **30680, 40103**
20 3944
25 .... **52719, 65139**
73 5363
74 5363
100 .... **17171, 29716, 64208**
101 .... **17171, 18057, 29557, 29716, 33055, 33700, 33715, 33731, 40104 40190, 44091, 53254, 53296, 54539, 68791**
.... 427
102 .... **17171, 29557**
103 .... **34010, 41612, 52042**
104 .... **29716**
109 .... **33871**
123 .... 4142, 7235
129 .... **34010**
135 .... **17172**
136 .... **53305, 65276**
137 .... **53305, 65276**
139 .... **53305, 65276**
161 .... **17171, 29557**
164 5153
165 .... **34010**
166 .... **43580, 50301**
168 5363
170 .... **52719, 65139**
171 .... **52719, 65139**
172 .... **53312**
.... 5363
173 5363
174 .... **52719, 65139**
176 3322
178 3322
179 .... **64526**
182 .... **27959, 59697**
.... 5363
184 .... **27959, 34010, 59697**

Note: Boldface page numbers indicate 1993 changes.

FIGURE 5-4 *(Continued)*

3–31–94
Vol. 59 No. 62

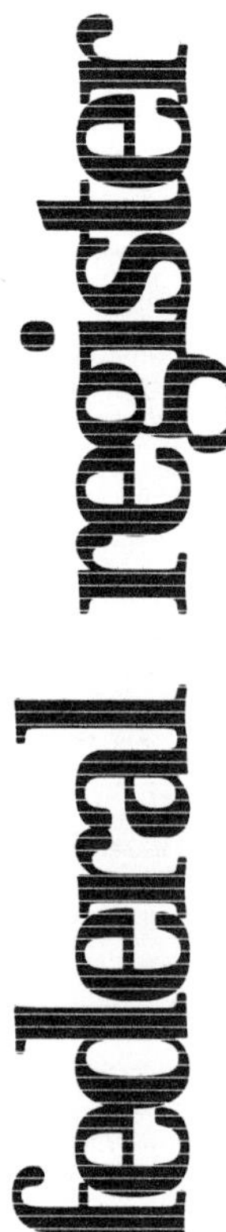

Thursday
March 31, 1994

United States
Government
Printing Office
SUPERINTENDENT
OF DOCUMENTS
Washington, DC 20402

OFFICIAL BUSINESS
Penalty for private use, $300

SECOND CLASS NEWSPAPER
Postage and Fees Paid
U.S. Government Printing Office
(ISSN 0097–6326)

FIGURE 5-4 *(Continued)*

i

Reader Aids

Federal Register
Vol.59, No. 62
Thursday, March 31, 1994 — **Last Federal Register for March**

INFORMATION AND ASSISTANCE

Federal Register

Index, finding aids & general information 202-523-5227
Public inspection desk 523-5215
Corrections to published documents 523-5237
Document drafting information 523-3187
Machine readable documents 523-3447

Code of Federal Regulations

Index, finding aids & general information 523-5227
Printing schedules 523-3419

Laws

Public Laws Update Service (numbers, dates, etc.) 523-6641
Additional information 523-5230

Presidential Documents

Executive orders and proclamations 523-5230
Public Papers of the Presidents 523-5230
Weekly Compilation of Presidential Documents 523-5230

The United States Government Manual

General information 523-5230

Other Services

Data base and machine readable specifications 523-3447
Guide to Record Retention Requirements 523-3187
Legal staff 523-4534
Privacy Act Compilation 523-3187
Public Laws Update Service (PLUS) 523-6641
TDD for the hearing impaired 523-5229

ELECTRONIC BULLETIN BOARD

Free Electronic Bulletin Board service for Public 202-275-1538,
Law numbers, and Federal Register finding aids. .... or 275-0920

FEDERAL REGISTER PAGES AND DATES, MARCH

9613-9916 1
9917-10046 2
10047-10264 3
10265-10568 4
10569-10720 7
10721-10938 8
10939-11174 9
11175-11472 10
11473-11698 11
11699-11896 14
11897-12142 15
12143-12522 16
12523-12794 17
12795-13178 18
13179-13428 21
13429-13638 22
13639-13864 23
13865-14082 24
14083-14356 25
14357-14540 28
14541-14734 29
14735-15032 30
15033-15312 31

CFR PARTS AFFECTED DURING MARCH — **This list is cumulative for March**

At the end of each month, the Office of the Federal Register publishes separately a List of CFR Sections Affected (LSA), which lists parts and sections affected by documents published since the revision date of each title.

3 CFR

Proclamations:
6651 10049
6652 10265
6653 10723
6654 10725
6655 10727
6656 11175
6657 13639
6658 14357
6659 14729
6660 14731

Administrative Orders:
Memorandums:
March 10, 1994 14079
Presidential Determinations:
No. 94—15 of February 18, 1994 10047
No. 94—16 of March 16, 1994 14081
No. 94—17 of March 20, 1994 14735
No. 94—18 of March 22, 1994 14737

Executive Orders:
12759 (Revoked in part by EO 12902) 11463
12840 (Superseded by EO 12903) 11473
12873 (See 12902) 11463
12901 10721
12902 11463
12903 11473
12904 13179
12905 14733

5 CFR

531 11699
532 .... 11699, 11701, 13181, 13641
550 11699
575 11699
582 14541
591 13844
831 12143
838 12143
837 10267
842 12143
890 .... 12143, 12144
1200 14739
1201 14739
2638 12145

Proposed Rules:
1630 14371
1980 ....

7 CFR

2 14083
54 13642
246 11475
248 11508
300 9613
301 .... 11177, 11659, 12795, 13181
319 .... 9917, 13181
321 9917
457 9614
735 15033
800 13865
810 10569
905 .... 10051, 12523
907 10052
908 10052
911 13429
917 10053
927 12524
932 12526
944 .... 11529, 12523
946 15039
955 .... 12527, 13866
959 .... 12149, 13430
979 .... 13430, 15041
980 11529
981 13432
985 12151
989 .... 12153, 12528
993 10228
999 11529
1011 13643
1094 10056
1098 13644
1106 11180
1150 13434
1211 11897
1250 12154
1413 10574
1413 10574
1464 10939
1475 9918
1703 11702
1786 13616
1924 9805
1930 9805
1942 .... 11530, 12155
1944 9805

Proposed Rules:
28 12862
29 14124
52 13252
300 13256
301 12553
318 13256
955 12554
959 11008
1004 10326
1250 13460
1427 9674
1499 12201
1744 10327
1753 10327
1942 12201
1980 .... 12201, 14371, 14769

8 CFR

212 13868

FIGURE 5-4 *(Continued)*

ii **Federal Register** / Vol. 59, No. 62 / Thursday, March 31, 1994 / Reader Aids

Proposed Rules:
103 ... 14779
208 ... 14779
236 ... 14779
242 ... 14779
274a ... 14779

9 CFR
51 ... 12530
78 ... 12530, 14359
91 ... 9616
92 ... 9617, 10729
94 ... 12533, 12535, 13183
145 ... 12795
147 ... 12795
317 ... 12157, 12536, 14528
318 ... 12536
381 ... 12157, 14528
Proposed Rules:
78 ... 9938
92 ... 9679
94 ... 9939, 9941
101 ... 9681
113 ... 9681, 13257, 13896
160 ... 12863
301 ... 10246
317 ... 12462, 12472
318 ... 10246
381 ... 10230, 12462, 12472

10 CFR
20 ... 14085
21 ... 14085
30 ... 14085
35 ... 14085
40 ... 14085
50 ... 10267, 14085, 14087
70 ... 14085
72 ... 14085
73 ... 14085
171 ... 12539
Proposed Rules:
Ch. II ... 9682
50 ... 14373
170 ... 12555
171 ... 12555
Ch. III ... 9682
430 ... 10334, 10464
Ch. X ... 9682
1102 ... 14789

11 CFR
104 ... 10057
Proposed Rules:
8 ... 11211, 14022
102 ... 14794

12 CFR
3 ... 10946
205 ... 10678
264b ... 12805
567 ... 12806
608 ... 13187
614 ... 11898
615 ... 11898, 12811
650 ... 9622
707 ... 13435
Proposed Rules:
205 ... 10684, 10698
225 ... 12202
327 ... 9687
550 ... 13461
552 ... 13461
562 ... 13461
563 ... 13461
571 ... 13461
701 ... 10334, 11937

13 CFR
121 ... 12811
123 ... 10953, 10955
124 ... 12811
Proposed Rules:
108 ... 12864
121 ... 11938

14 CFR
25 ... 13870, 13875, 14740
39 ... 10057, 10270, 10272, 10273, 10275, 10279, 10575, 10734, 10735, 11182, 11531, 11533, 11713, 11716, 12158, 13437, 13439, 13440, 13442, 13444, 13446, 13645, 14545, 14743, 15042
71 ... 9627, 9919, 9920, 10739, 10740, 10741, 10742, 10743, 10744, 10745, 10746, 10747, 10956, 10957, 11534, 11535, 12159, 13194, 13195, 13196, 13647, 13648, 13878, 14547, 14744
73 ... 10748
91 ... 10958, 11692
95 ... 15044
97 ... 11182, 11183, 12816, 12817, 12821
157 ... 10262
300 ... 10060
302 ... 10060
303 ... 10060
325 ... 10060
385 ... 10060
Proposed Rules:
Ch. I ... 11009, 13897, 14794
25 ... 14571
39 ... 10336, 10338, 10340, 10759, 11733, 11735, 11737, 11739, 11939, 11940, 11942, 11944, 11946, 11947, 12203, 12205, 12207, 12558, 12560, 12865, 13898, 14124, 14795, 14797, 14799, 14800
71 ... 10040, 10084, 10760, 11010, 11222, 11223, 11224, 11561, 11562, 11563, 11564, 11565, 12208, 12209, 12874, 12875, 12876, 13260, 13261, 13262, 13263, 13663, 14573, 14574, 14576, 14577, 14578, 14803, 14804, 14805, 15136, 15137, 15138
91 ... 12740
121 ... 15308
129 ... 15308
135 ... 12740, 15308

15 CFR
770 ... 13196
771 ... 10958, 13196, 14360
772 ... 10958
773 ... 10958, 12824, 13196
774 ... 10958, 13196
778 ... 10958, 12824
779 ... 13449
785 ... 14360
786 ... 10958
787 ... 10958
799 ... 10958, 12824, 13879
Proposed Rules:
777 ... 13900
946 ... 9921
990 ... 9688

16 CFR
Proposed Rules:
1500 ... 10761
1700 ... 13264

17 CFR
1 ... 11544
5 ... 11544
9 ... 10228
12 ... 9631
21 ... 10228
30 ... 10281
31 ... 11544
143 ... 10228
156 ... 10228
190 ... 10228
200 ... 12543
211 ... 12748
231 ... 12748
240 ... 10984
241 ... 12748
Proposed Rules:
1 ... 9689
240 ... 12759, 12767, 13275
275 ... 13464

18 CFR
Ch. I ... 9682
4 ... 10576
154 ... 11546
157 ... 11546
271 ... 10577
284 ... 11546
385 ... 11546
388 ... 11546
401 ... 11458
Proposed Rules:
284 ... 11011, 11566, 12210, 12877

19 CFR
4 ... 10283, 11898, 13198, 13664, 14022
12 ... 11547
24 ... 15046
102 ... 11547
123 ... 10283, 13198
134 ... 11547
141 ... 13198
171 ... 14745
173 ... 13198
175 ... 13450, 13452, 14548
181 ... 15047
Proposed Rules:
4 ... 11225, 12878
10 ... 11225
12 ... 11225, 14806
24 ... 13644
101 ... 12879
102 ... 11225
134 ... 11225, 14579
141 ... 14808
146 ... 10342
152 ... 14580
175 ... 10764, 12032, 14579
177 ... 11225

20 CFR
200 ... 15048
404 ... 11899, 14746
416 ... 11899, 12544
Proposed Rules:
404 ... 11949
416 ... 10766, 11949
422 ... 12211
626 ... 10769
1005 ... 10769

21 CFR
Ch. I ... 14366
5 ... 14362, 14549, 15049
7 ... 14362
10 ... 14362
12 ... 14362
20 ... 15050
25 ... 14362
58 ... 13200
60 ... 14362
73 ... 10578
74 ... 11718
101 ... 14362, 15049, 15050, 15051
105 ... 15049
109 ... 14362
130 ... 15049, 15051
155 ... 15051
172 ... 10986, 14549
176 ... 14549
177 ... 9925, 10986, 14549
178 ... 10064, 10065, 13649, 14549
179 ... 14549
184 ... 14362, 14549
314 ... 13200, 14362
330 ... 14362
442 ... 12545
450 ... 9638
500 ... 14362
509 ... 14362
510 ... 14366
520 ... 14362
522 ... 14362, 14366, 14367
524 ... 14362
558 ... 12547, 14362, 14367
808 ... 14362
821 ... 15052
886 ... 10283
1010 ... 14362
1030 ... 14362
1240 ... 14362
1250 ... 14362
1308 ... 10718, 12828, 15052
1310 ... 13881
Proposed Rules:
101 ... 11872, 14126
123 ... 10085
203 ... 11842
205 ... 11842
334 ... 15139
351 ... 13284
356 ... 11836
806 ... 13828
1240 ... 10085
1308 ... 10720
1310 ... 12562

22 CFR
40 ... 15298
42 ... 15298
Proposed Rules:
89 ... 13904

23 CFR
625 ... 14748
Proposed Rules:
657 ... 11956

24 CFR
8 ... 14090
12 ... 14091

FIGURE 5-4 *(Continued)* No listing for part 1316 of 21 C.F.R. means there were no changes to 21 C.F.R. part 1316 in March 1994.

Latest Federal Register available to author

4-22-94
Vol. 59 No. 78

federal register

Friday
April 22, 1994

United States
Government
Printing Office
SUPERINTENDENT
OF DOCUMENTS
Washington, DC 20402

OFFICIAL BUSINESS
Penalty for private use, $300

SECOND CLASS NEWSPAPER
Postage and Fees Paid
U.S. Government Printing Office
(ISSN 0097-6326)

FIGURE 5-4 *(Continued)*

i

Reader Aids

Federal Register
Vol. 59, No. 78
Friday, April 22, 1994

Cumulative for April 1994

INFORMATION AND ASSISTANCE

Federal Register

Index, finding aids & general information 202-523-5227
Public inspection desk 523-5215
Corrections to published documents 523-5237
Document drafting information 523-3187
Machine readable documents 523-3447

Code of Federal Regulations

Index, finding aids & general information 523-5227
Printing schedules 523-3419

Laws

Public Laws Update Service (numbers, dates, etc.) 523-6641
Additional information 523-5230

Presidential Documents

Executive orders and proclamations 523-5230
Public Papers of the Presidents 523-5230
Weekly Compilation of Presidential Documents 523-5230

The United States Government Manual

General information 523-5230

Other Services

Data base and machine readable specifications 523-3447
Guide to Record Retention Requirements 523-3187
Legal staff 523-4534
Privacy Act Compilation 523-3187
Public Laws Update Service (PLUS) 523-6641
TDD for the hearing impaired 523-5229

ELECTRONIC BULLETIN BOARD

Free Electronic Bulletin Board service for Public 202-275-1538,
Law numbers, and Federal Register finding aids. .... or 275-0920

FEDERAL REGISTER PAGES AND DATES, APRIL

CFR PARTS AFFECTED DURING APRIL

At the end of each month, the Office of the Federal Register publishes separately a List of CFR Sections Affected (LSA), which lists parts and sections affected by documents published since the revision date of each title.

FIGURE 5-4 *(Continued)*

ii **Federal Register** / Vol. 59, No. 78 / Friday, April 22, 1994 / Reader Aids

1 ... 17464
20 ... 17464
30 ... 17464
40 ... 17464
55 ... 17464
70 ... 17464
73 ... 17464
435 ... 18293
600 ... 18473
830 ... 15843
Proposed Rules:
20 ... 17746
30 ... 19147
32 ... 17286
40 ... 19147
50 ... 17499, 19147
61 ... 17052
70 ... 19147
72 ... 19147
430 ... 15868, 18502
436 ... 17204, 19150
1101 ... 16978

11 CFR
102 ... 17267

12 CFR
268 ... 16096
Ch. V ... 18474
503 ... 18474
504 ... 18474
505 ... 18474
515 ... 18474
544 ... 18474
552 ... 18474
561 ... 18474
Proposed Rules:
3 ... 18328
304 ... 15869
Ch. VI ... 15664
348 ... 18764
500 ... 18979
545 ... 18979
552 ... 18979
563 ... 18979
563b ... 18979
574 ... 18879
704 ... 18503

13 CFR
107 ... 16898, 16933
121 ... 16513, 16953
302 ... 15328
305 ... 15328
Proposed Rules:
120 ... 15872
121 ... 19150

14 CFR
39 ... 15329, 15332, 15613, 13853, 15854, 17467, 17681, 17683, 17685, 17686, 17687, 18294, 18709, 18712, 18713, 18714, 18715, 18717, 18718, 18720, 18722, 18952, 18955, 18957, 18958, 18960, 18961, 19127
61 ... 17644
71 ... 15616, 15617, 15618, 18296, 18724, 18725, 18726
91 ... 17550
93 ... 15332
97 ... 15519, 16119, 18476, 18478, 18726
141 ... 17644
1209 ... 18730
Proposed Rules:
1 ... 19296
21 ... 19114
25 ... 19296
27 ... 17156
29 ... 17156
34 ... 17640
39 ... 15348, 15873, 15875, 16151, 16574, 17288, 18768, 19151, 19152, 19154
61 ... 17162
71 ... 15665, 15666, 15667, 15668, 15669, 15670, 15671, 16153, 16155, 17055, 17056, 18329, 18506, 18770
91 ... 15350
121 ... 17166, 18456
125 ... 18456
135 ... 15350, 18456

15 CFR
286 ... 19129
771 ... 15621
774 ... 15621

16 CFR
Proposed Rules:
22 ... 18004
236 ... 18005
252 ... 18005
253 ... 18006
429 ... 18007
444 ... 18009

17 CFR
190 ... 17468
270 ... 15501
Proposed Rules:
210 ... 16576
230 ... 16576
239 ... 16576
270 ... 16576
274 ... 16576

18 CFR
141 ... 15333
161 ... 15336
250 ... 15336
284 ... 16537
Proposed Rules
284 ... 15672, 15877

19 CFR
4 ... 18479
10 ... 17473
42 ... 17474
101 ... 16121
122 ... 16121
175 ... 16895
Proposed Rules:
177 ... 18771

21 CFR
131 ... 17689
173 ... 15623
201 ... 18982
207 ... 18982
336 ... 16981
338 ... 16982
343 ... 18507
520 ... 17691, 17693, 19133
556 ... 17922
558 ... 15339, 15624, 17476, 17922, 18296, 19133
Proposed Rules
101 ... 16577
123 ... 16578
331 ... 17747
352 ... 16042
700 ... 16042
740 ... 16042
1240 ... 16578

22 CFR
126 ... 15624
145 ... 18730
502 ... 18963
514 ... 16983
Proposed Rules:
42 ... 18010
502 ... 17057, 18772

24 CFR
24 ... 18481
50 ... 17194, 19100
55 ... 19100
58 ... 19100
92 ... 18626
200 ... 19100
574 ... 17194
888 ... 16408
941 ... 18482
945 ... 17652
960 ... 17652
3280 ... 19072
Proposed Rules:
290 ... 17500
905 ... 18666
913 ... 18666
964 ... 18666
990 ... 18666

25 CFR
248 ... 16756
Proposed Rules:
20 ... 16720
40 ... 18460
113 ... 16760
256 ... 16726

26 CFR
1 ... 15501, 15502, 16984, 17154, 17477, 18746, 18747
15a ... 18747
602 ... 17154
Proposed Rules:
1 ... 15877, 17747, 18011, 18048, 18772
31 ... 18057

27 CFR
Proposed Rules:
4 ... 15878

28 CFR
36 ... 17442
522 ... 16406
540 ... 15812
545 ... 15812, 16406
551 ... 16406
Proposed Rules:
0 ... 15880

29 CFR
1601 ... 18751
1904 ... 15594, 16895
1910 ... 15339, 16334, 17478
1915 ... 17478
1917 ... 15339, 17478
1918 ... 17478
1926 ... 17478
2606 ... 17694
2610 ... 17922
2616 ... 17694
2617 ... 17694
2619 ... 17924
2622 ... 17922
2644 ... 17927
2676 ... 17924
Proposed Rules:
1903 ... 18508
1910 ... 15968, 18443
1915 ... 15968, 17290, 18443
1926 ... 15968, 18443
1928 ... 15968, 18443

30 CFR
75 ... 18485
206 ... 17479
756 ... 17748
901 ... 17928
904 ... 17931
906 ... 17931
914 ... 17928
915 ... 17931
917 ... 17928
918 ... 17931
920 ... 17928
924 ... 17928
925 ... 17931, 19134
926 ... 17931
931 ... 17931
935 ... 17928
938 ... 17928
943 ... 17931
944 ... 16538, 17931
944 ... 17931
946 ... 17928
948 ... 17928
Proposed Rules:
220 ... 17504
764 ... 16156
906 ... 16578
914 ... 18330, 19155
942 ... 16156

31 CFR
500 ... 16775
505 ... 16775
520 ... 16775
580 ... 15342, 16548

32 CFR
90 ... 16123
91 ... 16123
199 ... 16136
246 ... 19137
247 ... 19137
Proposed Rules:
77 ... 15673
91 ... 16157
989 ... 17061

33 CFR
1 ... 16558
100 ... 16560, 16561
117 ... 16562, 18298
150 ... 17480
151 ... 16985, 18700
162 ... 16563
165 ... 17482, 18485, 18486, 18487
Proposed Rules:
26 ... 16780
110 ... 16580, 16783
125 ... 16783

FIGURE 5-4 *(Continued)* — **No changes or proposed changes to part 1316 of 21 C.F.R.**

Citations for Administrative Law

The following are sample citations to the *Federal Register* and the Code of Federal Regulations:

56 Fed. Reg. 23000 (1992).	(page 23000 of volume 56 of the *Federal Register,* published in 1992)
21 C.F.R. § 1316.71 (1992).	(section 17 of part 1316 of volume 21 of the Code of Federal Regulations, 1992 version)

In the preceeding citation for the *Federal Register,* "56" is the volume, "23000" is the page number, and "(1992)" is the year of publication. In the citation for the Code of Federal Regulations, "21" is the title, "1316" is the part, "71" is the section, and "(1992)" is the year of publication.

NOTE ON COMPUTER-ASSISTED LEGAL RESEARCH

You can research the primary sources discussed in this chapter on LEXIS and WESTLAW the same way as you research cases. Determine the correct library and then search using either key words or a citation. The search may also be possible using plain English or menus. (See the "Note on Computer-Assisted Research" in Chapter 4 for an explanation of these research methods.) For some jurisdictions, the on-line services may include the annotated version of the primary source and the same indexes you would find if researching using hard copy. In addition, you may be able to do research on legislative history on-line. Be sure to check the user's manual accompanying the on-line service to determine what information is accessible on-line.

All of the primary sources discussed in this chapter can be updated using LEXIS or WESTLAW. Using the computer to make sure you have the latest version of statutes and administrative regulations, in particular, is usually much faster than searching manually using hard copy. CALR allows you access that you would not otherwise have to recently passed statutes which have not yet been printed.

Almost the same capability of researching constitutions, statutes, and administrative law may be available using a CD-ROM containing the appropriate database. If your CD contains your state constitution, statutes, and administrative law, you can research those primary sources. CDs are updated periodically by the publisher, which sends the owner a replacement CD. The replacement CD contains all the information on the prior CD plus any more recent information available. Research would be fairly current using a recently received CD, but would probably be more current (from a few days to several months) using an on-line service.

SUMMARY

- Constitutions, statutes, court rules, and administrative law, like cases, are primary authority.
- The United States Constitution sets forth the fundamental principles of governance for the country; state constitutions set forth the fundamental principles of governance for the states.
- To find how a provision of a contitution has been interpreted by the courts, consult an annotated version of the constitution.
- Federal and state statutes first appear as slip laws and then as session laws (arranged chronologically). They are codified (grouped by subject matter).
- To understand a statute, you must read the text of the statute and any annotations summarizing how the stature has been interpreted by the courts.
- The Federal Rules of Civil Procedure, the Federal Rules of Criminal Procedure, and the Federal Rules of Evidence govern litigation procedure in federal trial courts.
- Similar sets of rules govern litigation procedure in state trial courts.
- Separate sets of court rules govern litigation procedure in federal and state appellate courts.
- Administrative agencies promulgate administrative regulations which have the force of law.
- Federal administrative regulations are published chronologically in the *Federal Register* and are later codified in the code of Federal Regulations.
- State administrative regulations are generally published in similar fashion.
- Computer-assisted legal research may be used to research the primary sources discussed in this chapter.

RESEARCH ASSIGNMENTS

Legal Research Assignment—Constitutions

1. What do the following articles of the United States Constitution deal with?
   a. Article I.
   b. Article II.
   c. Article III.
2. What is the citation to the portion of your state's constitution dealing with the following matters?
   a. The executive branch.
   b. The legislative branch.
   c. The judicial branch.
3. Which provision of the United States Constitution contains the "enumerated powers" of Congress?
4. Which provision of the United States Constitution is commonly known as the "supremacy clause"?

5. a. Which provision of the United States Constitution is frequently cited as giving people the right to own handguns?
   b. If your state constitution guarantees the same right, give the citation to that provision.
6. a. Which provision of the United States Constitution guarantees the right to a speedy and public trial?
   b. If your state constitution guarantees the same right, give the citation to that provision.
7. a. Which provision of the United States Constitution deals with freedom of the press?
   b. Which provision of your state constitution deals with freedom of the press?
8. What 1868 change to the United States Constitution made much of the Bill of Rights applicable to state governments as well as the federal government?
9. a. In what set of books would you be able to research how case law has interpreted the United States Constitution?
   b. In what set of books would you be able to research how case law has interpreted your state's constitution?
10. a. Which provision of the United States Constitution specifically guarantees a right to privacy?
    b. If your state constitution guarantees the right to privacy, give the citation to that provision.
11. a. What is the citation to the Florida Supreme Court case in which the court interpreted the Florida Constitution's right to privacy as guaranteeing a minor's right to an abortion?
    b. What was the issue raised in *Jones v. State,* 18 F.L.W. D1375 (Fla. Dist. Ct. App. June 4, 1993)?
    c. How did the *Jones* court answer the issue?
12. a. Which provision of the United States Constitution guarantees "the right of the people to be secure in their persons, houses, papers and effects"?
    b. If your state constitution guarantees the same right, give the citation to that provision.
13. a. What question was considered by the United States Supreme Court in *Minnesota v. Dickerson,* 61 U.S.L.W. 4544 (1993)?
    b. How did the Court answer the question?
14. How did the United States Supreme Court, in a 1986 case, interpret the fourteenth amendment to the United States Constitution with regard to jury selection? Give the citation to that 1986 case.
15. a. Which provision of the United States Constitution guarantees free speech?
    b. If your state constitution guarantees the same right, give the citation to that provision.

16. a. How has the United States Supreme Court applied this free speech guarantee to "Son of Sam" laws designed to prevent criminals from profiting from crime-related books, movies, and other publicity?
    b. Give the citation to this case.
17. In *Edenfield v. Fane,* ____ U.S. ____, 113 S. Ct. 1792, 123 L. Ed. 2d 543 (1993), what is the wording of the Florida Board of Accountancy's rule which the United States Supreme Court held violated the United States Constitution's free speech guarantee?
18. a. Which provision of the United States Constitution prohibits laws "establishing" religion?
    b. If your state constitution guarantees the same right, give the citation to that provision.
19. Answer the following questions concerning *Lee v. Weisman,* 505 U.S. ____, 112 S. Ct. 2649, 120 L. Ed. 2d 467 (1992) and *Jones v. Clear Creek Independent School District,* 977 F.2d 963 (5th Cir. 1992):
    a. In *Lee,* what did the Court hold concerning prayers offered at public school commencement exercises?
    b. In light of the decision reached in *Lee,* the United States Supreme Court vacated the Fifth Circuit's decision in *Jones v. Clear Creek Independent School District* and remanded it for the lower court to make a further determination in accordance with *Lee.* The fifth circuit did so in *Jones v. Clear Creek Independent School District,* 977 F.2d 963 (5th Cir. 1992). When *Jones* went up to the United States Supreme Court a second time, the Court denied review. Because the Court denied review, the Fifth Circuit decision stands. Read *Jones* in light of *Lee* and explain what the *Jones* court held concerning school prayers.
20. Which provision of the United States Constitution prohibits cruel and unusual punishment? If your state constitution contains a similar prohibition, give the citation to that provision.
21. a. According to two United States Supreme Court cases decided in 1988 and 1989, at what age does the death penalty violate, and at what age does the death penalty not violate, the United States Constitution's guarantee against cruel and unusual punishment? Give the citations to the two cases.
    b. In *Arave v. Creech,* ____ U.S. ____, 113 S. Ct. 1534, 123 L. Ed. 2d 188 (1993), what was the wording of the Idaho statute which the trial judge relied on in sentencing Mr. Creech to death and which the United States Supreme Court ruled did not violate the United States Constitution's guarantee against cruel and unusual punishment?
    c. According to *Jordan v. Gardner,* 986 F.2d 1521 (9th Cir. 1993), what treatment of female prisoners constitutes cruel and unusual punishment?

Legal Research Assignment—Statutes

Note: You may research questions 8 through 12 in United States Code Service or United States Code Annotated instead of United States Code.

1. Name the set of books containing federal statutes arranged in chronological order.
2. Name the set of books containing the official codified version of federal statutes.
3. Name two sets of books containing the codified version of federal statutes and annotations to those statutes.
4. Name the set of books for your state containing session laws.
5. Name the set of books for your state containing state statutes arranged in chronological order.
6. Name the set of books for your state containing the official codified version of state statutes.
7. Name the set of books for your state containing the codified version of state statutes and annotations to those statutes.
8. a. What right does 15 U.S.C. § 1635 give consumers who mortgage their homes to secure payment for home improvements? When must this right be exercised?
   b. What do §§ 206 and 207 of 29 U.S.C. cover? What is the popular name of the act within which these sections are found?
   c. Under 50 U.S.C. App. § 520, what type of defendant in a lawsuit is given protection against a default judgment being entered against him or her? What is the popular name of 50 U.S.C. App. §§ 501–591?
9. a. What does Title 18 of the United States Code deal with?
   b. What does Title 21 of the United States Code deal with?
   c. What does Title 26 of the United States Code deal with?
10. a. What is the citation of the federal statute that makes armed carjacking a crime?
    b. What is the citation of the federal statute that makes it illegal for a pilot to fly a commercial airplane while under the influence of alcohol?
    c. After being acquitted in state court, the police officers involved in the Rodney King incident were tried in federal court for deprivation of Mr. King's civil rights. Give the citation to the applicable federal statute.
11. a. What is the citation for the Americans with Disabilities Act of 1990? (In the citation, give the numbers for all sections that are part of the Act.)
    b. What is the citation of the federal statute that prohibits job discrimination on the basis of race, religion, or sex?
    c. What is the citation of the federal statute that prohibits job discrimination on the basis of age?
12. The federal statutes contain a "speedy trial" rule requiring that a criminal defendant be brought to trial within a certain time after publication of the information or indictment or the defendant's initial appearance. Give the time period and state the authority for your answer.
13. Does your state have any gun control laws? Explain what limitations are placed on the purchase of guns and state the authority for your answer.

14. Does your state have a statute or statutes specifically making it a crime to access someone else's computer without authorization? If so, state the authority.
15. Does your state have a statute or statutes making money intended to be used to purchase illegal drugs subject to forfeiture? If so, state the authority.
16. In your state, who may be adopted? State the authority.
17. If you wanted to change your name, what procedure would you have to follow? State the authority.
18. Does your state have a statute or statutes making "stalking" a crime? If so, state the authority. Looking at the annotations to the law, can you tell whether the constitutionality of the law has been tested? Explain and provide the citation for any cases cited.
19. Give the citation for your state statute allowing a child to be tried as an adult for violation of state law. What ages are covered by the statute?
20. Does your state have a "hate crimes" law? If so, state the authority. Looking at the annotations to the law, can you tell whether the constitutionality of the law has been tested? Explain and provide the proper citation for any cases cited.
21. In your state, what is the legal blood alcohol level for a motorist? State the authority.
22. Does your state have a "shield" statute giving news reporters the right to keep sources confidential in connection with active news-gathering? If so, state the authority.
23. Does your state have a statute prohibiting the unlicensed practice of law? If so, state the authority.
24. If your state has a state-run lottery, what portion of the money goes to prizes? State the authority.
25. State the procedure, if there is one, in your state for making a living will (directing whether you want medical treatment if you are terminally ill). State the authority.
26. In your state, may a business club restrict membership to white males? State the authority.
27. In your state, what are the requirements for use of automobile seat belts and car seats? State the authority.
28. In your state, is flying an airplane while under the influence of alcohol legal? State the authority.
29. In your state, is it legal for an unmarried man and woman to live together? State the authority.
30. In 1993, the Florida legislature passed a new statute authorizing breast-feeding in public. Give the citation to the statute in Florida Session Law Service and state the section number from Florida Statutes assigned to the statute.

Legal Research Assignment—Court Rules

1. In what set of books would you find the Federal Rules of Civil and Criminal Procedure?
2. In what set of books would you find the Federal Rules of Evidence?
3. In what set of books would you find the rules of civil and criminal procedure for your state?
4. In what set of books would you find the rules of evidence for your state?
5. Using the Federal Rules of Civil Procedure, answer questions a and b:
   a. What information must be contained in the caption of a motion and a pleading?
   b. What is the authority for your answer?
   c. Using your state's rules of civil procedure, what are the answers to a and b?
6. Using the Federal Rules of Civil Procedure, answer questions a and b:
   a. What is the time period within which a defendant must serve an answer to a complaint?
   b. What is the authority for your answer?
   c. Using your state's rules of civil procedure, what are the answers to a and b?
7. Using the Federal Rules of Civil Procedure, answer questions a and b:
   a. What methods may be used to obtain discovery?
   b. What is the authority for your answer?
   c. Using your state's rules of civil procedure, what are the answers a and b?
8. Using the Federal Rules of Civil Procedure, answer questions a and b:
   a. May a party's failure to comply with a discovery order be a ground for dismissal of an action?
   b. What is the authority for your answer?
   c. Using your state's rules of civil procedure, what are the answers to a and b?
9. Using the Federal Rules of Civil Procedure, answer questions a through c:
   a. How many peremptory challenges of jurors does a plaintiff have when there is only one defendant in a civil action?
   b. What is the authority for your answer?
   c. In what two ways do peremptory challenges differ from challenges for cause?
   d. Using your state's rules of civil procedure, what are the answers to a and b of this question?
10. Using the evidence code or rules of your state, answer the following questions:
    a. What privileges are recognized?
    b. How may someone who has a privilege lose it?
    c. What is the authority for your answers?

11. Using the evidence code or rules of your state, answer the following questions:
    a. Does an attorney-client privilege exist when the services of a lawyer were sought or obtained to aid someone to commit a crime?
    b. What is the authority for your answer?
12. Using the Federal Rules of Evidence, answer questions a and b:
    a. How is "relevant evidence" defined?
    b. What is the authority for your answer?
    c. Using the evidence code or rules of your state, how is "relevant evidence" defined?
    d. What is the authority for your answer?
13. Using the Federal Rules of Evidence, answer questions a and b:
    a. How is "hearsay" defined?
    b. What is the authority for your answer?
    c. Using the evidence code or rules of your state, how is "hearsay" defined?
    d. What is the authority for your answer?
14. Using the Federal Rules of Evidence, answer question a:
    a. What rule allows a judge to exclude witnesses from the courtroom so they cannot hear the testimony of other witnesses?
    b. Using the evidence code or rules of your state, what is the answer to a?
15. Using the Federal Rules of Criminal Procedure, answer questions a and b:
    a. What must a judge do before accepting a guilty plea?
    b. What is the authority for your answer?
    c. Using the rules of criminal procedure of your state, what are the answers to a and b?
16. a. If your state has a speedy trial rule in its rules of criminal procedure, requiring the defendant to be brought to trial within a certain period of time, what is that period of time?
    b. What is the authority for your answer?
17. Using the Federal Rules of Criminal Procedure, answer questions a and b:
    a. What report must the judge review before imposing sentence?
    b. What is the authority for your answer?
    c. If your state's rules of criminal procedure contain sentencing guidelines, what is the purpose of those guidelines?
    d. What is the authority for your answer?
18. Using the Federal Rules of Appellate Procedure, answer questions a through c:
    a. What is the time period within which civil appeals as of right must be filed?
    b. What must be done to file an appeal?
    c. What is the authority for your answer?
    d. Using your state's rules of civil procedure and appellate procedure, what are the answers to a, b, and c?

19. Using the rule of civil procedure or the appellate rules for your state, what rule, if any, specifies correct citation form for court documents?
20. Using the Federal Rules of Appellate Procedure, answer questions a and b:
    a. What are the parts of an appellate brief?
    b. What is the authority for your answer?
    c. Using your state's rules of appellate procedure, what are the answers to a and b?
21. Using the Federal Rules of Appellate Procedure, answer questions a and b:
    a. What are the grounds for not allowing oral argument?
    b. What is the authority for your answer?
    c. Using your state's rules of appellate procedure, what are the answers to a and b?
22. Using the Federal Rules of Appellate Procedure, answer questions a and b:
    a. Who decides whether an appeal may be heard or reheard en banc?
    b. What is the authority for your answer?
    c. Using your state's rules of appellate procedure, what are the answers to a and b?
23. Using the Rules of the Supreme Court of the United States, answer questions a and b:
    a. What are the ways in which the Court obtains jurisdiction, other than original jurisdiction?
    b. What is the authority for your answer?
    c. Using the rules of the highest court in your state, what are the answers to a and b?
24. Using the Rules of the Supreme Court of the United States, answer questions a and b:
    a. On what size of paper are typed briefs to be submitted to the Court?
    b. What is the authority for your answer?
    c. Using the rules of the highest court in your state, what are the answers to a and b?
25. Using the Rules of the Supreme Court of the United States, answer questions a and b:
    a. What are the parts of an appellant's or petitioner's brief?
    b. What is the authority for your answer?
    c. Using the rules of the highest court in your state, what are the answers to a and b?

Legal Research Assignment—Administrative Law

1. a. What is the name of the set of books containing the codified version of federal administrative rules?
   b. What is the name of the publication containing new administrative rules not found in the code?

2. a. What is the name of the set of books containing the codified version of your state's administrative rules?
   b. What is the name of the publication containing new administrative rules not found in the code?
3. a. What federal government agency is the subject of Title 17 of the Code of Federal Regulations?
   b. What federal government agency is the subject of Title 26 of the Code of Federal Regulations?
   c. What federal government agency is the subject of Title 50 of the Code of Federal Regulations?
4. a. What is the purpose of the Note at 16 C.F.R. Part 17 (1993)?
   b. What is the purpose of 16 C.F.R. §§ 1615.1-1616.65 (1993)?
   c. What is the purpose of 16 C.F.R. §§ 1501.1-1501.5 (1993)?
   d. What is the purpose of 16 C.F.R. §§ 238.0-238.4 (1993)?
   e. What is the purpose of 16 C.F.R. §§ 233.1-233.5 (1993)?
5. a. What is the citation to the rules promulgated under the Magnuson-Moss Warranty Act?
   b. What is the citation to the rules requiring care labels (stating whether the item is recommended to be machine-washed or dry cleaned) in clothing?
   c. What is the citation to the rules requiring clothing labels to state the fabric content and the country of origin?
   d. What is the citation to the rule listing wildlife determined to be "Endangered" or "Threatened" species?
   e. What is the citation to the rule listing plants determined to be "Endangered" or "Threatened" species?
6. What is the definition in the Code of Federal Regulations for the following terms, and what is the authority for your answer?
   a. "beer."
   b. "wine."
   c. "milk."
   d. "cream."
7. Locate the federal regulations concerning the Code of Federal Regulations and the *Federal Register* and answer the following questions:
   a. How often is each book of the Code of Federal Regulations updated?
   b. What is the authority for your answer to a?
   c. What categories of documents are published in the *Federal Register*?
   d. How often is the *Federal Register* published?
   e. What is the authority for your answer to c and d?
8. Locate the federal regulations in the Code of Federal Regulations concerning chewing tobacco and answer the following questions:
   a. What is the name of the federal act authorizing enactment of the regulations?
   b. What is the wording for the three warnings, one of which is required to be placed on advertisements and packages of chewing tobacco?
   c. What is the authority for your answers to a and b?

9. Locate the federal regulations in the Code of Federal Regulations concerning labeling of alcoholic beverages and answer the following questions:
   a. What is the wording for the warning required to be placed on alcoholic beverages?
   b. What is the effective date of the labeling regulation?
   c. What is the authority for your answers to a and b?
10. Locate the federal regulations in the Code of Federal Regulations concerning inspection of meat and poultry and answer the following questions:
    a. What is the wording on the official inspection legend for beef carcasses?
    b. What is the wording on the official inspection legend for chicken?
    c. What is the authority for your answers to a and b?
11. Locate the federal regulations in the Code of Federal Regulations concerning grading of Florida oranges and answer the following questions:
    a. What types of fruit are covered by the regulations?
    b. What are the names of the various grades of oranges?
    c. What is the authority for your answers to a and b?
12. Answer the following questions and state the authority for your answers:
    a. When may a petition for pardon be filed by someone seeking executive clemency?
    b. Is a federal prisoner eligible for parole?
    c. In whose name must a patent application be made?
    d. May lawn darts be sold?
13. Answer the following questions and state the authority for your answers:
    a. What is the maximum distance allowed between slats on full-size baby cribs?
    b. What must a seller of mail-order merchandise do when the seller is unable to ship merchandise within the applicable time period?
    c. How long does a consumer who purchased a consumer item in a "door-to-door" sale have to cancel the purchase, and how long after receiving the buyer's cancellation notice does the seller have to refund any money paid?
    d. May someone operate a brewery in his or her home?
14. What do the following titles of your state's administrative code deal with? (If your state's administrative code is divided into something other than titles, answer the following questions substituting the applicable word for the word *title*.)
    a. What does title 21 deal with?
    b. What does title 6 deal with?
    c. What does title 20 deal with?
    d. What does title 10 deal with?

15 a. What is the citation for your state's administrative rules dealing with title insurance?
   b. What is the citation for your state's administrative rules dealing with driver licenses?

   c. What is the citation for your state's administrative rules dealing with your school, college, or university?
   d. What is the citation for your state's administrative rules dealing with licensing of medical doctors?
   e. What is the citation for your state's administrative rules dealing with sales tax?
16. Using your state's administrative rules, answer the following questions concerning abused and neglected children:
   a. What state department or agency has the responsibility of protecting abused and neglected children?
   b. What is the citation for the administrative rules dealing with child protective services?
   c. What do "abuse" and "neglect" mean?
   d. What is the authority for your answer to c?
17. Using your state's administrative rules, answer the following questions concerning amusement rides at public fairs:
   a. What rule or rules govern the testing of amusement rides?
   b. What state department or agency is responsible for inspecting amusement rides to make sure they are safe?
   c. What documentary evidence shows that an amusement ride has been safety tested?
18. Answer the following questions about the board, commission, or agency heading your state's university system:
   a. What is the name of the entity heading your state's university system?
   b. What is the citation to the rules concerning the entity?
   c. What are the principal responsibilities of the entity?
   d. What is the statutory authority for the entity?
19. Answer the following questions regarding your state's administrative code:
   a. Where are title insurance rates found?
   b. What administrative rule allows drivers licensed out-of-state to drive in your state?
   c. Concerning licensing of medical doctors, what is the definition of "foreign medical graduate"?
   d. Is a mail order company with retail stores in your state subject to your state's sales tax?

CHAPTER 6
Shepard's Citators

OUTLINE

Shepardizing Procedure
Note on Computer-Assisted Legal Research

COMMON LEGAL SOURCES AND FINDING TOOLS

Note: Sources used in this chapter are indicated by boldface type.

Primary Sources	Secondary Sources	Finding Tools
reporters	treatises	American Law Reports
constitutions	law review articles	legal encyclopedias
statutes	legal periodicals	digests
administrative regulations	law dictionaries	*Index to Legal Periodicals*
court rules	legal thesauruses	loose-leaf services
loose-leaf services	continuing legal education publications	**Shepard's Citators**
	Restatements	
	American Law Reports	
	legal encyclopedias	
	loose-leaf services	

Shepard's Citations are named after Frank Shepard, who started his citator business in 1873 in Chicago. Shepard's citators are sets of indexes which enable you to look up cases, statutes, and regulations to discover if they have been cited. Shepard's allows you to find out the current status of cases, statutes, and regulations (whether they are still good law) and allows you to locate more recent law concerning the issue you are researching.

Shepardizing involves consulting these sets of books, commonly called "Shepard's," to determine whether the authority you have found has been cited in any source. Shepard's will also tell you whether your authority is still good law. If your authority is a case, it is not good law if it has been reversed or overruled. If it was affirmed on appeal, you probably will want to cite the higher court opinion. If your authority is a statute, it is not good law if it has been repealed, amended, or held unconstitutional.

Although there are sets of Shepard's which allow you to shepardize virtually any primary source, this chapter concentrates on shepardizing cases. Once you know the shepardizing procedure for cases, you can use the same procedure to shepardize statutes, court rules, and administrative regulations.

There are two important reasons for shepardizing. The first reason, alluded to earlier, is that when you are researching, you do not want to rely on authority that is not still good law. For an attorney, relying on a case that has been reversed can mean instant malpractice, exposure to ridicule from fellow attorneys, or harsh criticism from judges and a severe loss of attorney credibility. If this happened because the paralegal forgot to shepardize and the attorney relied on the paralegal's research, the paralegal can lose his or her job. In short, do not forget to shepardize!

The second reason for shepardizing is to locate more recent cases dealing with the same legal principle found in the case you are shepardizing. Remember the doctrine of stare decisis? When a court renders a decision, the court will back up its reasoning by citing other cases that are precedent for the case being decided. Shepardizing allows you to locate every subsequent case that cited your case. The Shepard's sample pages contained in this chapter are ones you would find if you were to shepardize *Florida v. Jimeno.* Shepardizing tells you the location of every subsequent citation to *Jimeno.* Shepardizing even allows you to locate subsequent cases discussing the same legal principle contained in a particular headnote from *Jimeno.*

SHEPARDIZING PROCEDURE

Although some students find the shepardizing procedure difficult at first, you will gain confidence in your ability to shepardize after you do it a few times. Sample pages from Shepard's United States Citations have been reprinted for you in this chapter. These are the pages you would find if you were to shepardize *Florida v. Jimeno,* 114 L. Ed. 2d 297 (1991). The explanation of the shepardizing procedure was designed to walk you through shepardizing *Jimeno* step by step. You will probably find yourself reading the procedure several times before you understand the concept. First, read the procedure as you follow along, looking at the sample pages. Then read the procedure again by itself and test yourself by "shepardizing" *Jimeno* using the sample pages. After you have mastered the procedure, follow up by doing some of the shepardizing exercises at the end of this chapter.

Getting Organized

The first thing to do is get organized. If you do not shepardize systematically, you may miss something. You must locate the correct set of Shepard's to use and be ready to record the results of your shepardizing. The Shepard's set you will need is customarily located near the reporters containing cases shepardized in that Shepard's set. The citators used to shepardize United States Supreme Court decisions is called "Shepard's United States Citations." The Shepard's for Federal Reporter and Federal Supplement is called "Shepard's Federal Citations." There are Shepard's for all the regional reporters as well. The Shepard's for Southern Reporter is "Shepard's Southern Citations." Shepard's even publishes citators allowing you to shepardize the cases from only one state, even though the state cases are printed in a regional reporter. For example, Southern Reporter contains cases from Louisiana, Mississippi, Alabama, and Florida. Shepard's Southern Citations allows you to shepardize cases from all four states, but Shepard's Florida Citations allows you to shepardize only Florida cases. Some libraries carry the state-specific Shepard's rather than the Shepard's for the regional reporter, because that set is all that is usually needed for that state.

Once you find the correct Shepard's set, line up the volumes you will need to use. The set usually contains burgundy-colored hardbound volumes. It may also contain gold, red, and white paperbound volumes. Find the most recent paperbound volume. The date is in the upper right-hand corner of the cover. Because Shepard's is fairly current, you should be looking for a month that is within three months of the month in that you are doing your research. Then look on the front cover of the most recent Shepard's for the legend "WHAT YOUR LIBRARY SHOULD CONTAIN." Below that is the list of Shepard's you need to shepardize. For example, the June 1993 Shepard's United States Citations (Figure 6-1) lists a number of hardbound volumes. Then it lists the January 1993 Semiannual Cumulative Supplement, the May 1993 Cumulative Supplement, and the June 1993 Advance Sheet.

The next step is to determine which volumes of the ones listed on the front cover of the June 1993 volume you will need to use. *Jimeno* is a 1991 case, so it would not appear in any Shepard's prior to 1991. Look at the spines of the hardbound volumes. They will often give you the volume numbers of the reporters covered therein. When you look at the spines of the

LEGAL TERMS

shepardizing
using a citator.

VOL. 92 JUNE 1993 NO. 1

Shepard's United States Citations

ADVANCE SHEET EDITION (IN TWO PARTS)
PART 1B CASES

(USPS 605470)

IMPORTANT NOTICE

A 1991-1993 Hardbound Supplement for Shepard's United States Citations, Cases will be published in June, 1993 and delivered by July 31, 1993.

Do not destroy the January, 1993 gold paper-covered Semiannual Cumulative Supplement (Parts 1A, 1B, 1C and 1D) for Shepard's United States Citations, Cases.

WHAT YOUR LIBRARY SHOULD CONTAIN
PART 1, CASES

1988 Bound Volumes (Vols. 1A, 1B, 1C, 2A, 2B, 2C)*
1984 Bound Volumes (Vols. 3, 4, 5, 6)*
1984-1986 Bound Supplement (Vols. 7A and 7B)*
1986-1988 Bound Supplement (Vols. 8, 9, 10, 11, 12)*
1988-1990 Bound Supplement (Vols. 13, 14, 15, 16, 17)*
1990-1991 Bound Supplement (Vols. 18, 19)*
**Supplemented with:*
–January, 1993 Semiannual Cumulative Supplement Vol. 91 No. 8 (Parts 1A, 1B, 1C and 1D)
–May, 1993 Cumulative Supplement Vol. 91 No. 12 (Part I)
–June, 1993 Advance Sheet Vol. 92 No. 1 (Parts 1A and 1B)

PART 2, STATUTES

Please refer to the current supplement cover for Part 2, Statutes.

RECYCLE YOUR OUTDATED SUPPLEMENTS

When you receive new supplements and are instructed to destroy the outdated versions, please consider taking these paper products to a local recycling center to help conserve our nation's natural resources. Thank you.

FIGURE 6-1 Cover from Shepard's United States Citations. (From Shepard's United States Citations. Reproduced by permission of Shepard's/McGraw-Hill. Further reproduction is strictly prohibited.)

hardbound volumes for volume 114 of L. Ed. 2d, you find that volume 114 of L. Ed. 2d is not contained in any of these hardbound volumes. Notice from the list on the front cover of the June 1993 Shepard's that each of the

January, May, and June issues is published in more than one part. Determine that part of each issue you need to use by looking at the top of the pages. You want to find the part of each issue that says "Lawyers' Edition, United States Supreme Court Reports, 2d Series" across the top of the page and "Vol. 114" in the upper corner or someplace on the page. You will need to use Part 1B of the January 1993 issue, Part 1 of the May 1993 issue, and Part 1B of the June 1993 issue.

It is important that you check each of the issues you have identified, because they are *not* cumulative. This means that each of the Shepard's volumes listed on the front of the latest Shepard's issue contains different information from any other volumes. If you miss checking one of the Shepard's volumes, you may be missing information telling you that the case was reversed or affirmed on appeal. An easy way to make sure you don't miss checking any of the volumes is to make a chart like the one following. Along one edge of the chart, put the citation of the case you are shepardizing and identify the Shepard's volumes to be checked along an adjoining side of the chart. As you check a particular issue, place a check mark next to it to show that you have checked that volume. A chart is especially helpful if you are shepardizing a number of cases at the same time or you are not able to shepardize the issues in order because someone else is using the other volumes.

	Jan. 1993	May 1993	June 1993
114 L. Ed. 2d 297	X	X	X

Abbreviations

The first few pages of each Shepard's volume contain useful information that you will refer to often when you are learning how to shepardize. There are several pages entitled "Abbreviations–Reports" (Figure 6-2). If you are not sure what an abbreviation used in Shepard's stands for, you should consult this table. For example, "A2d" is the abbreviation for "Atlantic Reporter, Second Series." Another page is entitled "Abbreviations—Analysis" (Figure 6-3). This page contains abbreviations dealing with the history of the case. For example, "a" stands for "affirmed," "r" stands for "reversed," "s" stands for "same case," and "v" stands for "vacated." Other abbreviations on this page deal with the treatment of the case. For example, "e" means that the case cited explained the case you are shepardizing; "f" means that the case cited the case you are shepardizing as controlling the later court's decision; "j" means that the case you are shepardizing was cited in the dissenting opinion of the case cited; and "o" means that the cited case expressly overruled the case you are shepardizing. If you are shepardizing statutes, refer to the page that contains abbreviations for statutes.

ABBREVIATIONS—REPORTS

AA–Antitrust Adviser, Third Edition (Shepard's, 1987)
AABA–Atwood & Brewster, Antitrust and American Business Abroad (Shepard's, 1981)
A2d–Atlantic Reporter, Second Series
Ab–Abstracts
AB–American Bankruptcy Reports
ABA–American Bar Association Journal
ABA(2)–American Bar Association Journal, Part 2
AbD–Abbott's Court of Appeals Decisions (N.Y.)
AbN–Abstracts, New Series
ABn–American Bankruptcy Reports, New Series
AbP–Abbott's Practice Reports (N.Y.)
AbPn–Abbott's Practice Reports, New Series (N.Y.)
AC–American Annotated Cases
AD–American Decisions
ADC–Appeal Cases, District of Columbia Reports
Add–Addison's Reports (Pa.)
Advo–Givens, Advocacy (Shepard's, 1985)
Advo(3)–Givens, Advocacy, Third Edition (Shepard's, 1992)
AE(2)–Acret, Architects and Engineers, Second Edition (Shepard's, 1984)
AE(2s)–Acret, Architects and Engineers, Second Edition, Supplement (Shepard's, 1984)
AEn–Buck, Alternative Energy (Shepard's, 1982)
AFW–Newberg, Attorney Fee Awards (Shepard's, 1987)
AgD–Eglit, Age Descrimination (Shepard's, 1982)
AgL–Davidson, Agriculture Law (Shepard's, 1981)
AGSS–Laritz, Attorney Guide to Social Security Disability Claims (Shepard's, 1986)
Aik–Aiken's Reports (Vt.)
AL–Turley, Aviation Litigation (Shepard's, 1986)
A^2–American Law Reports, Second Series
A^3–American Law Reports, Third Series
A^4–American Law Reports, Fourth Series
A^5–American Law Reports, Fifth Series
Ala–Alabama Supreme Court Reports
AlA–Alabama Appellate Court Reports
Alk–Alaska Reports
Allen–Allen's Reports (Mass.)
AR–American Law Reports
ARF–American Law Reports, Federal
AMP–Bauernfeind, Income Taxation: Accounting Methods and Periods (Shepard's, 1983)
AN–Abbott's New Cases (N.Y.)
AntNP–Anthon's Nisi Prius Cases (N.Y.)
AOA–Anderson's Ohio Appellate Unreported Decisions
AR–American Reports
ARAP–Analytical Review: A Guide to Analytical Procedures (Shepard's, 1988)
ARD–Application for Review Decisions
Ark–Arkansas Reports
ARm–O'Reilly, Administrative Rulemaking (Shepard's, 1983)
AS–American State Reports
ASV–Eck, Asset Valuation (Shepard's, 1991)
At–Atlantic Reporter
AtSN–Attorney Sanctions Newsletter (Shepard's)
Az–Arizona Reports
AzA–Arizona Court of Appeals Reports
Bar–Barbour's Supreme Court Reports (N.Y.)
BCh–Barbour's Chancery Reports (N.Y.)
Binn–Binney's Reports (Pa.)
Blackf–Blackford's Reports (Ind.)
Bland–Bland's Chancery Reports (Md.)
Bos–Bosworth's Reports (N.Y.)
Boy–Boyce's Reports (Del.)
BP–Drake & Mullins, Bankruptcy Practice (Shepard's, 1980)
BP(2)–Drake, Bankruptcy Practice, Second Edition (Shepard's, 1990)
Bradb–Bradbury's Pleading & Practice Reports (N.Y.)
Bradf–Bradford's Surrogate's Court Reports (N.Y.)
Bray–Brayton's Reports (Vt.)
Breese–Breese's Reports (Ill.)
BRW–Bankruptcy Reporter (West)
BTA–United States Board of Tax Appeals Reports
BTCL–Givens, Business Torts and Competitor Litigation (Shepard's, 1989)
Bur–Burnett's Reports (Wis.)

FIGURE 6-2 First page of abbreviations from Shepard's United States Citations. (From Shepard's United States Citations. Reproduced by permission of Shepard's/McGraw-Hill. Further reproduction is strictly prohibited.)

ABBREVIATIONS—ANALYSIS

History of Case

a	(affirmed)	Same case affirmed on rehearing.
cc	(connected case)	Different case from cited but arising out of same subject matter or intimately connected therewith.
m	(modified)	Same case modified on rehearing.
r	(reversed)	Same case reversed on rehearing.
s	(same case)	Same case as case cited.
S	(superseded)	Substitution for former opinion.
v	(vacated)	Same case vacated.
US	cert den	Certiorari denied by U.S. Supreme Court.
US	cert dis	Certiorari dismissed by U.S. Supreme Court.
US	reh den	Rehearing denied by U.S. Supreme Court.
US	reh dis	Rehearing dismissed by U.S. Supreme Court.
US	app pndg	Appeal pending before the U.S. Supreme Court.

Treatment of Case

c	(criticised)	Soundness of decision or reasoning in cited case critised for reasons given.
d	(distinguished)	Case at bar different either in law or fact from case cited for reasons given.
e	(explained)	Statement of import of decision in cited case. Not merely a restatement of the facts.
Ex	(Examiner's decision)	Citation in Examiner's decision.
f	(followed)	Cited as controlling.
h	(harmonized)	Apparent inconsistency explained and shown not to exist.
j	(dissenting opinion)	Citation in dissenting opinion.
L	(limited)	Refusal to extend decision of cited case beyond precise issues involved.
o	(overruled)	Ruling in cited case expressly overruled.
p	(parallel)	Citing case substantially alike or on all fours with cited case in its law or facts.
q	(questioned)	Soundness of decision or reasoning in cited case questioned.

FIGURE 6-3 Table of case abbreviations from Shepard's United States Citations. (From Shepard's United States Citations. Reproduced by permission of Shepard's/McGraw-Hill. Further reproduction is strictly prohibited.)

Shepardizing

We will look at a page from each of the January, May, and June 1993 Shepard's volumes that you would find if you were shepardizing *Florida v. Jimeno,* 114 L. Ed. 2d 297 (1991), and determine what the information on those pages means. First let's look at the page from January 1993 (Figure 6-4). You know that you are looking at the correct page because it says "Lawyers' Edition, United States Supreme Court Reports, 2d Series" and "Vol. 114" at the top. Be sure that you have the correct series and volume for the reporter. Then look down the columns for "**297**," the first page of the case, at the top of the first column. Everything after "**297**" and before the next number in bold, "**307**," has to do with *Jimeno.* The information in parentheses, "(111SC1801)," on the line after "**297**" is a parallel

Lawyer's Edition, United States Supreme Court Reports, 2d Series Vol.114

—297—
(111SC1801)
s112L256a
Fla
s550So2d1176
s564So2d1083
s588So2d233
f117L2609
Cir. DC
DkDC 90-
[3178
f936F2d[2]1334
1936F2d21334
936F2d1335
956F2d297
j956F2d299
959F2d[4]996
Cir. 1
f793FS[4]376
f793FS[5]376
Cir. 2
967F2d86
f967F2d[1]87
f967F2d[4]87
f967F2d[5]88
j967F2d90
781FS[3]179

Cir. 4
j962F2d312
f966F2d[3]877
Cir. 5
d948F2d[1]906
d948F2d[2]906
d948F2d[1]907
d948F2d[2]907
j948F2d909
965F2d[4]1356
965F2d[2]1358
j965F2d1361
970F2d[3]101
787FS[4]680
e791FS[1]1166
791FS[4]1166
791FS[5]1166
Cir. 7
d938F2d[2]788
957F2d[2]501
Cir. 8
946F2d[1]62
Cir. 9
965F2d[4]803
965F2d[5]803
f785FS[1]1428
Cir. 10

f970F2d[4]698
774FS[4]1315
774FS[5]1315
Cir. 11
949F2d1119
Ala
602So2d491
Calif
235CA3S5
235CA3S9
286CaR767
286CaR770
Colo
826P2d1285
D C
507A2d473
Fla
582So2d1258
584So2d239
584So2d240
590So2d511
594So2d266
603So2d92
Ill
22711A1047
591N2923
596N21268

La
585So2d529
Md
325Md212
325Md281
88MdA175
88MdA186
594A2d598
594A2d604
600A2d114
600A2d434
Mo
825SW345
N C
103NCA188
405S2366
N D
474NW251
Utah
825P2d705
Va
419S2862
Wash
63WAp722
821P2d1268

Parallel citation
Same case
Docket number
Jimeno cited as controlling
Refers to headnote 2 of Jimeno
Page 1334 of volume 936 of Federal Reporter, Second Series
United States Second Circuit Court of Appeals
Circuit court cases
District court case

FIGURE 6-4 The *Jimeno* case reference in Shepard's United States Citations. (From Shepard's United States Citations. Reproduced by permission of Shepard's/McGraw-Hill. Further reproduction is strictly prohibited.)

citation to *Jimeno* in Supreme Court Reporter. If you look at *Jimeno* as reprinted in Chapter 1 or Appendix A of this book, you will see that the citation given is "111 S.Ct. 1801." The "s" next to "112LE561" on the following line stands for "same case" and means that whatever is on that volume and page also has something to do with *Jimeno.* This is the citation for the United States Supreme Court granting certiorari. You would know this either by pulling 112 L. Ed. 2d 561 and reading it or by reading the third page of *Jimeno.* The third page of *Jimeno* gives the same citation for the court granting certiorari. You might have also expected that this was the citation for the Court granting certiorari because it is a few volumes lower in number than the volume containing *Jimeno.* Because of the slightly lower volume number, whatever is printed on 112 L. Ed. 2d 561 happened a year or so before *Jimeno* was decided.

On the third, fourth, and fifth lines below "**297**," there are three citations to the same case in Southern Reporter Second Series. Because *Jimeno* originally started in the state courts in Florida, those citations are probably to the lower court decisions. Looking at the syllabus on the first page of *Jimeno,* you see that "550So2d1176" is the citation to the decision from the Florida District Court of Appeal and "564So2d1083" is the citation to the decision from the Florida Supreme Court. You could also find this information by looking in volumes 550 and 564 of Southern Reporter Second Series. The reference "588So2d233" could be the citation to the same case on remand, because from the "s" you know it is the same case and the volume number is higher than the other two citations. You can check this by pulling volume 588 of Southern Reporter Second Series.

Glancing down the following two columns of citations, you notice that the decisions are first grouped by United States circuit, and then by states for state court decisions. Notice that after each federal circuit name, citations for circuit cases are given, as well as district cases within the circuit. For example, below "Cir. 2" (meaning United States Second Circuit Court of Appeals), there are citations to Federal Reporter Second Series and to Federal Supplement. The citations to Federal Reporter would be to circuit court cases and the citations to Federal Supplement are to district court cases. You know this because Federal Reporter contains only circuit court opinions and Federal Supplement contains only district court opinions. "DkDC 90–3178" gives the docket number of a District of Columbia case. The open bracket ([) in front of "3178" indicates that 3178 is part of the prior citation, but the number was too long to fit on the same line.

The citation "f936F2d²1334" means that *Jimeno* was cited on page 1334 of volume 936, Federal Reporter Second Series. The only way to know what case cited *Jimeno* is to pull volume 936 of Federal Reporter Second Series and look at page 1334. "1334" is the page on that *Jimeno* is cited and may or may not be the first page of the case. The "f" in front of "936" means that *Jimeno* was cited as controlling. The "2" refers to headnote 2 of *Jimeno* and means that the subsequent case concerned the same legal principle dealt with in headnote 2 of *Jimeno.*

Now look at Figure 6-5. This is the page from the May 1993 issue of Shepard's United States Citations that you would use to shepardize *Jimeno.* Even though the upper left-hand corner of the page says "Vol. 113," you know that you are on the right page because "**Vol. 114**" appears in the second column of the page. Page number "**297**" appears near the middle of the next-to-last column on the page. You should be reading the information below "**297**" and above "**307**." There is less information for *Jimeno* in the May 1993 volume than in the January volume. This page shows that *Jimeno* was cited in a number of United States circuit and district court opinions and in state court opinions from Arizona, California, Florida, Illinois, Missouri, and Virginia.

Notice that in the second column of the same page from May 1993, several of the page numbers are followed by "Case 2." When cases are short, several cases may be printed on one page of the reporter. Because shepardizing is done by page number, when more than one case begins on the same page, you need to look under the page number and find the case by the order in which the case appears on the page. If two cases begin on the same page and you are shepardizing the second case, you need to look under "Case 2."

Finally, look at Figure 6-6. You know that you are on the right page because "**Vol. 114**" appears in the middle of the first column and "**297**" appears near the bottom of the second column. The information for *Jimeno* in the June 1993 volume is even less. During the time period covered by the June volume, *Jimeno* was cited by a federal circuit court ("Dk8" tells us that the docket number is that of an Eighth Circuit Court of Appeals case) and state courts from Connecticut, Georgia, and Virginia.

You may not find anything in a Shepard's volume for the case you are shepardizing. This means nothing more than that the case you are shepardizing was not cited during the period covered by the volume. If you do not find anything, it is a good idea to double-check that you are looking under the right series reporter, volume, and page.

NOTE ON COMPUTER-ASSISTED LEGAL RESEARCH

Shepardizing may also be done on WESTLAW, LEXIS, or a CD-ROM edition of Shepard's. Using one of these computer-assisted legal research services to shepardize is much faster than manually checking all applicable issues of Shepard's, and there is probably less chance of error. Shepardizing using an on-line service will give more current information than shepardizing using the hard copy. The Shepard's CD-ROM may or may not give more current information than the hard-copy Shepard's, depending on when the Shepard's CD-ROM was last updated in comparison to the hard copy. The Shepard's CD-ROMs are currently updated monthly. Some editions of Shepard's on CD-ROM may include textual explanations of the importance of new citations found by shepardizing.

Vol. 113 Lawyer's Edition, United States Supreme Court Reports, 2d Series

—722—
Case 1
Cir. 6
974F2d698

—722—
Case 2
Cir. 6
j973F2d473

—724—
Case 6
Cir. 7
Dk7 91-3698
Dk7 91-3935

—724—
Case 7
Cir. 7
Dk7 88-1387

—725—
Case 6
Cir. 11
973F2d904

—732—
Case 3
Cir. 3
975F2d962

—734—
Case 4
Fla
604So2d464

—735—
Case 1
Fla
604So2d464

—735—
Case 2
Cir. 3
143BRW657

—736—
Case 1
Tex
837SW155

—736—
Case 4
Tex
825SW247

Vol. 114

—26—
Cir. 2
f801FS[1]1281
f801FS[5]1281
Cir. 5
eDk5 91-6208
Dk5 92-3622
e975F2d[2]1162
Cir. 9
Dk9 90-
[16810
Ariz
840P2d1019
Mich
491NW561
N Y
586NYS2d
[460
29COA231§ 2

—49—
Cir.2
Dk2 92-7709
Cir. 5
Dk5 91-2891
Cir. 7

—81—
Case 6
Cir. 1
Dkl 92-1639

—83—
Case 7
Mo
836SW60
838SW58

—105—
Case 4
Cir. 7
Dk7 91-2390
972F2d1466

—108—
Case 3
Cir. 10

—134—
Cir. 5
Dk5 91-5115
Cir. 9
e795FS[1]968
804FS83

—152—
Cir. 1
971F2d[9]828
797FS310
Cir. 3
Dk3 92-1483
Cir. 5
974F2d30
Cir. 9
795FS1463
Cir. 10
Dk10 91-
[4152
794FS[4]1539
Ill
601N21269
Okla
838P2d4

—277—
Cir. DC
798FS[3]45
Cir. 1
Dk1 92-1224
973 F2d [1]42
974F2d[3]228
Cir. 2
798FS[2]920
Cir. 3
f972F2d[1]1368
802FS1272
804FS653
Cir. 5
Dk5 92-3144
Dk5 91-5673
Dk5 92-8369
fDk5 91-1807
Dk5 91-1807
974F2d[1]656
977F2d[1]927
Cir. 6
Dk6 91-4071
eDk6 91-4071
Cir. 7
Dk7 91-1933
d976F2d[2]1032
e976F2d1061
978F2d413
801FS[4]225
Cir. 8
Dk8 91-3517
j973F2d1390
976F2d[3]464
803FS1580
Cir. 9
jDk9 91-
[35146
Cir. 10
Dk10 91- [1169
975F2d729
f804FS[1]276
Cir. 11
9721F2d[3]1236
f802FS[1]442
CIT
801FS748

—297—
Cir. 5
f801FS[4]1575
Cir. 8
935F2d[1]985
Cir. 9
d798FS[2]1468
Cir. 10
Dk10 92-
[3083
973F2d[4]1535
975F2d[4]1455
Cir.11
Dkl: 91-
[5719
Ariz.
838P2d1345
Calif
9CA4th1406
12CaR2d173
Fla
604So2d503
Ill
231I1A798
233I1A494
599N2194
Mo
839SW662
840SW221
Va
423S2206

State court opinions

—307—
Fla
604So2d516

—337—
Cir. 1
d146BRW158
Cir. 5
d144BRW351
Cir. 6
144BRW364
Cir. 8
f974F2d[1]991
974F2d[4]992
d143BRW[1]
[706
143BRW[4]707
Cir. 9
1143BRW746
144BRW98
e144BRW[1]99
e144BRW[2]99
Tex
835SW655
835SW657
Wis
493NW729

—350—
Cir. 1
146BRW55
e146BRW[1]57
146BRW[8]57
cir. 8
f143BRW[1]705
147BRW[3]41

—366—
pDk9 90-
[55333
Cir. 2
802FS[1]921

—385—
Cir. 3
976F2d854

—395—
Cir. 2
Dk2 92-2289
973F2d121
Cir. 3
Dk3 91-1821

Continued

FIGURE 6-5 State court opinions in Shepard's United States Citations. (From Shepard's United States Citations. Reproduced by permission of Shepard's/McGraw-Hill. Further reproduction is strictly prohibited.)

—486—
Cir. 11
eDk11 91-
[5028
—494—
Ark
cc842SW428
Cir. 11
806FS[1]1558
806FS[2]1558
—517—
Cir. 5
Vol. 114
—26—
Cir. 3
805FS[4]1137
805FS[5]1137
Cir. 9
Dk9 90-
[16810
N Y
590NYS2d
[498

—49—
Cir. DC
DkDC 91-
[3057
Cir. 5
980F2d[8]989
Cir. 9
Dk9 91-
[35662
Cir. 7
jDk7 92-1680
Cir. 8
Dk8 92-2245
fDk8 93-1650
N M
845P2d138
—297—
Cir. 8
Dk8 92-2599
Conn
30CtA175
Ga
206GaA152
424L[2]834

Va
14VaA851
—307—
Cir. 4
Dk4 90-5913
fDk4 90-5913
Cir. 8
Dk8 92-1330
14VaA1049
14VaA1050
14VaA1062
—432—
Cir. 9
Dk9 92-
[10165
Dk9 92-
[50191
dDk9 92-
[50191
Dk9 89-
[55869
Dk9 92-
La
609So2d1018

Mont
844P2d109
Ohio
605NL[2]50
Pa
617A2d721
—649—
Cir. 8
Dk8 92-2599
—660—
Cir. 3
—78—
Dkl 92-1559
eDkl 92-1559
Dkl 92-1559
Cir. 1
e807FS16
Cir. 2
806FS[8]16
f807FS18
—96—
Cir. 5
805FS[3]441

—123—
—288—
Cir. 4
980F2d950
—321—
Cir. 1
Dk1 92-2157
Dk1 92-2148
fDkl 92-1983
Dk1 92-1983
Cir. 2
Dk2 92-7306
e807FS[3]441
144FRD[1]202
Cir. 5
—410—
Cir. 5
eDk8 92-1870
—447—
Mich
495NW394

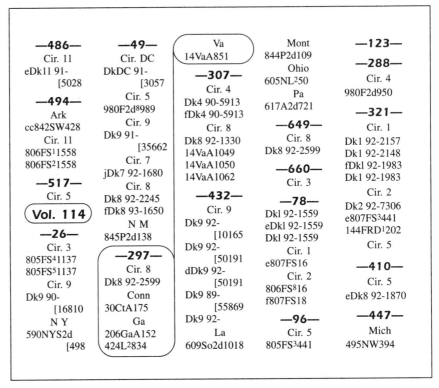

FIGURE 6-6 Updated *Jimeno* case references in Shepard's United States Citations. (From Shepard's United States Citations. Reproduced by permission of Shepard's/McGraw-Hill. Further reproduction is strictly prohibited.)

A comparison of the difference in cost to the client between shepardizing using a CALR service and using the hard-copy Shepard's could be made by comparing the costs involved and the accuracy of the results obtained. The costs of the CALR service include the cost of the service and the amount of billable time expended. The costs of shepardizing manually include the cost of the subscription and the amount of attorney time expended. The timeliness of shepardizing using a CALR service may outweigh any additional cost over shepardizing using the hard copy. In addition, the researcher shepardizing using CALR can print out a copy of the shepardizing request and the results. The printout could be kept in the appropriate file and referred to if a question arose later as to whether a particular authority had been shepardized. Some attorneys now consider it legal malpractice to have missed a recent authority available on WESTLAW or LEXIS, but not yet available in the hard copy of Shepard's.

SUMMARY

- Shepardizing involves consulting sets of books, commonly called citators or "Shepard's", to determine whether the authority you have found has been cited in any source.
- The two reasons for shepardizing are to discover whether your authority is still good law and to locate more recent authority dealing with the same legal principle found in the authority you are shepardizing.
- To shepardize an authority, consult each volume of the appropriate Shepard's set to see whether your authority has been cited in any other source.
- Shepardizing must be done systematically or you may miss something.
- Check to determine that you are shepardizing under the correct volume and series of the correct reporter and that you have consulted every applicable Shepard's volume.
- Consult the abbreviation tables at the beginning of each Shepard's volume to determine what an abbreviation stands for.
- Single-letter abbreviations in the left-hand margin of a column of a Shepard's citator indicate whether an authority has been affirmed, reversed, or vacated.
- Other single-letter abbreviations indicate the treatment of the authority you are shepardizing in other sources.
- Shepard's case citations are grouped by court: federal courts in descending order and then state court decisions arranged alphabetically.
- Shepardizing may also be done on WESTLAW, LEXIS, or a CD-ROM edition of Shepard's.

RESEARCH ASSIGNMENTS

Legal Research Assignment—Shepardizing

1. What is the name of the Shepard's you would use to shepardize decisions of the United States Supreme Court?
2. What is the name of the Shepard's you would use to shepardize decisions of the United States district and circuit courts?
3. What is the name of the Shepard's you would use to shepardize decisions of the state courts of your state?
4. a. What is the citation for the case that overruled *Plessy v. Ferguson,* 163 U.S. 537, 16 S. Ct. 1138, 41 L. Ed. 256 (1896)?
   b. What is the citation for the case that overruled *Wolf v. Colorado,* 338 U.S. 25, 69 S. Ct. 1359, 93 L. Ed. 1782 (1949)?
   c. What is the citation for the case that overruled *Monroe v. Pape,* 365 U.S. 167, 81 S. Ct. 473, 5 L. Ed. 2d 492 (1961)?

5. The following cases were appealed to the United States Circuit Court. Give the proper citation to the following cases on appeal:
   a. *Sexton v. Gibbs,* 327 F. Supp. 134.
   b. *United States v. Walker,* 751 F. Supp. 199.
   c. *McKay v. Hammock,* 542 F. Supp. 972.
6. a. What is the proper citation to *Sexton v. Gibbs,* 327 F. Supp. 134, including subsequent history?
   b. What is the proper citation to *United States v. Walker,* 751 F. Supp. 199, including subsequent history?
   c. What is the proper citation to *McKay v. Hammock,* 542 F. Supp. 972, including subsequent history?
7. The following cases were later decided by the United States Supreme Court. Give the proper citation to the decision of the following cases in the United States Supreme Court:
   a. *Sokolow v. United States,* 831 F.2d 1413.
   b. *Jacobson v. United States,* 916 F.2d 467.
8. a. What is the proper citation to *Sokolow v. United States,* 831 F.2d 1413, including subsequent history?
   b. What is the proper citation to *Jacobson v. United States,* 916 F.2d 467, including subsequent history?
9. The following cases were later decided by the United States Circuit Court and United States Supreme Court. Give the proper citation to the decision of the following cases in the United States Supreme Court:
   a. *Cipollone v. Liggett Group, Inc.,* 693 F. Supp. 208.
   b. Weisman v. Lee, 728 F. Supp. 68.
10. a. What is the proper citation to *Cipollone v. Liggett Group, Inc.,* 693 F. Supp. 208, including subsequent history?
    b. What is the proper citation to *Weisman v. Lee,* 728 F. Supp. 68, including subsequent history?
11. a. What is the proper citation to *United States v. Parcel of Land, Buildings, Appurtenances, & Improvements, 92 Buena Vista Avenue,* 738 F. Supp. 854, including subsequent history?
    b. What is the proper citation to *International Society for Krishna Consciousness, Inc. v. Lee,* 721 F. Supp. 572, including subsequent history?
12. a. What is the proper citation to *Medious v. Department of Highway Safety & Motor Vehicles,* 534 So. 2d 729, including subsequent history?
    b. What is the proper citation to *State v. Jimeno,* 550 So. 2d 1176, including subsequent history?
    c. What is the proper citation to *Inciarrano v. State,* 447 So. 2d 386, including subsequent history?
    d. What is the proper citation to the United States Supreme Court case that cited *Doe v. Sarasota-Bradenton Florida Television Co.,* 436 So. 2d 328?

13. a. What is the proper citation to the case that explained the importance of *Jacobson v. United States,* 916 F.2d 467? (Use only the hardbound Shepard's volumes to answer this question.)
    b. What is the proper citation to the case that followed *Sexton v. Gibbs,* 327 F. Supp. 134?
    c. What is the proper citation to the case that distinguished *Sexton v. Gibbs,* 327 F. Supp. 134?
    d. What is the proper citation to the case that followed *Jacobson v. United States,* 916 F.2d 467?
    e. What is the proper citation to the case that distinguished *State v. Jimeno,* 550 So. 2d 1176?
14. a. What is the citation of the case printed at 7 A.L.R. 2d 1280?
    b. What is the citation of the case printed at 3 A.L.R. 5th 1119?
    c. What is the citation of the A.L.R. Fed. article citing *Cipollone v. Liggett Group, Inc.,* 693 F. Supp. 208?
    d. What is the citation of the A.L.R. article citing *Medious v. Department of Highway Safety & Motor Vehicles,* 534 So. 2d 729?
15. a. What is the proper citation to the case that cited *Sokolow v. United States,* 831 F.2d 1413 in its dissenting opinion?
    b. What is the proper citation to the United States Supreme Court case that cited *McKay v. Hammock,* 730 F.2d 1367 in its dissenting opinion?
    c. What is the proper citation to the case that cited *Sexton v. Gibbs,* 327 F. Supp. 134 in its dissenting opinion?
    d. What is the proper citation to the case that cited *Medious v. Department of Highway Safety & Motor Vehicles,* 534 So. 2d 729 in its dissenting opinion?
16. a. What is the proper citation to the case that follows the point set forth in headnote 2 of *Sokolow v. United States,* 831 F.2d 1413? (Use only the hardbound Shepard's volumes.)
    b. What is the proper citation to the case that follows the point set forth in headnote 4 of *Jacobson v. United States,* 916 F.2d 467? (Use only the hardbound Shepard's volumes.)
    c. What is the proper citation to the case that follows the point set forth in headnote 1 of *Weisman v. Lee,* 728 F. Supp. 68? (Use only the hardbound Shepard's volumes.)
    d. What is the proper citation to the case that follows the point set forth in headnote 7 of *Medious v. Department of Highway Safety & Motor Vehicles,* 534 So. 2d 729? (Use only the hardbound Shepard's volumes.)
17. Has *Doe v. Sarasota-Bradenton Florida Television Co.,* 436 So. 2d 328 (1983) ever been cited in a law review article? If so, give the citation to the law review article, including the volume and page on which *Doe* was cited.
18. Using Shepard's United States Case Names Citator, look up the following cases and give the proper citation to each:
    a. The 1973 United States Supreme Court decision *Roe v. Wade.*

b. The 1963 United States Supreme Court decision *Gideon v. Wainright.*
c. The 1968 United States Supreme Court decision *Terry v. Ohio.*
d. The 1966 United States Supreme Court decision *Miranda v. Arizona.*
e. The 1991 United States Supreme Court decision *California v. Acevedo.*

19. Using Shepard's Federal Case Names Citator, look up the following cases and give the proper citation to each:
    a. The 1989 United States Circuit Court decision *Melear v. Spears.*
    b. The 1986 United States Circuit Court decision *United States v. $41,305.00 in Currency & Traveler's Checks.*
    c. The 1991 United States District Court decision *United States v. $14,500.00 in United States Currency.*
    d. The 1991 United States District Court decision *United States v. Borromeo.*
20. Using Shepard's Florida Case Names Citator, look up the following cases and give the proper citation to each:
    a. The 1992 Florida state court decision *In re Forfeiture of 1985 Ford Ranger Pickup Truck.*
    b. The 1987 Florida state court decision *In re Forfeiture of $6,003.00 in U.S. Currency.*
    c. The 1992 Florida state court decision *Brown v. State.*
21. a. What does "ABA(2)" stand for?
    b. What does "BRW" stand for?
    c. What does "FRD" stand for?
    d. What does "CR" stand for?
    e. What does "HLR" stand for?
    f. What does "YLJ" stand for?

CHAPTER 7
Overview of the Research Process

OUTLINE

Gathering Information
Identifying Key Terms
Learning about the General Topic
Locating Primary Sources
Note on Computer-Assisted Legal Research

COMMON LEGAL SOURCES AND FINDING TOOLS

Primary Sources	Secondary Sources	Finding Tools
reporters	treatises	American Law Reports
constitutions	law review articles	legal encyclopedias
statutes	legal periodicals	digests
administrative regulations	law dictionaries	Shepard's Citators
court rules	legal thesauruses	*Index to Legal Periodicals*
loose-leaf services	continuing legal education publications	loose-leaf services
	Restatements	
	American Law Reports	
	legal encyclopedias	
	loose-leaf services	

Step 1—Gather and study all relevant information for search and seizure problem:

- statements of Williams brothers
- statement of witnesses
- police report
- cash receipt
- newspaper articles on forfeiture
- car trader magazines
- home mortgage documents
- police videotape
- court documents from class action

Now that you have learned about the basic types of law books a legal researcher would use, it is time to discuss how to use them together. This chapter also discusses basic research strategies. Throughout the chapter, the Williams search and seizure problem from Appendix A is used as an example.

Before you start researching, you need to get organized. One way to organize your research is to keep a research journal in which you record any relevant information you have found. A research journal may seem time consuming at the beginning of your research. However, the time you spend writing in your research journal should help you focus your research. Refer to the Figure 7-1 for tips on keeping a research journal. Reviewing your research journal from time to time will remind you of what avenues of research you have pursued. Keep thinking of other key words, topics, and sources you could use and don't forget to check each of the primary and secondary sources you have learned about in this book.

GATHERING INFORMATION

The length of time you spend researching in the law library will probably be shortened by the time you spend organizing and gathering information beforehand. If you start researching without gathering all relevant

RESEARCH JOURNAL

Purposes:

1. To document your progress in researching a legal problem.
2. To document the development of your factual and legal analysis of a legal problem.

Procedure:

1. Log in the date and time you spent on the legal problem.
2. Note key terms, legal issues, citations, legal sources consulted, etc.
3. Describe how you spent your time (reading, researching, discussing, reflecting, writing) and how your understanding of the legal problem was affected.
4. Note any ideas you came up with that may be useful in understanding the problem.
5. Pose questions frequently to keep your thinking focused.
6. Note what research avenues did and did not lead to answers.
7. Record the results of shepardizing.
8. Reread previous entries and make comments on the facing pages.

FIGURE 7-1 Research journal tips.

information, you may spend hours researching a question that could have been answered by reviewing pertinent documents or gathering more facts.

If you were given the assignment to research the Williams search and seizure problem, you would start by reviewing the information you have. This means that you would carefully read the fact pattern contained in Appendix A. Then you would gather all other relevant information. If possible, you would talk to the Williams brothers, the officer, and anyone else who might have information. Gather any documents related to the incident. The documents might include materials substantiating the Williamses' story, such as car trader magazines and any paperwork showing how the brothers raised the $35,000 in cash. You might be able to obtain materials from the sheriff's office or the DEA. Any reports concerning the incident and a copy of the receipt the brothers signed would be important. The incident may have been videotaped from the patrol car. If so, it would be extremely important to obtain a copy of the videotape. You could obtain copies of newspaper articles describing similar stops by Volusia County sheriff officers, and you should obtain a copy of any relevant documents filed in the civil rights class action lawsuit. Relevant newspaper articles are reproduced in Appendix A.

Step 2—Identify key terms:

- fourth amendment
- search and seizure
- car automobile
- vehicle
- forfeit
- civil rights
- race discrimination

IDENTIFYING KEY TERMS

The next step is to review all the information you have gathered and use it to identify key terms and issues. The key terms can be used to start your research in the indexes to secondary or primary sources. From the search and seizure problem, you might make a list of the following terms: "search and seizure," "car," "drug courier profile," "Fourth Amendment," "class action," and "civil rights." Because the indexes you consult may use words other than the ones you have identified, brainstorm to identify other words with similar meanings or related words. A legal thesaurus might be helpful at this point. From branstorming and consulting a legal thesaurus, you might think of "dispossession," "forfeit," "vehicle," "automobile," and "race discrimination." As you progress in your research, add any other key words you find to your list.

Step 3—Learn more about the area of law you are researching through:

- legal encyclopedias
- ALR annotations
- loose-leaf services
- treatises
- textbooks
- law review articles
- legal periodicals

Note the following in your learning journal:

- citations to relevant authority
- possible issues
- applicable jurisdiction (federal, state, or local)

Make a checklist of publications to review

LEARNING ABOUT THE GENERAL TOPIC

If you know little or nothing about the area of law involved in the problem you are researching, a good beginning point in your research is to read a textual explanation of that area of the law. Legal encyclopedias and American Law Reports are the two most widely available sources of this type of information. Check to see whether your library has any loose-leaf services that cover the area you are researching. Use the key words you have identified to locate relevant topics in legal encyclopedias, relevant annotations in American Law Reports, and relevant materials in loose-leaf services.

Step 4—Locate primary authority by:

1. using citations found in secondary authority;
2. using indexes to find relevant statutes, constitutional provisions; adminstrative regulations, and court rules; and
3. using digests to find relevant cases.

By looking in the index to *American Jurisprudence* and American Law Reports, someone researching the search and seizure problem would locate the following materials:

36 Am. Jur. 2d *Forfeitures and Penalties* (1968).
Annotation, *Effect of Forfeiture Proceedings under the Controlled Substances Act or Similar Statute on Lien against Property Subject to Forfeiture,* 1 A.L.R.5th 317 (1992).

Chapter 2 contains a copy of a page from this *American Jurisprudence* topic and the first page of this *American Jurisprudence* annotation.

Law review and legal periodical articles may give you even more specific information. *Index to Legal Periodicals* is a good source to use to locate these articles either by subject or by author. Familiarize yourself with other resources available in your library, including treatises and hornbooks. A legal textbook covering the area of law you are researching may be another good place to start. Appendix A contains a textual explanation of some aspects of search and seizure and the exclusionary rule. It is entitled "Search and Seizure and the Exclusionary Rule" and contains information adapted from a criminal law textbook.

As you read about the topic you are researching, note in your journal anything that may be helpful to you later (citations to relevant authority, possible issues, and applicable jurisdiction (federal, state, or local)). Also make a checklist of the publications to review. Make sure to list primary and secondary sources and finding tools for federal, state, and local jurisdictions.

If you are knowledgeable in the topic you are researching or have a primary source to work with, you may want to start researching in primary sources first. Even a knowledgeable researcher would be glad to quickly locate a law review or legal periodical article on point. The article usually saves the researcher time by summarizing the law in the area and citing relevant authority. The researcher can pull the cited authority, read it, update it, and pursue another avenue of research.

LOCATING PRIMARY SOURCES

Using Secondary Sources, Indexes, and Digests

Armed with general knowledge about search and seizure and civil forfeiture, you are ready to locate primary sources. There is no one right place to start to locate primary sources. You may first want to locate primary sources by using the citations noted in your research journal. If you think the problem involves a statute, constitution, administrative regulation, or court rule, consult the appropriate index.

For example, you would find the text of the fourth amendment by looking in the index to the Constitution under "search and seizure." You would find the federal forfeiture statute (21 U.S.C. 881) by looking in the index to the United States Code or an annotated code under "forfeiture"; you would find the federal court rule governing class actions (Rule 23) by looking in the index to the Federal Rules of Civil Procedure under "class action"; you would find the federal administrative regulations governing forfeiture (21 C.F.R. §§ 1316.71–1316.81) in the index to the Code of Federal Regulations under "forfeiture." Chapter 5 contains copies of those materials.

Consult a digest to find relevant cases. You can find cases in the digest either by consulting the Descriptive-Word Indexes (located at the end of the digest set) or reviewing a topic outline (printed at the beginning of each topic). When you locate a primary source, use the primary source to locate other primary sources. For example, you could look in the descriptive word index to Federal Practice Digest 4th under "search and seizure." The index would tell you that there is a digest topic "Searches and Seizures." You could look at the outline at the beginning of the topic to identify relevant key numbers. You would find *Florida v. Jimeno* under various key numbers of the topic.

Step 5—Once you have found primary authority, use the primary authority to locate other primary authority.

If you have a statute or constitutional provision:

1. Pull any primary authority referenced in the statute or constitutional provision.
2. Consult an annotated code or constitution.
3. Shepardize.

If you have a relevant case:

1. Pull any cases referenced in the known case.
2. Use the headnotes of the known case to locate other cases in the digest.
3. Shepardize.

By Using Other Primary Authority

What do you do after you find a relevant statutory or constitutional provision? Once you find a relevant statutory or constitutional provision, there are three ways to use the provision to locate other primary authority. First, read the provision carefully and note any cross-references to other statutory or constitutional authority. Then pull the authorities referenced. Also examine how the provision fits with other statutory or constitutional provisions. You may find definitions of terms or related statutory provisions.

The second way is to consult an annotated code or constitution. Locate the applicable statute or constitutional provision and begin reading the references following the provision. The references may refer you to related constitutional provisions, statutes, and administrative regulations, as well as digest topics, legal encyclopedia topics, and law review articles. Then read the case summaries. If a reference or case summary involves the same question you are researching, make a note of the citation, pull the authority, and read it. A third way to locate other authority is to shepardize your constitutional or statutory provision.

What do you do after you find a relevant case? Once you find a relevant case, there are three ways to use the case to locate other cases. The first way is to read the relevant case and note the citations to earlier cases cited in it. Then pull and read any of those earlier cases which seem helpful. A second way is to make note of relevant headnotes from the case, locate the same digest topic in the digest, and read the digest annotations to locate more cases. A third way of locating cases is to shepardize the relevant case. Shepardizing will give you citations to later cases citing the case being shepardized. The relevant case may also give you citations to other primary sources, such as statutes, constitutional provisions, court rules, or administrative regulations.

When are you finished with your research? You are probably finished when you have checked each of the primary and secondary sources and you keep coming up with the same authorities. Before you stop, double-check to make sure you have shepardized any authorities you intend to use and follow any other avenues of research suggested by the information you obtain from shepardizing.

NOTE ON COMPUTER-ASSISTED LEGAL RESEARCH

If you have access to computer-assisted legal research, take advantage of it in your research if possible. You may want to do all your research on the computer, use a combination of CALR and traditional research, or use CALR only for shepardizing. If you are researching an area of the law with which you are not familiar, you may want to do some reading in a legal encyclopedia, an American Law Report, or a law review article and then complete your research on the computer. CALR allows you to search by key words found in primary sources, rather requiring you to know the legal terminology under which a legal principle is indexed. CALR also allows certain searches, such as by judge and attorney, that are impossible using hard copy.

If your educational institution has a special educational rate allowing unlimited on-line research for the same basic fee, cost would not be a factor in planning or executing your searches. Cost is a real factor, however, if the on-line service you are using charges for on-line time. On the job, if you are charged for on-line time, you may find yourself doing more research in the hard copy and using the on-line service after carefully formulating a query and using the on-line service for shepardizing.

A fascinating feature of the on-line services and, to some extent, of the CD-ROMs is *linking*. Linking allows you to instantly move from the source you are reading to another cited source. For example, you may be reading a case that cites a particular statute. While reading the case, you would like to refer to the statutory language. CALR allows you, with the touch of a few buttons, to jump to the text of the statute, read the statute, and jump back to the case.

On-line services give you access to secondary sources such as treatises and law reviews. News sources such as newspapers may also be available. The types of information available on-line are continually growing. Consult your manual for a complete listing of the libraries and information available on-line.

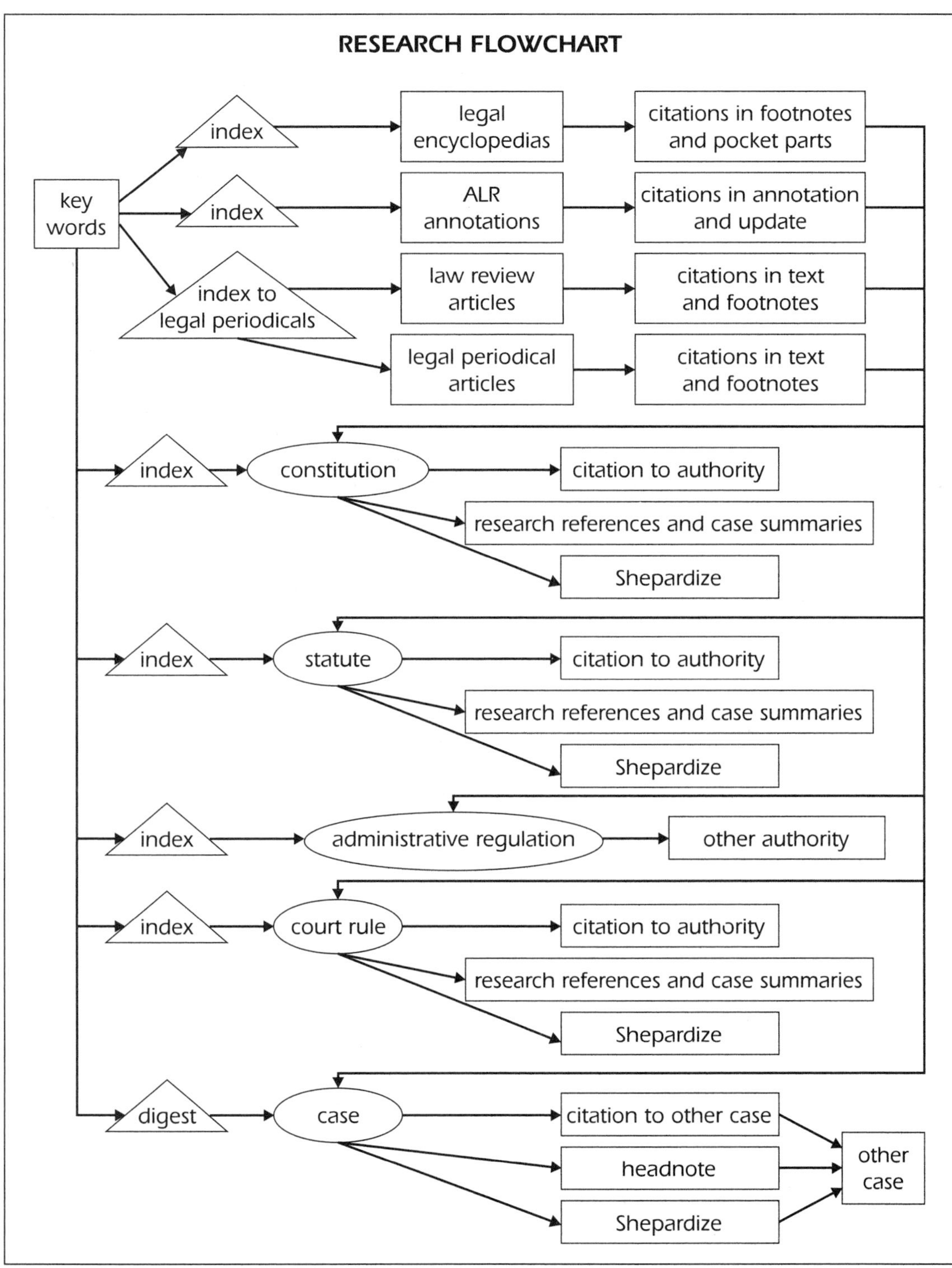

Research flowchart.

SUMMARY

- Before you start researching in the law library, gather and organize information and read all pertinent documents.
- Throughout the research process, take notes of what you have found, citations to relevant authority, and ideas for other avenues of research.
- Review all the information you have gathered and use it to identify key terms and issues.
- You may want to learn more about the area of law you are researching by consulting secondary sources such as legal encyclopedias, American Law Reports annotations, loose-leaf services, and law review articles.
- Locate primary authority by using citations found in secondary authority, indexes, and digests.
- Use primary authority to locate other primary authority through reading cited primary authority, case summaries in annotated codes and constitutions, and shepardizing.
- You are probably finished with your research when you have checked each of the main primary and secondary sources and keep coming up with the same authorities.
- Consult the Research Flowchart in this chapter to develop a research strategy or explore other avenues of research.
- Computer-assisted legal research may allow certain searches, such as by judge and attorney, that are impossible using hard copy.

EXERCISES

1. Pick one of the research problems from Appendix G.
2. Research the problem you have chosen.
3. List the citations to any relevant legal sources.
4. Using your research, write the answers(s) to the selected research problem.

PART II
Legal Writing

CHAPTER 8
Introduction to Legal Writing

OUTLINE

IMPORTANCE OF GOOD LEGAL WRITING TO THE LAW

Good legal writing is vitally important to those professionally involved with the law. Attorneys, judges, and paralegals are in the business of communicating, and their success depends in great part on how well they write. As explained in this chapter, the goal of a legal document may be to inform, to persuade, or to record information, depending on the document. Serious problems with meeting any of these goals may have negative consequences. For the judge, a poorly written opinion or order may result in reversal on appeal. For the attorney, errors in legal writing may result in loss of a case, loss of a client, litigation of ambiguously written legal documents, legal malpractice lawsuits, or professional sanctions. A paralegal may lose a job over a poorly written document.

This chapter briefly discusses the many different types of legal documents, and this book devotes an entire chapter to some of the most important ones—client opinion letters, contracts, law office memos, memoranda of law, pleadings, and appellate briefs. Chapter 9 discusses fundamentals of writing that apply to all types of legal documents. Appendix D of this book explains how to avoid some of the most common mechanical errors in legal writing and provides exercises for you to practice what you have learned. Appendix B explains citation rules and Appendix C explains rules for quotations and short-form citations. Appendixes B and C also provide exercises for you to practice what you have learned.

Don't be intimidated by legal writing. Although certain things, such as citation form and the format for some legal documents, are peculiar to legal writing, legal writing in many ways is not that different from the writing you have done in the past. You can think of learning legal writing as fine-tuning the writing skills you already have. In addition, just because you are doing legal writing does not mean that you leave your common sense behind. You will often have to draw on your own experience in analyzing problems and in brainstorming to arrive at solutions.

Writing is not easy—not for good writers, nor even for professional writers. Your writing will improve with practice and a good grasp of the fundamentals. This book is designed to give you practice in legal writing and to explain those fundamentals.

WRITING AS COMMUNICATION

The purpose of all writing, including legal writing, is to communicate. For centuries, legal writing has been criticized for being wordy and hard to understand because of the use of Latin phrases and legal terms. Although not universally accepted, the trend is to write legal documents in plain English. (Statutes in some states require consumer contracts to be written in plain English.) Writing in plain English means writing so the document can be easily understood. It requires good organization and format combined with elimination of excess words, Latin phrases, and unnecessary legal terms. This book stresses writing legal documents in plain English. Keep in mind the plain English lessons from this book and practice plain English whenever possible.

One common-sense thing you have probably done in your past writing is to think of your audience. You need to do the same in legal writing. Before you start writing, determine who your audience will be. For a client letter, it will be the client. For a memorandum of law, it will be the judge and opposing counsel. For a contract, it will be the parties to the contract. These are the obvious answers. Then think who else must understand what you have written. For example, documents designed to record information, such as deeds, contracts, and wills, may end up being litigated. A cautious writer of those types of documents will keep in mind the attorneys who might litigate and the judge who might interpret the meaning of those documents.

While writing, ask yourself whether your intended (and perhaps your unintended) audience will understand your communication. If you are writing to the client, will the client understand what you have written? If not, explain your message in simpler terms. Are the words you use too abstract or inexact? If so, use more specific words or explain yourself in more detail. Are any words too ambiguous? If so, try defining any ambiguous words. (Being abstract, inexact, or ambiguous is acceptable only if your client doesn't suffer and it is impossible to be more concrete, exact, or precise because necessary information is not known.)

Your ultimate goal is to have your reader comprehend what you have written. If you think your reader will have trouble doing so, revise your document. Even if your reader will understand what you have written, can you add more transitional language or signposts to make the document easier to understand? (The terms *transitional language* and *signposts* are explained in Chapter 9.) One way to determine whether your writing is easy to understand is to read the document out loud. Revise the parts of the document that do not sound right when being read out loud. Another way is to have someone else not familiar with the subject matter read your document. Ask that person what passages were hard to understanding and revise them.

A Warning Against Communicating Too Much

Although this book stresses communicating and writing in plain English, you must be careful not to communicate too much. If you were playing poker, you wouldn't let the other players see your hand. Just as you guard your poker hand, an attorney representing the client's best interests guards against certain information being disclosed and is careful about how information is presented. Care in word choice is extremely important because anything in writing may easily be used against the writer later. An attorney dealing with a confidential matter may refrain from putting the matter in writing for this very reason. If the information is adverse to the client, it may be better to communicate the information orally rather than to put it in writing.

In contrast, a paper trail is often useful as proof of exactly what was communicated. Some information should be written so that it can have legal effect now and be referred to later (contracts, wills, deeds, court documents). An attorney may put advice or information in writing in case there is any question later as to what the attorney communicated. A client opinion is often put in writing so the client can study it in detail and refer to it later; putting the advice in writing also protects the attorney if the client tries to apply the advice to some future situation beyond the scope of the opinion letter. Certain information may be given to an opposing attorney in writing to furnish proof that the opposing attorney was made aware of the information.

ELIMINATION OF MECHANICAL ERRORS

Communicating is the fun part of legal writing. The other necessary, though tedious, part is eliminating mechanical errors. You must do your best to eliminate mechanical errors for two reasons. First, you want your reader to concentrate on your message and not be distracted by mechanical errors. Second, a reader who spots a number of mechanical errors will begin to wonder if the writer was sloppy. If the writer didn't take the time to proofread for typographical and spelling errors, perhaps the writer's sloppiness extended to legal research too. You don't want to lose your credibility over a few easily eliminated mechanical errors.

In this author's experience, students typically have trouble with three categories of mechanical errors. You are already familiar with the first category of mechanical errors from your previous writing experience. These errors, which include problems with apostrophes, antecedents, spelling, run-on sentences, sentence fragments, parallel construction, and sequence of tenses, are discussed in Appendix D.

The second category of mechanical errors will be new to you if you have not had previous legal writing experience. This category includes problems with quotations and citations. The rules for quotations and citations are discussed in Appendixes C and D.

Third-category mechanical errors include errors other than errors in quotations and short form citations that are peculiar to legal writing. This category includes research errors such as quoting from a headnote or case syllabus, not using plain English, not giving a page reference to material from a primary or secondary source, not quoting exactly, plagiarizing, using contractions in formal legal documents, using the word "I" in formal legal documents, and elegant variation (using more than one word to refer to the same thing). These errors are discussed in Chapter 9.

TYPES OF LEGAL WRITING

The purposes of legal documents are to inform, to persuade, to record information, and to set forth the law to be followed. The balance of this chapter discusses the different types of legal documents falling within the first three categories: documents designed to inform, persuade, or record information. Cases, statutes, court rules, and administrative rules and regulations are specialized types of legal writing that set forth the law. You are already somewhat familiar with the substance and format of these documents from your legal research course, although further discussion of them is beyond the scope of this book.

Legal Writing Designed to Inform

The purpose of a transmittal letter, a client letter, a letter to a third party, an opinion letter, or a law office memo is to inform. (The client letter and the letter to a third party are also dealt with in the following section because another purpose of those documents is to persuade.) As the name suggests, a *client letter* is written to the client. The subject matter of a client letter may be anything from a simple cover letter explaining a document attached to the letter, to a letter containing basic facts such as the date and time of a closing, to a letter answering a legal question the client has asked. The first two types of client letters are often referred to as *transmittal letters.* The purpose of a transmittal letter is to communicate basic information. The letter answering a legal question the client has asked is often referred to as a *client opinion letter.* It is the most complicated and takes care to write. The transmittal letter and the client opinion letter are the subject of Chapter 10.

A client letter and a letter to a third party may be similar in subject matter, but usually differ in treatment of that subject matter. The two letters will likely differ in substance and wording because certain things may be discussed in confidence with the client that would not be revealed to a third party. Care in word choice is essential, because anything contained in a letter may later be used against the writer should the matter be litigated.

Be careful not to confuse a client opinion letter with an opinion letter. When attorneys refer to an *opinion letter,* they usually mean a formal letter written by an attorney in which the attorney gives an opinion as to whether a transaction is legal. The attorney writing the opinion letter is the attorney for one of the parties to the transaction. For example, an opinion letter may be required in a loan closing, a securities offering, or a real estate closing. The opinion letter is usually addressed to one of the other parties to the transaction. Its status is that of professional work product, and the party may sue the attorney who wrote the letter if the transaction does not turn out as the attorney stated in the letter. This type of opinion letter is beyond the scope of this book, but the client opinion letter is discussed extensively in Chapter 10.

The *law office memo* is used to inform the reader of the results of legal research. The information in the law office memo is used by the client or the attorney to solve the problem researched. The law office memo is discussed extensively in Chapter 13.

Legal Documents Designed to Persuade

As previously discussed, a second purpose of the client letter and the letter to a third party is to persuade. This is also the purpose of a pleading, a memorandum of law, and an appellate brief. The job of the attorney is to represent the client's best interests by persuading others that the client's argument is the one that should be adopted.

Let's think for a moment how the client's argument is formulated. Imagine that two parties have a contract dispute. The attorneys have in front of them the same contract and, if they have competently performed their legal research, the same primary and secondary authority. Each attorney reviews the contract and any authority in the light most favorable to the client. Just as there are two sides to every story, there are at least two arguments that can be made on the same set of facts. Each attorney will argue that the contract interpretation most favorable to the client applies and distinguish any interpretation not supporting the client's position. If the law seems to be contrary to the client's position, the attorney can argue for a change in the law or can argue that the law should not be enforced because it is unconscionable or unconstitutional.

A client letter, a letter to a third party, a pleading, a memorandum of law, and an appellate brief may all contain the same legal argument. The differences among them are the time frame in which each is used and the format. Let's take a closer look at each of these documents.

Although the client letter and the letter to a third party may be used at any time, they are often used as persuasive documents prior to or in anticipation of litigation. Both types of letters analyze a problem and argue persuasively that the problem should be resolved in a certain way. The letter to a third party may conclude by saying that the client will be forced to file a lawsuit if the third party does not resolve the problem as suggested in the letter. After the lawsuit has been filed, the letter to that third party may also be used as a persuasive document in pretrial settlement negotiations.

Pleadings are formal statements by the parties to a lawsuit setting forth their claims or defenses. Examples of pleadings include a complaint, an answer, and a counterclaim. The format and basic substance of civil pleadings are governed by the Federal Rules of Civil Procedure for federal courts and by state rules of civil procedure for state courts.

A **memorandum of law** is a written document containing the attorney's argument substantiated by relevant authority. At the trial level, an attorney may prepare, or may be required to prepare, a memorandum of law, the purpose of which is to persuade the judge to reach a particular decision. The format for a memorandum of law is discussed extensively in Chapter 14.

An *appellate* **brief** is a formal statement by a party submitted to the appellate court. When a case is appealed, each attorney submits a written statement to the appellate court to persuade the court of the correctness of the client's position. An appellate brief argues the facts of the case and the applicable law, supported by citations of authority. The format for an appellate brief is discussed extensively in Chapter 15.

Legal Documents Designed to Record Information

The primary purpose of a deed, contract, will, case brief, or a corporate document is to record information so the information can be referred to later. These documents are sometimes referred to as *planning documents* because they set forth a plan of what will happen in the future so the parties can avoid litigation. Well-written planning documents should prevent rather than encourage litigation. Let's look at these planning documents.

A **deed** is a document by which real property or an interest in real property is transferred from one person to another. A deed contains the names of the parties, the date, the operative words transferring the property, and the property description. A **warranty deed** contains title covenants (promises made by the person transferring the property that certain things are

LEGAL TERMS

pleadings
Formal statements by the parties to an action setting forth their claims or defenses. . . . The various kinds of pleadings, and the rules governing them, are set forth in detail in the Federal Rules of Civil Procedure and, with respect to pleading in state courts, by the rules of civil procedure of the several states. These rules of procedure abolished common law pleading.

memorandum of law
A written statement submitted to a court for the purpose of persuading [the court] of the correctness of one's position. It is similar to a brief, although usually not as extensive.

brief
1. A written statement submitted to a court for the purpose of persuading [the court] of the correctness of one's position. A brief argues the facts of the case and the applicable law, supported by citations of authority. 2. A text that an attorney prepares to guide him or her in the trial of a case. Called a *trial brief*, it can include lists of questions to be asked of various witnesses, points to be covered, and arguments to be made. 3. An outline of the published opinion in a case, made by an attorney or a paralegal for the purpose of understanding the case.

true concerning title to the property), whereas a **quitclaim deed** does not. Although there are similarities in the format for deeds from state to state, real property transactions are largely creatures of state law, so the law of the state in which the property is located should be consulted as to any particular format required.

A **contract** is an agreement entered into to do or refrain from doing a particular thing. The contract must be supported by adequate **consideration** (that which is given in exchange for performance or the promise to perform), must involve an undertaking that is legal to perform, and must be based on mutuality of agreement and obligation between at least two competent parties. The format for a contract is extensively discussed in Chapter 11.

A **will** is an instrument by which a person makes a disposition of his or her property, to take effect after death. A will contains the name of the person making the will, the date, the operative words willing that person's property, and the property description. In contrast to a deed, a will is revocable during a person's lifetime. Although there are similarities in the format for wills from state to state, wills are also largely creatures of state laws, so the law of the state in which the property is located should be consulted as to any particular format required.

A *case brief* is an outline or summary of a published court opinion. One reason to brief a case is to understand the case better by identifying its important parts. The other reason to brief a case is to be able to refer to the case brief to refresh one's memory without having to read the whole case over again. Although the format for a case brief varies from person to person, some standard parts of a case brief are the case citation, the facts, the history of the case, the issue(s), the answer(s), the reasoning, and the result.

Corporate documents are those documents necessary, usual, or permitted for the establishment and operation of a corporation. Because the corporation is a creature of statute, it comes into existence only upon compliance with the requirements of state statute. Generally, state statutes require articles of incorporation or a corporate charter to be filed with the secretary of state and an incorporation fee to be paid. Other corporate documents include bylaws, rules, and minutes. The format for corporate documents is beyond the scope of this book.

deed
A document by which real property, or an interest in real property, is conveyed from one person to another.

warranty deed
A deed that contains title covenants.

quitclaim deed
A deed that conveys whatever interest the grantor has in a piece of real property, as distinguished from the more usual deed which conveys a fee and contains various covenants, particularly title covenants. A quitclaim deed is often referred to simply as a "quitclaim."

contract
An agreement entered into, for adequate consideration, to do, or refrain from doing, a particular thing. The Uniform Commercial Code defines a contract as the total legal obligation resulting from the parties' agreement. In addition to adequate consideration, the transaction must involve an undertaking that is legal to perform, and there must be mutuality of agreement and obligation between at least two competent parties.

SUMMARY

- Good legal writing is vitally important to attorneys, judges, and paralegals.
- The trend is to write legal documents in plain English (writing so the document can be easily understood).
- Your ultimate goal is to have your reader understand what you have written.
- Legal writing also involves eliminating mechanical errors. This book tells you how to eliminate mechanical errors common to writing in general and how to avoid errors in quotations and citations, as well as how to prevent mechanical errors peculiar to legal writing.

- The purposes of legal documents are to inform, to persuade, to record information, and to set forth the law to be followed.
- This book devotes a chapter to the transmittal letter (designed to inform) and the client opinion letter (designed to inform and persuade); a chapter to the contract (designed to record information); a chapter to pleadings (designed to persuade); a chapter to the law office memo (designed to inform); a chapter to the memorandum of law (designed to persuade); and a chapter to the appellate brief (designed to persuade).
- The purpose of a transmittal letter is to communicate information. The client opinion letter answers a client's legal question.
- A contract is an agreement between two or more parties entered into to do or to refrain from doing a particular thing.
- Pleadings are formal statements by the parties to a lawsuit setting forth their claims or defenses.
- The law office memo is used to inform the reader of the results of legal research.
- A memorandum of law is a document, usually filed with the court, that contains the attorney's argument substantiated by relevant authority.
- An appellate brief is a formal statement by a party submitted to the appellate court.

EXERCISES

1. Why is good legal writing important to the legal profession?
2. How does legal writing resemble or differ from writing you have done in the past?
3. Who are the audiences for the different types of legal writing referred to in this chapter?
4. Is it always a good idea for legal writing to communicate as much as possible?
5. Where could you look in this book to find out how to eliminate mechanical errors from legal writing?
6. Name types of legal writing not covered in depth in this book.
7. What is the purpose of these types of legal writing?

LEGAL TERMS

consideration
The reason a person enters into a contract; that which is given in exchange for performance or the promise to perform; the price bargained and paid; the inducement. Consideration is an essential element of a valid and enforceable contract. A promise to *refrain* from doing something one is entitled to do also constitutes consideration.

will
An instrument by which a person (the *testator*) makes a disposition of his or her property, to take effect after his or her death.

CHAPTER 9
Fundamentals of Writing

OUTLINE

Writing Process
Structure
Mechanical Errors

This chapter introduces writing fundamentals that apply to all types of legal writing. The first part of the chapter discusses the writing process, from the prewriting stage, to writing, to editing and proofreading. The second part of the chapter discusses organization and then explains the use of topic sentences, transitional language and signposts, paragraphing, and format. The third part of the chapter discusses errors peculiar to legal writing other than errors in quotations and short form citations. These errors include quoting from a headnote or case syllabus, not using plain English, not giving a page reference to material from a primary or secondary source, not quoting exactly, plagiarizing, using contractions in formal legal documents, using the word "I" in formal legal documents, and elegant variation (using more than one word to refer to the same thing).

WRITING PROCESS

The writing process should have three steps:

1. Prewriting;
2. Writing; and
3. Editing and proofreading.

The novice writer often plunges into writing without going through the prewriting step and may not spend enough time on the third step. Some of you will be slow to be convinced and some of you will never be convinced that all three steps are necessary. If your professor doesn't force you to proceed through all three steps by requiring you to turn in an outline, a written document, and a revision of the written document, try completing the three steps on your own. You will be pleased with the results.

Prewriting

Prewriting involves performing any necessary research, formulating a writing plan, and outlining. Don't skimp on any of these activities. Your research strategy should include good notetaking and case briefing as you go along. You may spend a little more time doing research, but a little extra time on research should shorten the time you spend formulating your writing plan and outlining.

From time to time, you may need to pause and collect your thoughts. Mentally review what you have accomplished and think about the direction in which you are heading. You need to pay attention to detail yet not lose sight of the big picture.

The research required to write letters, deeds, contracts, and wills may be limited to gathering facts and identifying the information to be included. In writing a law office memo, a memorandum of law, or an appellate brief, your research usually will be more extensive than for other types of documents. Performing research may mean various things, from gathering facts by reviewing documents and interviewing people to doing legal research in the law library. You should complete the research, as much as possible, before you start writing, or you may find yourself backtracking later.

As you do your research, start to decide what your writing plan will be. In other words, how will you organize your facts and the results of your research to make sense to your reader? As you look at the information in front of you, you will probably identify a number of ideas you want to communicate to your reader. In formulating your plan, you must decide on a scheme for arranging these ideas and developing them for the reader.

Your plan is somewhat dictated by the type of document you are writing. Find out the standard format for that type of document. For certain documents, such as deeds and wills, you will probably want to follow the organizational format customarily used in your area, but don't depend entirely on the recognized format. Make any organizational changes necessary to make sure your reader understands what you have written. The format for court documents may be dictated by court rule. Even though you must follow the overall organizational framework set out in the rule, make sure you have good internal organization.

If you are writing a law office memo, a memorandum of law, or an appellate brief, prewriting should involve developing a thesis. Think about your facts in relation to the results of your research—then try to step back and look at the whole picture. If you think about it long enough, you will find a central idea that runs through your facts and research material. This is your thesis. Think of your thesis as the border to a puzzle. Once you have established your thesis, use it as a framework and fit your facts and research material within it.

Try to develop a flow chart or "road map" as part of the writing plan for your law office memo, memorandum of law, or appellate brief. (An example of a flowchart for a search and seizure problem is included in Appendix A.) A flowchart should help you understand the legal analysis applicable to the legal problem you are researching. If you can complete a flowchart, you are probably on the right track with your legal analysis. Frequent reference to your flowchart will help you write your outline. If you cannot construct a flowchart because you cannot make sense of your research, you either need to spend more time to fit the pieces together or you need to do more research.

Once you have completed your flowchart, start writing an outline. The outline can be as brief or as detailed as you like. An outline that does not contain very much detail does not take as long to write, but is less helpful in the writing process. An outline that is too skeletal is not very useful. Include enough information in your outline to organize yourself before you start writing and determine whether your legal analysis flows. A more detailed outline takes more time to write, but should speed up the writing process and cut down on revision time. An example of an outline for an office memo on the search and seizure problem is included in Appendix A.

If your writing plan is not clear, your writing will be unclear. If your writing is unclear, your reader will end up doing the organization which should have been your job. A reader saddled with this task will not enjoy reading what you have written and may become very frustrated in the attempt.

STRUCTURE

Overall Organization and Organization Within Sections

Good organization is essential for readability. Depending on the complexity of your document, you may have various levels of organization, but your document must be well arranged at each level. Section headings provide overall organization. Then you must organize your writing within each section and you must organize what you say within each paragraph and each sentence.

For example, a discussion—the reasoning portion of a legal document—should contain an introduction, explain the relevant law, and apply the law to the facts. The conclusion may be part of the body of the document or may be in a separate section. In explaining the relevant law and applying it to the facts, the body of the discussion should develop the idea introduced in the introduction and lead up to the conclusion. Develop the idea step by step so you don't lose your reader along the way; explain even the most obvious steps. Just because you can see the connection between steps two and four does not necessarily mean that your reader will be able to unless the connection is spelled out. The development can be logical or chronological, depending on the nature of the discussion.

Organization of a Law Office Memo

To understand what was explained in the preceding section, let's look at the various levels of organization of a law office memo. The overall organizational framework is set by the typical office memo format: heading, facts, issue(s), answer(s), reasoning, and conclusion. This is the first level of organization.

The key to the second level of organization is your formulation of the issue(s). An issue must be well organized to contain as much information as possible while still being readable. If you have more than one issue, carefully consider the order in which you will present the issues. The way you formulate your issues dictates everything else in the office memo. Look at your issues and decide what facts are relevant or significant to them. These are the only ones that you should include in the facts section. Your answers, as the term implies, are simply answers to your issues and should mirror the issues. The reasoning section flows from the issues because it tells the reader how you got from issue to answer. The conclusion is a more detailed statement of your answers.

The reasoning section should contain an introduction, an explanation of relevant law, and an application of the law to the facts. If you have more than one issue, you may want to begin the reasoning section by explaining everything applicable to all the issues first and then discuss each issue separately. For example, you may create an overall introduction in which you state the law relevant to all issues, with the balance of the reasoning section broken up into the same number of sections as there are issues. You may visually break up the reasoning section for your reader by using headings for each issue (such as "reasoning for issue one") and so on. More levels of organization may be needed if you have subissues within issues.

Organization at the Paragraph Level

The final levels of organization are at the paragraph and sentence levels. You will lose your reader, even if your overall organization and the organization within the various sections are good, if your paragraphs and sentences are not well organized. In this section we look at organization at the paragraph level. We'll look at organization at the sentence level in the next section.

Remember your English teacher talking to you about topic sentences? Most paragraphs need topic sentences (although a paragraph reciting a string of chronological events might get along without one.) A *topic sentence* summarizes the idea being discussed in the paragraph. The rest of the paragraph should develop and expand on the idea introduced in the topic sentence. Because the reader will best remember the first and last sentences of the paragraph, the topic sentence is usually, but not always, in one of those two positions.

Look at the preceding paragraph. The first sentence in the paragraph caught the reader's attention. The second sentence is the topic sentence that contains the main idea of the paragraph: namely, that paragraphs usually need topic sentences. The rest of the paragraph expands on the idea contained in the topic sentence. The rest of the paragraph gives an exception to the use of topic sentences, explains what a topic sentence does, explains how the rest of the paragraph relates to the topic sentence, and gives the typical location of the topic sentence.

If your discussion sounds disjointed, check your paragraph structure. Do you deal with a single idea in each paragraph? If you have more than one idea in a paragraph, split up the paragraph so you give each idea its own paragraph. Do you have a topic sentence? If not, write a sentence that contains the essence of the rest of your paragraph. Did you develop the idea introduced in the topic sentence? If not, decide what else you can say about the idea and add it to the paragraph. If you cannot develop a topic sentence, perhaps the idea should be part of another paragraph or should be eliminated.

Word Order Within Sentences

Although readers may enjoy a challenge, don't challenge your reader too often with unconventional word order. Most sentences should follow the conventional structure for English sentences: subject, verb, and object (if any). Your reader should easily understand your sentences without having to hunt for the subject and the verb. Help your reader by keeping the subject, verb, and object close together and near the beginning of the sentence. Every now and then you may want to vary the conventional subject/verb/object structure to emphasize certain words. Because your reader will remember the beginning and end of your sentence better than the middle of the sentence, put the information you want to emphasize either at the beginning or at the end of the sentence.

The following are "mixed-up" sentences from student writing. Read them, determine which word-order rules have been broken, and decide how the sentences can be corrected.

1. The United States Supreme Court in two cases had to determine whether an investigatory stop was based on reasonable suspicion.
2. Trooper Vogel testified that the appellants, based on a reasonable suspicion created by a drug courier profile, were hauling drugs.
3. In *Smith,* relying on a drug courier profile Trooper Vogel stopped a car.

Here are suggested corrections to the preceding sentences. They are only suggestions. You may come up with better answers.

1. In two cases the United States Supreme Court had to determine whether an investigatory stop was based on reasonable suspicion.
2. Trooper Vogel testified that he had a reasonable suspicion that the appellants were hauling drugs and that his suspicion was based on the drug courier profile.
3. In *Smith,* Trooper Vogel stopped a car in reliance on the drug courier profile.

Transitional Language and Signposts

Be kind to your reader by using transitional language and signposts as frequently as possible. Think of the textbooks you have been assigned to read this semester. You probably dread trying to read one or two of them, but you may actually enjoy reading another. Even the most impenetrable subject matter can be made less so through use of transitional language and signposts. In contrast, easier subject matter can seem just as impenetrable without transitional language and signposts. After you read this section, it would be interesting for you to take a look at your textbooks and analyze the authors' writing styles for use of transitional language and signposts.

Transitional language provides a transition or link between what you have just written and what you are going to write about. For example, the first sentence in this chapter provides a subject matter transition from Chapter 8 to Chapter 9 by explaining that Chapter 9 introduces the reader to the fundamentals of legal writing. Although transitional language introducing a new topic can be used anywhere in the paragraph, it is usually used at the beginning of the paragraph (as it was in the example) or at the end. Use of transitional language at the end of a paragraph allows the writer to introduce the topic of the next paragraph. The writer can then emphasize the new topic by discussing it again immediately in the first sentence of the new paragraph. You can also use transitional words such as "although," "even if," "after," "before," and "because" to show the reader the relationship between sentences in a paragraph.

Signposts are words or phrases that point the reader in the right direction and provide a framework for understanding the document. The signposts in the first paragraph of this chapter are the words "the first part of the chapter," "the second part of the chapter," and "the third part of the chapter." They make it easier for the reader to understand the chapter by preparing the reader to expect the chapter to discuss three main topics: the writing process, writing structure, and certain kinds of mechanical errors. Signposts can also highlight main points in a discussion. For example, the words "the main issue before the court" tell the reader that that will be the central focus of the discussion and provide a context for the rest of the discussion.

Paragraphing and Tabulation

To paragraph or not to paragraph: that is the question. There is no one right paragraph length. Some paragraphs may be one sentence long, whereas other paragraphs may contain a number of sentences. One gauge of correct paragraph length is the subject matter of the paragraph. Each paragraph should discuss one main idea. If a paragraph is long and sounds disjointed, it may be because you are trying to discuss more than one idea in a single paragraph. Break the paragraph into shorter paragraphs.

Another gauge of correct paragraph length is readability. Each page of print should contain a minimum of two or three paragraphs. A reader faced with a long, solid block of print will retain less of what is written there than if the same material were broken up into a number of shorter paragraphs. A page containing a series of one- and two-sentence paragraphs is just as bad however. If you find yourself with a series of one- and two-sentence paragraphs, see whether your text is easier to read if you combine several paragraphs.

Tabulation can be used very effectively in legal writing when you have a list of items or activities. When you tabulate, you place each item or activity on a separate line. Each line, except for the last and next-to-last lines, usually ends with a semicolon. The next-to-last line ends with a semicolon and the word "and" or "or." The last line ends with a period.

The first page of this chapter contains an example of tabulation:

> The writing process should have three steps:
>
> 1. prewriting;
> 2. writing; and
> 3. editing and proofreading.

Compare the tabulated material with the following:

> The writing process should have three steps: prewriting, writing, and editing and proofreading.

The only difference between the two sentences is tabulation. Doesn't tabulation make the ideas easier to grasp?

MECHANICAL ERRORS

Legal writing students typically have trouble with three categories of mechanical errors. The first and second categories of mechanical errors are discussed in appendixes C and D. This section deals with a third category of mechanical errors: those other than errors in quotations and short form citations that are peculiar to legal writing. This section discusses the following errors:

1. Quoting from a headnote or case syllabus
2. Not using plain English
3. Not properly citing material from a primary or secondary source

4. Not quoting exactly
5. Plagiarizing
6. Using contractions in formal legal documents
7. Using the word "I" in formal legal documents
8. Elegant variation.

Quoting from a Headnote or Case Syllabus

The error that will most quickly identify you as a novice legal writer is quoting from a headnote or case syllabus. You should not use any material other than the opinion itself, because the material other than the opinion is not the law—it is unofficial and may even be wrong. It is appropriate to refer to or quote from the opinion itself because the opinion is the law. The material in the reporter, other than the opinion itself, was prepared by the publisher or the reporter for the court. The nonopinion material is usually, but not always, accurate; it may on occasion contain outright errors. Because the nonopinion material is a summary of the case, you may garner a different impression of what the law is from reading the nonopinion material than from reading the opinion itself. In addition, the summary may not refer to a part of the case important for your research. The only way to find that material is to read the whole case.

Not Using Plain English

Writing in plain English means writing so the document can easily be understood. It requires good organization and format combined with elimination of excess words, Latin phrases, and unnecessary legal terms and jargon. Organization and format were discussed in an earlier section of this chapter. Appendix D, on mechanical errors, discusses elimination of excess words and contains exercises allowing you to practice what you learn. This section discusses elimination of Latin phrases and unnecessary legal terms.

Some attorneys seem to think that the more Latin phrases and legal terms they include, the better their writing will be. The contrary is usually true. Although there are some Latin terms (like *res ipsa loquitur*) whose meaning is clear to attorneys but are hard to translate into English, use of most Latin terms is unnecessary and may alienate your reader. Eliminate all Latin terms if possible. When you have to use a Latin term, like *res ipsa loquitur,* do so with caution. If there is any question about whether your reader will understand the term, define it. You can often slip in a definition in a parenthetical phrase within the sentence without insulting your reader's intelligence.

The same thing holds true with legal terms. Eliminate any legal terms or words you think your reader will have trouble understanding and replace them with words your reader will comprehend. For example, attorneys often speak of "drafting" a document and having the client "execute" it. The client may be confused if the attorney's cover letter refers to the document the attorney has "drafted" and asks the client to "execute" the document. For the legally unsophisticated client, it is preferable to refer to the document the attorney has "written" and ask the client to "sign" it.

Res ipsa loquitur means "the thing speaks for itself." When a "thing" causes an injury, an inference arises that the injury was caused by the defendant's negligence, if the thing was under the exclusive control of the defendant and the occurence was such as in the ordinary course of events would not have happened if the defendant had used reasonable care. For example, the utility company may properly be held liable under the doctrine of *res ipsa loquitur* for a gas explosion that destroys a building in which the utility company's equipment is functioning imperfectly.

Not Properly Citing Material from Primary or Secondary Sources

Most students know they need to give a page reference when they quote from a case so the reader can quickly find and read the passage in the case. In legal writing, you must also give a page reference when you are referring to specific material from a case, even if you are not quoting the material. For example, you may give the facts from the case in your own words. As a courtesy, tell your reader the page or pages on which the facts are located so the reader can refer to that part of the case without reading the entire opinion. A reference to a specific page is sometimes referred to as a *pinpoint* or *locus citation* because the citation pinpoints or specifically locates the information for the reader. You do not have to give a page reference if you are referring to the case in general, rather than to specific material from the case, and you have previously given the full citation to the case.

A pinpoint citation may precede or follow the information to which it refers. The location is unimportant, but you must provide the pinpoint citation and locate it so the reader is clear as to what information is being referenced. In the next sample paragraph, the first pinpoint citation precedes the information being referenced, the second follows the information being referenced. *Terry* appears by itself in the middle of the paragraph because the case is being referred to in general terms.

> *Terry v. Ohio,* 392 U.S. 1, 27 (1968) was the landmark case that lowered the burden of proof necessary for a stop from probable cause to "reasonable suspicion." In *Terry,* the United States Supreme Court held that police officers may stop someone on the street to investigate possible drug activity so long as the stop is based on something more than "inarticulate hunches." *Id.* at 22.

Not Quoting Exactly

A writer's stock-in-trade is his or her credibility. You will lose your credibility quickly if you do not quote accurately. It is important that anything you quote—but especially primary sources—be accurate. If your quotations are not accurate, your reader will think, at best, that you are sloppy and, at worst, that you are intentionally misleading the reader. You must disclose to your reader any intentional alteration of quoted material.

Appendix C explains how to show alterations. If you quote a passage that was printed with a typographical error or other mistake, do not correct the passage. Instead, quote the passage as originally printed and insert "[sic]" after the mistake. "[Sic]" tells the reader that the mistake was that of the original author.

Plagiarizing

Plagiarism is adopting another writer's work as your own without giving proper credit to the other writer. Plagiarism occurs when you quote from a primary or secondary source without putting the language in quotation marks. It also exists when you have generally followed another writer's style and word choice even though not every word is the other writer's. Instead of plagiarizing, either quote the other writer directly or put the material entirely in your own words. To put the material in your own words, you need to know the substance of it well enough that you can retell it without referring back to the text.

Using Contractions

Most legal documents, except for letters and memos to business associates who are also friends, have a somewhat formal tone. Certain words, such as contractions, that are common in oral communication do not fit in formal legal documents because the tone of these words is too informal. When you are writing a legal document, think twice before you use a contraction, colloquialism, or slang. Such items do not belong in your document.

Using the Word "I"

When giving an opinion in a document such as a client letter, a law office memo, a memorandum of law, or an appellate brief, keep the word "I" out of your writing. Although you have a personal opinion and the legal opinion you give very likely coincides with your own opinion, your analysis must be backed up with the law rather than your personal opinion. Rephrase your sentences in third person (for example: "The virtual identity of the facts in the two cases means that . . .") instead of in first person singular (for example: "I think that . . ."). You can include your personal opinion in formal legal documents as long as you state it in impersonal language.

Elegant Variation

In the past, a teacher has probably suggested that you make your writing interesting by using as many different words as possible to refer to the same thing. This is called *elegant variation*. Elegant variation is terrific for most writing other than legal writing. In legal writing, though, pick a word to refer to something and use it whenever you refer to that same thing. For example, this book uses *attorney* to refer to a person licensed to practice law. It would be elegant variation to also refer to that person as a *lawyer, counselor,* and *practitioner.*

Elegant variation is not appropriate in legal writing because attorneys focus so intently on word choice. If in writing a contract, you first referred to the document as a "contract," you have defined the document as a contract. If you later refer to it as an "agreement," an attorney will wonder why you have changed the wording from "contract" to "agreement." The attorney will wonder whether the writer made a mistake or whether the writer was referring to two different documents, one of which was a contract and the other of which was an agreement. Although it may seem uncomfortable at first to keep using the same word over and over again, you will soon get used to it.

A legal thesaurus may profitably be used when you are trying to come up with the right term. Once you choose your term, stick with it throughout your document. A recently published legal thesaurus is *Ballentine's Thesaurus for Legal Research and Writing* by Jonathan Lynton, published in 1994 by Lawyers Cooperative Publishing and Delmar Publishers Inc.

SUMMARY

- The three steps of the writing process are prewriting, writing, and editing and proofreading.
- Before you start writing, perform any necessary research and formulate a writing plan.
- Develop a flowchart and/or outline before you start writing.
- Good organization is essential for readability.
- Carefully organize words within sentences, sentences within paragraphs, and paragraphs within an entire document.
- Overall organization may be dictated by the traditional format of the type of document you are writing.
- Most paragraphs need topic sentences.
- Do not challenge your reader too often with unconventional word order.
- Use transitional language to provide a link between what you have just written and what you are going to write about.
- Use signposts to point the reader in the right direction and provide a framework for understanding the document.
- Paragraph and tabulate to enhance readability.
- Make sure you know how to eliminate the eight mechanical errors discussed at the end of the chapter.

LEGAL TERMS

Plagiarism
Stealing a person's ideas or copying or adapting his or her creative composition . . . and passing it off as one's own.

EXERCISES

1. What should you do before you write?
2. How can you improve your prewriting step?
3. Take a document you have written and analyze it:
   a. How is the overall organization?
   b. Do you use topic sentences?
   c. Is the word order within sentences logical?
   d. Can you use more transitional language and signposts?
   e. Do you paragraph about the right amount, too often, or too infrequently?
   f. Can you make more use of tabulation?
4. Are you prone to any of the eight mechanical errors discussed in this chapter?

CHAPTER 10
Transmittal Letter and Client Opinion Letter

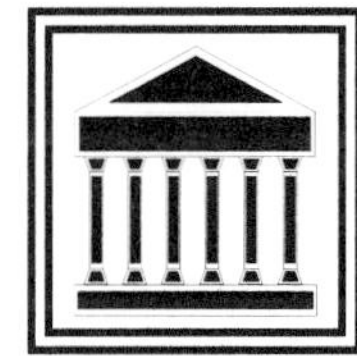

OUTLINE

Two types of letters attorneys often write to clients are the transmittal letter and the client opinion letter. This chapter explains the purpose and use of these letters and their proper format. It also includes a sample transmittal letter and a sample client opinion letter. The sample client opinion letter has been annotated to provide you with writing tips. It should be helpful to you to refer to the notes when you are writing your own client opinion letters.

PURPOSE OF THE TRANSMITTAL LETTER

One of the most common types of letters written in the law office is the *transmittal letter*, the cover letter used when forwarding a document or other information to the client or a third party. The purposes of the transmittal letter are to explain the information being transmitted, to instruct the recipient on any further action to be taken, and to cover any related matters. For example, the sample transmittal letter in Figure 10-1 is the cover letter for an attorney-client retainer agreement (the contract between the attorney and client memorializing the employment relationship between client and

Florida Attorney
Main Street
Anytown, Anystate 10001
May 4, 1995

Via facsimile number: (000) 000-0000
Confirmation number: (000) 000-1000

Esteemed Client
201 Oak Street
Anytown, Anystate 01110

Re: Attorney-Client Retainer Agreement

Dear Ms. Client:

It was a pleasure to meet with you in my office yesterday to discuss your potential lawsuit against Rack and Ruin, Inc. Enclosed are two copies of the Attorney-Client Retainer Agreement we discussed. The Agreement states the terms of our attorney-client relationship.

Please sign both copies of the Agreement on page 2 in the space provided for your signature and keep one copy of the Agreement for your files. Please return the second signed copy to me in the enclosed stamped self-addressed envelope.

I would like to meet with you again to discuss any paperwork you are able to find on Rack and Ruin, Inc. Once you have gathered any applicable information, please call my office and schedule an appointment with me.

Very truly yours,

Florida Attorney

FIGURE 10-1 Sample transmittal letter.

attorney). The transmittal letter explains to the client what the attached document is, asks the client to sign the two copies of the agreement and return one copy to the attorney, and suggests that the client set up an appointment with the attorney.

Another purpose of the transmittal letter is to document that the information attached to the letter was sent to the client and to document the instructions given. Usually the attorney places a copy of the transmittal letter and attachment in the client file. Later the attorney can refer to the file copy to learn what was sent to the client. If the client loses the transmittal letter or the attachment, the material can be resent.

STYLE OF LETTERS

Clients judge the competency of an attorney by the way the attorney presents himself or herself. Clients may lose confidence in the attorney if they spot errors in letters received from the attorney. In contrast, a clear but knowledgeable letter will strengthen the attorney-client relationship and may encourage the client to recommend the attorney to others.

The 10 style tips listed in the sidebar apply to both the transmittal letter and the client opinion letter. The list probably contains nothing new; most of the suggestions are a matter of common sense. They are things that you probably wish someone writing a letter to you would do.

Glance over the style tips and try to keep them in mind as you write your transmittal or client opinion letter. As you revise your letter, use the list as a checklist and make sure you have complied with it.

Style

Do:

1. Use plain English
2. Be precise and specific
3. Write at a level of formality appropriate for the recipient
4. Be consistent in maintaining the same level of formality throughout the letter
5. Keep your sentences fairly short
6. Break up each page of the text with paragraphs
7. State the purpose of the letter early in the letter (preferably in the "Re:" or in the opening line of the body of the letter)
8. Proofread the letter
9. Double-check that any enclosures are included
10. Note any special transmittal method other than regular mail (facsimile, certified mail, etc.).

PURPOSE OF THE CLIENT OPINION LETTER

From time to time, a client will ask an attorney a question that requires the attorney to do some research before giving the client the answer. After the attorney researches the question, the attorney may give the client the answer orally or in writing. The letter the attorney writes to the client explaining the answer is usually referred to as a *client opinion letter* because it gives the client the attorney's legal opinion. Another alternative is to tell the client the answer and follow up the conversation with a client opinion letter. The client opinion letter repeats what the client was told in the conversation and adds any supplementary information suggested by the conversation.

Generally, it is wise for the attorney to give the answer to the client's question in a client opinion letter. The client can reread the opinion letter as many times as necessary. Putting the opinion in writing means that the client will more likely understand the opinion as it was stated by the attorney. The client opinion letter usually states that the opinion it contains is limited by the facts stated in the letter and by the law as of the date of the letter. This language, and the fact that the opinion is in writing, protect the attorney to the greatest extent possible from having the attorney's advice misconstrued or applied in the future to a different set of facts. An attorney might decide not to put his or her opinion in writing if the subject matter of the opinion is confidential. Another reason not to put an opinion in writing is that a written opinion may be discoverable in litigation.

The main purpose of the client opinion letter is to answer the client's question, but the opinion letter does not merely contain the answer. A good client opinion letter also contains a statement of the facts on which the opinion was based, an explanation of applicable law, and an explanation of how the law applies to the facts. The tone of the client opinion letter is usually objective, rather than persuasive, because it explains the law, whether favorable or unfavorable to the client. There is no need to be persuasive and argue the client's position, because the letter is directed to the client.

Chapter 13, which discusses the law office memo, may appear very similar to what you read in this chapter. The reason is that both a client opinion letter and a law office memo require the same type of research and analysis to answer a legal question or problem. The client opinion letter and the law office memo differ in content because the audience is different. Unless the client is sophisticated, the client opinion letter should be stated in lay terms and include few quotations or citations. (If the client is sophisticated, he or she may be sent the law office memo itself rather than a separate client opinion letter.) Another difference is format. A client opinion letter more closely resembles a business letter, although it may have internal headings similar to those of law office memo.

FORMAT OF CLIENT OPINION LETTER

Although there is no one required format for client opinion letters, the format given in this chapter is fairly standard. As you read the explanation in this chapter, compare it with the sample client opinion letter in Figure 10-2.

Heading

The heading contains the name and address of the attorney, the date, the name and address of the client, and the subject matter (the "re"). The date is important because, unless otherwise stated in the letter, it is assumed that the opinion is based on the law current through the date of the letter. For ease of reading and reference, the "re" identifies the subject matter of the letter with a reasonable amount of detail.

Opening

The opening paragraph sets the stage. It typically reminds the client of the context of the client's question and reiterates the client's question. This is a good place to state any limitations on the opinion contained in the letter. The attorney typically states that the opinion is limited to the facts contained in the letter and the law of the state (or federal law, if federal law applies) as of the date of the letter. It is advisable to state that the opinion may be different given different facts or a different date.

Facts

The facts significant to the opinion are stated objectively in the facts section. If important facts are not known, this should be stated. It is wise to ask the client to review the facts and advise the attorney of any necessary additions or changes.

Answer

The answer section explains the answer to the client's question, with any necessary detail and clarification.

Explanation

In the explanation section, the attorney explains the law in lay terms and then explains how the law applies to the facts. The challenge is to back up the answer with the law yet explain it in a way the client can understand. Generally, the attorney does not use quotations or citations in this section, but they may be included if the client is sophisticated. Even if the client is not sophisticated, the opinion may quote the relevant portion of an important statute or case. If a source is quoted or a case is referred to specifically, the citation should be given. The subject matter content and the way it is presented must be geared to the particular client.

Closing

The closing is no different from the closing in any other business letter. The attorney may want to tell the client what action must to be taken and may direct the client to contact the attorney with any further questions concerning the opinion.

SAMPLE CLIENT OPINION LETTER

The sample client opinion letter in Figure 10-2 was written to a mother whose son had been arrested for possession of cocaine. The cocaine was found in the car trunk when the son's car was stopped on Interstate 95 in Florida. The son is originally from Florida but had been attending an out-of-state university. Prior to the arrest, the son had returned to Florida with a friend to visit his mother and to enjoy spring break. The mother hired the attorney to represent the son and has asked the attorney whether the cocaine found can be suppressed.

Florida Attorney
Main Street
Anytown, Florida 10001
July 6, 1995

Ms. Mom Campbell
Oak Street
Anytown, Florida 01110

Re: Whether cocaine found in the Campbell car when it was stopped on I-95 may be suppressed.

Dear Ms. Mom Campbell:

You hired me to represent your son who had been arrested for possession of cocaine on July 1, 1995. On July 2, 1995 I met with you and your son and you asked me whether the cocaine could be suppressed. This opinion is limited to the facts contained in the facts section of this letter and to federal law as of the date of this letter and is solely for your benefit and for the benefit of your son.[1]

Facts

The following facts were gathered from the July 2, 1995 interview with you and Mike Campbell, your son, and a review of the police report. Please contact me or have your son contact me if there are any inaccuracies to be corrected or any additions to be made.[2]

Your son and his best friend, John Doe, were driving north on I-95, returning from spring break in Florida, when they were stopped by members of a drug task force made up of Volusia County Sheriff officers and federal drug enforcement agents. The agents requested permission to search the car. When your son refused consent, the agents brought in a drug-sniffing dog, which alerted to the trunk of the car. The agents then claimed that the dog's actions gave them probable cause to search the trunk and gave your son the choice of either opening the trunk or waiting until the agents obtained a search warrant. After your son opened the trunk, the agents found two kilograms of cocaine in a brown paper bag. Your son and Doe were arrested and charged with possession with intent to distribute cocaine.

---

[1] This sentence protects the attorney by stating the persons who can rely on the opinion. Perhaps the attorney was trying to avoid having the other defendant (the son's best friend) rely on the letter, by stating that the letter's benefit is limited to the mother and son. This type of language is usually used when third parties who are not represented by the attorney may try to rely on the opinion.

[2] This language protects the attorney by requesting that both mother and son verify that the facts are accurate. The prior sentence identifies the source of the attorney's information.

FIGURE 10-2 Sample client opinion letter.

The agents claimed they stopped your son's car because your son did not use his turn signal when changing lanes and because the following facts fit a drug courier profile used by the Volusia County Sheriff officers:

1. The car was a large late-model one;
2. The car had out-of-state tags;
3. The car was being driven cautiously at the speed limit;
4. The car was being driven on a known drug corridor, I-95;
5. There were two passengers in the car;
6. The passengers were in their twenties;
7. The car was being driven in the early evening; and
8. The passengers were dressed casually.[3]

Altough not listed by the agents, your son and Doe believe the real reason they were stopped is because they are Afro-Americans.

Answer

The court should suppress the cocaine if your son files a motion to suppress. In opposition to the motion to suppress, the government will likely make two arguments.

One argument is that the agents had reasonable suspicion that your son's car contained illegal drugs. They will claim that their reasonable suspicion was based on the drug courier profile. The government should lose this argument because of the similarity between the facts in a recent case and your son's case. In the recent case, the court granted the defendant's motion to suppress the illegal drugs found because the stop violated the defendant's constitutional right to be free from unreasonable search and seizure.

The second argument is that the agents had probable cause to stop your son's car for his failure to signal when changing lanes. The government should also lose this argument based on the same recent case. That case explained that an officer may not stop a car for an alleged traffic violation if a reasonable officer would not have stopped the car absent an invalid purpose. Because a reasonable officer on the interstate highway would not have stopped a car for failure to signal when changing lanes, the court should also rule against the government on this argument.

---

3 When you have a list of items, make it easier for your reader to skim down the list by tabulating. Number each item, follow each item except for the last one with a semicolon, and place the word "and" after the semicolon following the next-to-last item. Make sure that you follow parallel construction for all items. If you are unsure what *parallel construction* means, refer to Appendix D.

FIGURE 10-2 *(Continued)*

Once the court rules against the government on the government's two arguments, the court should grant the motion to suppress because the cocaine would not have been found had the car not been stopped.

Explanation of the government's first argument

The fourth amendment to the United States Constitution protects your son "against unreasonable searches and seizures." The fourth amendment does not prohibit all searches and seizures—just *unreasonable* searches and seizures. The courts have allowed officers to stop cars on the highway to investigate a "reasonable suspicion" of illegal drug activity. In a case involving facts almost identical to those in your son's case, the court found that a highway stop was not reasonable under the fourth amendment even though the stop was made based on a drug courier profile. *United States v. Smith,* 799 F.2d 704, 712 (11th Cir. 1986).[4] (This was the recent case referred to in the preceding answer section.)

You will probably be interested to know more about *Smith* because the facts in that case are nearly identical to the facts in your son's case. This letter first gives you the facts from *Smith* and then compares them to the facts from your son's case.

Smith

One night in June of 1985, Trooper Robert Vogel, a Florida Highway Patrol trooper, and a DEA agent were observing cars traveling in the northbound lanes of I-95. They hoped to intercept drug couriers. When Smith's car passed through the arc of the patrol car headlights, Vogel noticed the following factors which matched his drug courier profile:

1. The car was traveling at 3:00 a.m.;
2. The car was a 1985 Mercury, a large late-model car;
3. The car had out-of state tags;

---

[4] "704" is the first page of *Smith* and "712" is the page on which the finding of the court referred to in the preceding sentence is located. As a courtesy to the reader, a page reference should be given when specific material from a case is referred to, even if the material is not directly quoted.

The two types of sentences in legal writing are textual sentences and citation sentences. A *textual sentence* is the type of sentence you have been writing all your life. It is a complete grammatical sentence with a subject and a verb. A *citation sentence* contains only citations. A *string citation* is a citation sentence with more than one citation. In a string citation, the citations should be separated by semicolons.

A sentence is more difficult to read when it contains a full case citation, especially if the citation is long. To avoid having to include a full citation in a textual sentence, you can refer to a case in very general terms or refer to a legal principle from a case and give the full citation to the case in a citation sentence following the textual sentence.

FIGURE 10-2 *(Continued)*

4. There were two occupants of the car who were around 30; and
5. The driver was driving cautiously and did not look at the patrol car as the Mercury passed through the arc of the patrol car headlights.

Id. at 705—06.[5]

The above drug courier profile is almost identical to the profile used by the officers in your son's case[6]. In both *Smith* and your son's case, the cars were traveling after dark, the cars were large late models with out-of-state tags, the cars were being driven "cautiously", and each car contained two passengers in their twenties or thirties. The differences between the two profiles are very minor. Your son and Doe were dressed casually, while it is not known how Smith and Swindell were dressed. Smith and Swindell did not look at Vogel as they passed. It is not known whether your son and Doe looked in the agents' direction as your son drove past. Your son and Doe claim that race was a factor in their stop even though it was not listed as such by the agents. Smith and Swindell's race is unknown.[7]

In *Smith,* Vogel followed the Mercury for a mile and a half and noticed that the Mercury "wove" several times, once as much as six inches into the emergency lane. Vogel pulled Smith over. When a drug dog alerted on the car, a DEA agent searched the trunk and discovered one kilogram of cocaine. Smith and his passenger, Swindell, were arrested and charged with conspiracy to possess cocaine with the intent to distribute it. *Id.* at 706. On appeal, the *Smith* court held that the stop of Smith's car violated Smith's constitutional rights and found that Smith's motion to suppress should have been granted. *Id.* at 712.

---

5 When you need to cite a block quotation or other material set off from the rest of the text, as is the tabulation here, bring the citation back to the left margin. "*Id.*" is used here because "*id.*" refers back to the immediately preceding citation, *Smith.* When citing inclusive pages with three or more digits, drop all but the last two digits of the second number and place an en dash or hyphen between the numbers.

6 This is an example of a topic sentence. A topic sentence contains one main idea summarizing the rest of the paragraph, with the rest of the paragraph developing the idea presented in the topic sentence. Most paragraphs should have topic sentences. The typical location of a topic sentence is the first sentence in the paragraph. Sometimes the topic sentence is the last sentence in the paragraph and pulls together the rest of the paragraph. Some paragraphs, typically narrative paragraphs, do not have a topic sentence.

If a paragraph sounds disjointed or unorganized, try it pulling together using a topic sentence. If a topic sentence does not help, think about breaking the paragraph up into more than one paragraph.

7 This paragraph applies the facts in *Smith* to the facts in *Campbell.* Applying facts from one case to another case involves explaining the similarities and differences between the two sets of facts. Instead of simply stating that the facts from the two cases are very similar, the paragraph specifically states which facts are the same. Sometimes, in the application, you must explain in what way the facts are similar if they are not identical.

You can either apply the *Smith* facts to *Campbell,* as done here, or you can wait until you have thoroughly discussed *Smith.* When you prepare your outline prior to writing the office memo, spend some time moving parts around to determine the best flow for your reasoning.

FIGURE 10-2 *(Continued)*

Just as there was nothing in the drug courier profile in your son's case to differentiate your son and Doe from other innocent college students returning from spring break in Florida, there was nothing in Vogel's drug courier profile to differentiate Smith and Swindell from other law-abiding motorists on I-95. It is usual to drive after dark to avoid heavy traffic or to complete an interstate trip. Although many motorists speed on the highways, motorists driving "cautiously" at or near the speed limit are simply obeying traffic laws. Many persons other than drug couriers drive large late model cars with out-of-state tags. A motorist between the ages of twenty and forty is not unusual.

Explanation of the government's second argument

In *Smith*, the government argued on appeal that the stop was valid either because Vogel had probable cause to stop the car for a traffic violation ("weaving") or because Vogel could have stopped the car on the suspicion from the "weaving" that Smith was driving drunk. The *Smith* court found that the cocaine should have been excluded from evidence because a reasonable officer would not have stopped Smith's car for the alleged traffic violation. *Id.* at 711.

Smith and your son's case are very similar in that, in both cases, the government claimed that the stop of a suspect car did not violate the driver's right against unreasonable search and seizure, because there was some irregularity in the way the car was being driven that gave the officer reason to stop the car. The driving "irregularities" are similar in that swerving six inches into the emergency lane and failing to use a turn signal in changing lanes are fairly minor infractions which did not appear to cause any safety hazard. If the driving irregularities are compared in terms of severity, your son's alleged failure to use his turn signal when changing lanes is by far less severe. If officers were to stop every car on the highway which failed to use its turn signal when changing lanes, a very high percentage of the cars traveling the highway would be pulled over.

I will be meeting with your son within the next few days and I anticipate filing a motion to suppress after that meeting. Should you or your son have any questions concerning this matter, do not hesitate to call me.

Very truly yours,

Florida Attorney

FIGURE 10-2 *(Continued)*

SUMMARY

- The transmittal letter is the cover letter used when forwarding a document or other information to the client or a third party.
- The client judges the competency of the attorney by the way the attorney presents himself or herself. A client letter may either cause the client to lose confidence in the attorney or may strengthen the attorney-client relationship.
- The client opinion letter answers the client's question and contains a statement of the facts, an explanation of applicable law, and an explanation of how the law applies to the facts.
- The format of the client opinion letter generally contains a heading, an opening, the facts, an answer, an explanation, and a closing.
- The client opinion letter should state that it is limited to the facts in the letter, to federal and/or state law of a certain date, and to the benefit of the client.
- Gear the language in the client opinion letter to the sophistication of the client.
- You may or may not want to include citations or quotations in the client opinion letter.

EXERCISES

1. What are important style tips to remember when writing a transmittal letter?
2. What does the heading of a client letter contain?
3. What does the opening of a client opinion letter contain?
4. What facts should a client opinion letter contain?
5. What does the answer section of a client opinion letter contain?
6. What does the explanation section of a client opinion letter contain?
7. What does the closing of a client opinion letter contain?

CHAPTER 11
Contracts

OUTLINE

On some occasion, you have probably been faced with a formidable-looking contract, filled with legalese, which someone expected you to sign. If you are like most people, you probably gave up reading after the first three "whereas" clauses, flipped to the signature line, and signed, hoping that you had not signed your life or car away. Attorneys have rightly been criticized for adhering to their old forms and producing contracts that are almost unintelligible to laypersons and to many other attorneys as well.

Contracts can be written in plain English so that you can understand what you are signing without the help of an attorney. In fact, some states require consumer contracts to be written in plain English. Contracts should be in plain English so the parties to the contract can read the contract and follow it in their performance.

This chapter is designed to give you:

1. Basic information about writing contracts
2. A few sample contract provisions
3. Practice in writing a contract.

The focus is on two types of contracts: contracts for the sale of goods and employment contracts. These two contract types were selected because they are among the most common and because, from your own experience, you probably can think of terms that should be included in them.

A word of caution is advisable here. This chapter gives you some familiarity with writing contracts, but does not license you to practice law. The sample contract provisions included in this chapter are very simple ones and may not be appropriate for certain situations. Statutory or case law may require the inclusion of certain provisions not covered in this chapter. Only an attorney can advise you on how to protect yourself adequately under a contract.

WHY BE FAMILIAR WITH SIMPLE CONTRACTS?

The advantage this chapter gives you is enough familiarity with simple contracts so that, when you read a contract, you can start asking questions and identifying potential problems. Some of the problems may be created by the contract requiring too much or by the contract not addressing certain of your concerns. If there are problems with the contract, the time to solve them is *before* you sign. After you sign, it is too late unless the other party is willing to amend the contract.

Read the contract carefully and decide whether you can perform all that is expected of you under the contract and whether the contract includes everything you expected. Even an onerous contract is enforceable, unless it is so onerous that it is unconscionable. Absence of a particular contract term may create as big a problem as inclusion of improper ones. You may not receive a benefit you have bargained for if it is not included in the contract. For example, if in an initial interview, your prospective employer promises you a bonus based on your performance, make sure your written contract includes the terms of the bonus.

WHY HAVE WRITTEN CONTRACTS?

Certain types of contracts traditionally were required to be in writing to be enforceable. These included a contract for the sale of goods for $500 or more, an employment contract for a term of one year or more, and a contract for the sale of real property. A writing was required for these important transactions because the temptation to defraud and opportunity for fraud by an unscrupulous party are great. Such contracts were thus required to be in writing to furnish tangible proof of the parties' agreement in the event of a dispute. Contracts required to be in writing are generally referred to as *falling within the Statute of Frauds.* Your state has its own version of the **Statute of Frauds**. It might be interesting for you to research which types of contracts are required to be in writing in your state.

Even if a contract is not legally required to be in writing, it is advisable to put a contract of any importance in writing. The written contract furnishes tangible proof of the parties' agreement. A contract spells out the basic terms of a transaction, the respective rights and obligations of the parties, and the remedies in the event of a breach. A written contract also memorializes necessary information so that it is readily accessible later. Should a dispute arise later, it may be resolved simply by consulting the written contract. Should the contract go to litigation, a well-written contract will protect you better than if you have to rely on imperfect recollection of the contract terms.

SUBSTANCE OF THE CONTRACT

A contract should include the material terms of the transaction. You may want to think of the essential contract terms as falling into three broad categories:

1. Parties and subject matter
2. Operative provisions
3. Contingencies.

For example, if you are purchasing a computer, the contract will contain your name and the name of the seller (the parties), the type of computer you are purchasing (the subject matter), the price and payment method (the operative provisions), and the warranty (contingency provision). Figure 11-1 is a bare-bones contract containing these essential terms, written in plain English. The contract is fine if nothing goes wrong. After you read the contract, think what problems you might have in purchasing a computer under such a contract and what contract provisions could be added to deal with those problems. Potential problems with this contract are discussed later in this chapter.

Negotiated and Unnegotiated Terms

Negotiated terms, as the phrase implies, are the terms of the contract that the parties talked about and agreed to. For example, in the contract in Figure 11-1, Mr. Jones and the salesperson for Computer Sales, Inc. probably discussed which computer Mr. Jones should purchase and negotiated the price. These are the negotiated terms in this transaction.

In addition to including all material, negotiated terms, a contract may contain terms the parties never formally negotiated. Certain contingencies happen often enough that the person writing the contract will provide for them. Whoever wrote the sample contract probably referred to the manufacturer's warranty because buyers usually want to know that their computers are covered by a warranty if they malfunction.

LEGAL TERMS

Statute of Frauds
A statute, existing in one or another form in every state, that requires certain classes of contracts to be in writing and signed by the parties. Its purpose is to prevent fraud or reduce the opportunities for fraud. A contract to guarantee the debt of another is an example of an agreement that the statute of frauds requires to be in writing.

Computer Contract

The parties to this Contract are Computer Sales, Inc., Anystreet USA, Anytown, Florida ("Seller") and J.A. Jones, Main Street, Anytown, Florida ("Buyer") and the date of this contract is July 1, 1995. Seller and Buyer agree as follows:

Seller will install the computer identified on Exhibit A to this contract (the "Computer") at the above address of the Buyer.

Buyer will pay Seller $2,000 for the Computer and the installation.

The Computer carries the manufacturer's warranty described in the computer instruction manual.

Computer Sales, Inc.

By: ____________
Computer Whiz, Pres.

____
J.A. Jones

FIGURE 11-1 Sample contract for sale of computer.

Depending on the subject matter of the contract, state or federal law may mandate inclusion of certain terms or disclosure of certain information. For example, federal law requires certain consumer protection language to be inserted in a contract if the sale was solicited at the buyer's home or the purchase was made on credit. A contract also typically contains **boilerplate** provisions, that is, provisions common to all legal documents of the same type. Typical contract boilerplate provisions include **notice**, **assignment**, choice of law, **attorney fees**, saving clause, and so on.

WRITING A CONTRACT

Although a contract can be written entirely from scratch, a person writing a contract usually tries to find one or more existing contracts that are similar to the one the person needs and use those contracts as a guide. An attorney may recall a similar matter the attorney has dealt with in the past and use the contract from that matter as a guide. In addition, attorneys typically maintain files of contracts which they use when appropriate.

Another option is to consult **forms** and formbooks. Attorneys may prepare their own forms or use commercially prepared forms. Some law firms develop their own formbooks for use by all the legal professionals in the firm. A law firm formbook may be just a ring binder containing copies of documents contributed by various attorneys in the firm. If you are lucky, the forms may also be stored on the law firm's central computer, or on disk, accessible to everyone in the firm. You should check your law library to see whether it contains any commercially prepared formbooks.

As the term implies, *formbooks* are volumes containing forms intended to be referred to as guides. There is a wide variety of formbooks. The forms contained in a particular publication may be much simpler than those contained in another formbook. Some forms are written in plain English; others are not. Office supply stores sell forms, either singly or in packages; and a law firm may stock certain of these forms for use in routine transactions. A number of formbooks are also available on computer disk.

Besides including forms, a formbook often contains checklists of typical provisions to be included in a particular type of contract. When writing or analyzing a contract, it is helpful to glance down the checklist to make sure the writer has included all necessary provisions. Some writers actually use a checklist from a formbook as a checklist and check off each item as either included in the contract or not needed. Later sections of this chapter contain a list of matters typically considered when writing a contract for the sale of goods and another list of matters typically considered when writing an employment agreement. You can use these lists as checklists in completing the exercises for this chapter.

In some states, the state bar association, or a bar-related not-for-profit corporation, is active in preparing all sorts of helpful state-specific materials, including forms. It would be useful for you to determine what materials are prepared in your state and whether nonattorneys can purchase them. For instance, in Florida, the Florida Bar has prepared, and the Florida Supreme Court has approved, forms for use by nonattorneys. The forms cover a number of matters commonly encountered by the average layperson. Although the "Contract for Sale and Purchase" (designed to be used when someone is selling a home) was approved a number of years ago, the rest of the forms were approved much more recently. The forms were prepared in response to criticism that everyone needs legal assistance from time to time, but few can afford to hire an attorney. Because these forms were approved by the Florida Supreme Court, a nonattorney using the forms cannot be prosecuted for unlicensed practice of law. The "Contract for Sale and Purchase" has been disseminated so widely throughout Florida that it has become the standard form to use in the sale of residential property.

Use of Contract Forms

Critics are fond of saying that all attorneys do is fill in forms—and they don't even do that personally. They have their secretaries do it. Is this criticism valid?

The advantage in using forms is that they cut down on the time and expense of preparing a contract. For example, if an attorney represents a developer of a residential subdivision, the attorney will probably write a

LEGAL TERMS

boilerplate language
Language common to all legal documents of the same type. Attorneys maintain files of such standardized language for use where appropriate.

notice
1. As defined by judicial decision, "information concerning a fact, actually communicated to a person by an authorized person, or actually derived by him from a proper source." ... 3. Information; intelligence; knowledge.

assignment
1. A transfer of property, or a right in property, from one person to another. 2. A designation or appointment.

attorney fees
Compensation to which an attorney is entitled for his or her services.

form
A printed instrument with blank spaces for the insertion of such details as may be required to make it a complete document.

contract for the sale of a lot and use it as a form when any lot in the subdivision is sold. This makes sense because very little differs in the various sales, other than the buyer, the purchase price, and the lot number. These terms can easily be filled in to correspond to the particular transaction. Other changes to the form contract can be made either by writing in the change and having the parties initial it or attaching an **addendum** (an appendix or addition) to the contract.

The disadvantage in using forms is that they may not be tailored to a particular transaction. A form should be analyzed to determine whether there is a valid reason for including each provision and whether any other provisions are necessary for the particular transaction. Attorneys must stay current on the law or must do the necessary legal research to make sure the contract reflects current law. A careless attorney who has a secretary or paralegal fill out a form without adequately supervising the work is inviting a legal malpractice lawsuit.

Ideally, an attorney will tailor the contract to the particular transaction by combining the best provisions from a number of forms with the negotiated terms and other information peculiar to the transaction. When doing this, the attorney must make sure the contract is consistent. Provisions taken from different forms should not contradict each other, and the same defined terms should be used throughout the contract. For example, if the contract starts out referring to the buyer as "Buyer," the contract should always refer to that person as "Buyer." If a provision borrowed from another contract refers to the buyer as the "Purchaser," the word "Purchaser" should be replaced by the word "Buyer" to be consistent.

CHECKLIST: SALE-OF-GOODS CONTRACT

The following is a list of matters to be considered when writing a contract for the sale of goods. As you read the list, keep in mind the computer contract in Figure 11-1. In a later section of this chapter, we review this list and determine what provisions should be added to that contract.

Computer Contract

1. **Parties and subject matter.**
   a. Definitions.
   b. Parties.
   c. Date of the contract.
   d. Description of goods.
2. **Operative provisions.**
   a. Price.
   b. Obligations of seller.
   c. Obligations of buyer.
   d. Time for performance.

3. **Contingencies.**
    a. Warranties.
    b. Transfer of title to goods and risk of loss.
    c. Excuse of performance.
    d. Remedies of seller.
    e. Remedies of buyer.
4. **Provisions required by statute or case law.**
5. **Boilerplate.**
    a. Modification or amendment of contract.
    b. Assignment of contract.
    c. Notice provision.
    d. Choice-of-law provision.
    e. Attorney fees.
    f. Saving clause.

Test your brainstorming ability by making a list of provisions to add to the computer contract in Figure 11-1 before you read the following sections.

THE PERFECT CONTRACT

If this were a perfect world, we wouldn't need contracts, because every transaction would be performed as planned. Because this is not a perfect world, we know that there will be problems (although we hope very minor ones) with every contract. The challenge in writing a "perfect" contract is to accurately state the negotiated provisions, to include any provisions required by statute or case law, and to predict everything that will happen between the parties as the contract is performed.

In looking at a contract, you may have wondered why you recognized such a small portion of the provisions (the parties, subject matter, and operative provisions) and what the balance of the terms were doing in the contract. The provisions with which you may not be familiar are the ones included just in case something unanticipated happens. The "just-in-case" provisions are categorized as contingencies, provisions required by statute or case law, and boilerplate.

If you were to compare a number of contracts for the sale of goods, you would notice provisions, other than the negotiated ones, that are similar from contract to contract. Through the years, certain problems in contract performance happened often enough that the just-in-case provisions began to be included in every contract. These provisions constitute a large portion of the contract because the potential problems are many and varied.

Although many of the just-in-case provisions are necessary, these provisions are probably the ones that make the contract hard to read. Someone attempting to write a plain English contract must analyze each provision of the traditional contract and determine whether there is a valid business reason for that provision. The choice should be made in light of the particular transaction to be covered by the new contract. Certain detailed provisions

LEGAL TERMS

addendum
An appendix or addition to a document.

that may be necessary in a commercial transaction may be overkill in a consumer transaction. The writer should not include provisions covering events that are extremely unlikely to occur, so long as the risk of loss is minimal. Boilerplate provisions should be written to correspond to the specifics of the transaction, with any unnecessary provisions eliminated.

In addition to the standard just-in-case provisions, other contingency provisions peculiar to a particular transaction may be needed. The writer must study the transaction to determine whether other provisions are needed. Based on the course of dealings between the parties or a party's past experience or reputation, the writer may feel the need to head off a potential problem peculiar to the parties or the subject matter of the contract.

Precise and Imprecise Language in Perfect Contracts

The language in a skillfully written contract precisely sets forth well-defined expectations and is purposefully imprecise when dealing with unknown future events. Usually the material terms of a transaction are stated precisely to coincide with the parties' expectations. If a time period for performance is involved, it is wise to state it exactly. Otherwise, performance within a "reasonable time" is sufficient and the transaction may never be completed. The language of just-in-case provisions is usually not precise because it is impossible to predict exactly what will happen.

The skill of an experienced attorney lies in knowing when to be precise and when to be imprecise. Although the material terms of a transaction are usually well defined, sometimes even some of the material terms must be purposefully vague. For example, if the buyer wants to buy all that the seller can produce of a certain item, but it is not known how much the seller will produce, the contract can require the seller to sell and the buyer to buy all that the seller produces. In contrast, a contingent provision may be written with a great deal of specificity if a particular contingency is fairly likely to occur. For example, if the seller has had great difficulty in the past obtaining an essential component of the item the seller is manufacturing, the contract may provide that the seller's performance is excused if the seller cannot obtain the essential component by a certain date.

What's Wrong with the Computer Contract?

In this section we review the sale-of-goods checklist and determine what provisions should be added to the computer contract. During this analysis, draw on your personal experience and your imagination of transactions that didn't work as planned. Think of the last time you purchased a large item. Did the item live up to the sales pitch? Was it delivered on time? Did the seller perform as expected? Were the payment terms satisfactory? And so on.

The following numbers correspond to the numbers in the checklist. The title, "Computer Contract," tells what type of document it is and identifies the subject matter. You could also add the names of the parties to the title.

Parties and subject matter.

1. a. In the computer contract we used the defined terms "Seller," "Buyer," and "Computer." Once you have given the definition of a term, you need only capitalize the term later in the contract when you refer to it, rather than giving the whole definition each time. Be careful that you use the same defined term throughout the contract. If you start out using "Buyer," do not use "Purchaser" later to refer to the same person. If you have a number of defined terms, you may want to include a definitions section near the beginning of the contract, in which you give definitions of all the terms used in the contract. That way, the reader knows to refer back to the definitions section when the reader sees a capitalized term. A definitions section is probably not needed in the computer contract because there are not a great number of defined terms.
   b. The parties are named. It is a good idea to also give their addresses and any other basic information in a contract. If you include that information in a contract, you can use the contract as a ready reference instead of having to consult a number of other sources.
   c. The date of a contract is often the date when the last of the parties signs the contract, or another date selected by the parties. The parties may have a reason for wanting the contract made on a certain date. The exact contract date would be important to know if time periods included in the contract start on the contract date.
   d. In the computer contract, it would be important for the Buyer to check Exhibit A and make sure that the Computer is the right one. If the Buyer was supposed to receive any other equipment, that equipment should also be listed on Exhibit A, or the Buyer may end up paying for it in addition to the contract price.

Operative provisions.

2. a. The price is given, but the payment terms are not—they should be. One payment option is having a portion of the purchase price due upon signing the contract, with the balance due upon installation of the Computer or the Buyer being billed for the balance. Another option is payment of the entire purchase price when the contract is signed. This may be required when the goods are being designed and manufactured specially for the Buyer. Another option is payment in full upon delivery.
   b. From the contract, we know that the Seller must supply and install the Computer. If the Seller has any other obligations, they should be stated in the contract. For example, the purchase price may include a certain number of hours of instruction and maintenance. It is to the Buyer's benefit to have this clearly stated in the contract.

c. The main obligation of the Buyer is to pay. As explained in 2.a., the payment terms should be included in the contract. Any other obligation of the Buyer should also be stated in the contract.

d. The contract does not state when the Computer is to be installed. If it is critical to the Buyer that the Computer be installed by a certain date, this should be stated in the contract. The Buyer may want to include a penalty that the Seller would have to pay for each day the Seller is late. Again, refer to 2.a. for the Buyer's payment terms.

Contingencies.

3. a. The contract does state that the Computer carries the manufacturer's warranties. If the Buyer expects any other warranties, they should be stated in the contract. If warranty service is vital to the Buyer, the Buyer may want to specify where the warranty service is to be done (does the service person come to the Buyer or does the Buyer have to take the computer in?) and how quickly any repairs will be made.

b. A transfer of title to goods and risk-of-loss provision most often is included when the goods are being manufactured specially for the Buyer. This provision would probably not be included in the computer contract unless the Seller were manufacturing the Computer for the Buyer. Should the specially manufactured goods be destroyed before they are delivered and paid for, two questions would be asked: "Who owned the goods when they were destroyed?" and "Who should bear the loss?" The parties can specify in a contract when ownership passes and who bears the risk of loss.

c. An excuse-of-performance provision is also often included when the goods are being manufactured specially for the Buyer. An **act of God** may excuse the Seller's performance. An *act of God* is an unusual, extraordinary, and unexpected act caused solely by the forces of nature or something outside the Seller's control. Examples are a flood that destroys the Seller's manufacturing facility or a war that makes it impossible for the Seller to continue manufacturing. This provision would probably not be included in the computer contract unless the Seller were manufacturing the Computer specially for the Buyer.

d. In general, remedies for breach of a contract include **damages**, **consequential damages**, **liquidated damages**, **injunction**, and **specific performance**. Unless otherwise stated, it is assumed that a party may sue for damages. A party may also sue for specific performance if the goods are unique. If there is a basis for a party demanding consequential or liquidated damages or an injunction, this information should be included in the contract. Because the only obligation of the Buyer under the computer contract is to pay the purchase price, the most likely remedy of the Seller is an action for damages to collect the balance of the purchase price. If the Seller would be

LEGAL TERMS

act of God
An unusual, extraordinary, and unexpected act caused solely by the forces of nature. A person cannot be held liable for an act of God.

damages
The sum of money that may be recovered in the courts as financial reparation for an injury or wrong suffered as a result of breach of contract or a tortious act.

satisfied with suing for damages, a remedy provision need not be included in the contract. The Seller could also sue for specific performance to force the Buyer to purchase the Computer if the Computer were being specially manufactured for the Buyer. If the Seller would like to sue for specific performance, it would be wise to specifically give the Seller this remedy in the contract.

e. If the Seller fails to deliver the Computer, the Buyer can sue for damages without having a damages provision included in the contract. Following the explanation in 3.d., the basis for any other remedy should be stated in the contract.

Provisions required by statute or case law.

4. The contract writer should research to determine what provisions, if any, are required by statute or case law.

Boilerplate.

5. a. This amendments-and-merger provision typically states that it contains the parties' entire understanding regarding the subject matter of the contract and that any modification must be in writing.
   b. Assignment of a contract is usually prohibited when performance is of a personal nature or the Seller relied on the creditworthiness of the person signing the contract as the Buyer.
   c. This notice provision contains the names and addresses of persons to whom notice is to be sent. This provision is probably not necessary in the computer contract because there is no requirement or mention of either party giving notice.
   d. If the parties are from different states and the contract is to be performed in a third state, it may be helpful to specify which state's law is to govern. This provision is probably unnecessary in the computer contract because the parties are located in the same town where the contract is to be performed.
   e. An attorney fee provision making the losing party responsible for the prevailing party's attorney fees is a very common provision. Otherwise, each party pays its own attorney fees, absent a statute providing for attorney fees.
   f. This common provision states that if one contract provision is ruled unenforceable, the rest of the contract should be enforced.

CHECKLIST: EMPLOYMENT CONTRACT

Now that you have some familiarity with common provisions of a contract for the sale of goods, it will be interesting to see how those provisions differ from the common provisions of an employment contract. The following is a checklist for a simple employment agreement.

consequential damages
Indirect losses; damages that do not result from the wrongful act itself, but from the result or the aftermath of the wrongful act.

liquidated damages
A sum agreed upon by the parties at the time of entering into a contract as being payable by way of compensation for loss suffered in the event of a breach of contract; a sum similarly determined by a court in a lawsuit resulting from breach of contract.

injunction
A court order that commands or prohibits some act or course of conduct. It is preventive in nature and designed to protect a plaintiff from irreparable injury to his or her property or property rights by prohibiting or commanding the doing of certain acts. An injunction is a form of equitable relief.

specific performance
The equitable remedy of compelling performance of a contract, as distinguished from an action at law for damages for breach of contract due to nonperformance. Specific performance may be ordered in circumstances where damages are an inadequate remedy.

Employment Contract

1. **Parties and subject matter.**
   a. Definitions.
   b. Parties.
   c. Date of the contract.
   d. Statement establishing the employer-employee relationship.
2. **Operative provisions.**
   a. Duration of the employment.
      i. Employment term.
      ii. Renewal of term.
   b. Compensation.
      i. Wages.
      ii. Other benefits.
   c. When compensation payable.
   d. Reimbursement of business expenses paid by employee.
   e. Duties of employee.
   f. Time employee will devote to employer's business.
3. **Contingencies.**
   a. Termination of contract prior to end of contract term.
      i. Reasons.
      ii. Termination procedure.
   b. Work product provision (work produced by employee while employed is owned by employer).
   c. Employee's duty not to disclose trade secrets and other information important to the business.
   d. Noncompetition provision (after leaving employer, employee may not compete with employer's business for a certain length of time and within a certain geographical area).
4. **Boilerplate.**
   a. Modification or renewal of contract.
   b. Notice provision.
   c. Choice-of-law provision.
   d. Saving clause.

Because an employment agreement governs an ongoing relationship between the employer and the employee, that relationship is much better defined than the relationship between the seller and the buyer in the computer contract. The employment agreement specifies the length of employment, the employee's duties and compensation, and the reasons and procedure for terminating the agreement. The work product, nondisclosure, and noncompetition provisions protect the employer against the employee taking advantage of what the employee has learned while on the job.

Think about a job you have held as you review this checklist. What were the material terms of the employment agreement? Jot down notes of the material terms next to the sections of the checklist entitled "Parties and subject matter" and "Operative provisions." Which of the "Contingencies" were spelled out in the employment agreement? If your employment agreement were written, which of the boilerplate provisions would be included? Now review the checklist again. Can you think of any terms that were left out?

CONTRACT STRUCTURE

Deciding what provisions to include is only part of writing a contract. The reader will have an easier time understanding a contract that is well organized and has an inviting format. Organization and format go hand-in-hand. A well-organized contract may not be easy to understand if the format is poor. Nevertheless, good format will not save poor organization.

Organization

The following are the traditional parts of a contract.

Introduction The introduction usually contains the names of the parties and the date. The contract must contain a statement that the parties agree to the remainder of the terms in the contract. This statement is typically contained either in the introduction or in the recitals.

Recitals This section of the contract states the basis for the contract and states that the parties agree to the remainder of the terms in the contract (if this latter statement was not included in the introduction). In contracts not written in plain English, you can recognize this section because it is usually headed "WITNESSETH:"; each paragraph of the section begins with "WHEREAS," and the section ends with some variation on the words: "Now, therefore, in consideration of the mutual covenants herein contained, and other good and valuable consideration, the receipt of which is hereby acknowledged, the parties to this agreement hereby agree as follows."

Be kind to your reader by replacing this traditional **legalese** with plain English. Title this section "Background of Contract," or simply "Background," instead of heading it "WITNESSETH:". Delete all the "WHEREAS"es. If this is where you state the parties' agreement, state it simply: "The parties agree as follows." Unless you make this section part of the body of the contract, the section is not normally numbered or lettered.

Because the terms of the computer contract were so simple, the contract did not contain this section. If it had, it might have looked something like this:

Background of Contract

Buyer desires to purchase a computer and Seller sells the type of computer Buyer desires.

LEGAL TERMS

legalese
The use by lawyers of specialized words and phrases, rather than plain talk, when it serves no purpose; legal jargon.

Body The body of the contract contains the parts of the contract discussed earlier in this chapter: the subject matter, the definitions section (if there is need for one), the operative provisions, the contingencies, and the boilerplate. For ease of reference, the sections and divisions within sections are numbered or lettered, as in an outline, and the sections are introduced by section headings.

Signatures The signature block contains signature lines for the parties signing and, if possible, should identify the persons signing. Preferably, the identification will be typewritten, but it may be handwritten legibly. Depending on the legal requirements of the contract, this section may contain lines for witnesses to sign and one or more notary blocks.

Good organization means that related terms are near each other and are placed in a logical order. Writing the contract using the four parts previously identified provides a framework for the contract. Then the information within each of the four parts must be organized as well. The order may be chronological or functional, or may follow some other scheme suited to the subject matter and the intended audience.

Format

Pick out one of your textbooks whose pages look inviting to read and one whose pages look uninviting. Now compare the pages of the two texts. Chances are that the more inviting page has wider margins, larger print, medium-length lines and paragraphs, double-spacing between sections, and underlined or boldfaced descriptive section headings. Reader-friendly format makes a page easier to read.

You can use that same reader-friendly format in writing contracts. Make your margins wide enough that they give the reader's eyes a place to rest. Line and paragraph length should be neither too long nor too short. The print should be no smaller than 10 or 12 point. Give the contract a title identifying what type of document it is. You may also want to include other information in the title, such as the subject matter and the parties. Underlined or boldfaced descriptive section headings make it easy to find relevant terms. You may want to break up a longer section into a number of sections or tabulate to make the section easier to read.

When deciding on format, do not forget to check for any statutory requirements. The signatures on certain documents, typically those to be recorded in the public records, may require witnesses and may be required to be notarized.

SUMMARY

- You should be familiar with simple contracts so that when you read a contract, you can ask questions and identify potential problems.
- Some contracts are required to be in writing. Even if not required, it is advisable to have a written contract.
- The three types of contract provisions are parties and subject matter, operative provisions, and contingencies.
- Contract terms may be negotiated or unnegotiated.
- Often an attorney uses a contract form as a basis for writing the contract rather than writing the contract entirely from scratch.
- Contract forms may be helpful but should not be followed mindlessly.
- Besides the three types of contract provisions listed here, contracts often include provisions required by statute or case law and boilerplate provisions.
- The challenge in writing the perfect contract is to accurately state the negotiated provisions, to include any provisions required by statute or case law, and to predict everything that will happen between the parties as the contract is performed.
- The perfect contract also requires good organization and format.

EXERCISES

Use what you have learned in this chapter to complete the following exercises.

1. Rewrite the computer contract, supplying any missing terms. In rewriting, think about substance, organization, and format.
2. Write a contract for the sale of goods. The terms can be taken from a real-life transaction or an imaginary one. In writing, think about substance, organization, and format.
3. Write an employment agreement. The terms of the agreement can be based on real life or can be imaginary. In writing, think about substance, organization, and format.

CHAPTER 12
Pleadings

OUTLINE

Pleadings are the formal statements made by the parties to an action setting forth their claims or defenses. This chapter explains the purpose, use, and format of the complaint and the answer and includes a sample complaint and answer.

The sample complaint and answer have been extensively annotated to provide you with writing tips. The notes to the sample complaint and answer are not part of the pleadings themselves. If the notes do not make sense to you right now, read them again when you are writing your own complaint and answer.

PURPOSE

A civil lawsuit begins with a party (who consequently becomes the **plaintiff**) filing a complaint with the court. The **complaint** is the initial pleading in a civil action, in which the plaintiff alleges a cause of action and asks that the wrong done to the plaintiff be remedied by the court. The purposes of the complaint are for the plaintiff to state what happened and to state the relief that the plaintiff is requesting from the court.

LEGAL TERMS

pleadings
Formal statements by the parties to an action setting forth their claims or defenses. The various kinds of pleadings, and the rules governing them, are set forth in detail in the Federal Rules of Civil Procedure and, with respect to pleading in state courts, by the rules of civil procedure of the several states. These rules of procedure abolished common law pleading.

plaintiff
A person who brings a lawsuit.

complaint
The initial pleading in a civil action, in which the plaintiff alleges a cause of action and asks that the wrong done him or her be remedied by the court.

The **answer** is a pleading in response to the complaint, made by the opposing party (known as the **defendant**). The answer may deny the allegations of the complaint, agree with them, state that the defendant is without knowledge of them, or introduce **affirmative defenses** intended to defeat the plaintiff's lawsuit or delay it. The purposes of the answer are for the defendant to reply to the claims the plaintiff raised in the complaint, to state the defendant's affirmative defenses, and to state related claims (called **counterclaims**) that the defendant has against the plaintiff.

Let's look for a moment at the sample complaint and answer included in this chapter. The plaintiff is Jake Carson and the defendant is Tom Harris. Jake and Tom ran against each other for the position of student body president at Collegiate University. The basis of Jake's suit is the statement Tom made about Jake in Tom's political skit, presented on the eve of the election. In the skit Tom stated to a student playing the part of Jake that "Jake" was HIV positive. Jake claims that the skit also depicted him as a homosexual. Jake was so outraged by the skit that he hired an attorney to sue Tom for slander and for depicting him in a "false light" as being a homosexual.

BASIC FORMAT

Court Rules

Once you determine the court in which the complaint will be filed, you must carefully review any applicable court rules and statutes. It might also be helpful to review court files to learn the format customarily used in the particular court.

Court rules may specify the contents of the complaint and the answer. For example, Rule 1.110 of the Florida Rules of Civil Procedure requires the complaint to "state a cause of action." The same rule requires the answer to "state in short and plain terms the pleader's defenses to each claim asserted and . . . [to] admit or deny the averments on which the adverse party relies."

Commonly, the court rules and official forms accompanying the court rules specify the format of the **caption** (the heading of the court paper) and the body of the pleading. For example, Form 1.901 of the Florida "Forms for Use with the Rules of Civil Procedure" gives the general form of the caption. (This form was followed for the caption of the sample pleadings contained in this chapter.)

Forms

Although pleadings can be written entirely from scratch, someone who must draft a pleading usually tries to find one or more other pleadings that are similar to the one the person is writing and use those pleadings as a guide. An attorney may recall a similar lawsuit the attorney has dealt with in the past and use a pleading from that matter as a guide.

Another option is to consult forms and formbooks. Court rules may have official forms appended to them. A number of commercial publishers publish *formbooks*, which are volumes containing forms that may be referred to as a guide, so a wide variety of formbooks is available. The forms contained in one particular publication may be much simpler than those contained in another formbook. Some formbooks are written in plain English, whereas others contain a lot of legalese.

If you use a form, you must tailor it to the particular situation you are dealing with. Just because material is contained in a form does not mean that the material is correct for your jurisdiction. Be sure to research the cause of action and defenses for your jurisdiction to make sure you have covered all the elements of the cause of action and have correctly stated the relief available and any affirmative defenses.

Besides forms, formbooks often contain checklists of typical provisions to be included in a particular type of pleading. When writing a pleading, it is helpful to glance down the checklist to make sure you have included all necessary provisions.

FORMAT OF THE COMPLAINT

This section gives a brief explanation of the various parts of the complaint. It might be helpful for you to read the rest of this section and the next section while comparing the explanation to the sample complaint and answer that appear later in this chapter.

Caption

The caption section contains the name of the court, the names of the parties, the case number, and the title of the pleading.

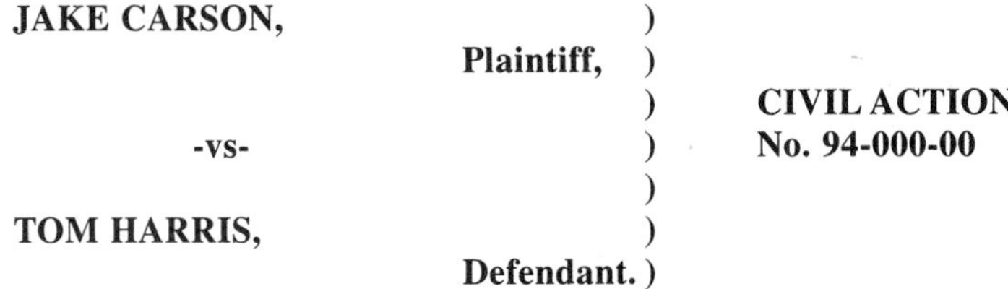

IN THE CIRCUIT COURT
OF THE NINTH JUDICIAL CIRCUIT
IN AND FOR ORANGE COUNTY, FLORIDA

JAKE CARSON,	)	
Plaintiff,	)	
	)	**CIVIL ACTION**
-vs-	)	**No. 94-000-00**
	)	
TOM HARRIS,	)	
Defendant.	)	

Introduction

After the caption and before the first numbered paragraph, an unnumbered sentence (called the *introductory clause* or *commencement*) states

LEGAL TERMS

answer
A pleading in response to a complaint. An answer may deny the allegations of the complaint, demur to them, agree with them, or introduce affirmative defenses intended to defeat the plaintiff's lawsuit or delay it.

defendant
The person against whom an action is brought.

affirmative defense
A defense that amounts to more than simply a denial of the allegations of the plaintiff's complaint. It sets up new matter which, if proven, could result in a judgment against the plaintiff even if all the allegations of the complaint are true.

counterclaim
A cause of action on which a defendant in a lawsuit might have sued the plaintiff in a separate action. Such a cause of action, stated in a separate division of a defendant's answer, is a counterclaim.

caption
A heading. As applied in legal practice, when "caption" is used to mean "heading," it generally refers to the heading of a court paper.

who is filing the complaint and who it is being filed against. The trend in some jurisdictions is to eliminate the introductory paragraph.

COMPLAINT

Plaintiff, JAKE CARSON, sues defendant, TOM HARRIS, and alleges:

Claims

The claims section (called the *body* or *charging portion* of the complaint) contains a series of numbered paragraphs telling the court why it has jurisdiction over the case and what has happened. Rule 8(a) of the Federal rules of Civil Procedure requires the complaint to contain "(1) a short and plain statement of the grounds upon which the court's jurisdiction depends" and "(2) a short and plaint statement of the ultimate facts showing that the pleader is entitled to relief." Rule 10(b) of the Federal Rules of Civil Procedure specifies the format for the body of the pleading:

> All averments of claim or defense shall be make in numbered paragraphs, the contents of each of which shall be limited as far as practicable to a statement of a single set of circumstances; and a paragraph may be referred to by number in all subsequent pleadings. Each claim founded upon a separate transaction or occurrence and each defense other than denials shall be stated in a separate count or defense whenever a separation facilitates the clear presentation of the matters set forth.

COUNT I—DEFAMATION

1. This is an action for damages that exceed $15,000.
2. In October 1993 plaintiff was a student at Collegiate University, a member of the Collegiate Beta Fraternity, and a candidate for student body president of Collegiate University.
3. In October 1993 defendant was a student at Collegiate University, a member of the Collegiate Alpha Fraternity, and a candidate for student body president of Collegiate University.
4. The October 20, 1993, issue of the Collegiate University student newspaper reported that plaintiff and defendant "were running neck and neck" in the student body president race.
5. On October 20, 1993, the day before the student body president election, plaintiff and defendant presented skits to Collegiate University students and faculty at the Collegiate University football stadium.
6. In defendant's skit, defendant portrayed "plaintiff's doctor" and another student portrayed plaintiff.
7. In defendant's skit, defendant, in the presence and hearing of plaintiff and the students and faculty watching the skit, maliciously and falsely announced that plaintiff had tested HIV positive, saying "you tested HIV positive."
8. In the student body president election on October 21, 1993, plaintiff received 10% of the vote and defendant received 90% of the vote.

9. Plaintiff at the time of defendant's statement was in good health and free from any disease, and the statements of defendant were wholly untrue.
10. As a result of defendant's slanderous statement, plaintiff suffered, and continues to suffer, great nervousness and mental anguish.
11. Plaintiff, as the direct result of defendant's statement, in addition to the nervousness and bodily injury, has been injured in plaintiff's good reputation in the Collegiate University community. Defendant published such false and slanderous statement about plaintiff to numerous students and faculty of Collegiate University, who have changed their attitude toward plaintiff, and who have begun to question plaintiff as to whether plaintiff has tested HIV positive, which the slanderous remark of defendant wrongly, maliciously, and untruthfully imputed to plaintiff.

COUNT II—FALSE LIGHT INVASION OF PRIVACY

12. Plaintiff realleges and incorporates paragraphs 1–8 above.
13. Prior to October 20, 1993, a rumor had circulated on the Collegiate University campus that plaintiff was a homosexual, and this rumor was traced back to defendant's fraternity.
14. Defendant's statement during the skit and the manner of its presentation, in light of the rumor that plaintiff was a homosexual, falsely depicted plaintiff as a homosexual.
15. Plaintiff is not a homosexual and defendant's depiction of plaintiff as a homosexual was highly offensive to plaintiff.
16. Defendant's depiction of plaintiff as homosexual was done with knowledge of its falsity or reckless disregard whether the depiction gave a false impression or not.
17. As a result of defendant's depiction of plaintiff as a homosexual, plaintiff suffered, and continues to suffer, great nervousness and mental anguish.
18. Plaintiff, as the direct result of defendant's depiction of plaintiff as a homosexual, in addition to the nervousness and bodily injury, has been injured in plaintiff's good reputation in the Collegiate University community. Such false depiction has been circulated also among plaintiff's personal friends, who have changed their attitude toward plaintiff, and who have begun to question whether plaintiff is a homosexual, which depiction defendant wrongly, maliciously, and untruthfully imputed to plaintiff.

Prayer for Relief

The **prayer** section of the complaint states that the plaintiff wants the court to do. Rule 8(a) of the Federal Rules of Civil Procedure requires the complaint to contain "a demand for judgment for the relief the pleader seeks." A plaintiff may ask the court for various types of damages, for an injunction, for specific performance, or for some other type of relief.

LEGAL TERMS

prayer
Portion of a bill in equity or a petition that asks for equitable relief and specifies the relief sought.

Plaintiff therefore requests judgment granting the following relief as to counts I and II:

A. an award of compensatory damages in an amount to be set at trial;
B. an award of punitive damages in an amount to be set at trial;
C. an award of costs and attorney's fees; and
D. such other relief as court deems appropriate.

JURY DEMAND

Plaintiff demands trial by jury.

Signature Block

The signature block usually contains the name of the attorney, the name and designation of the person the attorney is representing, the attorney's address, and the attorney's telephone number. Florida state courts and other courts require the attorney's bar membership number. Rule 11(a) of the Federal Rules of Civil Procedure requires the following:

> Every pleading, written motion, and other paper shall be signed by at least one attorney of record in the attorney's individual name, or, if the party is not represented by an attorney, shall be signed by the party. Each paper shall state the signer's address and telephone number, if any.

____
Florida Attorney
101 Main Street
Anytown, Florida
Attorney for plaintiff
(407) 000-0000
Bar No. 0000000

Verification

The **verification** is a notarized statement of the party, rather than of the attorney, "verifying" the statements contained in the complaint. Rule 11(a) of the Federal Rules of Civil Procedure dispenses with verification of court documents unless specifically required by an applicable rule or statute. You should check to determine whether verification is required by the court in which your complaint is being filed.

FORMAT OF THE ANSWER

Caption

The format of the caption for an answer is the same as that of the caption for the complaint.

IN THE CIRCUIT COURT
OF THE NINTH JUDICIAL CIRCUIT
IN AND FOR ORANGE COUNTY, FLORIDA

JAKE CARSON,	)	
Plaintiff,	)	
	)	**CIVIL ACTION**
-vs-	)	**No. 94-000-00**
	)	
TOM HARRIS,	)	
Defendant.	)	

Defenses

As noted earlier, the answer states the defendant's defense, admitting or denying plaintiff's claims. The answer also contains any affirmative defenses or counterclaims. Rule 8 of the Federal Rules of Civil Procedure quite specifically states how any denial is to be made:

> A party shall state in short and plain terms the party's defenses to each claim asserted and shall admit or deny the averments upon which the adverse party relies. If a party is without knowledge or information sufficient to form a belief as to the truth of an averment, the party shall so state and this has the effect of a denial. Denial shall fairly meet the substance of the averments denied. When a pleader intends in good faith to deny only a part or a qualification of an averment, the pleader shall specify so much of it as is true and material and shall deny only the remainder. Unless the pleader intends in good faith to controvert all the averments of the preceding pleading, the pleader may make denials as specific denials of the designated averments or paragraphs, or may generally deny all the averments except such designated averments or paragraphs as the pleader expressly admits; but, when the pleader does so intend to controvert all its averments, including averments of the grounds upon which the court's jurisdiction depends, the pleader may do so by general denial.
>
> * * *
>
> Averments in a pleading to which a responsive pleading is required, other than those as to the amount of damages, are admitted when not denied in the responsive pleading. Averments in a pleading to which no responsive pleading is required or permitted shall be taken as denied or avoided.

ANSWER

Defendant TOM HARRIS answers Plaintiff's complaint and says:

1. He admits paragraph 1 for jurisdictional purposes only and otherwise denies it insofar as it is applied to him.
2. He admits paragraph 2.
3. He admits paragraph 3.
4. He admits paragraph 4.

LEGAL TERMS

verification
A sworn statement certifying the truth of the facts recited in an instrument or document. Thus, . . ., a verified complaint is a pleading accompanied by an affidavit stating that the facts set forth in the complaint are true.

5. He admits paragraph 5.
6. He admits paragraph 6.
7. With respect to paragraph 7, he denies making the quoted statement maliciously or falsely. Otherwise he admits paragraph 7.
8. He is without knowledge of paragraph 8.
9. He is without knowledge of paragraph 9.
10. He is without knowledge of paragraph 10.
11. With respect to paragraph 11, he repeats his response to paragraphs 1 through 7.
12. He is without knowledge of paragraph 12.
13. He denies paragraph 13.
14. He denies paragraph 14.
15. He is without knowledge of paragraph 15.
16. He denies paragraph 16.
17. He is without knowledge of paragraph 17.
18. With respect to paragraph 18, he repeats his response to paragraphs 12 through 17.

Affirmative Defenses and Counterclaims

Rule 1.110 of the Florida Rules of Civil Procedure specifies the format for any affirmative defenses or counterclaims:

> All averments of claim of defense shall be made in consecutively numbered paragraphs, the contents of each of which shall be limited as far as practicable to a statement of a single set of circumstances, and a paragraph may be referred to by number in all subsequent pleadings. Each claim founded upon a separate transaction or occurrence and each defense other than denials shall be stated in a separate count or defense when a separation facilitates the clear presentation of the matter set forth.

FIRST AFFIRMATIVE DEFENSE

19. Defendant's skit was an obvious expression of humor and could not reasonably be understood as describing an actual fact about plaintiff or an actual event in which plaintiff participated.

SECOND AFFIRMATIVE DEFENSE

20. Plaintiff has failed to allege facts showing that defendant's skit was presented with falsity, negligence, actual malice, or reckless disregard for the truth.

A counterclaim, like the body of the complaint, would be followed by a prayer for relief.

Certificate of Service

If the attorney for the defendant serves the answer on the plaintiff attorney, a **certificate** *of service* must be included. No certificate of service was included in the complaint because the complaint was served on the defendant by the court, not by the plaintiff's attorney.

CERTIFICATE OF SERVICE

I furnished a copy of this answer to Florida Attorney, attorney for plaintiff, 101 Main Street, Anytown, Florida, by U.S. mail on ______, 19___.

____
Unnamed Attorney
Attorney for defendant
TOM HARRIS
100 Court Street
Anytown, Florida
(407) 880-0000
Florida Bar No. 100000

EVIDENTIARY FACTS, ULTIMATE FACTS, AND LEGAL CONCLUSIONS

An understanding of the terms *evidentiary facts*, *ultimate facts*, and *legal conclusions* is vital in drafting the allegations of a complaint. This section first explains what these terms mean. It then explains the relationship among the terms and drafting allegations.

Evidentiary facts are facts admissible in evidence. *Ultimate facts* are the facts in a case upon which liability is determined or based. Ultimate facts establish the elements of the cause of action. A *legal conclusion* is a statement of the result in a situation, which involves applying the law to a set of facts. A legal conclusion states an element of the cause of action. As shown in Figure 12–1, there is an overlap between evidentiary facts and ultimate facts and there is an overlap between ultimate facts and conclusions of law. To understand these terms, let's see how they relate to the sample complaint.

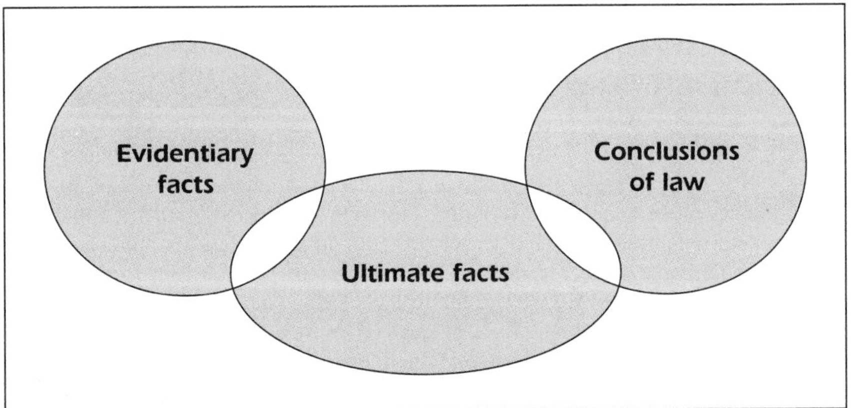

FIGURE 12-1 The relationship among facts and conclusions.

LEGAL TERMS

certificate
A formal or official written declaration intended as an authentication of the fact or facts set forth therein.

Evidentiary Facts

Paragraphs 2 through 6 and 8 of the sample complaint contain evidentiary facts. For example:

> In October 1993 plaintiff was a student at Collegiate University, a member of the Collegiate Beta Fraternity, and a candidate for student body president of Collegiate University.
>
> In October 1993 defendant was a student at Collegiate University, a member of the Collegiate Alpha Fraternity, and a candidate for student body president of Collegiate University.
>
> In defendant's skit, defendant portrayed "plaintiff's doctor" and another student portrayed plaintiff.

Paragraph 7 contains a mixture of evidentiary and ultimate facts. The kernel of the ultimate facts has been bracketed:

> In defendant's skit, defendant, [in the presence and hearing of] plaintiff and the students and faculty watching the skit, [maliciously and falsely announced] that plaintiff had tested HIV positive, saying "you tested HIV positive."

Ultimate Facts

Paragraphs 9 and 10 of the sample complaint contain ultimate facts (establishing elements of defamation):

> Plaintiff at the time of defendant's statement was in good health and free from any disease, and the statements of defendant were wholly untrue.
>
> As a result of defendant's slanderous statement, plaintiff suffered, and continues to suffer, great nervousness and mental anguish.

Conclusions of Law

Paragraph 11 of the sample complaint contains conclusions of law:

> Plaintiff, as the direct result of defendant's statement, in addition to the nervousness and bodily injury, has been injured in plaintiff's good reputation in the Collegiate University community. Defendant published such false and slanderous statement about plaintiff to numerous students and faculty of Collegiate University, who have changed their attitude toward plaintiff, and who have begun to question plaintiff as to whether plaintiff has tested HIV positive, which the slanderous remark of defendant wrongly, maliciously, and untruthfully imputed to plaintiff.

The essence of paragraph 11 is that:

Tom Harris made a defamatory statement about Jake Carson;
Tom Harris published the statement to numerous students and faculty of Collegiate University; and
The statement damaged Jake Carson's reputation.

Drafting Allegations

Now that you have an idea of the difference among evidentiary facts, ultimate facts, and conclusions of law, let's see how these terms relate to drafting allegations. The body of the complaint will contain evidentiary facts, ultimate facts, and conclusions of law. The complaint should be drafted so that the defendant admits as much as possible and denies as little as possible. The defendant is more likely to admit evidentiary facts than to admit ultimate facts, and will routinely deny conclusions of law. Therefore, the body of a complaint should, as much as possible, separate evidentiary facts from ultimate facts from conclusions of law. In the sample answer, the defendant admitted paragraphs 2 through 6 and part of paragraph 7. The paragraphs to which the defendant admitted contained evidentiary facts.

When drafting a complaint, use the list of things to do in Figure 12–2.

1. Separate evidentiary facts, ultimate facts, and conclusions of law. (The defendant will be more likely to admit allegations if evidentiary facts are separated from ultimate facts.)
2. Write in plain English. (Make your allegations clear to the judge.)
3. Place only one or two sentences in each numbered paragraph. (If a number of facts are included in a paragraph and one of the facts is wrong, the defendant may deny the whole paragraph.)
4. Do not include more evidentiary facts than necessary. (If you do, the plaintiff will be faced with proving facts not admitted.)
5. Use descriptive words for allegations favorable to the plaintiff; use abstract words for allegations adverse to the plaintiff. (The judge will more likely remember a description that brings a picture to mind than an abstract statement of adverse facts.)
6. Use objective rather than subjective language. (It is harder for the defendant to deny objectively stated facts.)

FIGURE 12-2 Tips for drafting a complaint.

SAMPLE COMPLAINT

IN THE CIRCUIT COURT
OF THE NINTH JUDICIAL CIRCUIT
IN AND FOR ORANGE COUNTY, FLORIDA

JAKE CARSON,	)	
Plaintiff,	)	
	)	CIVIL ACTION
- vs-	)	No. 94-000-00
	)	
TOM HARRIS,	)	
Defendant.	)[1]	

COMPLAINT[2]

Plaintiff, JAKE CARSON, sues defendant, TOM HARRIS, and alleges:[3]

---

[1] The caption contains the name of the court, the names of the parties, and the case number. There is one plaintiff and one defendant in this lawsuit. If there were more parties, all of them would be named in the caption of the initial complaint. In all other documents, only the first party on each side would be named, followed by "*et al.*" replacing all other parties. "*Et al.*" is short for "*et alia,*" meaning "and others." "JAKE CARSON, plaintiff vs. TOM HARRIS, Defendant" is often referred to as the **style** of the case. The case number is supplied by the court clerk. The number "95" indicates the year the case was filed. The next number indicates the order of filing. Cases are given consecutive numbers based on the order filed. For example, "100" would mean that the case was the one hundredth case filed in 1995. The sample complaint is unnumbered—"000"—to show that it is not an actual case.

[2] Rule 1.100 of the Florida Rules of Civil Procedure requires that court documents "indicate clearly the subject matter of the paper and the party requesting or obtaining relief." The form complaints at the end of the Florida Rules of Civil Procedure (see, for example, Forms 1.936–1.942) are simply named "COMPLAINT." Some jurisdictions may require the pleading name to indicate the relief requested, for example, "COMPLAINT FOR DAMAGES."

[3] This introductory clause (also referred to as the *commencement*) states who is suing whom. Notice that the introductory clause is not numbered.

This introductory clause is modeled on the one contained in the forms at the end of the Florida Rules of Civil Procedure: "Plaintiff, A.B., sues defendant, C.D., and alleges:" (see Forms 1.936–1.942). This plain English clause is much easier to read than the traditional introductory clause filled with legalese. For example, the introductory clause rewritten in legalese might look something like this:

> Now comes the above-named plaintiff, Jake Carson, by and through his attorney of record, Florida Attorney, and for cause of action and complaint against the defendant herein alleges unto this honorable court:

Write your pleadings in plain English, complying with the court rules of your jurisdiction. Plain English pleadings are easier for the client to understand and are less time-consuming in the long run.

COUNT I—DEFAMATION[4]

1. This is an action for damages that exceed $15,000.[5]
2. In October 1993 plaintiff was a student at Collegiate University, a member of the Collegiate Beta Fraternity, and a candidate for student body president of Collegiate University.[6]

For simplicity's sake, there is one plaintiff and one defendant in this sample complaint. For ease of reference, they are referred to as "Plaintiff" and "Defendant" throughout the complaint. If this were a real complaint, Jake might have also named the Alpha Fraternity and Collegiate University as defendants. Multiple defendants could be referred to by short forms established in the introductory clause. For example:

> Plaintiff, JAKE CARSON, sues Defendants, TOM HARRIS ("Defendant Harris"), ALPHA FRATERNITY ("Defendant Fraternity"), and COLLEGIATE UNIVERSITY ("Defendant University") and says:
>
> or
>
> Plaintiff, JAKE CARSON, sues Defendants, TOM HARRIS ("Harris"), ALPHA FRATERNITY ("Fraternity"), and COLLEGIATE UNIVERSITY ("University") and says:

Once you establish short forms, you should use them consistently throughout the rest of the complaint. For readability, you may want to put party names in all capital letters.

4 In a complaint with more than one count, the counts are usually numbered for ease of reference. The count heading may also state the cause of action (here "COUNT I—DEFAMATION" and "COUNT II—FALSE LIGHT INVASION OF PRIVACY") or relief sought. The relief sought in another complaint, for example, might be "SPECIFIC PERFORMANCE" and "DAMAGES." If the complaint contains a single count, the count need not be headed.

In this complaint, the background for both counts is alleged in numbered paragraphs 1 through 8. Paragraph 12 of Count II realleges paragraphs 1 through 8. Another way to organize the complaint is to provide a heading "COMMON ALLEGATIONS" after the introductory paragraph. The "COMMON ALLEGATIONS" section of the complaint would contain numbered paragraphs 1 through 8. Then the complaint would state:

COUNT I—DEFAMATION

> 9. Plaintiff realleges and incorporates paragraphs 1–8 above.

5 The paragraphs of the body of the complaint (sometimes referred to as the *charging portion* of the complaint) are numbered consecutively. In the body of the complaint, the plaintiff alleges the plaintiff's ultimate facts. This paragraph establishes the court's jurisdiction. In Florida, the circuit court handles cases with more than $15,000 in controversy.

6 Paragraphs 2 through 11 contain the evidentiary and ultimate facts on which the plaintiff relies. The two purposes of the body of the complaint are to:

1. give the defendant notice of the plaintiff's claims; and
2. include all the elements of the cause of action that the plaintiff alleges.

Before you write the body of the complaint, make a list of the elements of the cause of action. After you have completed the body of the complaint, double-check to make sure you have included ultimate facts needed for all elements.

LEGAL TERMS

style
Caption or heading; the caption of a case.

3. In October 1993 defendant was a student at Collegiate University, a member of the Collegiate Alpha Fraternity, and a candidate for student body president of Collegiate University.[7]
4. The October 20, 1993, issue of the Collegiate University student newspaper reported that plaintiff and defendant "were running neck and neck" in the student body president race.[8]
5. On October 20, 1993, the day before the student body president election, plaintiff and defendant presented skits to Collegiate University students and faculty at the Collegiate University football stadium.
6 In defendant's skit, defendant portrayed "plaintiff's doctor" and another student portrayed plaintiff.
7. In defendant's skit, defendant, in the presence and hearing of plaintiff and the students and faculty watching the skit, maliciously and falsely announced that plaintiff had tested HIV positive, saying "you tested HIV positive."
8. In the student body president election on October 21, 1993, plaintiff received 10% of the vote and defendant received 90% of the vote.
9. Plaintiff at the time of defendant's statement was in good health and free from any disease, and the statements of defendant were wholly untrue.
10. As a result of defendant's slanderous statement, plaintiff suffered, and continues to suffer, great nervousness and mental anguish.
11. Plaintiff, as the direct result of defendant's statement, in addition to the nervousness and bodily injury, has been injured in plaintiff's good reputation in the Collegiate University community. Defendant published such false and slanderous statement about plaintiff to numerous students and faculty of Collegiate University, who have changed their attitude toward plaintiff, and who have begun to question plaintiff as to whether plaintiff has tested HIV positive, which the slanderous remark of defendant wrongly, maliciously, and untruthfully imputed to plaintiff.

COUNT II—FALSE LIGHT INVASION OF PRIVACY

12. Plaintiff realleges and incorporates paragraphs 1–8 above.[9]
13. Prior to October 20, 1993, a rumor had circulated on the Collegiate University campus that plaintiff was a homosexual, and this rumor was traced back to defendant's fraternity.

---

[7] Paragraphs 2 and 3 identify the parties. Usually the parties are identified early in the complaint.

[8] Here the plaintiff begins to narrate what happened. The narrative is written in the past tense.

[9] Paragraph numbering is consecutive from one count to the next.

14. Defendant's statement during the skit and the manner of its presentation, in light of the rumor that plaintiff was a homosexual, falsely depicted plaintiff as a homosexual.
15. Plaintiff is not a homosexual and defendant's depiction of plaintiff as a homosexual was highly offensive to plaintiff.
16. Defendant's depiction of plaintiff as a homosexual was done with knowledge of its falsity or reckless disregard whether the depiction gave a false impression or not.
17. As a result of defendant's depiction of plaintiff as a homosexual, plaintiff suffered, and continues to suffer, great nervousness and mental anguish.
18. Plaintiff, as the direct result of defendant's depiction of plaintiff as a homosexual, in addition to the nervousness and bodily injury, has been injured in plaintiff's good reputation in the Collegiate University community. Such false depiction has been circulated also among plaintiff's personal friends, who have changed their attitude toward plaintiff, and who have begun to question whether plaintiff is a homosexual, which depiction defendant wrongly, maliciously, and untruthfully imputed to plaintiff.

Plaintiff therefore requests judgment granting the following relief as to counts I and II:[10]

A. an award of compensatory damages in an amount to be set at trial;
B. an award of punitive damages in an amount to be set at trial;
C. an award of costs and attorney's fees; and
D. such other relief as the court deems appropriate.[11]

JURY DEMAND

Plaintiff demands trial by jury.[12]

---

[10] This is the beginning line of the plaintiff's prayer for relief. The line is not numbered, but the various types of relief sought are lettered with capital letters. Traditionally, the first line of the prayer for relief would have read as follows:

> WHEREFORE, Plaintiff, JAKE CARSON, demands that this honorable court grant judgment for the following relief:

This line has been rewritten in the sample complaint to eliminate legalese. Also, the word "requests" (a word sounding less strident) has been substituted for "demands."

Another way to organize the complaint would be to have two prayer-for-relief sections—one following paragraph 11 and the other (as it is in the sample complaint) following paragraph 18.

[11] This catchall phrase typically is included in the prayer-for-relief because it allows the court to grant relief other than that specifically requested.

[12] Typically the plaintiff requests a jury trial. If the plaintiff decides later against a jury trial, the right may be waived.

____
Florida Attorney
101 Main Street
Anytown, Florida
Attorney for plaintiff
(407) 000-0000
Bar No. 0000000

SAMPLE ANSWER

IN THE CIRCUIT COURT
OF THE NINTH JUDICIAL CIRCUIT
IN AND FOR ORANGE COUNTY, FLORIDA

JAKE CARSON,)
Plaintiff,)
) CIVIL ACTION
- vs-) No. 94-000-00[13]
)
TOM HARRIS,)
Defendant.)

ANSWER[14]

Defendant TOM HARRIS answers Plaintiff's complaint and says:

1. He admits paragraph 1 for jurisdictional purposes only and otherwise denies it insofar as it is applied to him.
2. He admits paragraph 2.[15]
3. He admits paragraph 3.

---

[13] The case number is copied from the complaint.

[14] Because there is a single defendant, "ANSWER" is a sufficient title. If there were multiple defendants and the answer was that of all defendants, the pleading would be titled "DEFENDANTS' ANSWER." If the answer was that of less than all the defendants, the title should indicate the party filing the answer, for example, "ANSWER OF DEFENDANT COLLEGIATE UNIVERSITY."

[15] Here the defendant's numbered paragraphs correspond to the numbering of the paragraphs in the complaint. Another way to organize the answer would be for the defendant to list in a single numbered paragraph the paragraphs of the complaint admitted, to list in a single numbered paragraph the paragraphs of the complaint denied, and to list in a single numbered paragraph the paragraphs of the complaint of which defendant has no knowledge. For example:

2. He admits paragraphs 2 through 6.
3. He is without knowledge of paragraphs 8 through 11, 13, 15, 17, and 18.
4. He denies paragraphs 14 and 16.

4. He admits paragraph 4.
5. He admits paragraph 5.
6. He admits paragraph 6.
7. With respect to paragraph 7, he denies making the quoted statement maliciously or falsely. Otherwise he admits paragraph 7.[16]
8. He is without knowledge of paragraph 8.
9. He is without knowledge of paragraph 9.
10. He is without knowledge of paragraph 10.
11. With respect to paragraph 11, he repeats his response to paragraphs 1 through 7.
12. He is without knowledge of paragraph 12.
13. He denies paragraph 13.
14. He denies paragraph 14.
15. He is without knowledge of paragraph 15.
16. He denies paragraph 16.
17. He is without knowledge of paragraph 17.
18. With respect to paragraph 18, he repeats his response to paragraphs 12–17.

FIRST AFFIRMATIVE DEFENSE

19. Defendant's skit was an obvious expression of humor and could not reasonably be understood as describing an actual fact about plaintiff or an actual event in which plaintiff participated.

SECOND AFFIRMATIVE DEFENSE

20. Plaintiff has failed to allege facts showing that defendant's skit was presented with falsity, negligence, actual malice, or reckless disregard for the truth.

CERTIFICATE OF SERVICE

I furnished a copy of this answer to Florida Attorney, attorney for plaintiff, 101 Main Street, Anytown, Florida, by U.S. mail on _______, 19___.

____
Unnamed Attorney
Attorney for defendant
TOM HARRIS
100 Court Street
Anytown, Florida
(407) 880-0000
Florida Bar No. 100000

[16] Rule 1.110 of the Florida Rules of Civil Procedure requires the defendant to specify which part of the allegation is admitted and which part of the allegation is denied.

WHAT AN ANSWER!*

The following is an answer that was filed in a case earlier in this century. You may find the content of the answer (written very tongue-in-cheek) amusing. Aside from the interesting content, the answer is an example of how not to write an answer. You may want to try rewriting the answer using the tips included in this chapter. (Rewrite it in plain English, one or two sentences to a numbered paragraph, etc.)

A.D. BEATTY, et ux	IN THE DISTRICT COURT OF
-vs-	McCLENNAN COUNTY, TEXAS
MISSOURI-KANSAS-TEXAS	54th JUDICIAL DISTRICT
RAILROAD CO. OF TEXAS	

TO THE HONORABLE JUDGE OF SAID COURT:

Now comes the defendant, Missouri-Kansas-Texas Railroad Company of Texas, a corporation, and with leave of the Court first had and obtained files this its first amended original answer and cross-action herein and for such shows to the Court as follows:

1.

Defendant demurs generally to the allegations in plaintiff's petition contained and says the same are not sufficient in law to constitute a cause of action against it and of this it prays judgment of the Court.

2.

For further answer, if necessary, this defendant denies all and singular the allegations in said petition contained, and demands strict proof thereof.

3.

Answering further, if need there be, this defendant railroad company would reveal to the Court that in truth and in fact the plaintiff, Mrs. Hattie Beatty, for several nights prior to the occasion of which she now complains, had strolled by the signal tower in question and on each occasion persistently propositioned this defendant's employee at said tower, one Dockery, to engage with her in an ancient popular pastime.

That the said Dockery is an old and trusted employee, a man of over sixty winters with snow in his hair but with summer in his heart; that the faint odor of Beatty's perfume touched his delicate nostrils and the full red painted lips of his modern young aphrodite brought back youthful dreams to his aging head. Although the season was fall time, the sap began to rise in his erotic soul as in romantic springtime of yore. It was on the unlucky night of Friday the thirteenth of September, A.D. 1934, that the said Dockery finally succumbed to plaintiff's feminine allurements, the price being paid one dollar in advance.

That in all truthfulness the only mechanical contrivance or unique lever about the said tower in which the plaintiff expressed any interest whatsoever was that which was hung on the person of the said Dockery.

That this defendant Railroad Company had not equipped its said tower for any such passionate purpose and had, in fact, instructed its said employee to admit no visitors thereto, but that unbeknown to this defendant the said Dockery permitted the plaintiff to come into the crowded quarters of said tower to indulge with him in an session of Spanish athletics; that while she reclined upon cushioned chair and unfolded her female charms to his approach her bare knee did touch and open electric switch upon the wall of said tower, thereby creating an electrical contact quite different from the contact for which she was prepared; that either from shocked surprise at the seemingly remarkable amative powers of said Dockery or for other reasons unknown to this defendant the said plaintiff sank to the floor of said tower in an apparent swoon, leaving the said Dockery unrewarded and bewildered, with raiment disarranged and struggling desperately to operate his signals for a fast train which he discovered at that moment approaching unexpectedly upon defendant's tracks.

That as to this defendant the transaction in question was ultra vires and completely outside the scope of employment of the said Dockery, and clearly without benefit to this defendant corporation, except for the publicity that might possibly attend this proof to the world of the exemplary manner in which the M-K-T Railroad cares for and preserves the virility of its aging employees.

That if it would be held, however, that the said Dockery was, on the occasion in question, acting for this defendant railroad company, which is, as the Court has often heard plaintiff's counsel charge, a heartless and bloodless corporation, a poor creature of statute, without pride of ancestry or hope of posterity and physically incapable of becoming enraptured in the ethereal paroxysms of love, then in that event only this defendant pleads that the plaintiff was guilty of contributory negligence in the following respects: That the said Dockery urged the plaintiff to remove herself from the cushioned chair to the floor of the tower in order that his engagement might be fulfilled in the good old American way but that plaintiff proclaimed her proficiency and maintained her ability to handle the situation from her position in the chair and that she remained in said chair contrary to Dockery's urgent solicitations and entreaties and received the electric shock as a direct and proximate result of her insistence upon departing from well-recognized precedent; that plaintiff was negligent in failing to pursue her activities horizontally from the floor in the time-honored, accepted and orthodox style and that her failure so to do proximately contributed to the cause of her injuries, if any.

That if it should be held that the said Dockery was acting for the defendant railroad corporation and that through some manner of judicial reasoning unknown to it this defendant should be held to have enjoyed vicariously the benefits anticipated by the said Dockery from his relations with plaintiff, then in that event this defendant shows that there has been a complete failure of consideration in that there was no contract as agreed.

That, in any event, it is a matter of judicial knowledge that the business in which the plaintiff was engaged entails certain ordinary risks, one of the least of which is the risk of being shocked, and in this connection it is shown that the plaintiff held herself out as an expert in her art, while the said Dockery was to an observant eye a man fresh from the soil and reared to the manners of the pioneer country-side, a man entirely untrained to innovations of perpendicular postures and therefore completely unable to anticipate plaintiff's new-fangled hip and knee movements from a cushioned chair or to warn plaintiff of the probable consequences thereof, and that plaintiff assumed the risk of her injuries if any.

4.

And now, becoming actor herein only in the event the Court should hold that the said Dockery represented this defendant corporation in question which will never be admitted, this defendant shows as against plaintiff that its agent Dockery did pay to the said plaintiff one devalued dollar of the United States Currency and received no value therefor as agreed by the plaintiff, and that said dollar has never been returned to its owner and that under all the facts hereinabove alleged it is entitled to recover said sum.

WHEREFORE, this defendant Railroad Company prays that plaintiff take nothing in this suit, as did the said Dockery take nothing from plaintiff, and that in the alternative alleged it recover from the plaintiff the sum of one dollar and all costs of suit herein and that its virtue be in all things vindicated and that it further be relieved of all possible insinuations against its chastity that may arise as the result of this lawsuit, and for such other relief as it may merit.

NAMAN, HOWELL AND BROOKS
Attorneys for Defendant
Missouri-Kansas-Texas Railroad Co.

SUMMARY

- The complaint is the initial pleading in a civil action, in which the plaintiff alleges a cause of action and asks that the wrong done to the plaintiff be remedied by the court.
- The answer is a pleading by the defendant in response to the complaint.
- Pleadings must conform to applicable court rules and statutes.
- Pleading forms may be used to draft a pleading but must be tailored to the particular situation with which you are dealing.
- Generally the complaint contains a caption, claims, a prayer for relief, and a signature block.
- Generally the answer contains a caption, defenses, affirmative defenses and counterclaims, and a certificate of service.
- Evidentiary facts are facts admissible in evidence.
- Ultimate facts are the facts in a case upon which liability is determined or based.
- A legal conclusion is a statement of the result in a situation, which involves applying the law to a set of facts.
- When drafting the complaint, follow the six writing tips in Figure 12-2.

EXERCISES

Using the answer in *Beatty v. Missouri-Kansas-Texas Railroad,* answer the following questions:

1. What is contained in the caption?
2. What are the defendant's defenses?
3. How was the plaintiff injured?
4. What is the "cross-action"?
5. What relief does the defendant request?

NOTES

* Grateful thanks to Dr. Daniel Hall who supplied me with a copy of this answer.

CHAPTER 13
Law Office Memo

OUTLINE

Purpose and Uses
Style
Format

A *law office memo* is different from a *memorandum of law*. As the name suggests, the law office memo is seen only by those in the law office and by the client. In litigation, though, an attorney may be required by court rule, may be asked by the judge, or may feel the need to submit a memorandum of law. The purpose of the memorandum of law is to support and argue the client's position in the lawsuit. The tone of the memorandum of law is persuasive rather than objective. Because it is submitted to court, it is a matter of public record and a copy of the memorandum of law is delivered to opposing counsel.

One of the standard legal documents written by a paralegal or attorney is referred to as the "law office memo." (It may also be called an "office memo" or "interoffice memorandum.") This chapter includes a sample law office memo and explains the purpose and use of the office memo and its format. The first time you read this chapter, glance over the sample memo, noting its format. Then refer back to the sample as it is being analyzed in the balance of the chapter.

The sample office memo has been extensively annotated to provide you with writing and citation tips. If the notes do not make much sense to you right now, read them again after you have gone over the rules for citations and quotations contained in appendixes B and C. It might also be helpful to refer to the notes again when you are writing your own office memos.

PURPOSE AND USES

The footnotes in the sample office memo are not part of the law office memo itself. Although an office memo may contain footnotes, there are not usually more than one or two. The office memo you write should contain few or no footnotes.

Legal research is required when the client or the attorney is confronted with a legal problem and the answer to the problem is unclear. A client who is planning a business deal may be wondering how the deal can be structured most advantageously to minimize taxes. Often a client is contemplating suing someone. It is important for both the client and the attorney to know what the client's chances are of obtaining a favorable judgment and whether the client would be entitled to attorney fees. After a lawsuit has been filed, the attorney may need to have a procedural question researched.

The main purposes of the office memo are to record the law found as a result of the research, to explain how the researcher analyzed the law and applied it to the facts, and to propose a solution to the problem. At the moment he or she completes the research on a problem, the researcher is the "expert" on the legal principles involved, but any researcher will quickly forget some details of the research. Depending on the complexity of the questions, one hour, several hours, or several weeks of research might have been required. For a client being billed at an hourly rate, research is expensive but necessary. Writing an office memo allows both the client and the attorney to benefit from the research. The office memo can be read several times and discussed before a decision is made. Although you will find that your first office memo seems to take days to write, edit, and rewrite, the time spent by an experienced writer on an office memo is fairly small in comparison to the time spent doing the research.

Usually multiple copies of the law office memo are made, with one copy being kept by the researcher, one copy going to the attorney in the office who requested the research, one copy being placed in the client file, one copy going to the client (if the client is sophisticated enough to understand it), and one copy being placed in a research file in the office. The attorney and the client use their copies to decide how to resolve the problem discussed in the memo. The copy in the client file can be used later to quickly review the facts or the analysis underlying the decision made. Often the researcher has spent time pulling the facts together from various sources and organizing them. The memo may be used to quickly refresh memory on the facts without having to consult all the various sources, or to understand later why the particular decision was made. The copy placed in the research file may be used to aid in research; there may be further research to be done later on the same or a related problem. The researcher can quickly pull prior office memos and determine whether any of the research previously done can be used. If the researcher is lucky enough to find a prior office memo involving the same problem, all the researcher may have to do is to update the research from the date of the prior memo.

STYLE

A number of common style errors made in law office memos are easily avoidable if you know what to do and what not to do. Reading this section should help you avoid such errors. After you have written the first draft of your office memo, read this section again and make any necessary changes to your memo.

First of all, the tone of the office memo should be objective rather than persuasive. Choose words that are fairly neutral. For example, referring to the illegal drug problem as a "serious menace," as the *Smith* court did in the last paragraph of the opinion on which the sample is based, is fine for an opinion, but that language sounds too subjective for an office memo. Instead, substitute "serious problem."

Secondly, keep yourself out of the memo. Even if the office memo contains your opinion, keep the tone of the office memo as impersonal as possible and do not use the word "I." Instead of saying: "I think that . . . ," you might substitute: "Based on similar facts in *Smith* and *Campbell,* it is obvious that . . . ."

A third style tip is to avoid using contractions, slang, or any other informal expressions that are normally used in spoken rather than written communication. Although the tone of the office memo does not have to be so proper that it is uninviting to read, it should be somewhat formal. Contractions and slang lend too informal a tone to your office memo.

A fourth error is use of elegant variation. Your English composition teacher probably told you not to use the same word twice and to use synonyms to make your writing more interesting. This is fine for English composition, but not for legal writing. If you use two different words that mean the same thing, like "lawyer" and "attorney" or "purchaser" and "buyer," an attorney reading your writing will immediately want to know why you changed the wording. The attorney will also assume that there is some reason for the change. Perhaps you were referring to something different when you used a different word. When you refer to the same thing a second time, use the same reference term.

The final common style error is to use an abstract word when a more specific one is available. For example, in *Campbell* (the case on which the sample is based), the agents discovered cocaine in Campbell's car. Rather than talking about suppression of the "evidence" or the "drugs," tell your reader that Campbell filed a motion to suppress the "cocaine." It is just as easy to use the word "cocaine," it makes it easier for your reader to picture, and the word is more descriptive than "evidence" or "drugs."

FORMAT

Although there is no one correct format for office memos, the format given in this chapter is fairly standard. Another format frequently used has the same major sections but places the facts after the issues and answers. Ask your professor what format he or she prefers. You will need to do the same thing if you are asked to write an office memo for your job. Many law offices have a format that the attorneys prefer.

The following portion of this chapter tells you in general terms what to put in each section of the office memo. You may want to read the following sections while comparing them to the sample office memo.

To and From

These two sections contain the name of the person who assigned you to write the law office memo and your name. If the office memo will be read by persons other than the person who assigned you, you may want to add their names as well.

Re

Identify the subject matter of the office memo in a phrase with sufficient detail so a reader will know whether to read further.

Date

The memo should be dated with either the date you complete your research or the date you deliver it to your reader. The date is important for future reference because it is assumed that the research reflected in the memo is current up to the date of the memo or shortly before.

Facts

Clearly state significant facts which the reader needs to know to understand the reasoning section of the memo. Limit them to one or two paragraphs. The facts are the facts; do not invent "facts". If you do not know important facts, spend more time gathering them, or, if that is impossible, state what facts are not known. When important facts are unknown, you may have to assume facts and then base your research and your law office memo on the assumed facts. This is fine as long as you clearly state your assumptions and explain that your discussion and conclusions are based on those assumptions. You may even want to assume facts in the alternative and explain what conclusions you would reach based on other assumptions.

Issue(s) and Answer(s)

You should spend considerable time writing your issues and answers because they are the heart of your memo. You may have an idea of what your issues will be before you begin your research, so write down your issues at this preliminary stage. As you perform your research and write your office memo, you will probably find yourself revising your issues and answers several times.

An issue and the corresponding answer should each be one sentence in length while giving the reader the most information possible. An issue is usually stated in the form of a question and the answer is a full-sentence response to the issue. Usually there are the same number of issues as answers, with each issue being paired with an answer. Number your issues and answers to make understanding easier for your reader. If you find, in including as much information as possible in your issue and answer, that the issue and answer become unwieldy, experiment with splitting up that issue and answer into two issues and two answers.

Thesis Paragraph

The reasoning portion of your office memo should begin with a thesis paragraph. This paragraph should contain your *thesis*—the central idea of your memo. It should serve as a road map, giving your reader the big picture of your memo. Besides stating your thesis in your thesis paragraph, you may want to state your final conclusion in simple terms.

Rule of Law

The *rule of law* is the law contained in any legal sources which will, later in your memo, be applied to your facts. Usually the law is contained in primary sources, but sometimes you may have to rely on secondary sources (such as law review articles or legal periodicals) if there are no primary sources on point.

You need to clearly explain the rule of law to the reader so the reader has a solid basis for understanding the rest of your reasoning. If your law is contained in constitutional or statutory provisions, you may want to quote the relevant portions of those provisions. Leave out any portions of the provisions that are irrelevant and indicate any omissions by the use of ellipses. If the provisions are very simple, you may want to explain them in your own words rather than quoting them. If your law is from case law, explain enough about the precedent case so the reader can understand what the case stands for and can better comprehend your application of the case to the facts of the current problem. You may need to devote one or more paragraphs to explaining the significant facts of an important case if you will later be comparing the facts of that case to the facts of the current problem. Your readers will be able to understand the rest of your reasoning better if you have first given them a good foundation in the rule of law.

Application of Law to Facts

Many students spend so much energy explaining the rule of law that they do not have time or energy for the application; thus, they skip from the rule of law to the conclusion. This is a fatal error because the application is the most important part of the office memo. Omission of the application in the office memo results in a reduction of the student's grade, severely hampers the reader's understanding, and greatly lessens the memo's utility.

When applying the law to the facts, you must lead the reader step by step from the law to your conclusion. You must specifically explain why a constitutional or statutory provision applies or does not apply to the facts before explaining the consequences of the application. When applying case law, specifically tell your reader what facts from a previous case are similar to and what facts are different from the facts in the memo and *explain why.* It is not sufficient to simply state that facts are similar or different without telling your reader which facts you are referring to and why. You may not be conscious of some of the steps you used in concluding that a particular case is or is not controlling. Try to consciously think of the steps you went through in moving from the law to the conclusion and then write those steps down on paper so your reader can follow and understand your analysis.

Your writing should be so clear that someone who has never read about that area of law before can understand your memo. You probably have a friend or relative who has a difficult time understanding detailed explanations. Picture yourself with that person and think of how you could explain your law office memo to that person. Have someone else who has no knowledge of that area of the law read your memo and tell you if there are any passages he or she could not understand. Rewrite those passages so almost anyone can understand them. Try reading your office memo out loud either to yourself or to someone else. A passage that seems perfectly clear when you read it silently may not sound very clear when read out loud. Rewrite any passages that are unclear or awkward.

Conclusion

Your conclusion should be a final paragraph that ties everything together. Remember that in applying case law to your facts you are guided by the **doctrine of stare decisis**. If the facts in a prior case from the same or a higher court are substantially similar, then the answer to the problem should be the same as the result reached by the court in the prior case. Summarize the similarities and differences between the case law used as authority and the facts of the memo and explain what cases you are relying on to reach your conclusion.

SAMPLE LAW OFFICE MEMO

To: Legal research and writing classes [attorney]
From: Your author [paralegal]
Re: Whether cocaine found in a car stopped on I-95 should be suppressed [case]
Date: February 7, 1995

Facts:

Mike Campbell[1] and his best friend, John Wright, were driving north on I-95, returning from spring break in Florida, when they were stopped by members of a drug task force made up of Volusia County Sheriff officers and federal drug enforcement agents. The agents requested permission to search the car. When Campbell refused consent, the agents brought in a drug dog which alerted to the trunk of the car. The agents then claimed that the dog's actions gave them probable cause to search the trunk and gave

---

[1] It is easier for your reader to understand if you refer to people by their names (a surname is sufficient) instead of as "appellant," "appellee," or similar terms. An alternative is to use terms such as "suspect" or "officer."

Campbell the choice of either opening the trunk or waiting until the agents obtained a search warrant. After Campbell opened the trunk, the agents found two kilograms of cocaine in a brown paper bag. Campbell and Wright were arrested and charged with possession with intent to distribute cocaine. Prior to trial they filed a motion to suppress the cocaine, claiming that it was the fruit of an unreasonable search and seizure.

The agents claimed that they stopped the Campbell car because Campbell did not use his turn signal when changing lanes and because the following facts fit a drug courier profile used by the Volusia County Sheriff officers:

1. The car was a large late model;
2. The car had out-of-state tags;
3. The car was being driven cautiously at the speed limit;
4. The car was being driven on a known drug corridor, I-95;
5. There were two passengers in the car;
6. The passengers were in their twenties;
7. The car was being driven in the early evening; and
8. The passengers were dressed casually.[2]

Although not listed by the agents, Campbell and Wright believe the real reason they were stopped is because they are Afro-Americans.

Issues:[3]

1. Did the agents have reasonable suspicion to stop the car for an illegal drug violation?
2. Did the agents have probable cause to stop the Campbell car for the driver's failure to signal when changing lanes?

Answers:[4]

1. Because the factors in the drug courier profile, even if taken together, did not support reasonable suspicion of illegal drug activity, the cocaine should be suppressed unless the agents had probable cause to stop the car for a traffic violation.

---

[2] When you have a list of items, make it easier for your reader to skim down the list by tabulating. Number each item, follow each item except for the last one by a semicolon, and place the word "and" after the semicolon following the next-to-last item. Make sure that you follow parallel construction for all items.

[3] Each issue should be a single-sentence question. Between the issue and the answer you should give your reader the most information possible. Often a reader will read the issues and the answers first to determine if he or she should read the whole memo. It is very frustrating for the reader if the reader cannot make that determination without reading the rest of the memo.

[4] Each answer should be a complete, single-sentence answer responding to an issue. Usually there are the same number of answers as there are issues. An exception would be, for example, if the issue is so broad that there are two parts to the answer. As noted previously, between the issue and the corresponding answer, give your reader the most information possible. If you find an issue and answer getting so long as to be unwieldy, try splitting them up into two issues and answers.

LEGAL TERMS

stare decisis
Means "standing by the decision." *Stare decisis* is the doctrine that judicial decisions stand as precedents for cases arising in the future. It is a fundamental policy of our law that, except in unusual circumstances, a court's determination on a point of law will be followed by courts of the same or lower rank in later cases presenting the same legal issue, even though different parties are involved and many years have elapsed.

2. Because a reasonable officer would not have stopped the car absent an invalid purpose, the stop violated the passengers' fourth amendment[5] right against unreasonable search and seizure and the cocaine should be suppressed as illegally obtained evidence.

Reasoning:[6]

Federal legislation makes possession of cocaine a crime and officers have the unenviable job of enforcing this legislation. One method used to diminish illegal drug activity is to cut down on the transportation of illegal drugs along the nation's highways.[7] Unfortunately, there is no accurate method to determine which cars on the highway are carrying drugs unless the cars are stopped and searched. Campbell and Wright's constitutional right against unreasonable search and seizure was violated when their car was stopped, because the agents did not have reasonable suspicion of illegal drug activity and the alleged traffic violation was a pretext for the stop.

The fourth amendment[8] to the United States Constitution guarantees "[t]he[9] right of the people to be secure in their persons, houses, papers, and effects against unreasonable searches and seizures" and allows a search warrant to be issued only upon "probable cause."[10] The fourth amendment

---

5 If you refer to a constitutional or statutory provision in an issue or answer by number, also give your reader a short explanation of the provision's subject matter. Otherwise your reader will be frustrated by not knowing why you cited a particular provision. It is usually better not to give case citations in issues or answers. Instead, state the rule of law from the case in your issue or answer and cite the case in the reasoning section of your memo.

6 You should begin the reasoning portion of your office memo with a thesis paragraph. A well-written thesis paragraph is a road map, providing the reader with a framework into which the balance of the memo can be placed. It also tells the reader your ultimate conclusion.

A *thesis* is the central idea running through the entire memo. The time you spend in developing your thesis, before you start writing, is well worth it. Once you find a central idea, it will be much easier to organize the writing of your memo. To find a thesis, think in broad terms of the problem or controversy which is the basis for your memo—the problem or controversy was what caused you to do the research in the first place. This memo concerns the delicate balance between society's interest in enforcing criminal drug statutes against the individual's constitutional right against unreasonable search and seizure. The courts recognize society's interest by prosecuting those believed to have violated criminal drug statutes, but the courts also recognize the individual's constitutional right by excluding any evidence obtained in violation of the individual's right.

7 Be sure to keep your tone objective rather than persuasive.

8 When quoting a constitutional or statutory provision, quote only the relevant portion. Set quotations of 50 words or more off from the rest of the text in a *quotation block* indented left and right but not enclosed in quotation marks. Other quotations should be run in as part of the paragraph, with the quoted language in quotation marks.

9 The brackets indicate a change in the quotation from the original. Here the "t" was upper case originally.

10 Periods and commas go inside quotation marks. Other punctuation is placed outside quotation marks unless that punctuation is part of the quotation.

does not prohibit all searches and seizures—just *unreasonable* searches and seizures. Although obtaining a search warrant before conducting a search is preferable, the courts have allowed a number of exceptions to the search warrant requirement over the years. One exception[11] is to investigate illegal drug activity and another exception is to investigate a traffic violation. These two exceptions are the ones involved in *Campbell* and are discussed in detail in this memo.

Terry v. Ohio, 392 U.S. 1 (1968)[12] was the landmark case that lowered the burden of proof necessary for a stop from probable cause to "reasonable suspicion." In *Terry*[13] the United States Supreme Court held that police officers could stop someone on the street to investigate possible drug activity so long as the stop is based on something more than an "unparticularized suspicion or 'hunch.'"[14] To reach the level of reasonable suspicion, the officer may rely on "reasonable inferences" from "unusual conduct." *Id.* at 27.[15] Such stops made on reasonable suspicion are often referred to as "Terry stops," after *Terry,* and the definition of Terry stops has been broadened to apply to car stops. Once a Terry stop is made, the officers would still need probable cause or consent to search a car.

In recent years, federal courts[16] have decided a number of cases in which the defendants filed motions to suppress claiming that the evidence seized from cars should be suppressed because of a violation of their right against unreasonable search and seizure. In a case involving facts almost identical to those in *Campbell*[17] above, the Eleventh Circuit Court of

---

[11] *Signposts* are words used to guide the reader in a particular direction. "One exception" and "a second exception" are signposts clearly identifying the two exceptions which are discussed in much more detail later in the memo.

[12] The first time you refer to a case by name, you must give the full citation. After that, you should use a short form citation.

Citations in the sample office memo are given in *Bluebook* form. Your professor may require you to cite according to some other citation rule (perhaps your state's citation rule). If so, always check the appropriate citation rule to make sure you are citing correctly. For example, Rule 9.800 of the Florida Rules of Appellate Procedure requires that parallel citations to United States Reports, Supreme Court Reporter, and United States Supreme Court Reports, Lawyers Edition be given for all United States Supreme Court cases.

[13] Once you have given the full citation for a case and are referring to the case in general terms, you can refer to it by using one or two of the words from the name of the case and underlining or italicizing the shortened name. Be sure the words you pick are not so common as to cause confusion. Here, for example, use *Terry* rather than *Ohio.*

[14] To indicate quotes within quotes, alternate double and single quotation marks, with double quotations being the outermost ones.

[15] "*Id.*" means that you are referring to the immediately preceding authority cited and "27" tells the page number on which your reader will find the material.

[16] Capitalize the word "court" only when referring to the United States Supreme Court or to the full name of any other court.

[17] You can refer to "*Campbell,*" with the underscore or italics showing it is a case, since Campbell and Wright have had charges filed against them. You should not refer to "*Williams*" as a case because no lawsuit has been filed.

Appeals found that a highway stop was not reasonable under the fourth amendment even though the stop was made based on a drug courier profile and the driver had allegedly committed a traffic violation. *United States v. Smith,* 799 F.2d 704, 712 (11th Cir. 1986).[18] Although the *Smith* court found that the *Smith* drug courier profile did not support reasonable suspicion, the use of drug courier profiles is not *per se* unconstitutional. *Id.* at 708 n.5.[19] The United States Supreme Court has allowed the use of drug courier profiles when all the factors of the drug courier profile taken together do support reasonable suspicion. *United States v. Sokolow,* 490 U.S. 1, 9 (1989). This memo will discuss *Smith*[20] and *Sokolow* and apply them to the above facts to answer the two issues being considered.[21]

Reasoning for issue one:[22]

One night in June 1985, Trooper Robert Vogel, a Florida Highway Patrol trooper, and a DEA agent were observing cars traveling in the northbound lanes of I-95, in hopes of intercepting drug couriers. When Smith's car passed through the arc of the patrol car headlights, Vogel noticed the following factors that matched his drug courier profile:

1. The car was traveling at 3:00 a.m.;
2. The car was a 1985 Mercury, a large, late-model car;
3. The car had out-of-state tags;

---

18 "704" is the first page of *Smith* and "712" is the page on which the finding of the court referred to in the preceding sentence is located. As a courtesy to the reader, a page reference should be given when specific material from a case is referred to even if the material is not directly quoted.

The two types of sentences in legal writing are textual sentences and citation sentences. A textual sentence is the type of sentence you have been writing all your life. It a complete grammatical sentence with a subject and a verb. A citation sentence contains only citations. A *string citation* is a citation sentence with more than one citation. In a string citation, the citations should be separated by semicolons.

A sentence is more difficult to read when it contains a full case citation, especially if the citation is long. To avoid having to include a full citation in a textual sentence, you can refer to a case in very general terms or refer to a legal principle from a case and give the full citation to the case in a citation sentence following the textual sentence.

19 This reference is to footnote 5 of *Smith* located on page 708.

20 Delete excess words by writing "*Smith*" instead of "the *Smith* case" or "the case of *Smith*."

21 This sentence contains transitional language helping the reader make the transition from the introductory material contained in the first part of the reasoning section to the reasoning for issue one. Your reader will understand your memo better if you make transitions from one paragraph to the next as smooth as possible by using transitional language.

22 The material that applies to both issues was placed in the preceding section. The material in this section of the memo applies to issue one. Some of the material in this section, such as some of the facts from *Smith,* also apply to issue two. Rather than state the *Smith* facts all over again in the next section, you can refer the reader back to this section, if necessary.

4. There were two occupants of the car who were around 30; and
5. The driver was driving cautiously and did not look at the patrol car as the Mercury passed through the arc of the patrol car headlights.

799 F.2d at 705–06.[23]

The above drug courier profile is almost identical to the *Campbell* profile.[24] In both *Smith* and *Campbell* the cars were traveling after dark; the cars were large late models with out-of-state tags; the cars were being driven "cautiously"; and each car contained two passengers in their twenties or thirties. The differences between the two profiles are very minor. Campbell and Wright were dressed casually, while it is not known how Smith and Swindell were dressed. Smith and Swindell did not look at Vogel as they passed. It is not known whether Campbell and Wright looked in the agents' direction as Campbell drove past. Campbell and Wright claim that race was a factor in their stop even though it was not listed as such by the agents. Smith and Swindell's race is unknown.[25]

In *Smith,* Vogel followed the Mercury for a mile and a half and noticed that the Mercury "wove" several times, once as much as six inches into the emergency lane. Vogel pulled Smith over. When a drug dog alerted on

---

23 When you need to give the source of a block quote or other material set off from the rest of the text, as is the tabulation here, bring the citation back to the left margin. "*Id.*" cannot be used here because "*id.*" would refer back to the immediately preceding citation, *Sokolow,* instead of to *Smith.* Where "*id.*" cannot be used, give the volume number of the reporter, the abbreviation for the reporter, "at," and the page number. You could precede this short form citation by "*Smith,*" if *Smith* had not been cited for a page or more or the reader might confuse the citation with another case, especially one from the same volume of the same reporter. This is not necessary here because *Smith* has been cited fairly recently.

When citing inclusive pages with three or more digits, drop all but the last two digits of the second number and place a hyphen or en dash between the numbers.

24 This is an example of a topic sentence. A topic sentence contains one main idea summarizing the rest of the paragraph, with the rest of the paragraph developing the idea presented in the topic sentence. Most paragraphs should have topic sentences. The typical location of a topic sentence is the first sentence in the paragraph. Sometimes the topic sentence is the last sentence in the paragraph and pulls together the rest of the paragraph. Some paragraphs, typically narrative paragraphs like the preceding paragraph, do not have a topic sentence.

If a paragraph sounds disjointed or unorganized, try pulling it together using a topic sentence. If a topic sentence does not help, think about breaking the paragraph up into more than one paragraph.

25 This paragraph applies the facts in *Smith* to the facts in *Campbell.* Applying facts from one case to another case involves explaining the similarities and differences between the two sets of facts. Instead of simply stating that the facts from the two cases are very similar, the paragraph specifically states which facts are the same. Sometimes in the application you need to explain in what way the facts are similar if they are not identical.

You can either apply the *Smith* facts to *Campbell,* as done here, or you can wait until you have thoroughly discussed *Smith.* When you prepare your outline prior to writing the office memo, spend some time moving parts of your reasoning around to determine the best flow for your reasoning.

the car, a DEA agent searched the trunk and discovered one kilogram of cocaine. Smith and his passenger, Swindell, were arrested and charged with conspiracy to possess cocaine with the intent to distribute it. Smith and Swindell's motions to suppress the cocaine were denied and they were tried and convicted. *Id.* at 706.

The issue before the appellate court was whether the stop of Smith's car was reasonable. *Id.*[26] This is the same basic issue that will be before the *Campbell* court when it considers Campbell and Wright's motion to suppress. The *Smith* court held that the stop of Smith's car could not be upheld as a valid Terry stop, *id.* at 708, finding that "Trooper Vogel stopped the car because [Smith and Swindell] . . .[27] matched a few nondistinguishing characteristics contained on a drug courier profile and, additionally, because Vogel was bothered by the way the driver of the car chose not to look at him." *Id.* at 707.

Just as there was nothing in the *Campbell* drug courier profile to differentiate Campbell and Wright from other innocent college students returning from spring break in Florida, there was nothing in Vogel's drug courier profile to differentiate Smith and Swindell from other law-abiding motorists on I-95. It is usual to drive after dark to avoid heavy traffic and to complete an interstate trip.[28] Although many motorists speed on the highways, motorists driving "cautiously" at or near the speed limit are simply obeying traffic laws. Many people other than drug couriers drive large, late-model cars with out-of-state tags. A motorist between the ages of twenty and forty is not unusual.

The contrast between the *Campbell* and *Smith* drug courier profiles which do not support reasonable suspicion and the *Sokolow* drug courier profile which was held to support reasonable suspicion is instructive. *Sokolow,* 490 U.S. at 3. DEA agents found 1,063 grams of cocaine inside Sokolow's carry-on luggage when he was stopped in Honolulu International Airport based on the following profile:

1. He had paid $2,100 in cash for two airplane tickets from a roll of $20 bills which appeared to contain $4,000;
2. He was ticketed under a name other than his own;
3. He traveled to Miami, a known drug source, and back;

---

26 When you are referring to material from the same page as the material you referred to in the last citation, use just "*id.*"

27 "Smith and Swindell" are in brackets because this wording inserted into the quotation by the person writing the memo. The ellipsis (...) shows that something was omitted from the original wording of the quotation. Your quotations must exactly match the wording and punctuation of the authority the quotation comes from. If you are sloppy in quoting and your reader discovers that you have taken liberties with the quoted material, your reader may suspect that you are sloppy in other ways—perhaps even in your research.

28 No page reference is needed if you have already given the facts in the cases you are using as authority and are referring to those cases in general.

4. Although his round trip flight lasted 20 hours, he stayed in Miami only 48 hours;
5. He appeared nervous;
6. He was about 25 years old;
7. He was dressed in a black jumpsuit and was wearing gold jewelry which he wore during both legs of the round trip flight; and
8. Neither he nor his companion checked any luggage.[29]

Id. at 3–5. The Court explained that the above drug courier profile must be evaluated in light of "the totality of the circumstances—the whole picture." *Id.* at 8 (quoting *United States v. Cortez,* 449 U.S. 411, 417 (1981)).[30] "Any one of these factors [in the drug courier profile] is not by itself proof of any illegal conduct and is quite consistent with innocent travel. But we think taken together they amount to reasonable suspicion." *Id.* at 9. The *Sokolow* dissent would have found that all of the factors even if "taken together" did not amount to reasonable suspicion. In criticizing the use of a drug courier profile to stop suspects, the dissent noted "the profile's 'chameleon-like way of adapting to any particular set of observations' " "subjecting innocent individuals to unwarranted police harassment and detention." *Id.* at 13 (Marshall, J., dissenting)[31] (quoting *Sokolow v. United States,* 831 F.2d 1413, 1418 (9th Cir. 1987), *rev'd,* 490 U.S. 1 (1989)[32]).

As predicted in the *Sokolow* dissent, Smith, Swindell, Campbell, and Wright were subjected to "unwarranted police harassment and detention" even though the factors in the respective drug courier profiles, even if "taken together," did not amount to reasonable suspicion. In contrast, several of the *Sokolow* factors, such as carrying such a large amount of cash and traveling a long distance to stay a relatively short period of time, are unusual or even suspicious in and of themselves. Each of the *Smith* and *Campbell* factors was not at all out of the ordinary alone and certainly taken together did not amount to reasonable suspicion.

Conclusion[33] for issue one:

Because the drug courier profiles in *Smith* and *Campbell* are virtually identical and are in sharp contrast to the *Sokolow* drug courier profile, the *Campbell* court should find that there was not reasonable suspicion

[29] Only those facts from *Sokolow* that are relevant to the discussion of *Smith* are given.

[30] When you are quoting from a case which in turn quotes from another case, identify the second case by putting its name and cite in parentheses following the citation for the case you are quoting.

[31] You must identify the type of opinion from which you are quoting if it is other than the majority opinion.

[32] Subsequent history must be given for the lower court decision in *Sokolow.*

[33] Your conclusion section at the end of a reasoning section ties together your previous discussion and reaches a conclusion. The difference between the conclusion section for issue one and answer one is that answer one is a more condensed, one-sentence version of the conclusion section.

to stop Campbell and the stop on that ground was an unconstitutional violation of Campbell and Wright's right to be free from unreasonable search and seizure. Unless the agents had probable cause to investigate the alleged traffic violation, the court should suppress the cocaine as the fruit of an unconstitutional search and seizure.

Reasoning for issue two:

In *Smith,* the government argued on appeal that the stop was valid either because Vogel had probable cause to stop the car for a traffic violation ("weaving") or because Vogel could have stopped the car on the suspicion from the "weaving" that Smith was driving drunk. In responding to the government's arguments, the court set forth the following test. "[I]n determining whether an investigative stop is invalid as pretextual, the proper inquiry is whether a reasonable officer *would*[34] have made the seizure in the absence of illegitimate motivation." 799 F.2d at 708. Applying this test to *Smith,* the court concluded that "a reasonable officer would not have stopped the car absent an additional, invalid purpose," rejected "the traffic stop rationale . . . as pretextual," and found that the cocaine should have been excluded from evidence. *Id.* at 711.

In making its decision, the *Smith* court followed *United States v. Cruz,* 581 F.2d 535 (5th Cir. 1978) (en banc)[35] (this decision is binding on the United States Eleventh Circuit Court of Appeals because it occurred before the Fifth Circuit was split into the Fifth and Eleventh Circuits in 1981).[36] In Cruz, an officer speculated that a car the officer had passed had made an illegal u-turn on the highway because the suspect car did not follow the patrol car over a hill and, after turning the patrol car around, the officer observed the suspect car travelling in the opposite direction. The officer stopped the suspect car because of the illegal u-turn. After stopping the car and questioning its occupants, the officer arrested the occupants for violation of immigration laws. The Fifth Circuit "held the stop an unreasonable seizure under the fourth amendment because its purported rationale was merely a pretext for an invalid purpose." 799 F.2d at 710.

Cruz, Smith, and *Campbell* are very similar in that in all three cases, the government claimed that the stop of a suspect car did not violate the driver's right against unreasonable search and seizure because there was

---

[34] The word "would" was italicized in the material being quoted. You can emphasize words from a quotation by underlining or italicizing them so long as you note the change in parentheses following the citation for the quotation with "(emphasis added)."

[35] An *en banc* decision is usually an important one, because the entire membership of the court sits rather than the usual three-judge panel, and it is reserved for consideration of important legal issues.

[36] These two phrases in parentheses are explanatory parentheticals. They are not technically necessary but are added to the end of the citation to give the reader more information.

some irregularity in the way the car was being driven that gave the officer reason to stop the car. The driving "irregularities" are similar in that making a u-turn, swerving six inches into the emergency lane, and failing to use a turn signal in changing lanes are fairly minor infractions which did not appear to cause any safety hazard. If the three driving irregularities are compared in terms of severity, Campbell's alleged failure to use his turn signal when changing lanes is by far the least severe of the three. If officers were to stop every car on the highway which failed to use its turn signal when changing lanes, a very high percentage of the cars traveling the highway would be pulled over.

Conclusion for issue two:

The *Cruz* and *Smith* courts rejected the traffic stop rationale as pretextual. Both *Cruz* and *Smith* are binding on the *Campbell* court. Following the mandatory authority of those two decisions, the *Campbell* court should also reject as pretextual the stop of Campbell's car for failure to signal when changing lanes. This is because the "traffic violation" in *Campbell* is similar to, but so much less severe than, the alleged traffic violations in *Smith* and *Cruz* that a reasonable officer would not have stopped Campbell absent a "hunch" that the car contained illegal drugs. Because the agents did not have reasonable cause to stop Campbell to investigate for illegal drug activity and the stop for Campbell's failure to signal when changing lanes was pretextual, the stop violated Campbell and Wright's right against unreasonable search and seizure. Because their fourth amendment right was violated by the stop and the agents would not have found the cocaine if they had not first stopped the car on I-95, the cocaine should be suppressed as the **fruit of the poisonous tree**.

SUMMARY

- The office memo records the results of legal research, explains how the researcher analyzed the law and applied it to the facts, and proposes a solution to the problem.
- The tone of the office memo is objective rather than persuasive.
- Generally the office memo contains a heading (to and from, re, and date); facts; issue(s) and answer(s); a thesis paragraph; the rule of law; the application of the law to the facts; and the conclusion.
- Refer to people by their names or terms such as "suspect" or "officer" instead of "appellant," "appellee," or similar terms.
- Each issue and each answer should be a single sentence.
- Between the issue and the answer, you should give your reader the most information possible.
- Usually there are the same number of answers as issues.

LEGAL TERMS

fruit of the poisonous tree doctrine
The constitutional law doctrine that evidence, including derivative evidence, obtained as the result of an illegal search is inadmissible.

- If you refer to a consitutional or statutory provision in an issue or answer by number, also give your reader a short explanation of the provision's subject matter.
- A thesis is the central idea running through the entire memo.
- Quote only the relevant portion of constitutions or statutes.
- The first time you refer to a case by name, give the full citation; after that, use a short form citation.

EXERCISES

1. Pick one of the research problems from Appendix G.
2. Research the problem you have chosen.
3. Write an office memo summarizing and explaining your research.

CHAPTER 14
Memorandum of Law

OUTLINE

Purpose
Style
Organization
Format

One of the standard legal documents written by a litigation attorney for submission to court is what is referred to in this book as a **memorandum of law**. (Some attorneys refer to it as a *trial brief,* a *trial-level brief,* or a *memorandum of points and authorities.*) This chapter explains the purpose, use, and format of the memorandum of law and includes a sample memorandum of law.

The sample memorandum of law has been extensively annotated to provide you with writing and citation tips. If the notes do not make much sense to you right now, read them again after you have gone over the rules for citations and quotations contained in Appendixes B and C in this book. It might also be helpful to you to refer to the notes again when you are writing your own memorandum of law.

LEGAL TERMS

memorandum of law A written statement submitted to a court for the purpose of persuading [the court] of the correctness of one's position. It is similar to a brief, although usually not as extensive.

PURPOSE

In litigation, an attorney may be required by court rule, may be asked by the judge, or may feel the need to submit a written document called a *memorandum of law.* For example, Rule 3.01 of the Local Rules for the United States District Court for the Middle District of Florida requires any party filing a motion to also file "a brief or legal memorandum with citation of authorities in support of the relief requested." The rule gives the party opposing the motion 10 days to file a "brief or legal memorandum" in opposition. As a court document, the memorandum of law is a matter of public record, and a copy of it is delivered to opposing counsel. The purposes of the memorandum of law are to explain the client's position in a lawsuit and to convince the judge to rule in the client's favor.

Let's look for a moment at the sample memorandum of law in this chapter, written by Mike Campbell's attorney. You may recall from prior chapters that Mike was arrested for possession of cocaine. The cocaine was found in Mike's car after he was stopped on the interstate by DEA agents. Mike's position is that, because the stop of his car was unconstitutional, the cocaine should be suppressed as illegally obtained evidence from an unconstitutional search and seizure. If Mike's attorney can convince the judge that the cocaine should be suppressed, the charge against Mike will have to be dropped for lack of evidence. Mike's attorney would formally request the judge to suppress the cocaine by filing a motion to suppress and, as required by local rule, a memorandum of law supporting the motion. Once Mike's attorney has filed the motion to suppress the cocaine and the supporting memorandum of law, the government attorney will file a motion in opposition to the motion to suppress and a memorandum of law supporting the government's motion in opposition.

The circumstances surrounding Mike's arrest can be viewed from two perspectives: Mike's perspective and the perspective of the DEA agents. Mike would argue that the agents singled him out on the hunch that because he is Afro-American, he might be carrying illegal drugs. The agents then violated his constitutional right against unreasonable search and seizure by stopping and searching his car. The government would argue that the agents could have pulled Mike over either because of a traffic violation or because Mike fit a drug courier profile. In the agents' experience, persons who fit the drug courier profile often carry drugs. The drug courier profile, although not entirely accurate, has been the law enforcement officer's best weapon in the war against the illegal drug trade.

The tone of a memorandum of law is persuasive, in contrast to the law office memo, which is objective in tone. In her memorandum of law, Mike's attorney will try to persuade the judge that Mike's view of the facts is more accurate and is supported by case law interpretation of the fourth amendment. In the government's memorandum of law in opposition to Mike's motion to suppress, the government attorney will try to persuade the judge that Mike's motion to suppress should not be granted because the government's view of the facts is more accurate and applicable case law supports denial of the motion to suppress.

Although Mike's attorney has to represent Mike's best interests, this duty is tempered by the attorney's ethical duty as an officer of the court. Rule 4-3.3 of the Rules Regulating the Florida Bar states: "A lawyer shall not knowingly . . . make a false statement of material fact or law to a tribunal . . . [or] fail to disclose to the tribunal legal authority in the controlling jurisdiction known to the lawyer to be directly adverse to the position of the client and not disclosed by opposing counsel." Attorney ethics rules in other states contain similar wording. Thus, Mike's attorney has a dual role. She is an advocate for Mike's best interests as well as an advisor to the court. Mike's attorney must present Mike's side of the story, but may not invent or change facts. In presenting the law in support of Mike's position, the attorney may not intentionally mislead the court and must disclose law "directly adverse" to Mike's position which the government has failed to disclose.

An *officer of the court* is anyone who is an employee of the court or a person who, although not an employee of the court, is obligated to conduct himself or herself in a manner that furthers the administration of justice (example: any attorney admitted to practice before the court).

STYLE

An attorney must work very hard to build credibility with the judge and must work just as hard not to lose this credibility. You must build credibility in your writing by making absolutely sure that the facts and the law are stated accurately. Choose words that emphasize the client's position but are not obviously biased. The memorandum will be more credible if you include adverse facts and law as well as facts and law in the client's favor. The judge will be comparing your memorandum with that of opposing counsel to see how you have dealt with adverse facts and law. Your failure to deal with adverse facts and law may make the judge think you are doing a sloppy job, and you will quickly lose your credibility. Of course, adverse facts and law need only be mentioned and should not be dwelled upon. A well-organized memorandum will emphasize favorable facts and law and will downplay unfavorable ones. (See the next section of this chapter for tips on organization.)

The appearance of the memorandum should be inviting, with enough descriptive headings to allow the judge to glance through the memorandum and "see" the flow of your writing. When you have completed the first draft of the memorandum, review it critically. Does it appear reader-friendly? Are the pages broken up into a number of paragraphs? Is the print large enough to be easily read? Are the margins wide enough to give the reader's eyes a chance to rest? Can you make it easier to spot headings by putting them in bold type or underlining them? If not, make any necessary changes.

ORGANIZATION

When you are having trouble writing a memorandum of law, picture yourself as a busy judge with a heavy case load and ask yourself what you would find helpful in a memorandum of law. A busy judge does not have the luxury of time to pore over a lengthy, disorganized memorandum containing a convoluted legal argument. The judge will be more inclined to read a shorter memorandum that is straightforward, well organized, and just long enough to get the point across. If you can squeeze the issues and short answers into the first two pages, you will have the judge's attention.

Remember that a reader will pay more attention to the beginning and the end than to the middle of sections within the memorandum. Put any information you want to emphasize either at the beginning or at the end of a section. For example, in the facts section, focus the reader's attention on the client by referring to the client first and retelling the facts from the client's perspective. Diffuse the opposing party's case by including any significant adverse facts, but downplay them by briefly mentioning them in the light most favorable to the client midway through the facts section.

Do something similar with the argument section. If there is an easy way for the judge to dispose of the case in the client's favor, put the argument supporting that easy ruling first. Otherwise, put the strongest argument first. "Bury" any adverse law which must be disclosed in the middle of the argument section. A duty to disclose adverse law does not mean that it has to be discussed in detail. Refer to it, distinguish it, and move on. Do the same with the opposing party's counterarguments. Refer to them briefly and then focus on the client's argument. The best defense is a good offense.

The same organizational tip as for sections of the memorandum applies for sentences and paragraphs. If you want your reader to focus on particular words in a sentence, rearrange your sentence to put those words first or last in the sentence. The focus will be even greater if rearranging the sentence changes the grammatical structure from the typical subject-verb-object structure of English sentences. Be careful that you do not change from the typical structure too often, though, or the atypical structure will become routine and lose its impact. In addition, sentences written other than with the subject, verb, and object, in that order, are harder for the reader to understand.

The reader will pay more attention to the first and last sentences in a paragraph than to the middle of the paragraph. For that reason, make your topic sentence either the first or the last sentence in the paragraph. Put any information you want to make sure the reader does not miss in the first or last sentences. If the important information is more than can fit in the first and last sentences of the paragraph, consider splitting the paragraph into a number of paragraphs. Put adverse information three-quarters of the way through the paragraph to deemphasize it.

FORMAT

Although there is no one right format for a memorandum of law, the format given in this chapter is fairly standard. The format should be modified to conform to any applicable court rules and to the format customarily used for a particular court. For example, Rule 1.05 of the Local Rules of the United States District Court for the Middle District of Florida requires all documents filed with the court to be typewritten, to be double-spaced, to be on 8.5-by-11-inch paper, to have 1.25-inch margins, to be signed personally by the attorney, and to include the attorney's name, the attorney's Florida Bar identification number, the firm name and address, and the attorney's telephone number below the signature line. Rule 3.01 requires the memorandum of law to be no longer than 20 pages in length (absent prior court permission) and to contain "citation of authorities." Other than that, the form of the memorandum of law is not specified. (To save space, the sample memorandum of law included in this chapter is single-spaced rather than being double-spaced as required by the local rule.)

The balance of this section gives a brief explanation of the various parts of the memorandum of law. It might be helpful for you to read the rest of this section while comparing the explanation to the sample memorandum of law.

Caption

The caption contains the name of the court, the names of the parties, the case number, and the title of the pleading. After the title of the pleading and before the questions presented section, it is customary to include a sentence stating who is submitting the memorandum and why it is being submitted.

Questions Presented

The questions section contains several numbered questions to be considered by the judge. The questions should be stated in the light most favorable to the client and should be worded so that the judge can easily reach an answer favorable to the client. Give as much information as possible in each question without sacrificing readability. There should be enough information so that the judge understands a question without having to refer to other sections of the memorandum.

Each question should contain a combination of law and facts, and should ask how the law applies to the facts. Because the facts section of the memorandum follows rather than precedes the questions presented section, the judge will not have read the facts before reading the questions. The judge will have an easier time understanding the facts if the law in each question precedes the facts. Using this order, the law will serve as a framework into which the judge can fit the facts.

Facts

The writer should create empathy for the client by painting a picture of the facts from the client's perspective. Choose descriptive words and incorporate a fair amount of detail when recounting facts favorable to the client. State the facts as specifically as possible to make them memorable. If the picture is created in sufficient detail, your picture will come to the judge's mind when he or she considers the case. Relevant adverse facts upon which opposing counsel is likely to rely can be mentioned briefly, in broad terms, and with little detail, using bland, uninteresting language.

Highlight your client's view of the facts. Focus the reader's attention on the client by referring to the client first and calling the client by name. Try telling the facts in the order the client perceived them rather than in strict chronological order. This ordering of the facts will make it easier for the judge to understand the client's position.

Choose your words carefully. The words chosen should reflect favorably on the client without conveying an argumentative or adversarial tone. The writer may lose credibility if the language is too exaggerated or overly biased. Well-stated facts are so subtly persuasive that the judge can believe they are stated objectively.

Argument

The argument section is the longest and most complex portion of the memorandum of law. This section is divided into a number of subsections by headings called *point headings.* An introductory portion of the argument section may precede the first main point heading. The introductory material contains a thesis paragraph and may explain law applicable to all the point headings in the memorandum. Each subsection following a point heading should explain the applicable rule of law and apply the rule of law to the facts. The last paragraph in the point heading subsection may contain the conclusion for the point heading, or the conclusion for all point headings may be contained in the conclusion section.

Even though the tone of the memorandum of law is persuasive and the tone of the law office memo is objective, the basic structure of the argument section of a memorandum of law should be similar to the structure of the reasoning section of a law office memo. You should present one or more thesis paragraphs, you should set forth the rule of law, and you should apply the rule of law to the facts of the case. Refresh your memory of how to write the thesis paragraph(s), the rule of law, and the application of law to facts by rereading those portions of the "Format" section of Chapter 13.

Although opposing counsel and others will read the memorandum of law, the intended and primary audience is the judge. The judge is not your adversary and may become your ally on the strength of the memorandum of law. Make the judge your ally by advising the judge as to why ruling in the client's favor is the correct solution to the problem. In most cases the judge has some discretion in making decisions. If you can convince the judge that he or she is your ally, the judge may use this discretion in your client's favor. Therefore, although the tone of the memorandum of law is persuasive, it should be subtly persuasive. Shy away from an argumentative or demanding tone of voice that may prejudice the judge against the client.

Thesis Paragraph

If an introductory portion of the argument section precedes the first main point heading, it should begin with a thesis paragraph. Besides stating your thesis in your thesis paragraph, you may want to use this paragraph to state your final conclusion in simple terms. If your argument section begins with a point heading rather than with an introductory portion, you should either follow your first point heading with a thesis paragraph or include a short thesis paragraph after each of your point headings. For a more detailed explanation of how to write a thesis paragraph, reread the thesis paragraph portion of the "Format" section of Chapter 13.

A main *point heading* answers one of the questions in the questions presented section of the memorandum, with the main point headings appearing in order corresponding to the order of the questions presented. The word *heading* is used because a point heading serves as a heading to one portion of the argument section. Main point headings are often written in all capitals or underlined to make them stand out from the rest of the memorandum. They may also be numbered with roman numerals or lettered with capital letters. A complex issue may call for several point headings for subissues under a main point heading.

Rule of Law

A busy judge does not have the time to do extensive independent research before ruling on a motion. A judge will appreciate a step-by-step explanation of the current status of applicable law—either to acquaint the judge with an unfamiliar area of the law or to update the judge's knowledge. Be careful to advise rather than lecture the judge on the law. A judge will appreciate a clear explanation of the law, but a judge who is being lectured may take offense. For the judge's easy reference, you may want to provide copies of the cases you have cited in the memorandum. For a more detailed explanation of how to write the rule of law, reread the rule of law portion of the "Format" section of Chapter 13.

Application of Law to Facts

After stating the rule of law, you must carefully lead the reader step by step from the law to your conclusion. For a detailed explanation of how to apply the rule of law to the facts, reread the application of law to facts portion of the "Format" section of Chapter 13.

Either the argument section or the conclusion section should contain one or more paragraphs summarizing your argument. This summary serves the same purpose as the conclusion section of a law office memo: it ties the facts to the rule of law and reaches a conclusion. Customarily, this summary is part of the argument rather than the conclusion section. Look through some recent memoranda of law filed with the court to determine what the custom is in your area. If the summary is part of the argument section, you can either put a summary of the answers to all of the questions presented at the end of the argument section, or have a summary paragraph at the end of each subsection within your argument.

Conclusion

The conclusion section of a memorandum of law specifically requests the judge to take a particular action or actions. The motion that accompanies Mike Campbell's memorandum of law is a motion to suppress the evidence found in Mike's car. If the evidence is suppressed, the government will probably have to drop the charge against Mike for lack of evidence. Therefore, the conclusion section of the memorandum of law should request the judge to suppress the evidence and to dismiss the charge against Mike.

As stated previously, you should include a summary of your argument in the conclusion section if you have not included it in the argument section.

SAMPLE MEMORANDUM OF LAW

UNITED STATES DISTRICT COURT
MIDDLE DISTRICT OF FLORIDA
ORLANDO DIVISION

UNITED STATES OF AMERICA,

Plaintiff,

v. Case No. 93-000-CR-ORL-00[1]

MICHAEL CAMPBELL and JOHN WRIGHT,

Defendants.

______________________________/

MEMORANDUM IN SUPPORT OF DEFENDANT CAMPBELL'S MOTION TO SUPPRESS[2]

Defendant Michael Campbell submits this memorandum of law in support of defendant's motion to suppress the evidence seized from the defendant's car.[3]

---

[1] This is the docket number written as required by Rule 1.03(a) of the Local Rules of the United States District Court for the Middle District of Florida. The first part of the docket number, "93," is an abbreviation for "1993" (the year in which the case was filed). Were this a real case, the number of the case would be substituted for "000," the second part of the docket number. Cases in the Orlando division of the district are consecutively numbered corresponding to the order in which they are filed. The third part of the docket number, "CR," indicates that this is a criminal rather than a civil case (abbreviated "CIV"), and "ORL" indicates that this is an Orlando division case. The last two digits give the number of the judge to whom the case is assigned. As Middle District of Florida judges are appointed, they are numbered in sequence and the numbers are used to identify which judge is handling a particular case.

[2] Use a descriptive title to identify the type of document (a memorandum of law), why it is being filed (in support of a motion to suppress), and the party filing the document (defendant Campbell). From the title, the judge should learn at a glance important information about the document without having to read the text of the document.

[3] Use a short introductory sentence to explain why the document is being submitted. It does not hurt to lay out the explanation like this in a full sentence even though it repeats information from the title of the document.

Questions presented:[4]

1. Did the law enforcement officer violate Mike Campbell's constitutional right against unreasonable search and seizure when the law enforcement officer stopped Mike's out-of-state tagged Lincoln Continental that Mike was driving on I-95 in the early evening at the speed limit when the only other information the officer had was that Mike and his passenger were Afro-American, were in their twenties, and wore beach attire?
2. Did the officer violate Mike Campbell's constitutional right against unreasonable search and seizure when the officer followed the Campbell car for a distance and then pulled the car over when Mike failed to signal when changing lanes?

Facts:[5]

Mike Campbell and his best friend had decided, like thousands of other college students, to enjoy a Florida spring break. After Mike promised to drive carefully, Mike's father let Mike borrow his car, a brand new Lincoln Continental. After arriving in Florida, Mike and his friend spent every waking moment of their break on the beach. In the early evening on the last day of vacation, they went straight from the beach to their car to begin the long trip back to school, calculating that they would have just enough driving time to make it back for their first class. Mike was driving north on I-95, thinking about the promise he had made to his father, when he saw patrol cars parked in the median, one with its lights shining across the northbound lanes. Almost immediately after driving through the arc of the patrol car's headlights, Mike looked in the rear-view mirror and saw the patrol car pull out behind him. The patrol car followed Mike for a distance. When Mike changed lanes without using his turn signal, the patrol car put on its flashing lights and pulled Mike over.

---

4 Each of these questions asks how the law applies to the facts. Notice the word choice. The questions are worded from Mike's perspective and Mike is referred to by name. Specific facts are included in the questions for a number of reasons. The judge's decision to grant or deny the motion to suppress turns on whether the facts were sufficient to justify the stop, making the facts extremely important. Because the factors in the drug courier profile and the nature of the alleged traffic violation are generally favorable to Mike, they are detailed so that they are easy to remember. The way the questions are worded paints the judge a picture of the scene which the judge can use as a framework when reading the rest of the memorandum. The most important facts should be laid out in the questions, or the judge will not be familiar with them, because the facts section follows the questions presented section.

5 The facts are told from Mike's perspective and in the order he perceived them. Mike is referred to by name to create empathy, whereas the other persons are not. The wording was chosen to be subtly persuasive rather than obviously biased. Compare this statement of the facts with the facts contained in the law office memo in Chapter 13.

An officer got out of the patrol car, walked over to Mike's car, and asked for Mike's driver's license and car registration. As Mike handed over his license and the registration, he noticed the officer eying Mike's beach attire suspiciously. When Mike told the officer they were heading back to school from spring break, the officer commented, "We don't see too many blacks down here over spring break." Still holding the license and registration, the officer asked Mike whether the officer could search the car and said, "You don't have anything to hide, do you?" Hoping that if he answered "no" they could be on their way, Mike answered, "No." The officer said, "Wait here," turned around, walked back to the patrol car, and got in. Mike could not have left even if the officer had not told him to wait, because the officer still had Mike's license and car registration.

Forty-five minutes later, another patrol car pulled up and an officer got out with a dog. The officer led the dog around the car. The dog circled the car once and then stopped and pawed the car's trunk. The officer motioned Mike to roll down his window. The officer told him that the dog had detected drugs in the trunk of Mike's car. The officer told Mike that Mike could either open the car trunk or wait there whatever time was necessary for the officer to obtain a search warrant. Feeling that he had no choice, Mike opened the trunk. Both officers started pulling Mike's and his friend's belongings out of the trunk and tossing them on the ground. One of the officers found a brown paper bag containing cocaine wedged in a bottom corner of the trunk. Mike and his friend were arrested and were charged with possession with intent to distribute cocaine.

Argument:

The fourth amendment[6] to the United States Constitution guarantees "[t]he[7] right of the people to be secure in their persons, houses, papers, and effects against unreasonable searches and seizures" and allows a search warrant to be issued only upon "probable cause."[8] A search warrant requirement was spelled out in the amendment to safeguard this important right. Over the more than two hundred years since the amendment was adopted, the individual's right against unreasonable search and seizure has been jealously guarded.

Although the time and level of evidence needed to obtain a search warrant protect the individual's constitutional right, the courts have allowed two exceptions to the search warrant requirement, both of which the government argues are applicable here and allowed them to stop the

---

6 When quoting a constitutional or statutory provision, quote only the relevant portion. Set quotations of 50 words or more off from the rest of the text in a quotation block indented left and right but not enclosed in quotation marks. Other questions should be part of the paragraph, with the quoted language in quotation marks.

7 The brackets indicate a change in the quotation from the original. Here the "t" was upper case originally.

8 Periods and commas go inside quotation marks; other punctuation is placed outside the quotation marks unless it is part of the quotation.

Campbell car. The first exception[9] requires a minimum of "reasonable suspicion" of illegal activity to stop a car and question its occupants. *Terry v. Ohio*, 392 U.S. 1, 27 (1968).[10] The second exception allows an officer to stop a car to investigate a traffic violation as long as the traffic violation is not a pretext for the stop. *United States v. Smith*, 799 F.2d 704, 709 (11th Cir. 1986).

Defendant Campbell's motion to suppress should be granted because neither of the two exceptions to the search warrant requirement apply here. The officer stopped Campbell's car on a mere "hunch" and a reasonable officer would not have stopped Campbell's car for the alleged traffic violation except to follow up on a hunch. This memorandum will first explain why there was not enough evidence to justify an investigatory stop and then why the alleged traffic violation did not justify the stop.[11]

A. Because the information the officer relied on to stop the Campbell car was no more than a mere "hunch," the evidence should be suppressed unless the officer had probable cause to stop the car for a traffic violation.[12]

Terry[13] was the landmark case that lowered the burden of proof necessary for a stop from probable cause to "reasonable suspicion." Such stops made on reasonable suspicion are often referred to as "Terry stops,"

---

9 *Signposts* are words used to guide the reader in a particular direction. "One exception" and "a second exception" are signposts clearly identifying the two exceptions, which are discussed in much more detail later in the memo.

10 The first time you refer to a case by name, you must give the full citation. After that, you should use a short form citation.

Citations in this sample memorandum of law are given in *Bluebook* form. Your professor may require you to cite according to some other citation rule (perhaps your state's citation rule). If so, always check the appropriate citation rule to make sure you are citing correctly. For example, Rule 9.800 of the Florida Rules of Appellate Procedure requires that parallel citations to United States Reports, Supreme Court Reporter, and United States Supreme Court Reports, Lawyers Edition be given for all United States Supreme Court cases.

11 This introductory portion of the argument section contains three paragraphs. The first paragraph is the thesis paragraph and quotes the relevant portion of the fourth amendment. The second paragraph lays out in general terms the law applicable to the rest of the memorandum. The third paragraph contains a statement of the conclusion. Don't leave the judge in suspense. Tell the judge your conclusion up front. The third paragraph also contains signposts. With these signposts, the reader will expect the portion of the memorandum following the first point heading to discuss the drug courier profile and the portion of the memorandum after the second point heading to discuss the alleged traffic violation.

12 This point heading answers the first question presented.

13 Once you have given the full citation for a case, and are subsequently referring to the case in general terms, you can refer to it by using one or two words from the name of the case and underlining them. Be sure the words you pick are not so common as to cause confusion. Here, for example, use *Terry* rather than *Ohio*.

after *Terry*, and the definition of Terry stops has been broadened to apply to car stops. The new reasonable suspicion standard allows a police officer to stop and briefly question someone, but is still designed to protect the innocent traveler, singled out because of certain immutable personal characteristics such as race, sex, and age, from being subjected to "overbearing or harassing" law enforcement tactics. 392 U.S. at 14–15 n.11. A stop made only on an "unparticularized suspicion or 'hunch'"[14] is unconstitutional. Assuming the officer has the requisite reasonable suspicion for a Terry stop, the officer would still need probable cause or consent to search a car.[15]

Smith involved almost identical facts to those being considered here. In *Smith* the government argued that a highway stop was constitutionally permitted based either on a drug courier profile or on Smith's alleged commission of a traffic violation. 799 F.2d at 705.[16] Smith filed a motion to suppress, claiming that the evidence seized from his car should be suppressed because of the violation of his right against unreasonable search and seizure. *Id.* at 706.[17] The Eleventh Circuit Court of Appeals found that the *Smith* drug courier profile did not support reasonable suspicion, reversed the lower court's denial of Smith's motion to suppress, and vacated Smith's conviction. *Id.* at 712.

One night in June 1985, Trooper Robert Vogel, a Florida Highway Patrol trooper, and a DEA agent were observing cars traveling in the northbound lanes of I-95, in hopes of intercepting drug couriers. When Smith's car passed through the arc of the patrol car headlights, Vogel noticed the following factors that matched his drug courier profile:

1. The car was traveling at 3:00 a.m.;
2. The car was a 1985 Mercury, a large, late-model car;
3. The car had out-of-state tags;
4. There were two occupants of the car who were around 30; and
5. The driver was driving cautiously and did not look at the patrol car as the Mercury passed through the arc of the patrol car headlights.

---

[14] To indicate quotes within quotes, alternate double and single quotation marks, with double quotations being the outermost ones.

[15] This discussion of *Terry* is written to support Mike's motion and to convince the judge to rule in Mike's favor. Compare it with the discussion of *Terry* contained in the law office memo in Chapter 13. There the *Terry* discussion was more balanced.

[16] Once you have cited a case in full, you should use a short form citation the next time you refer to material from the case. This short form citation contains the volume number and the abbreviation for the reporter in which *Smith* is printed, "at," and the page on which the "government's argument" is found in *Smith.* To learn more about short form citations, refer to Appendixes B and C, which explain quotations and short form citations.

[17] You should use "*id.*" here instead of repeating "799 F.2d" because this citation is to the same volume of the same reporter cited in the immediately preceding citation. You still need "at 706" because the referenced material appears on page 706 instead of on page 705, the page of the previously referenced material.

Id. at 705–06.[18]

The above drug courier profile is almost identical to the *Campbell* profile.[19] In both *Smith* and this case, the cars were traveling after dark; the cars were large late models with out-of-state tags; the cars were being driven "cautiously"; and each car contained two passengers in their twenties or thirties. The differences between the two profiles are very minor. Campbell and his friend were dressed casually, while it is not known how Smith and Swindell were dressed. Smith and Swindell did not look at Vogel as they passed. It is not known whether Campbell looked in the agents' direction as Campbell drove past. Campbell claims that race was a factor in the stop even though it was not listed as such by the agents. Smith and Swindell's race is unknown.[20]

In *Smith*, Vogel followed the Mercury for a mile and a half and noticed that the Mercury "wove" several times, once as much as six inches into the emergency lane. Vogel pulled Smith over. When a drug dog alerted on the car, a DEA agent searched the trunk and discovered one kilogram of cocaine. Smith and his passenger, Swindell, were arrested and charged with conspiracy to possess cocaine with the intent to distribute it. Smith and Swindell's motions to suppress the cocaine were denied and they were tried and convicted. *Id.* at 706.

The issue before the appellate court was whether the stop of Smith's car was reasonable. *Id.*[21] This is the same basic question to be answered by this court in determining whether Campbell's motion to suppress

---

18 When you need to cite a block quote or other material set off from the rest of the text, as is the tabulation here, bring the citation back to the left margin. When citing inclusive pages with three or more digits, drop all but the last two digits of the second number and place a hyphen or an en dash between the numbers.

19 This is an example of a topic sentence. A topic sentence contains one main idea summarizing the rest of the paragraph, with the rest of the paragraph developing the idea presented in the topic sentence. Most paragraphs should have topic sentences. The typical location of a topic sentence is the first sentence in the paragraph. Sometimes the topic sentence is the last sentence in the paragraph and pulls together the rest of the paragraph. Some paragraphs, typically narrative paragraphs like the preceding paragraph, do not have topic sentences.

If a paragraph sounds disjointed or unorganized, try pulling it together using a topic sentence. If a topic sentence does not help, think about breaking the paragraph up into more than one paragraph.

20 This paragraph applies the facts in *Smith* to the facts in *Campbell*. Applying facts from one case to another case involves explaining the similarities and differences between the two sets of facts. Instead of simply stating that the facts from the two cases are very similar, the paragraph specifically states which facts are the same. Sometimes in the application you need to explain in what way the facts are similar if they are not identical.

You can either apply the *Smith* facts to *Campbell* midway in discussing *Smith* as done here or you can wait until you have thoroughly discussed *Smith*. When you prepare your outline prior to starting to write the memorandum of law, spend some time moving parts of your "argument" section around to determine the best flow.

21 When you are referring to material from the same page as the material you referred to in the last citation, use just "*id.*"

should be granted. The *Smith* court held that the stop of Smith's car could not be upheld as a valid Terry stop, *id.* at 708, finding that "Trooper Vogel stopped the car because [Smith and Swindell][22] . . . matched a few nondistinguishing characteristics contained on a drug courier profile and, additionally, because Vogel was bothered by the way the driver of the car chose not to look at him." *Id.* at 707.

Just as there was nothing in the *Campbell* drug courier profile to differentiate Campbell and his friend from other innocent college students returning from spring break in Florida, there was nothing in Vogel's drug courier profile to differentiate Smith and Swindell from other law-abiding motorists on I-95. It is usual to drive after dark to avoid heavy traffic or to complete an interstate trip.[23] Although many motorists speed on the highways, motorists driving "cautiously" at or near the speed limit are simply obeying traffic laws. Many people other than drug couriers drive large, late-model cars with out-of-state tags. A motorist between the ages of twenty and forty is not unusual.

The contrast between the *Campbell* and *Smith* drug courier profiles, which do not support reasonable suspicion, and another courier profile which was held to support reasonable suspicion is marked. *United States v. Sokolow,* 490 U.S. 1, 3 (1989).[24] In *Sokolow*, DEA agents found 1,063 grams of cocaine inside Sokolow's carry-on luggage when he was stopped in Honolulu International Airport based on the following profile:

1. He had paid $2,100 in cash for two airplane tickets from a roll of $20 bills which appeared to contain $4,000;
2. He was ticketed under a name other than his own;
3. He traveled to Miami, a known drug source, and back;
4. Although his round trip flight lasted 20 hours, he stayed in Miami only 48 hours;
5. He appeared nervous;
6. He was about 25 years old;
7. He was dressed in a black jumpsuit and was wearing gold jewelry which he wore during both legs of the round-trip flight; and
8. Neither he nor his companion checked any luggage.[25]

---

[22] "Smith and Swindell"is in brackets because this wording was inserted into the quotation by the person writing the memo. The ellipsis (. . .) shows that something was omitted from the original wording of the quotation. Your quotations must exactly match the wording and punctuation of the authority the quotation comes from. If you are sloppy in quoting and your reader discovers that you have taken liberties with the original material, the reader may suspect that you are sloppy in other ways—perhaps even in your research.

[23] No page reference is needed if you have already given the facts in the cases you are using as authority and you are referring to those cases in general.

[24] To avoid including a full citation in a textual sentence, *Sokolow* is referred to in general terms and the citation to *Sokolow* is given in a separate citation sentence. Including the full citation in the sentence makes the sentence harder to read and understand.

[25] Only those facts from *Sokolow* which are relevant to the discussion of *Smith* are given.

Id. at 3–5. The Court held that the *Sokolow* drug courier profile did support reasonable suspicion. *Id.* at 11.

The *Sokolow* dissent would have found that all of the factors, even if "taken together," did not amount to reasonable suspicion. In criticizing the use of a drug courier profile to stop suspects, the dissent noted "the profile's 'chameleon-like way of adapting to any particular set of observations'" "subjecting innocent individuals to unwarranted police harassment and detention." *Id.* at 13 (Marshall, J., dissenting)[26] (quoting *Sokolow v. United States,* 831 F.2d 1413, 1418 (9th Cir. 1987), *rev'd,* 490 U.S. 1 (1989)[27])

As predicted in the *Sokolow* dissent, Smith, Swindell, Campbell, and Campbell's friend were subjected to "unwarranted police harassment and detention" even though the factors in the respective drug courier profiles, even if "taken together," did not amount to reasonable suspicion. In contrast, several of the *Sokolow* factors, such as carrying such a large amount of cash and traveling a long distance to stay a relatively short period of time, are unusual or even suspicious in and of themselves. Each of the *Smith* and *Campbell* factors was not at all out of the ordinary alone and certainly taken together did not amount to reasonable suspicion.

B. Because the alleged traffic violation was only a pretext to allow the officer to investigate his "hunch," the evidence found in the trunk of Mike Campbell's car should be suppressed as the fruit of an unconstitutional search and seizure.

In *Smith*, the government argued on appeal that the stop was valid either because Vogel had probable cause to stop the car for a traffic violation ("weaving") or because Vogel could have stopped the car on the suspicion from the "weaving" that Smith was driving drunk. In responding to the government's arguments, the court set forth the following test. "[I]n determining whether an investigative stop is invalid as pretextual, the proper inquiry is whether a reasonable officer *would*[28] have made the seizure in the absence of illegitimate motivation." 799 F.2d at 708. Applying this test to *Smith*, the court concluded that "a reasonable officer would not have stopped the car absent an additional, invalid purpose," rejected "the traffic stop rationale . . . as pretextual," and found that the cocaine should have been excluded from evidence. *Id.* at 711.

---

26 You must identify the type of opinion from which you are quoting if it is other than the majority opinion.

27 This explanatory parenthetical tells the reader that the material Marshall is quoting came from the lower court decision in *Sokolow*. If you are quoting something which in turn quotes another source, you should identify the original source, as is done here. Subsequently history must be given for the lower court decision in *Sokolow*.

28 The word "would" was italicized in the material being quoted. You can emphasize words from a quotation which were not emphasized originally by underlying or italicizing them so long as you note the change by including "(emphasis added)" at the end of the citation.

In making its decision, the *Smith* court followed *United States v. Cruz*, 581 F.2d 535 (5th Cir. 1978) (en banc)[29] (this decision is binding on the United States Eleventh Circuit Court of Appeals because it occurred before the Fifth Circuit was split into the Fifth and Eleventh Circuits in 1981).[30] In *Cruz*, an officer speculated that a car the officer had passed had made an illegal u-turn on the highway because the suspect car did not follow the patrol car over a hill and, after turning the patrol car around, the officer observed the suspect car travelling in the opposite direction. The officer stopped the suspect car because of the illegal u-turn. After stopping the car and questioning its occupants, the officer arrested the occupants for violation of immigration laws. The Fifth Circuit "held the stop an unreasonable seizure under the fourth amendment because its purported rationale was merely a pretext for an invalid purpose." 799 F.2d at 710.

Cruz, *Smith*, and *Campbell* are very similar in that in all three cases, the government claimed that the stop of a suspect car did not violate the driver's right against unreasonable search and seizure because there was some irregularity in the way the car was being driven that gave the officer reason to stop the car. The driving "irregularities" are similar in that making a u-turn, swerving six inches into the emergency lane, and failing to use a turn signal in changing lanes are fairly minor infractions which did not appear to cause any safety hazard. If the three driving irregularities are compared in terms of severity, Campbell's alleged failure to use his turn signal when changing lanes is by far the least severe of the three. If officers were to stop every car on the highway which failed to use its turn signal when changing lanes, a very high percentage of the cars traveling the highway would be pulled over.

In both *Smith* and *Campbell*, the chronology of events suggests that the officers followed Smith and Campbell on the hunch that they might be involved in some illegal activity. Having a police car follow another car would, in most instances, make the car's driver nervous and the nervousness would probably increase as the distance the police car followed the other car increased. A nervous driver is much more likely to make a small driving mistake than one who is not nervous. Both Smith and Campbell finally made small driving mistakes after being followed for a considerable distance and the officers relied on the driving mistakes in pulling Smith and Campbell over. A reasonable officer would not have followed Campbell for such a distance based only on a hunch, waiting for Campbell to make a small driving mistake.

---

[29] An *en banc* decision is usually an important one, because the entire membership of the court sits rather than the usual three-judge panel, and it is reserved for consideration of important legal issues.

[30] These two phrases in parentheses are explanatory parentheticals. They are not technically necessary, but are added to the end of the citation to give the reader more information.

Because the drug courier profiles in *Smith* and *Campbell* are virtually identical and are in sharp contrast to the *Sokolow* drug courier profile, this court should find that there was not reasonable suspicion to stop Campbell and the stop on that ground was an unconstitutional violation of Campbell's right to be free from unreasonable search and seizure. Unless the agents had probable cause to investigate the alleged traffic violation, this court should suppress the cocaine as the fruit of an unconstitutional search and seizure.

Following the *Cruz* and *Smith* courts, which rejected the traffic stop rationale as pretextual, and whose decisions are binding here, this court should also reject the stop of Campbell's car for failure to change lanes as pretextual. This is because the traffic violation here is similar to, but so much less severe than, the alleged traffic violations in *Smith* and *Cruz* that a reasonable officer would not have stopped Campbell absent a "hunch" that the car contained illegal drugs. Because the agents did not have reasonable suspicion to stop Campbell to investigate for illegal drug activity and the stop for Campbell's failure to change lanes was pretextual, the stop violated Campbell's right against unreasonable search and seizure. Because Campbell's fourth amendment right was violated by the stop and the agents would not have found the cocaine if they had not first stopped the car on I-95, the cocaine should be suppressed as the fruit of the poisonous tree.

Conclusion:

For the reasons set forth above, defendant Campbell requests this court to grant his motion to suppress and to dismiss the charge against him for lack of evidence.

Respectfully submitted,

____

Florida Attorney, Esq.
Florida Bar Number 000000
Law Firm
Main Street
Anytown, Fla.

SUMMARY

- In litigation, an attorney may be required by court rule, may be asked by the judge, or may feel the need to submit a memorandum of law to the court.
- The purposes of the memorandum of law are to explain the client's position in a lawsuit and to convince the judge to rule in the client's favor.

- The tone of the memorandum of law is persuasive.
- Although the attorney has to represent the client's best interest, this duty is tempered by the attorney's ethical duty as "an officer of the court."
- Build your credibility by stating the facts and the law accurately.
- Use a format that makes your memorandum of law reader-friendly.
- Organize the document to highlight important information and to obscure adverse information which you feel obligated to include.
- Comply with any court rules and the format customarily used for the particular court.
- The parts of a standard memorandum of law are the caption, the question presented, the facts, the argument, the thesis paragraph, the rule of law, the application of law to the facts, and the conclusion.

EXERCISES

1. Pick one of the research problems from Appendix G.
2. Research the problem you have chosen.
3. Write a memorandum of law using your research.

CHAPTER 15
Appellate Brief

OUTLINE

Purpose
Format

When a case is appealed, the attorneys for the parties submit *appellate briefs* to the appellate court. This chapter explains the purpose, use, and format of the appellate brief and includes a sample appellate brief.

Much of the substance of the sample appellate brief is similar to that of the sample memorandum of law in Chapter 14. To avoid repetition, the annotations from the memorandum of law are not repeated in the appellate brief. You may want to go back later and reread the notes to the sample memorandum of law from Chapter 14.

An *appellate brief* is a written statement submitted to an appellate court to persuade the court of the correctness of one's position. An appellate brief argues the facts of a case, supported by specific page references to the record, and the applicable law, supported by citations of authority.

The *record* is the file containing the papers the lower court transmits to the appellate court. The parties usually designate those papers they desire to become part of the record on appeal. Rule 10(a) of the Federal Rules of Appellate Procedure lists the typical papers making up the record: "the original papers and exhibits filed in the district court, the transcripts of the proceedings, if any, and a certified copy of the docket entries prepared by the clerk of the district court." Statements of fact and statements about the history of the case included in the appellate briefs are required to be supported by specific page references to the record.

PURPOSE

When a party loses in a lower court and appeals, the appellate court's job is to review what the lower court did to determine whether the lower court committed reversible error. In its review, the appellate court examines the record of the lower court proceedings and reads the appellate briefs. Once the record on appeal is transmitted to the appellate court and appellate briefs are filed, the appellate court may rule on the appeal solely on the strength of the documents filed with the appellate court, or it may hear oral argument. During oral argument, the attorney for each party has an allotted period of time to argue the client's position in the case and respond to questions posed by the appellate judges.

The appellate briefs play a major role in the appeal. You might think of the appellate briefs as guidebooks to the case. They contain the arguments of the parties, they assist the appellate court in determining the issues to be decided on appeal, and they explain the applicable law and facts. Of course, because the appellate briefs are designed to persuade the appellate court of the correctness of the respective parties' positions, the **appellant's** brief is written from the appellant's perspective and the **appellee's** brief is written from the appellee's perspective.

The appellant's brief is filed first and gives the appellant's reasons why the appellate court should reverse or otherwise modify the lower court decision. Court rules give the appellee a certain period of time after the appellant's brief is filed to file the appellee's brief. The appellee's brief gives the appellee's reasons why the lower court decision should be affirmed.

In reviewing a lower court decision, the appellate court must follow the standard of review. The standard of review is the nature and extent of the action the appellate court may take in reviewing the lower court decision. The standard is different depending on whether the appellate court is reviewing a finding of fact, a ruling of law, or a ruling on a question involving both law and fact. Because the trial court was in the best position to judge the credibility of the witnesses, the trial court's finding of fact is given great deference. The appellate court is bound to follow the trial court's finding of fact unless a jury finding was unreasonable or a trial judge's finding was clearly erroneous. When deciding a question of law or a question involving both law and fact, the appellate court is free to reach a ruling different from that of the trial court.

Keep in mind the standard of review when writing the appellate brief. If you represent the appellee and the question for review is one of fact, emphasize that the trial court's finding of fact must be deferred to unless unreasonable or clearly erroneous. Whether the issue is one purely of fact, purely of law, or of mixed fact and law is rarely clear-cut. If you represent the appellant, try to characterize the issue as one of law or of fact and law so that the appellate court will not have to defer to the decision of the trial court.

If you represent the appellee, use the lower court decision in the appellee's favor to your advantage. Do not hesitate to rely on the reasoning of the lower court. You may even want to quote particularly well-worded passages of the lower court's opinion. Although an appellate court is not bound by the trial court's ruling on a question of law or a mixed question of fact and law, sometimes it helps to remind the appellate court that, after studying the issue, the lower court ruled in the appellee's favor.

Let's compare the appellate brief with the memorandum of law. Of the legal documents covered in this book, the appellate brief is most similar to the memorandum of law. Because both the memorandum of law and the appellate brief are persuasive in tone and are designed to convince the reader of the correctness of the client's position, much of the substance of the two documents will be similar. Although similar in tone and purpose, the two documents differ in two respects. As explained earlier, the appellate brief differs from the memorandum of law in the standard of review by the appellate court. The different standard of review in the appellate court will probably dictate some change in the wording of the issues and argument portions of the appellate brief from the questions presented and argument sections of the memorandum of law. Another difference is format. Aside from complying with page size and other such mundane requirements, attorneys writing memoranda of law generally follow the format customary in their area rather than having to follow a certain format specified by court rule. In contrast, the format for appellate briefs is usually specified in detail in the applicable court rules.

At this point, you should probably reread the preceding chapter on the memorandum of law (Chapter 14). Except for differences in the standard of review and format, assume that the explanation of the memorandum of law from that chapter applies to the appellate brief.

FORMAT

The first step in writing an appellate brief is to check applicable court rules to determine the format required by the court. For a case being appealed to a federal circuit court, you would review the Federal Rules of Appellate Procedure. The United States Supreme Court has its own set of rules which must be consulted for documents submitted to it. For a case being appealed to the intermediate appellate court of your state, check the rules of appellate procedure for your state. The court of last resort of your state may have its own set of rules which must be consulted for documents submitted to it, or it may use the same rules as the state intermediate appellate courts. In addition to the rules referred to in this paragraph, many courts have local rules that must be complied with.

Failure to follow court rules for appellate briefs may have serious consequences. The least serious of the consequences is attorney embarrassment if the failure to comply is pointed out by the clerk of the court, by opposing counsel, or by a judge. The most serious consequence is the clerk's office refusing to file an appellate brief that fails to comply with applicable appellate rules.

The rules for appellate briefs cover a number of matters. They usually specify the major sections required to be included in the appellate brief and may specify their content. The rules may also mandate certain more mundane matters, such as paper size, type size, and maximum page length. For example, Rule 28 of the Federal Rules of Appellate Procedure states the sections required for the appellate brief, gives a brief explanation of the information to be included in each section, and limits appellate briefs to 50 pages. Rule 32 requires appellate briefs to be double-spaced in at least 11 point type on 8.5-by-11-inch paper, with typed material not exceeding 6.5 by 9.5 inches. (To save space, the sample appellate brief contained in this chapter is single rather than double-spaced.) Rule 32 also specifies the information required on the cover of the appellate brief and the color of the cover.

The format used in this chapter complies with Rule 28 of the Federal Rules of Appellate Procedure. The following are the sections of an appellate brief required by Rule 28.

LEGAL TERMS

appellant
A party who appeals from a lower court to a higher court.

appellee
A party against whom a case is appealed from a lower court to a higher court.

Table of Contents

The table of contents should include the titles of the sections of the brief and the wording of the point headings as well as the page references.

Table of Cases, Statutes, and Other Authorities

This table (alphabetically arranged) contains references to the pages of the brief on which the listed authorities are cited.

Statement of Subject Matter Jurisdiction

Rule 28 requires "a statement of the basis for **subject matter jurisdiction** in the district court or agency, with citation to applicable statutory provisions and with reference to the relevant facts to establish such jurisdiction."

Statement of Appellate Jurisdiction

Rule 28 requires

> a statement of the basis for jurisdiction in the court of appeals, with citation to applicable statutory provisions and with reference to the relevant facts to establish such jurisdiction; the statement shall include relevant filing dates establishing the timeliness of the appeal or petition for review and
>
> (a) shall state that the appeal is from a final order or a final judgment that disposes of all claims with respect to all parties or, if not,
>
> (b) shall include information establishing that the court of appeals has jurisdiction on some other basis.

Statement of Issues Presented for Review

The issues are the questions you are suggesting that the appellate court consider. Word the issues so the appellate court can easily reach a decision in your client's favor. Often the appellee will start an issue with the words, "Did the trial court properly find that" or "Did the trial court properly rule that." Such wording suggests that the trial court decision was correct. In contrast, the appellant would start the same issue with the words, "Did the trial court err in." This wording suggests that there was something wrong with the trial court's decision.

Statement of the Case

Rule 28 requires that the statement "first indicate briefly the nature of the case, the course of proceedings, and its disposition in the court below."

Statement of the Facts

Rule 28 requires that the statement contain "the facts relevant to the issues presented for review, with appropriate references to the record." For ease of reference, the appellant's brief usually has an appendix attached to it, containing copies of the parts of the record referenced in the appellant's brief. The abbreviation "(A.3)" would reference page three of the appendix.

Legal Argument

Rule 28 states: "The argument may be preceded by a summary. The argument shall contain the contentions of the appellant with respect to the issues presented, and the reasons therefor, with citations to the authorities, statutes and parts of the record relied on." As in the memorandum of law, use point headings to make the brief reader-friendly. The brief should contain one or more major point headings for major sections and may contain subheadings within a major section to divide that major section into subsections. The major point headings should be equal in number to the issues presented, should answer the issues, and should appear in the same order as the issues presented.

Legal Conclusion

Rule 28 requires "[a] short conclusion stating the precise relief sought."

SAMPLE APPELLATE BRIEF

IN THE
UNITED STATES COURT OF APPEALS
FOR THE ELEVENTH CIRCUIT

CASE NO. 93-0000

UNITED STATES OF AMERICA,
Appellee,
v.
MICHAEL CAMPBELL and JOHN WRIGHT,
Appellants.

LEGAL TERMS

subject matter jurisdiction
The jurisdiction of a court to hear and determine the type of case before it.

APPEAL OF A CRIMINAL CONVICTION FROM THE
UNITED STATES DISTRICT COURT
FOR THE MIDDLE DISTRICT OF FLORIDA
ORLANDO DIVISION

BRIEF FOR APPELLANT CAMPBELL

Florida Attorney, Esq.
Florida Bar Number 000000
Law Firm
Main Street
Anytown, Fla.

TABLE OF CONTENTS

TABLE OF AUTHORITIES

CASES

FEDERAL RULES OF APPELLATE PROCEDURE

UNITED STATES CODE

UNITED STATES CONSTITUTION

STATEMENT OF SUBJECT MATTER JURISDICTION IN THE UNITED STATES DISTRICT COURT

The defendant, Michael Campbell, was indicted in the United States District Court for the Middle District of Florida on March 16, 1993. The indictment charged him with violating 21 U.S.C. § 841(a)(1) for possession with intent to distribute a quantity of cocaine. (A. 21). Defendant received a jury verdict of guilty on May 18, 1993 and was sentenced on July 12, 1993 to a term of three years. (A. 25).

STATEMENT OF JURISDICTION

This is an appeal from the final judgment of the United States District Court for the Middle District of Florida in a criminal case pursuant to a motion under Rule 4(b) of the Federal Rules of Appellate Procedure. Jurisdiction in the United States Court of Appeals for the Eleventh Circuit is invoked under 28 U.S.C. § 1291, which provides that the Court of Appeals has jurisdiction from all final decisions of the United States District Court. Defendant was sentenced on July 12, 1993. On July 20, 1993, a timely Notice of Appeal was filed from which this appeal follows. (A. 25, 27).

STATEMENT OF THE ISSUE

Did the trial court err in admitting evidence seized from defendant Mike Campbell's car where a law enforcement officer pursued the Campbell car after he observed Mike and his friend, two Afro-American college students in their twenties in beach attire, traveling on I-95 in the early evening at the speed limit in an out-of-state tagged Lincoln Continental and where the law enforcement officer pulled the Campbell car over when it failed to signal when changing lanes? (A. 3-4).

STATEMENT OF THE CASE

On March 14, 1993, United States Drug Enforcement Agents stopped the defendant, Michael Campbell, on I-95 because he fit their drug courier profile and for his failure to signal when he changed lanes. (A. 3-4). After the agents found cocaine in the trunk of Campbell's car, he was arrested and taken into custody. (A. 5). He was provided an initial detention hearing on March 15, 1993. (A. 20). On March 16, 1993, an indictment was filed charging him with a violation of 21 U.S.C. § 841(a)(1) for possession with intent to distribute a quantity of cocaine. He was arraigned the same day and he entered a plea of not guilty. (A. 21).

A trial date was set for May 17, 1993 for a jury trial. Prior to trial defendant filed a motion to suppress the cocaine found in the trunk of defendant's car. The district court denied the motion and the trial began on May 17, 1993. (A. 22). Defendant received a jury verdict of guilty on May 18, 1993. (A. 24). Defendant was sentenced on July 12, 1993 to a term of three years. (A. 25).

STATEMENT OF THE FACTS

Mike Campbell and his best friend had decided, like thousands of other college students, to enjoy a Florida spring break. After Mike promised to drive carefully, Mike's father let Mike borrow his car, a brand new Lincoln Continental. After arriving in Florida, Mike and his friend spent every waking moment of their break on the beach. In the early evening on the last day of vacation, they went straight from the beach to their car to begin the long trip back to school, calculating that they would have just enough driving time to make it back for their first class. (A. 1-2). Mike was driving north on I-95, thinking about the promise he had made to his father, when he saw patrol cars parked in the median, one with its lights shining across the northbound lanes. Almost immediately after driving through the arc of the patrol car's headlights, Mike looked in the rear-view mirror and saw the patrol car pull out behind him. The patrol car followed Mike for a distance. When Mike changed lanes without using his turn signal, the patrol car put on its flashing lights and pulled Mike over. (A. 3-4).

An officer got out of the patrol car, walked over to Mike's car, and asked for Mike's driver's license and car registration. As Mike handed over his license and the registration, he noticed the officer eying Mike's beach attire suspiciously. When Mike told the officer they were heading back to school from spring break, the officer commented, "We don't see too many blacks down here over spring break." Still holding the license and registration, the officer asked Mike whether the officer could search the car and said, "You don't have anything to hide, do you?" Hoping that if he refused they could be on their way, Mike answered, "No." The officer said, "Wait here," turned around, walked back to the patrol car, and got in. Mike could not have left even if the officer had not told him to wait because the officer still had Mike's license and car registration. (A. 3-4).

Forty-five minutes later, another patrol car pulled up and an officer got out with a dog. The officer led the dog around the car. The dog circled the car once and then stopped and pawed the car's trunk. The officer motioned Mike to roll down his window. The officer told him that the dog had detected drugs in the trunk of Mike's car. The officer told Mike that Mike could either open the car trunk or wait there whatever time was necessary for the officer to obtain a search warrant. Feeling that he had no choice, Mike opened the trunk. Both officers started pulling Mike's and his friend's belongings out of the trunk and tossing them on the ground. Wedged in a bottom corner of the trunk, one of the officers found a brown paper bag containing cocaine. Mike and his friend were arrested and charged with possession with intent to distribute cocaine. (A. 4-5).

SUMMARY OF ARGUMENT

The fourth amendment to the United States Constitution guarantees "[t]he right of the people to be secure in their persons, houses, papers, and effects against unreasonable searches and seizures" and allows a search warrant to be issued only upon "probable cause." A search warrant requirement was spelled out in the amendment to safeguard this important right. Over the more than two hundred years since the amendment was adopted, the individual's right against unreasonable search and seizure has been jealously guarded.

Although the time and level of evidence needed to obtain a search warrant protect the individual's constitutional right, the courts have allowed two exceptions to the search warrant requirement, either of which the government argues is applicable here and allowed its agents to stop the Campbell car. The first exception requires a minimum of "reasonable suspicion" of illegal activity to stop a car and question its occupants. *Terry v. Ohio,* 392 U.S. 1, 27 (1968). The second exception allows an officer to stop a car to investigate a traffic violation so long as the traffic violation is not a pretext for the stop. *United States v. Smith,* 799 F.2d 704, 709 (11th Cir. 1986).

Defendant Campbell's motion to suppress should have been granted because neither of the two exceptions to the search warrant requirement applies here. The officer stopped Campbell's car on a mere "hunch" and a reasonable officer would not have stopped Campbell's car for the alleged traffic violation except to follow up on a hunch. The argument section of this brief will first explain why there was not enough evidence to justify an investigatory stop and then why the alleged traffic violation did not justify the stop.

ARGUMENT

THE EVIDENCE FOUND IN THE TRUNK OF DEFENDANT CAMPBELL'S CAR SHOULD HAVE BEEN SUPPRESSED AS THE FRUIT OF AN UNCONSTITUTIONAL SEARCH AND SEIZURE BECAUSE THE DRUG COURIER PROFILE DID NOT SUPPORT THE REASONABLE SUSPICION NECESSARY FOR AN INVESTIGATORY STOP AND A REASONABLE OFFICER WOULD NOT HAVE STOPPED CAMPBELL FOR FAILURE TO SIGNAL WHEN CHANGING LANES.

A. Because the information the officer relied on to stop the Campbell car was no more than a mere "hunch," the evidence should be suppressed unless the officer had probable cause to stop the car for a traffic violation.

Terry was the landmark case that lowered the burden of proof necessary for a stop from probable cause to "reasonable suspicion." Such stops made on reasonable suspicion are often referred to as "Terry stops," after *Terry,* and the definition of Terry stops has been broadened to apply to car stops. The new reasonable suspicion standard allows a police officer to stop and briefly question someone, but is still designed to protect the innocent traveler, singled out because of certain immutable personal characteristics such as race, sex, and age, from being subjected to "overbearing or harassing" law enforcement tactics. 392 U.S. at 14-15 n.11. A stop made only on an "unparticularized suspicion or 'hunch'" is unconstitutional. Assuming the officer has the requisite reasonable suspicion for a Terry stop, the officer would still need probable cause or consent to search a car.

Smith involved almost identical facts to those being considered here. In *Smith* the government argued that a highway stop was constitutionally permitted based either on a drug courier profile or on Smith's alleged commission of a traffic violation. 799 F.2d at 705. Smith filed a motion to suppress, claiming that the evidence seized from his car should be suppressed because of the violation of his right against unreasonable search and seizure. *Id.* at 706. The Eleventh Circuit Court of Appeals found that the *Smith* drug courier profile did not support reasonable suspicion, reversed the lower court's denial of Smith's motion to suppress, and vacated Smith's conviction. *Id.* at 712.

One night in June 1985, Trooper Robert Vogel, a Florida Highway Patrol trooper, and a DEA agent were observing cars traveling in the northbound lanes of I-95, in hopes of intercepting drug couriers. When Smith's car passed through the arc of the patrol car headlights, Vogel noticed the following factors that matched his drug courier profile:

1. The car was traveling at 3:00 a.m.;
2. The car was a 1985 Mercury, a large, late-model car;
3. The car had out-of-state tags;
4. There were two occupants of the car who were around 30; and
5. The driver was driving cautiously and did not look at the patrol car as the Mercury passed through the arc of the patrol car headlights.

Id. at 705-06.

The above drug courier profile is almost identical to the profile in this case. In both *Smith* and this case, the cars were traveling after dark; the cars were large, late models with out-of-state tags; the cars were being driven "cautiously"; and each car contained two passengers in their twenties or thirties. The differences between the two profiles are very minor. Campbell and his friend were dressed casually, while it is not known how Smith and Swindell were dressed. Smith and Swindell did not look at Vogel as they passed. It is not known whether Campbell looked in the agents' direction as Campbell drove past. Campbell claims that race was a factor in the stop even though it was not listed as such by the agents. (A. 3-4). Smith and Swindell's race is unknown.

In *Smith,* Vogel followed the Mercury for a mile and a half and noticed that the Mercury "wove" several times, once as much as six inches into the emergency lane. Vogel pulled Smith over. When a drug dog alerted on the car, a

DEA agent searched the trunk and discovered one kilogram of cocaine. Smith and his passenger, Swindell, were arrested and charged with conspiracy to possess cocaine with the intent to distribute it. Smith and Swindell's motions to suppress the cocaine were denied and they were tried and convicted. *Id.* at 706.

The issue before the appellate court was whether the stop of Smith's car was reasonable. *Id.* This is the same basic question before the court in determining whether Campbell's motion to suppress should have been granted. The *Smith* court held that the stop of Smith's car could not be upheld as a valid Terry stop, *id.* at 708, finding that "Trooper Vogel stopped the car because [Smith and Swindell] . . . matched a few nondistinguishing characteristics contained on a drug courier profile and, additionally, because Vogel was bothered by the way the driver of the car chose not to look at him." *Id.* at 707.

Just as there was nothing in the Campbell drug courier profile to differentiate Campbell and his friend from other innocent college students returning from spring break in Florida, there was nothing in Vogel's drug courier profile to differentiate Smith and Swindell from other law-abiding motorists on I-95. (A. 3-4). It is usual to drive after dark to avoid heavy traffic or to complete an interstate trip. Although many motorists speed on the highways, motorists driving "cautiously" at or near the speed limit are simply obeying traffic laws. Many people other than drug couriers drive large, late-model cars with out-of-state tags. A motorist between the ages of twenty and forty is not unusual.

The contrast between the *Campbell* and *Smith* drug courier profiles, which do not support reasonable suspicion, and another courier profile which was held to support reasonable suspicion is marked. *United States v. Sokolow,* 490 U.S. 1, 3 (1989). In *Sokolow,* DEA agents found 1,063 grams of cocaine inside Sokolow's carry-on luggage when he was stopped in Honolulu International Airport based on the following profile:

1. He had paid $2,100 in cash for two airplane tickets from a roll of $20 bills which appeared to contain $4,000;
2. He was ticketed under a name other than his own;
3. He traveled to Miami, a known drug source, and back;
4. Although his round-trip flight lasted 20 hours, he stayed in Miami only 48 hours;
5. He appeared nervous;
6. He was about 25 years old;
7. He was dressed in a black jumpsuit and was wearing gold jewelry which he wore during both legs of the round-trip flight; and
8. Neither he nor his companion checked any luggage.

Id. at 3-5. The Court held that the *Sokolow* drug courier profile did support reasonable suspicion. *Id.* at 11.

The *Sokolow* dissent would have found that all of the factors, even if "taken together," did not amount to reasonable suspicion. In criticizing the use of a drug courier profile to stop suspects, the dissent noted "the profile's 'chameleon-like way of adapting to any particular set of observations'" "subjecting innocent individuals to unwarranted police harassment and detention." *Id.* at 13 (Marshall, J., dissenting) (quoting *Sokolow v. United States,* 831 F.2d 1413, 1418 (9th Cir. 1987), *rev'd,* 490 U.S. 1 (1989)).

As predicted in the *Sokolow* dissent, Smith, Swindell, Campbell, and Campbell's friend were subjected to "unwarranted police harassment and detention" even though the factors in the respective drug courier profiles, even if "taken together," did not amount to reasonable suspicion. In contrast, several of the *Sokolow* factors, such as carrying such a large amount of cash and traveling a long distance to stay a relatively short period of time, are unusual or even suspicious in and of themselves. Each of the *Smith* and *Campbell* factors was not at all out of the ordinary alone and certainly taken together did not amount to reasonable suspicion. (A. 3-4).

B. Because the alleged traffic violation was only a pretext to allow the officer to investigate his "hunch," the evidence found in the trunk of Mike Campbell's car should be suppressed as the fruit of an unconstitutional search and seizure.

In *Smith,* the government argued on appeal that the stop was valid either because Vogel had probable cause to stop the car for a traffic violation ("weaving") or because Vogel could have stopped the car on the suspicion from the "weaving" that Smith was driving drunk. In responding to the government's arguments, the court set forth the following test. "[I]n determining whether an investigative stop is invalid as pretextual, the proper inquiry is whether a reasonable officer *would* have made the seizure in the absence of illegitimate motivation." 799 F.2d at 708. Applying this test to *Smith,* the court concluded that "a reasonable officer would not have stopped the car absent an additional, invalid purpose," rejected "the traffic stop rationale . . . as pretextual," and found that the cocaine should have been excluded from evidence. *Id.* at 711.

In making its decision, the *Smith* court followed *United States v. Cruz,* 581 F.2d 535 (5th Cir. 1978) (en banc) (this decision is binding on the United States Eleventh Circuit Court of Appeals because it occurred before the Fifth Circuit was split into the Fifth and Eleventh Circuits in 1981). In *Cruz,* an officer speculated that a car the officer had passed had made an illegal u-turn on the highway because the suspect car did not follow the patrol car over a hill and, after turning the patrol car around, the officer observed the suspect car travelling in the opposite direction. The officer stopped the suspect car because of the illegal u-turn. After stopping the car and questioning its occupants, the officer arrested the occupants for violation of immigration laws. The Fifth Circuit "held the stop an unreasonable seizure under the fourth amendment because its purported rationale was merely a pretext for an invalid purpose." 799 F.2d at 710.

Cruz, Smith, and *Campbell* are very similar in that, in all three cases, the government claimed that the stop of a suspect car did not violate the driver's right against unreasonable search and seizure because there was some irregularity in the way the car was being driven that gave the officer reason to stop the car. The driving "irregularities" are similar in that making a u-turn, swerving six inches into the emergency lane, and failing to use a turn signal in changing lanes are fairly minor infractions which did not appear to cause any safety hazard. (A. 3-4). If the three driving irregularities are compared in terms of severity, Campbell's alleged failure to use his turn signal when changing lanes is by far the least severe of the three. If officers were to stop every car on the highway which failed to use its turn signal when changing lanes, a very high percentage of the cars traveling the highway would be pulled over.

In both *Smith* and *Campbell,* the chronology of events suggests that the officers followed Smith and Campbell on the hunch that they might be involved in some illegal activity. Having a police car follow another car would in most instances make the car's driver nervous and the nervousness would probably increase as the distance the police car followed the other car increased. A nervous driver is much more likely to make a small driving mistake than one who is not nervous. Both Smith and Campbell finally made small driving mistakes after being followed for a considerable distance, and the officers relied on the driving mistakes in pulling Smith and Campbell over. (A. 3-4). A reasonable officer would not have followed Campbell for such a distance based only on a hunch, waiting for Campbell to make a small driving mistake.

Because the drug courier profiles in *Smith* and *Campbell* are virtually identical and are in sharp contrast to the *Sokolow* drug courier profile, this court should find that there was not reasonable suspicion to stop Campbell and the stop on that ground was an unconstitutional violation of Campbell's right to be free from unreasonable search and seizure. Unless the agents had probable cause to investigate the alleged traffic violation, this court should suppress the cocaine as the fruit of an unconstitutional search and seizure.

Following the *Cruz* and *Smith* courts, which rejected the traffic stop rationale as pretextual, and whose decisions are binding here, this court should also reject the stop of Campbell's car for failure to change lanes as pretextual. This is because the "traffic violation" here is similar to, but so much less severe than, the alleged traffic violations in *Smith* and *Cruz* that a reasonable officer would not have stopped Campbell absent a "hunch" that the car contained illegal drugs. Because the agents did not have reasonable cause to stop Campbell to investigate for illegal drug activity and the stop for Campbell's failure to change lanes was pretextual, the stop violated Campbell's right against unreasonable search and seizure. Because Campbell's fourth amendment right was violated by the stop and the agents would not have found the cocaine if they had not first stopped the car on I-95, the cocaine should be suppressed as the fruit of the poisonous tree.

CONCLUSION

For the reasons set forth above, defendant Campbell requests this court to reverse the district court's denial of his motion to suppress, vacate his conviction, and remand the case to the district court.

Respectfully submitted,

____

Florida Attorney, Esq.
Florida Bar Number 000000
Law Firm
Main Street
Anytown, Fla.

SUMMARY

- The appellate brief is a written statement submitted to the appellate court to persuade the court of the correctness of one's position.
- When a party loses in a lower court and appeals, the appellate court's job is to review what the lower court did to determine whether the lower court committed reversible error.
- The standard of review is different depending on whether the appellate court is reviewing a finding of fact, a ruling of law, or a ruling on a question involving both law and fact.
- The appellate court is bound to follow the trial court's finding of fact unless a jury finding was unreasonable or a trial judge's finding was clearly erroneous.
- When deciding a question of law or a question involving both law and fact, the appellate court is free to reach a ruling different from that of the trial court.
- The appellate brief is persuasive in tone.
- Follow any applicable court rules (including local rules) governing the appellate brief.
- Rule 28 of the Federal Rules of Appellate Procedure requires:
    - A table of contents
    - A table of authorities cited
    - A statement of subject matter jurisdiction
    - A statement of appellate jurisdiction
    - A statement of the issues
    - A statement of the case
    - A statement of the facts
    - An argument
    - A conclusion.

EXERCISES

1. Pick one of the research problems from Appendix G.
2. Research the problem you have chosen.
3. Write an appellate brief using your research.

APPENDIX A

Search and Seizure

INTRODUCTION

The search and seizure problem and the primary sources contained in this appendix are referred to throughout this book and will be the basis of many of the research and writing exercises you will perform. The first time you read this appendix, read the problem carefully and skim the following section to gain some familiarity with the law you might find in the law library if you were researching the problem. The search and seizure topic was selected because it is fairly easy to understand and seems to be interesting to most students. In addition, you will be learning some substantive law as you read and work through the exercises.

THE WILLIAMS SEARCH AND SEIZURE PROBLEM

Ralph Williams is the owner of All-Right Paint Shop in a small town in New Jersey. The shop is in the business of repainting cars. Ralph had been operating the paint shop for 10 years when he decided that he would like to open a new business selling antique cars. (He had gotten the idea from advertisements for antique cars in car-trader magazines.) He thought that he would buy a few antique cars now and then would open the new business after he had a number of cars in stock. The money to buy the first cars would come from profits from the paint business and a home equity loan on his home. Ray Williams, Ralph's brother, offered to quit his job to manage the new business as soon as the brother had built up an inventory of a few cars.

After thoroughly reading the advertisements in the car-trader magazines, the brothers decided to head to Miami to look for antique cars. On a friend's advice, the brothers carried $35,000 in cash. The friend had told them that car dealers, especially in the Miami area, require cash. The friend also cautioned them that he had read articles about a large number of cars being stopped by Volusia County sheriff officers on Interstate 95 in Florida. The articles said that cash was taken from a number of cars, although no arrests were made. The stops typically were made in the evening or early morning hours. Most of the cars stopped had rental or out-of-state tags. Almost three-quarters of the drivers were male, 85 percent were black, and just over half were between 18 and 29 years of age. Three-quarters of the cars stopped contained two or more occupants.

The trip from New Jersey to Florida was uneventful. The brothers stopped only for gasoline and food and took turns driving. As it grew dark, Ralph dozed off in the passenger seat, waking up off and on while Ray drove. Ralph noticed several times when he woke up that Ray seemed to be tired, too. He was driving below the 55-mph speed limit, and was letting the car weave ever so slightly within its lane. At one point Ralph grabbed the wheel and steered it back into the lane as the car's outside front tire crossed the center line. When Ralph asked Ray whether he was too tired to drive, Ray said that he was a little tired but would get some coffee at the next rest stop. Ray did not notice that, about the time his car was weaving, he had passed an unmarked police car parked on the shoulder of the road. The officer in the unmarked car had observed Ray weaving and the officer radioed ahead to other officers to be on the watch for Ray's car.

A few minutes later, Ray saw two marked patrol cars parked in the median, one with its lights shining across the southbound lanes of traffic and the other with its headlights shining across the northbound lanes of traffic. As Ray learned later, the patrol cars contained sheriff officers and DEA agents participating in a joint drug task force. Ray kept his eyes on the road while passing the patrol cars and then glanced in the rear-view mirror. The patrol car pointing in his direction was pulling out onto I-95. As if in a bad dream, Ray watched as the patrol car came up behind him, put on its flashing lights, and pulled him over.

Ray was so nervous his hand was shaking as he handed over his driver's license and car registration. The officer examined Ray's driver's license and car registration and asked the brother where they were going. They said they were going to Miami on business. The officer returned the license and registration and was turning back to his patrol car when he said, "You don't mind if I search your car, do you?" The brothers were too surprised to say anything. Without giving them a chance to respond, the patrolman immediately opened the back door of the car and started examining the inside of the car with his flashlight. He picked up the cash box from the floorboard behind the front passenger seat, opened it, and found the $35,000 in cash.

When he saw the cash, the officer said, "This is an awful lot of cash to be carrying around. Where did you boys get this kind of money?" He looked at them in disbelief as they told him their story. Then he said, "I don't know whether I believe your story. I'll have to take this with me." When the brothers asked when they could get their money back, the patrolman suggested they contact the local Drug Enforcement Agency office in the morning and gave them the telephone number. The brothers signed a receipt and the patrolman left.

The brothers decided to go to the nearest rest stop and wait until they could call the DEA office. When they called the office, they were told they would have to file suit to get the money back. They were understandably upset, believing that the patrolman chose not to believe their story because they are Afro-Americans.

A short time later, Ray and Ralph read about a civil rights class action lawsuit filed in federal court in Florida. The named plaintiff alleged that her constitutional right against unreasonable search and seizure was violated when a sheriff's deputy seized $19,000 from her. Because the plaintiff's story seemed similar to their own, the brothers thought they might be members of the class. They decided to consult an attorney to determine what to do.

EXAMPLES OF PRIMARY SOURCES FOUND AFTER RESEARCHING SEARCH AND SEIZURE PROBLEM

As more fully explained in Chapter 1, primary sources contain the law itself. This section contains an example of each of the various types of primary sources. The examples were selected to allow you to glimpse primary sources as they appear printed in the law books you might find in your law library if you had researched the search and seizure problem.

This section contains the Fourth Amendment to the United States Constitution, a federal forfeiture statute, a search and seizure case, the federal court rule governing class actions, and federal administrative regulations concerning forfeiture. As you glance over these examples, try to understand the basic subject matter and notice the format of the various sources. There is no need at this point to scrutinize these examples in detail. Read the primary source again when you read a chapter dealing with that type of primary source.

THE U.S. CONSTITUTION, AMENDMENT IV [1791].

The right of the people to be secure in their persons, papers, and effects, against unreasonable searches and seizures, shall not be violated, and no warrants shall issue but upon probable cause, supported by oath or affirmation, and particularly describing the place to be searched and the persons or things to be seized.

Driver sues, says I-95 seizure biased

□ A motorist who says Volusia deputies stopped him and took his $265,000 because he is black is suing for $2 million.

By Jeff Brazil

OF THE SENTINEL STAFF

A Maryland man is suing the Volusia County Sheriff's Office, claiming deputies used a racially biased "profile" and violated search and seizure laws when they stopped him on Interstate 95 and confiscated his $265,000.

The federal lawsuit, filed in Orlando, alleges that Sheriff Bob Vogel's Special Enforcement Team stopped Aubrey Marcus Duncan, 52, of Fort Washington, Md., on April 25, 1991, because he is black.

It says deputies improperly detained him for more than an hour while they summoned a drug-sniffing dog to search for contraband. Duncan was not arrested, nor were any drugs found, but deputies seized his money because they believed it was intended to be used in a drug transaction, the suit states.

The suit, which asks for $2 million in damages, is the first of its kind against Vogel's anti-drug squad. The sheriff's team has seized more than $8 million, mostly from Interstate 95 motorists, and kept more than half after negotiating settlements with drivers.

"Somebody must challenge what these deputies are doing," said Duncan's attorney, Dean Mosley, who said he hopes other motorists stopped and detained by the team during the past four years will follow suit.

Vogel could not be reached for comment. In the past, he has said that race is not a factor in his team's traffic stops.

Duncan is awaiting sentencing on narcotics charges in an unrelated case in New Jersey, but Mosley said the drug case should have no bearing on the civil rights case.

"They have nothing to do with each other," he said. "The bottom line is, they violated Mr. Duncan's constitutional rights. They took his money. And, as a result, he couldn't settle with the IRS. He lost his house because he couldn't pay his mortgage. He couldn't even pay for his cancer treatments."

Duncan's suit comes at a time when law enforcement's use of drug courier profiles is coming under increased scrutiny from judges and lawmakers across the country. Defense lawyers and civil rights advocates believe police are targeting minorities.

Most police officials say they do not single out people based on race, and they contend that such profiles—characteristics that arouse officers' suspicions—are a valuable law enforcement tool.

"[The suits] are happening in pockets all over," said Nancy Hollander, president of

Is your money safe if you are Afro-American? (Reprinted with permission of the Orlando *Sentinel.*)

the National Association of Criminal Defense Lawyers.

In June 1992, Circuit Judge William C. Johnson, Jr. ordered the Sheriff's Office to give Duncan his money back, saying the agency violated Fourth Amendment protections against illegal search and seizure.

The Sheriff's Office, maintaining it had evidence Duncan was involved in narcotics, asked for a rehearing, but Johnson denied the request. The Internal Revenue Service later put a lien on Duncan's money, saying the self-proclaimed professional gambler owed back taxes.

Two months later, in October, Duncan was arrested in New Jersey after a state police officer stopped the car he was riding in for speeding. Inside, police said officers found four kilos of cocaine and a pound of heroin.

(Continued)

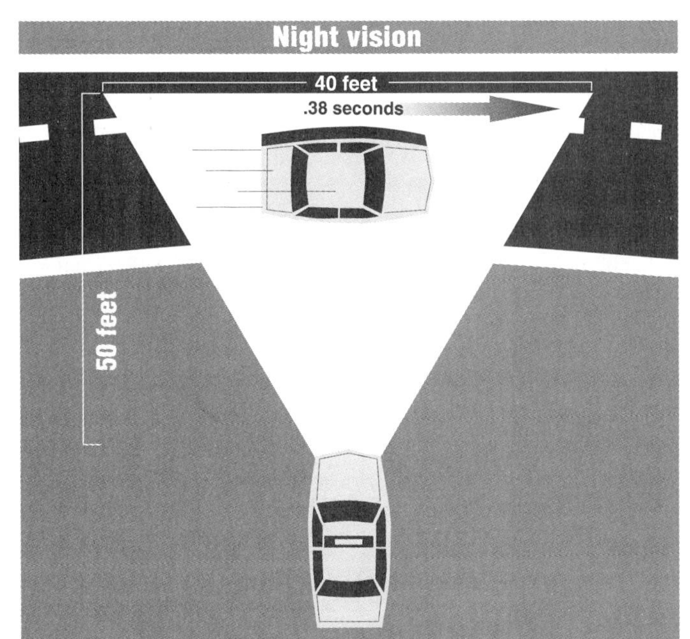

MARK BOIVIN/SENTINEL

At night, deputies look for drug traffickers by shining headlights and spotlights across Interstate 95. They say they're looking for traffic violations, driver's age, radar detectors, cellular telephones or CB antennas on out-of-state cars. Critics say they look for dark-skinned drivers. Whatever the object, there is little time. Headlights on their 1990 Chevrolet Caprices cast a 40-foot-wide beam at 50 feet. At 72 mph, average interstate speed, cars cross the lighted area in .38 seconds.

Source: Dr. David Moore. General Motors headlights specialist

MARK BOIVIN/SENTINEL

Do officers on I-95 have "reasonable suspicion" for the stops? (Reprinted with permission of the Orlando *Sentinel.*)

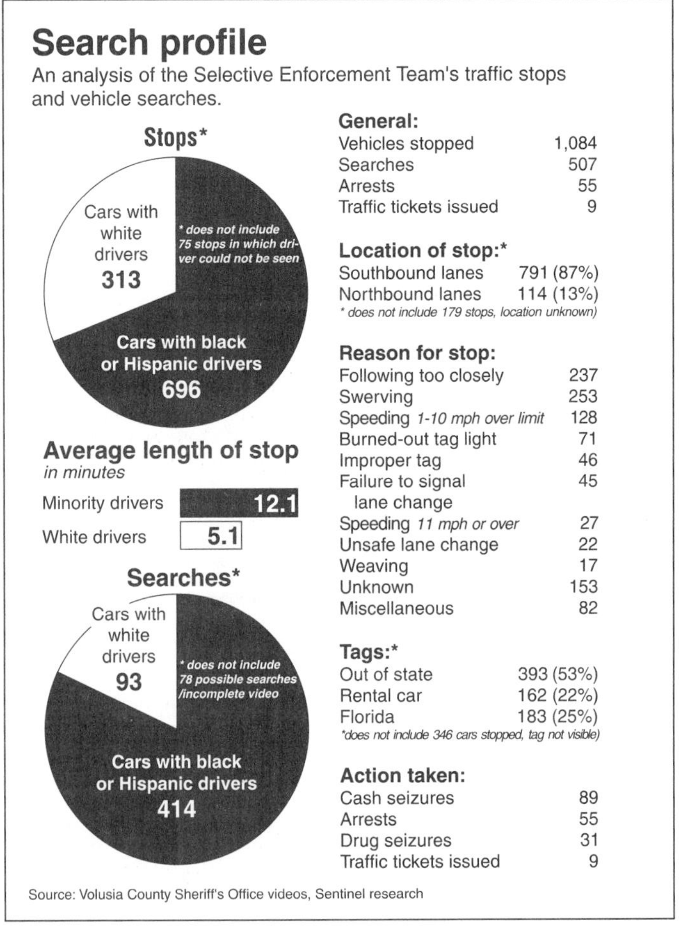

Search profile

An analysis of the Selective Enforcement Team's traffic stops and vehicle searches.

Stops*

Cars with white drivers 313

Cars with black or Hispanic drivers 696

* does not include 75 stops in which driver could not be seen

Average length of stop

in minutes

Minority drivers	12.1
White drivers	5.1

Searches*

Cars with white drivers 93

Cars with black or Hispanic drivers 414

* does not include 78 possible searches /incomplete video

General:

Vehicles stopped	1,084
Searches	507
Arrests	55
Traffic tickets issued	9

Location of stop:*

Southbound lanes	791 (87%)
Northbound lanes	114 (13%)

** does not include 179 stops, location unknown)*

Reason for stop:

Following too closely	237
Swerving	253
Speeding *1-10 mph over limit*	128
Burned-out tag light	71
Improper tag	46
Failure to signal lane change	45
Speeding *11 mph or over*	27
Unsafe lane change	22
Weaving	17
Unknown	153
Miscellaneous	82

Tags:*

Out of state	393 (53%)
Rental car	162 (22%)
Florida	183 (25%)

**does not include 346 cars stopped, tag not visible)*

Action taken:

Cash seizures	89
Arrests	55
Drug seizures	31
Traffic tickets issued	9

Source: Volusia County Sheriff's Office videos, Sentinel research

(Continued)

NAACP files suit against Sheriff Vogel

☐ **The class action suit says the Volusia County sheriff singled out black and Hispanic motorists for cash-seizure stops on I-95.**

By Steven Berry

OF THE SENTINEL STAFF

Lawyers for the NAACP Friday filed a class action suit in federal court accusing Volusia County Sheriff Bob Vogel of singling out blacks and Hispanics for his cash-seizure traffic stops on Interstate 95.

Would the Williams brothers be members of this class? (Reprinted with permission of the Orlando *Sentinel.*)

Attorneys Charles Burr of Tampa and E.E. "Bo" Edwards of Nashville filed the suit in U.S. Middle District Court in Orlando.

They filed it on behalf of Florida's National Association for the Advancement of Colored People, Selena Washington of Charleston, S.C., and all other blacks and Hispanics who were not arrested when their cash was seized by Volusia deputies while traveling I-95 between 1989 and 1992.

Cheryl Downs, Vogel's spokeswoman, said Friday that Vogel could not comment on the suit until he got a copy of it.

He has 20 days to file an answer with the court.

Washington, 43, was one of the motorists highlighted in an *Orlando Sentinel* investigative report last year on Vogel's cash-seizure operation.

Deputies on Vogel's five-person Selective Enforcement Team took $19,000 from Washington on April 24, 1990. She said she had borrowed the money from her father and friends to buy building materials to repair her home, which had been damaged by Hurricane Hugo.

Deputies found no drugs in her car, and she did not have a criminal record.

Vogel gave her $15,000 back eight months later as an out-of-court settlement.

Washington said Friday she planned to offer to testify at congressional hearings on Capitol Hill next week. The hearings, called by the House Committee on Government Operations, are to investigate cash-seizure practices of law enforcement agencies around the country.

Vogel seized more than $8 million—most of it from I-95—in 262 seizure cases. One of four involved an arrest. Of the seizures in which there was no arrest, 90 percent were from black and Hispanic motorists.

Out of more than 1,000 traffic stops that deputies videotaped, 70 percent involved blacks and Hispanics.

The suit claims Vogel used a race-based profile to choose which motorists to stop and search for drugs. It says his deputies seized any money they found even though they did not find drugs and did not arrest them.

The suit asks the court to return all the money seized from the plaintiffs and for an unspecified amount of punitive damages.

(Continued)

You may be drug free, but is your money?

☐ Cocaine is found on the cash of 8 non-users. The test suggests that a drug dog would detect cocaine on almost anyone's money.

By Jeff Brazil and Steve Berry

OF THE SENTINEL STAFF

Uriel Blount Jr. is a circuit judge. He has never snorted cocaine. But his money has traces of the illegal drug on it.

Leesburg Police Chief Jim Brown hasn't snorted cocaine either. His money has traces, too.

Would your money pass the test? (Reprinted with permission of the Orlando *Sentinel*.)

The same is true of State Sen. Dick Langley, Sanford Mayor Betty Smith, Daytona Beach Community College President Philip Day and *Orlando Sentinel* Editor John Haile.

Each recently agreed to help *The Orlando Sentinel* test the theory that most currency in Florida is tainted with tiny amounts of cocaine. Without warning, reporters approached them and offered an even trade for money in their wallets.

The money was tested: most samples tested positive.

In Florida the presence of cocaine, even in microscopic amounts, is critical. It has been a key factor in justifying the seizure of tens of millions of dollars.

South Florida reigns supreme in seizing drug money. But no Florida agency north of Fort Lauderdale seizes more than the Volusia County Sheriff's Office. Under Sheriff Bob Vogel, it has earned a national reputation for cash seizures along Interstate 95.

One legal proof the agency uses is an alert signal by a drug-sniffing dog. If the dog wags his tail or barks when sniffing for drugs, it constitutes legal "probable cause" to believe that the money is tainted.

The newspaper's test, however, suggests that the odds are that a drug dog would detect cocaine on almost anyone's money in this state, according to toxicologist Wayne Morris.

Morris has testified in hundreds of criminal cases that as much as 90 percent of currency in some cities tests positive for cocaine. "If you took 10 samples from any major city in America, I'd be surprised if any one of them didn't come up positive," he said.

The reason: Cocaine adheres to what it touches.

The contamination spreads through a variety of means. Cocaine users roll bills like straws to inhale the drug into their nostrils. Dealers hide money and drugs together. They "launder" cash profits by injecting the money into circulation. Seized money is deposited into banks, intermingling with other bills.

Besides Blount, Brown, Langley, Smith, Day and Haile, the newspaper obtained money from the Rev. Hal Marchman, founder of a Volusia County drug-treatment center, Orange County Chairman Linda Chapin and from a Publix cash-drawer in DeLand.

Vogel was asked to participate but would not, saying "That strikes me as somewhat offensive."

Vogel said the newspaper was "getting into personal and theatrical issues. We are not writing stories for the *Sentinel* or any other newspaper—at least I'm not."

Vogel would not allow the agency's dogs to be used in a sniff test of the samples.

"We're not going to call into question the credibility of our dogs by doing something like that," said Nancy Jones, Vogel's legal adviser.

In April the samples were taken to Morris, the toxicologist. He is a former crime-laboratory specialist for the Florida Department of Law Enforcement and now owns Morris Forensics Inc. in Winter Park.

The 57 bills—in denominations of $1, $5, $10 and $20—were tested with a gas chromatograph. To confirm findings, bills also were tested in a mass spectrometer.

The results: Six of nine samples carried detectable amounts of cocaine. The grocery-store sample was "borderline."

Samples from Marchman and Chapin were clean. Both were carrying new bills when asked to participate. Morris had predicted that they would test clean; the money hadn't circulated.

"The fact that you can get a negative on a new bill basically makes the argument," Morris said. "If it's been in circulation long enough, it'll be tainted."

Of six positive samples, only tiny amounts of cocaine—invisible to the eye—were present. But all were well within the range of a drug dog's detection ability, Morris said. Dogs' ability to smell is thousands of times more sensitive than humans.

Brown said, "I think you're on to a good story."

Haile, whose money had the most cocaine, said: "Based on what I've heard about tainting of money by drugs, I'm not surprised."

(Continued)

The question is whether finding traces of drugs on money in Florida really says anything about who is dealing in drugs.

Blount said that many in law enforcement know that most money is tainted. That's why Vogel wouldn't "play the game," Blount said. "I think [he] knew what you were going to get."

Mel Stack, forfeiture attorney for the Sheriff's Office, said the agency has been downplaying the dog's role.

But dozens of lawyers interviewed for this series of reports said the agency continues to use dog alerts as grounds for confiscations and "as a legal hammer" during negotiations.

(Continued)

FRIDAY, May 31, 1991

Court broadens police-search rules

COMPILED FROM WIRE REPORTS

No warrant needed if probable cause exists

WASHINGTON—The Supreme Court overturned two of its own precedents Thursday and expanded the ability of police officers who do not have a court warrant to search bags, suitcases and other containers they find in vehicles.

The court ruled that as long as the police have probable cause to believe that drugs or other illegal items are in a container, they can open and examine it without a warrant regardless of whether they have a reason to search the car.

The 6-3 court majority said its ruling had not significantly changed the law.

But Justice John Paul Stevens, writing a stinging dissent, said the decision would "result in a significant loss of individual privacy" and "support the conclusion that this court has become a loyal foot soldier in the . . . fight against crime."

Voting with Stevens were Justices Thurgood Marshall and Byron White.

The ruling continued the court's trend in recent years of expanding the authority of the police to search individuals and their property while diminishing the privacy protections of the Fourth Amendment, which bars unreasonable searches and seizures.

Just last week the court ruled in a case from Miami that when police obtain a motorist's consent to search a car, they do not need a warrant to look inside closed containers within the vehicle. In Thursday's case, the police opened a paper bag in a car trunk without the owner's consent and without a valid reason to search the car itself. But police found marijuana in the bag and arrested the driver.

In their ruling, Justice Harry Blackmun, Chief Justice William Rehnquist and all four appointees of Presidents Reagan and Bush, scrapped 1977 and 1979 decisions that had required police to obtain a warrant before searching a container found in a vehicle.

Those decisions, a product of a more liberal court, were based on what the justices saw as the need to protect the privacy of an individual's personal luggage—even when the police had reason to suspect the luggage contained illegal items.

Newspaper article on *Florida v. Jimeno.* (Reprinted with permission of the Orlando *Sentinel.*)

FLORIDA v. JIMENO
Cite as 111 S.Ct. 1801 (1991)

FLORIDA, Petitioner

v.

Enio JIMENO et al.

No. 90–622.

Argued March 25, 1991.

Decided May 23, 1991.

State defendant's suppression motion for paper bag in defendant's automobile was granted by the Circuit Court, Dade County, Fredricka G. Smith, J., and State appealed. The Florida District Court of Appeal, 550 So.2d 1176, affirmed, and application for review was filed. The Florida Supreme Court, Grimes J., 564 So.2d 1083, approved decision. Certiorari was granted. The Supreme Court, Chief Justice Rehnquist, held that criminal suspect's right to be free from unreasonable searches was not violated when, after he gave police officer permission to search his automobile, officer opened closed container found within car that might reasonably hold object of search.

Reversed and remanded.

Justice Marshall dissented and filed opinion in which Justice Stevens joined.

1. Searches and Seizures ⚷23

Touchstone of Fourth Amendment is reasonableness. U.S.C.A. Const.Amend. 4.

2. Searches and Seizures ⚷23

Fourth Amendment does not proscribe all state-initiated searches and seizures; it merely proscribes those which are unreasonable. U.S.C.A. Const.Amend. 4.

3. Searches and Seizures ⚷186

Standard for measuring scope of suspect's consent to search under fourth Amendment is that of "objective" reasonableness, i.e., what would typical reasonable person have understood by exchange between officer and suspect. U.S.C.A. Const. Amend. 4.

4. Searches and Seizures ⚷53, 147, 186

Scope of search is generally defined by its expressed object. U.S.C.A. Const. Amend. 4.

5. Searches and Seizures ⚷186

Narcotics suspect's fourth Amendment right to be free from unreasonable searches was not violated when, after he gave police officer permission to search his car, officer opened folded, brown paper bag on floorboard on passenger side and found kilogram of cocaine therein; suspect had not placed any explicit limitation on scope of search and it was objectively reasonable for officer to conclude that suspect's general consent included consent to search closed containers within car which might bear drugs. U.S.C.A. Const.Amend. 4.

6. Searches and Seizures ⚷186

If police wish to search closed containers within car, they need not separately request permission to search each container, although suspect may delimit as he chooses the scope of a search to which he consents. U.S.C.A. Const. Amend. 4.

*Syllabus**

Having stopped respondent Jimeno's car for a traffic infraction, police officer Trujillo, who had been following the car after overhearing Jimeno arranging what appeared to be a drug transaction, declared that he had reason to believe that Jimeno was carrying narcotics in the car, and asked permission to search it. Jimeno consented, and Trujillo found cocaine inside a folded paper bag on the car's floorboard. Jimeno was charged with possession with intent to distribute cocaine in violation of Florida law, but the state trial court granted his motion to suppress the cocaine on the ground that his consent to search the car did not carry with it specific consent to open the bag and examine its contents. The Florida District Court of Appeal and Supreme Court affirmed.

Held: A criminal suspect's Fourth Amendment right to be free from unreasonable

Florida v. Jimeno. (Reprinted with permission from the National Reporter System, copyright by West Publishing Company.)

searches is not violated when, after he gives police permission to search his car, they open a closed container found within the car that might reasonably hold the object of the search. The Amendment is satisfied when, under the circumstances, it is objectively reasonable for the police to believe that the scope of the suspect's consent permitted them to open the particular container. Here, the authorization to search extended beyond the car's interior surfaces to the bag, since Jimeno did not place any explicit limitation on the scope of the search and was aware that Trujillo would be looking for narcotics in the car, and since a reasonable person may be expected to know that narcotics are generally carried in some form of container. There is no basis for adding to the Fourth Amendment's basic test of objective reasonableness a requirement that, if police wish to search closed containers within a car, they must separately request permission to search each container. Pp. 1803–1804.

564 So.2d 1083 (Fla.1990), reversed and remanded.

REHNQUIST, C.J., delivered the opinion of the Court, in which WHITE, BLACKMUN, O'CONNOR, SCALIA, KENNEDY, and SOUTER, JJ., joined.

MARSHALL, J., filed a dissenting opinion, in which STEVENS, J., joined.

Michael J. Neimand, Miami, Fla., for petitioner.

John G. Roberts, Jr., Washington, D.C., for the U.S., as amicus curiae, supporting the petitioner, by special leave of Court.

Jeffrey S. Weiner, Miami, Fla., for respondent.

Chief Justice REHNQUIST delivered the opinion of the Court.

In this case we decide whether a criminal suspect's Fourth Amendment right to be free from unreasonable searches is violated when, after he gives a police officer permission to search his automobile, the officer opens a closed container found within the car that might reasonably hold the object of the search. We find that it is not. The Fourth Amendment is satisfied when, under the circumstances it is objectively reasonable for the officer to believe that the scope of the suspect's consent permitted him to open a particular container within the automobile.

This case began when a Dade County police officer, Frank Trujillo, overheard respondent, Enio Jimeno, arranging what appeared to be a drug transaction over a public telephone. Believing that respondent might be involved in illegal drug trafficking, Officer Trujillo followed his car. The officer observed respondent make a right turn at a red light without stopping. He then pulled respondent over to the side of the road in order to issue him a traffic citation. Officer Trujillo told respondent that he had been stopped for committing a traffic infraction. The officer went on to say that he had reason to believe that respondent was carrying narcotics in his car, and asked permission to search the car. He explained that respondent did not have to consent to a search of the car. Respondent stated that he had nothing to hide, and gave Trujillo permission to search the automobile. After two passengers stepped out of respondent's car, Officer Trujillo went to the the passenger side, opened the door, and saw a folded, brown paper bag on the floorboard. The officer picked up the bag, opened it, and found a kilogram of cocaine inside.

Respondent was charged with possession with intent to distribute cocaine in violation of Florida law. Before trial, he moved to suppress the cocaine found in the bag on the ground that his consent to

*The syllabus constitutes no part of the opinion of the Court but has been prepared by the Reporter of Decisions for the convenience of the reader. See *United States v. Detroit Lumber Co.,* 200 U.S. 321, 337, 26 S.Ct. 282, 287 50 L.Ed. 499.

(*Continued*)

search the car did not extend to the closed paper bag inside of the car. The trial court granted the motion. It found that although respondent "could have assumed that the officer would have searched the bag" at the time he gave his consent, his mere consent to search the car did not carry with it specific consent to open the bag and examine its contents. No. 88–23967 (Cir. Ct. Dade Cty., Fla., Mar. 21, 1989); App. to Pet. for Cert. A–6.

The Florida District Court of Appeal affirmed the trial court's decision to suppress the evidence of the cocaine. 550 So.2d 1176 (Fla. 3d DCA 1989). In doing so, the court established a *per se* rule that "consent to a general search for narcotics does not extend to 'sealed containers within the general area agreed to by the defendant.'" *Ibid.* (citation omitted). The Florida Supreme Court affirmed, relying upon its decision in *State v. Wells,* 539 So.2d 464 (1989) aff'd on other grounds, 495 U.S. ____, 110 S.Ct. 1632, 109 L.Ed.2d 1 (1990). 564 So.2d 1083 (1990). We granted certiorari to determine whether consent to search a vehicle may extend to closed containers found inside the vehicle. 498 U.S. ____, 111 S.Ct. 554, 112 L.Ed.2d 561 (1990), and we now reverse the judgment of the Supreme Court of Florida.

[1–3] The touchstone of the Fourth Amendment is reasonableness. *Katz v. United States,* 389 U.S. 347, 360, 88 S.Ct. 507, 516, 19 L.Ed.2d 576 (1967). The Fourth Amendment does not proscribe all state-initiated searches and seizures; it merely proscribes those which are unreasonable. *Illinois v. Rodriguez,* 497 U.S. ____, 110 S.Ct. 2793, 111 L.Ed.2d 148 (1990). Thus, we have long approved consensual searches because it is no doubt reasonable for the police to conduct a search once they have been permitted to do so. *Schneckloth v. Bustamonte,* 412 U.S. 218, 219, 93 S.Ct. 2041, 2043, 36 L.Ed.2d 854 (1973). The standard for measuring the scope of a suspect's consent under the Fourth Amendment is that of "objective" reasonableness—what would the typical reasonable person have understood by the exchange between the officer and the suspect? *Illinois v. Rodriguez, supra,* at ____, 110 S.Ct., at 2798–2802; *Florida v. Royer,* 460 U.S. 491, 501–502, 103 S.Ct. 1319, 1326–1327, 75 L.Ed.2d 229 (1983) (opinion of WHITE, J.); *id.,* at 514, 103 S.Ct., at 1332 (BLACKMUN, J., dissenting). The question before us, then, is whether it is reasonable for an officer to consider a suspect's general consent to a search of his car to include consent to examine a paper bag lying on the floor of the car. We think that it is.

[4, 5] The scope of a search is generally defined by its expressed object. *United States v. Ross,* 456 U.S. 798, 102 S.Ct. 2157, 72 L.Ed.2d 572 (1982). In this case, the terms of the search's authorization were simple. Respondent granted Officer Trujillo permission to search his car, and did not place any explicit limitation on the scope of the search. Trujillo had informed respondent that he believed respondent was carrying narcotics, and that he would be looking for narcotics in the car. We think that it was objectively reasonable for the police to conclude that the general consent to search respondent's car included consent to search containers within that car which might bear drugs. A reasonable person may be expected to know that narcotics are generally carried in some form of a container. "Contraband goods rarely are strewn across the trunk or floor of a car." *Id.,* at 820, 102 S.Ct., at 2170. The authorization to search in this case, therefore, extended beyond the surfaces of the car's interior to the paper bag lying on the car's floor.

The facts of this case are therefore different from those in *State v. Wells, supra,* on which the Supreme Court of Florida relied in affirming the suppression order in this case. There the Supreme Court of Florida held that consent to search the trunk of a car did not include authorization to pry open a locked briefcase found inside the trunk. It is very likely unreasonable to

(Continued)

think that a suspect, by consenting to the search of his trunk, has agreed to the breaking open of a locked briefcase within the trunk, but it is otherwise with respect to a closed paper bag.

[6] Respondent argues, and the Florida trial court agreed with him, that if the police wish to search closed containers within a car they must separately request permission to search each container. But we see no basis for adding this sort of superstructure to the Fourth Amendment's basic test of objective reasonableness. Cf. *Illinois v. Gates,* 462 U.S. 213, 103 S.Ct. 2317, 76 L.Ed.2d 527 (1983). A suspect may of course delimit as he chooses the scope of the search to which he consents. But if his consent would reasonably be understood to extend to a particular container, the Fourth Amendment provides no grounds for requiring a more explicit authorization. "[T]he community has a real interest in encouraging consent, for the resulting search may yield necessary evidence for the solution and prosecution of crime, evidence that may ensure that a wholly innocent person is not wrongly charged with a criminal offense." *Schneckloth v. Bustamonte, supra,* at 243, 93 S.Ct., at 2056.

The judgment of the Supreme Court of Florida is accordingly reversed, and the case remanded for further proceedings not inconsistent with this opinion.

It is so ordered.

Justice MARSHALL, with whom Justice STEVENS joins, dissenting.

The question in this case is whether an individual's general consent to a search of the interior of his car for narcotics should reasonably be understood as consent to a search of closed containers inside the car. Nothing in today's opinion dispels my belief that the two are not one and the same from the consenting individual's standpoint. Consequently, an individual's consent to a search of the interior of his car should not be understood to authorize a search of closed containers inside the car. I dissent.

In my view analysis of this question must start by identifying the differing expectations of privacy that attach to cars and closed containers. It is well established that an individual has but a limited expectation of privacy in the interior of his car. A car ordinarily is not used as a residence or repository for one's personal effects, and its passengers and contents are generally exposed to public view. See *Cardwell v. Lewis,* 417 U.S. 583, 590, 94 S.Ct. 2464, 2469, 41 L.Ed.2d 325 (1974) (plurality opinion). Moreover, cars "are subjected to pervasive and continuing governmental regulation and controls," *South Dakota v. Opperman,* 428 U.S. 364, 368, 96 S.Ct. 3092, 3096, 49 L.Ed.2d 1000 (1976), and may be seized by the police when necessary to protect public safety or to facilitate the flow of traffic, see *id.,* at 368–369, 96 S.Ct., at 3096–3097.

In contrast, it is equally well established that an individual has a heightened expectation of privacy in the contents of a closed container. See, *e.g., United States v. Chadwick,* 433 U.S. 1, 13, 97 S.Ct. 2476, 2484, 53 L.Ed.2d 538 (1977). Luggage, handbags, paper bags, and other containers are common repositories for one's papers and effects, and the protection of these items from state intrusion lies at the heart of the Fourth Amendment. U.S. Const., Amdt. 4 ("The right of the people to be secure in their . . . papers, and effects, against unreasonable searches and seizures, shall not be violated"). By placing his possessions inside a container, an individual manifests an intent that his possessions be "preserve[d] as private," *United States v. Katz,* 389 U.S. 347, 351, 88 S.Ct. 507, 511, 19 L.Ed.2d 576 (1967), and thus kept "free from public examination," *United States v. Chadwick, supra,* 433 U.S., at 11, 97 S.Ct., at 2483.

The distinct privacy expectations that a person has in a car as opposed to a closed

(Continued)

container do not merge when the individual uses his car to transport the container. In this situation, the individual still retains a heightened expectation of privacy in the container. See *Robbins v. California,* 453 U.S. 420, 425, 101 S.Ct. 2841, 2845, 69 L.Ed.2d 744 (1981) (plurality opinion); *Arkansas v. Sanders,* 442 U.S. 753, 763–764, 99 S.Ct. 2586, 2592–2593, 61 L.Ed.2d 235 (1979). Nor does an individual's heightened expectation of privacy turn on the type of container in which he stores his possessions. Notwithstanding the majority's suggestion to the contrary, see *ante,* at 1804, this Court has soundly rejected any distinction between "worthy" containers, like locked briefcases, and "unworthy" containers, like paper bags.

> "Even though such a distinction perhaps could evolve in a series of cases in which paper bags, locked trunks, lunch buckets, and orange crates where placed on one side of the line or the other, the central purpose of the Fourth Amendment forecloses such a distinction. For just as the most frail cottage in the kingdom is absolutely entitled to the same guarantees of privacy as the most majestic mansion, so also may a traveler who carries a toothbrush and a few articles of clothing in a paper bag or knotted scarf claim an equal right to conceal his possessions from official inspection as the sophisticated executive with the locked attaché case." *United States v. Ross,* 456 U.S. 798, 822, 102 S.Ct. 2157, 2171, 72 L.Ed.2d 572 (1982) (footnotes omitted).

Because an individual's expectation of privacy in a container is distinct from, and far greater than, his expectation of privacy in the interior of his car, it follows that an individual's consent to a search of the interior of his car cannot necessarily be understood as extending to containers in the car. At the very least, general consent to search the car is ambiguous with respect to containers found inside the car. In my view, the independent and divisible nature of the privacy interests in cars and containers mandates that a police officer who wishes to search a suspicious container found during a consensual automobile search obtain additional consent to search the container. If the driver intended to authorize search of the container, he will say so; if not, then he will say no.** The only objection that the police could have to such a rule is that it would prevent them from exploiting the ignorance of a citizen who simply did not anticipate that his consent to search the car would be understood to authorize the police to rummage through his packages.

According to the majority, it nonetheless is reasonable for a police officer to construe generalized consent to search an automobile for narcotics as extending to closed containers, because "[a] reasonable person may be expected to know that narcotics are generally carried in some form of a container." *Ante,* at 1804. This is an interesting contention. By the same logic a person who consents to a search of the car from the driver's seat could also be deemed to consent to a search of his person or indeed of his body cavities, since a reasonable person may be expected to know that drug couriers frequently store their contraband on their persons or in their body cavities. I suppose (and hope) that even the majority would reject this conclusion, for a person who consents to the search of his *car* for drugs certainly does not consent to a search of things *other than his car* for drugs. But this example illustrates that if there is a reason for not treating a closed container as something "other than" the car in which it sits, the reason cannot be based on intuitions about where people carry drugs. The majority, however, never identifies a reason for conflating the distinct privacy expectations that a person has in a car and in closed containers.

**Alternatively, the police could obtain such consent in advance by asking the individual for permission to search both the car and any closed containers found inside.

(Continued)

The majority also argues that the police should not be required to secure specific consent to search a closed container, because " '[t]he community has a real interest in encouraging consent.' " *Ante,* at 1804, quoting *Schneckloth v. Bustamonte,* 412 U.S. 218, 243, 93 S.Ct. 2041, 2056, 36 L.Ed.2d 854 (1973). I find this rationalization equally unsatisfactory. If anything, a rule that permits the police to construe a consent to search more broadly than it may have been intended would discourage individuals from consenting to searches of their cars. Apparently, the majority's real concern is that if the police were required to ask for additional consent to search a closed container found during the consensual search of an automobile, an individual who did not mean to authorize such additional searching would have an opportunity to say no. In essence, then, the majority is claiming that "the community has a real interest" not in encouraging citizens to *consent* to investigatory efforts of their law enforcement agents, but rather in encouraging individuals to be *duped* by them. This is not the community that the Fourth Amendment contemplates.

Almost 20 years ago, this Court held that an individual could validly "consent" to a search—or, in other words, waive his right to be free from an otherwise unlawful search—without being told that he had the right to withhold his consent. See *Schneckloth v. Bustamonte, supra.* In *Schneckloth,* as in this case, the Court cited the practical interests in efficacious law enforcement as the basis for not requiring the police to take meaningful steps to establish the basis of an individual's consent. I dissented in *Schneckloth,* and what I wrote in that case applies with equal force here.

"I must conclude, with some reluctance, that when the Court speaks of practicality, what it really is talking of is the continued ability of the police to capitalize on the ignorance of citizens so as to accomplish by subterfuge what they could not achieve by relying only on the knowing relinquishment of constitutional rights. Of course it would be "practical" for the police to ignore the commands of the Fourth Amendment, if by practicality we mean that more criminals will be apprehended, even though the constitutional rights of innocent people go by the board. But such a practical advantage is achieved only at the cost of permitting the police to disregard the limitations that the Constitution places on their behavior, a cost that a constitutional democracy cannot long absorb." 412 U.S., at 288, 93 S.Ct., at 2079.

I dissent.

(Continued)

§ 881. Forfeitures

(a) Subject property. The following shall be subject to forfeiture to the United States and no property right shall exist in them:

(1) All controlled substances which have been manufactured, distributed, dispensed, or acquired in violation of this title.

(2) All raw materials, products, and equipment of any kind which are used, or intended for use, in manufacturing, compounding, processing, delivering, importing, or exporting any controlled substance in violation of this title.

(3) All property which is used, or intended for use, as a container for property described in paragraph (1) or (2).

Federal forfeiture statute. (Courtesy of Lawyers Cooperative Publishing.)

(4) All conveyances, including aircraft, vehicles, or vessels, which are used, or are intended for use, to transport, or in any manner to facilitate the transportation, sale, receipt, possession, or concealment of property described in paragraph (1) or (2), except that—

(A) no conveyance used by any person as a common carrier in the transaction of business as a common carrier shall be forfeited under the provisions of this section unless it shall appear that the owner or other person in charge of such conveyance was a consenting party or privy to a violation of this title or title III; and

(B) no conveyance shall be forfeited under the provisions of this section by reason of any act or omission established by the owner thereof to have been committed or omitted by any person other than such owner while such conveyance was unlawfully in the possession of a person other than the owner in violation of the criminal laws of the United States, or of any State.

(5) All books, records, and research, including formulas, microfilm, tapes, and data which are used, or intended for use, in violation of this title.

(6) All moneys, negotiable instruments, securities, or other things of value furnished or intended to be furnished by any person in exchange for a controlled substance in violation of this title, all proceeds traceable to such an exchange, and all moneys, negotiable instruments, and securities used or intended to be used to facilitate any violation of this title, except that no property shall be forfeited under this paragraph, to the extent of the interest of an owner, by reason of any act or omission established by that owner to have been committed or omitted without the knowledge or consent of that owner.

(b) Seizure pursuant to Supplemental Rules for Certain Admiralty and Maritime Claims. Any property subject to forfeiture to the United States under this title may be seized by the Attorney General upon process issued pursuant to the Supplemental Rules for Certain Admiralty and Maritime Claims by any district court of the United States having jurisdiction over the property, except that seizure without such process may be made when—

(1) The seizure is incident to an arrest or a search under a search warrant or an inspection under an administrative inspection warrant;

(2) The property subject to seizure has been the subject of a prior judgment in favor of the United States in a criminal injunction or forfeiture proceeding under this title;

(3) the Attorney General has probable cause to believe that the property is directly or indirectly dangerous to health or safety; or

(4) the Attorney General has probable cause to believe that the property has been used or is intended to be used in violation of this title.

In the event of seizure pursuant to paragraph (3) or (4) of this subsection, proceedings under subsection (d) of this section shall be instituted promptly.

(c) Custody of Attorney General. Property taken or detained under this section shall not be repleviable, but shall be deemed to be in the custody of the Attorney General, subject only to the orders and decrees of the court or the official having jurisdiction thereof. Whenever property is seized under the provisions of this title, the Attorney General may—

(1) place the property under seal;

(2) remove the property to a place designated by him; or

(3) require that the General Services Administration take custody of the property and remove it to an appropriate location for disposition in accordance with law.

(d) Other laws and proceedings applicable. The provisions of law relating to the seizure, summary and judicial

(Continued)

forfeiture, and condemnation of property for violation of the customs laws; the disposition of such property or the proceeds from the sale thereof; the remission or mitigation of such forfeitures; and the compromise of claims shall apply to seizures and forfeitures incurred, or alleged to have been incurred, under the provisions of this title, insofar as applicable and not inconsistent with the provisions hereof; except that such duties as are imposed upon the customs officer or any other person with respect to the seizure and forfeiture of property under the customs laws shall be performed with respect to seizures and forfeitures of property under this title by such officers, agents, or other persons as may be authorized or designated for that purpose by the Attorney General, except to the extent that such duties arise from seizures and forfeitures effected by any customs officer.

(e) Disposition of forfeited property. Whenever property is forfeited under this title the Attorney General may—

(1) retain the property for official use;

(2) sell any forfeited property which is not required to be destroyed by law and which is not harmful to the public;

(3) require that the General Services Administration take custody of the property and remove it for disposition in accordance with law; or

(4) forward it to the Bureau of Narcotics and Dangerous Drugs for disposition (including delivery for medical or scientific use to any Federal or State agency under regulations of the Attorney General).

The proceeds from any sale under paragraph (2) and any moneys forfeited under this title shall be used to pay all proper expenses of the proceedings for forfeiture and sale including expenses of seizure, maintenance of custody, advertising, and court costs. The Attorney General shall forward to the Treasurer of the United States for deposit in the general fund of the United States Treasury any amounts of such moneys and proceeds remaining after payment of such expenses.

(f) Forfeiture of schedule I substances. All controlled substances in schedule I that are possessed, transferred, sold, or offered for sale in violation of the provisions of this title shall be deemed contraband and seized and summarily forfeited to the United States. Similarly, all substances in schedule I, which are seized or come into the possession of the United States, the owners of which are unknown, shall be deemed contraband and summarily forfeited to the United States.

(g) Plants. (1) All species of plants from which controlled substances in schedules I and II may be derived which have been planted or cultivated in violation of this title, or of which the owners or cultivators are unknown, or which are wild growths, may be seized and summarily forfeited to the United States.

(2) The failure, upon demand by the Attorney General or his duly authorized agent, of the person in occupancy or in control of land or premises upon which such species of plants are growing or being stored, to produce an appropriate registration, or proof that he is the holder thereof, shall constitute authority for the seizure and forfeiture.

(3) The Attorney General, or his duly authorized agent, shall have authority to enter upon any lands, or into any dwelling pursuant to a search warrant, to cut, harvest, carry off, or destroy such plants.

§ 881. Forfeitures [from pocket part supplement]

(a) Subject property. [Introductory matter unchanged]

(1), (2) [Unchanged]

(3) All property which is used, or intended for use, as a container for property described in paragraph (1), (2) or (9).

(4) All conveyances, including aircraft, vehicles, or vessels, which are used, or are intended for use, to transport,

(Continued)

or in any manner to facilitate the transportation, sale, receipt, possession, or concealment of property described in paragraph (1), (2), or (9), except that—

(A) no conveyance used by any person as a common carrier in the transaction of business as a common carrier shall be forfeited under the provisions of this section unless it shall appear that the owner or other person in charge of such conveyance was a consenting party or privy to a violation of this title or title III;

(B) no conveyance shall be forfeited under the provisions of this section by reason of any act or omission established by the owner thereof to have been committed or omitted by any person other than such owner while such conveyance was unlawfully in the possession of a person other than the owner in violation of the criminal laws of the United States, or of any State; and

(C) no conveyance shall be forfeited under this paragraph to the extent of an interest of an owner, by reason of any act or omission established by that owner to have been committed or omitted without the knowledge, consent, or willful blindness of the owner.

(5), (6) [Unchanged]

(7) All real property, including any right, title, and interest (including any leasehold interest) in the whole of any lot or tract of land and any appurtenances or improvements, which is used, or intended to be used, in any manner or part, to commit, or to facilitate the commission of, a violation of this title punishable by more than one year's imprisonment, except that no party shall be forfeited under this paragraph, to the extent of an interest of an owner, by reason of any act or omission established by that owner to have been committed or omitted without the knowledge or consent of that owner.

(8) All controlled substances which have been possessed in violation of this title.

(9) All listed chemicals, all drug manufacturing equipment, all tableting machines, all encapsulating machines, and all gelatin capsules, which have been imported, exported, manufactured, possessed, distributed, or intended to be distributed, imported, or exported, in violation of a felony provision of this title or title III.

(10) Any drug paraphernalia (as defined in section 1822 of the Mail Order Drug Paraphernalia Control Act [21 USCS § 857]).

(11) Any firearm (as defined in section 921 of title 18, United States Code) used or intended to be used to facilitate the transportation, sale, receipt, possession, or concealment of property described in paragraph (1) and (2) and any proceeds traceable to such property.

(b) Seizure pursuant to Supplemental Rules for Certain Admiralty and Maritime Claims. Any property subject to civil forfeiture to the United States under this title may be seized by the Attorney General upon process issued pursuant to the Supplemental Rules for Certain Admiralty and Maritime Claims by any district court of the United States having jurisdiction over the property, except that seizure without such process may be made when—

(1)–(3) [Unchanged]

(4) the Attorney General has probable cause to believe that the property is subject to civil forfeiture under this title.

In the event of seizure pursuant to paragraph (3) or (4) of this subsection, proceedings under subsection (d) of this section shall be instituted promptly.

The Government may request the issuance of a warrant authorizing the seizure of property subject to forfeiture under this section in the same manner as provided for a search warrant under the Federal Rules of Criminal Procedure.

(Continued)

(c) Custody of Attorney General. Property taken or detained under this section shall not be repleviable, but shall be deemed to be in the custody of the Attorney General, subject only to the orders and decrees of the court or the official having jurisdiction thereof. Whenever property is seized under any of the provisions of this title, the Attorney General may—

(1), (2) [Unchanged]

(3) require that the General Services Administration take custody of the property and remove it, if practicable, to an appropriate location for disposition in accordance with law.

(d) Other laws and proceedings applicable. The provisions of law relating to the seizure, summary and judicial forfeiture, and condemnation of property for violation of the customs laws; the disposition of such property or the proceeds from the sale thereof; the remission or mitigation of such forfeitures; and the compromise of claims shall apply to seizures and forfeitures incurred, or alleged to have been incurred, under any of the provisions of this title, insofar as applicable and not inconsistent with the provisions hereof; except that such duties as are imposed upon the customs officer or any other person with respect to the seizure and forfeiture of property under the customs laws shall be performed with respect to seizures and forfeitures of property under this title by such officers, agents, or other persons as may be authorized or designated for that purpose by the Attorney General, except to the extent that such duties arise from seizures and forfeitures effected by any customs officer.

(e) Disposition of forfeited property.

(1) Whenever property is civilly or criminally forfeited under this title the Attorney General may—

(A) retain the property for official use or, in the manner provided with respect to transfers under section 616 of the Tariff Act of 1930, transfer the property to any Federal agency or to any State or local law enforcement agency which participated directly in the seizure or forfeiture of the property;

(B) except as provided in paragraph (4), sell, by public sale or any other commercially feasible means, any forfeited property which is not required to be destroyed by law and which is not harmful to the public;

(C) require that the General Services Administration take custody of the property and dispose of it in accordance with law;

(D) forward it to the Bureau of Narcotics and Dangerous Drugs for disposition (including delivery for medical or scientific use to any Federal or State agency under regulations of the Attorney General); or

(E) transfer the forfeited personal property or the proceeds of the sale of any forfeited personal or real property to any foreign country which participated directly or indirectly in the seizure or forfeiture of the property, if such a transfer—

(i) has been agreed to by the Secretary of State;

(ii) is authorized in an international agreement between the United States and the foreign country; and

(iii) is made to a country which, if applicable, has been certified under section 481(h) of the Foreign Assistance Act of 1961 [22 USCS § 2291(h)].

(2)(A) The proceeds from any sale under subparagraph (B) of paragraph (1) and any moneys forfeited under this title shall be used to pay—

(i) all property expenses of the proceedings for forfeiture and sale including expenses of seizure, maintenance of custody, advertising, and court costs; and

(ii) awards of up to $100,000 to any individual who provides original information which leads

(Continued)

to the arrest and conviction of a person who kills or kidnaps a Federal drug law enforcement agent. Any award paid for information concerning the killing or kidnapping of a Federal drug law enforcement agent, as provided in clause (ii), shall be paid at the discretion of the Attorney General.

(B) The Attorney General shall forward to the Treasurer of the United States for deposit in accordance with section 524(c) of title 28, United States Code, any amounts of such moneys and proceeds remaining after payment of the expenses provided in subparagraph (A), except that, with respect to forfeitures conducted by the Postal Service, the Postal Service shall deposit in the Postal Service Fund, under section 2003(b)(7) of title 39, United States Code, such moneys and proceeds.

(3) The Attorney General shall assure that any property transferred to a State or local law enforcement agency under paragraph (1)(A)—

(A) has a value that bears a reasonable relationship to the degree of direct participation of the State or local agency in the law enforcement effort resulting in the forfeiture, taking into account the total value of all property forfeited and the total law enforcement effort with respect to the violation of law on which the forfeiture is based; and

(B) will serve to encourage further cooperation between the recipient State or local agency and Federal law enforcement agencies.

(4)(A) With respect to real property described in subparagraph (B), if the chief executive officer of the State involved submits to the Attorney General a request for purposes of such subparagraph, the authority established in such subparagraph is in lieu of the authority established in paragraph (1)(B).

(B) In the case of property described in paragraph (1)(B) that is civilly or criminally forfeited under this title, if the property is real property that is appropriate for use as a public area reserved for recreational or historic purposes or for the preservation of natural conditions, the Attorney General, upon the request of the chief executive officer of the State in which the property is located, may transfer title to the property to the State, either without charge or for a nominal charge, through a legal instrument providing that—

(i) such use will be the principal use of the property; and

(ii) title to the property reverts to the United States in the event that the property is used otherwise.

(f) Forfeiture of schedule I or II substances. (1) All controlled substances in schedule I or II that are possessed, transferred, sold, or offered for sale in violation of the provisions of this title; all dangerous, toxic, or hazardous raw materials or products subject to forfeiture under subsection (a)(2) of this section; and any equipment or container subject to forfeiture under subsection (1)(2) or (3) which cannot be separated safely from such raw materials or products shall be deemed contraband and seized and summarily forfeited to the United States. Similarly, all substances in schedule I or II, which are seized or come into the possession of the United States, the owners of which are unknown, shall be deemed contraband and summarily forfeited to the United States.

(2) The Attorney General may direct the destruction of all controlled substances in schedule I or II seized for violation of this title; all dangerous, toxic, or hazardous raw materials or products subject to forfeiture under subsection (a)(2) of this section; and any equipment or container subject to forfeiture under subsection (a)(2) or

(Continued)

(3) which cannot be separated safely from such raw materials or products under such circumstances as the Attorney General may deem necessary.

(g) [Unchanged]

(h) Property title, etc. vested in United States. All right, title, and interest in property described in subsection (a) shall vest in the United States upon commission of the act giving rise to forfeiture under this section.

(i) Stay of civil proceeding. The filing of an indictment or information alleging a violation of this title or title III, or a violation of State or local law that could have been charged under this title or title III, which is also related to a civil forfeiture proceeding under this section shall, upon motion of the United States and for good cause shown, stay the civil forfeiture proceeding.

(j) Venue. In addition to the venue provided for in section 1395 of title 28, United States Code [28 USCS § 1395], or any other provision of law, in the case of property of a defendant charged with a violation that is the basis for forfeiture of the property under this section, a proceeding for forfeiture under this section may be brought in the judicial district in which the defendant owning such property is found or in the judicial district in which the criminal prosecution is brought.

[(k)](l) Functions. The functions of the Attorney General under this section shall be carried out by the Postal Service pursuant to such agreement as may be entered into between the Attorney General and the Postal Service.

(Continued)

FEDERAL RULES OF CIVIL PROCEDURE FOR THE UNITED STATES DISTRICT COURTS

Rule 23. Class Actions

(a) Prerequisites to a Class Action. One or more members of a class may sue or be sued as representative parties on behalf of all only if (1) the class is so numerous that joinder of all members is impracticable, (2) there are questions of law or fact common to the class, (3) the claims or defenses of the representative parties are typical of the claims or defenses of the class, and (4) the representative parties will fairly and adequately protect the interests of the class.

(b) Class Actions Maintainable. An action may be maintained as a class action if the prerequisites of subdivision (a) are satisfied, and in addition:

(1) the prosecution of separate actions by or against individual members of the class would create a risk of

(A) inconsistent or varying adjudications with respect to individual members of the class which would establish incompatible standards of conduct for the party opposing the class, or

(B) adjudications with respect to individual members of the class which would as a practical matter be dispositive of the interests of the other members not parties to the adjudications or substantially impair or impede their ability to protect their interests; or

(2) the party opposing the class has acted or refused to act on grounds generally applicable to the class, thereby making appropriate final injunctive relief or corresponding declaratory relief with respect to the class as a whole; or

Fed. R. Civ. P. 23

(3) the court finds that the questions of law or fact common to the members of the class predominate over any questions affecting only individual members, and that a class action is superior to other available methods for the fair and efficient adjudication of the controversy. The matters pertinent to the findings include: (A) the interest of members of the class in individually controlling the prosecution or defense of separate actions; (B) the extent and nature of any litigation concerning the controversy already commenced by or against mem-bers of the class; (C) the desirability or undesirability of concentrating the litigation of the claims in the particular forum; (D) the difficulties likely to be encountered in the management of a class action.

(c) Determination by Order Whether Class Actions to be Maintained; Notice; Judgment; Actions Conducted Partially as Class Actions. (1) As soon as practicable after the commencement of an action brought as a class action, the court shall determine by order whether it is to be so maintained. An order under this subdivision may be conditional, and may be altered or amended before the decision on the merits.

(2) In any class action maintained under subdivision (b)(3), the court shall direct to the members of the class the best notice practicable under the circumstances, including individual notice to all members who can be identified through reasonable effort. The notice shall advise each member that (A) the court will exclude the member from the class if the member so requests by a specified date; (B) the judgment, whether favorable or not, will include all members who do not request exclusion; and (C) any member who does not request exclusion may, if the member desires, enter an appearance through counsel.

(3) The judgment in an action maintained as a class action under subdivision (b)(l) or (b)(2), whether or not favorable to the class, shall include and describe those whom the court finds to be members of the class. The judgment in an action maintained as a class action under subdivision (b)(3), whether or not favorable to the class, shall include and specify or describe those to whom the notice provided in subdivision (c)(2) was directed, and who have not requested exclusion, and whom the court finds to be members of the class.

(4) When appropriate (A) an action may be brought or maintained as a class action with respect to particular issues, or (B) a class may be divided into subclasses and each subclass treated as a class, and the provisions of this rule shall then be construed and applied accordingly.

(d) Orders in Conduct of Actions. In the conduct of actions to which this rule applies, the court may make appropriate orders: (1) determining the course of proceedings or prescribing measures to prevent undue repetition or complication in the presentation of evidence or argument; (2) requiring, for the protection of the members of the class or otherwise for the fair conduct of the action, that notice be given in such manner as the court may direct to some or all of the members of any step in the action or of the proposed extent of the judgment, or of the opportunity of members to signify whether they consider the representation fair and adequate, to intervene and present claims or defenses, or otherwise to come into the action; (3) imposing conditions on the representative parties or on intervenors; (4) requiring that the pleadings be amended to eliminate therefrom allegations as to representation of absent persons, and that the action proceed accordingly; (5) dealing with similar procedural matters. The orders may be combined with an order under Rule 16, and may be altered or amended as may be desirable from time to time.

(e) Dismissal or Compromise. A class action shall not be dismissed or compromised without the approval of the court, and notice of the proposed dismissal or compromise shall be given to all members of the class in such manner as the court directs.

(Continued)

21 CFR Ch. 11 (4-1-92 Edition)

PARTS 1314–1315—[RESERVED]

PART 1316—ADMINISTRATIVE FUNCTIONS, PRACTICES, AND PROCEDURES

Subpart A—Administrative Inspections

Sec.
1316.01 Scope of Subpart A.
1316.02 Definitions.
1316.03 Authority to make inspections.
1316.04 Exclusion from inspection.
1316.05 Entry.
1316.06 Notice of inspection.
1316.07 Requirement for administrative inspection warrant; exceptions.
1316.08 Consent to inspection.
1316.09 Application for administrative inspection warrant.
1316.10 Administrative probable cause.
1316.11 Execution of warrants.
1316.12 Refusal to allow inspection with an administrative warrant.
1316.13 Frequency of administrative inspections.

Subpart B—Protection of Researchers and Research Subjects

1316.21 Definitions.
1316.22 Exemption.
1316.23 Confidentiality of identity of research subjects.
1316.24 Exemption from prosecution for researchers.

Subpart C—Enforcement Proceedings

1316.31 Authority for enforcement proceeding.
1316.32 Notice of proceeding; time and place.
1316.33 Conduct of proceeding.
1316.34 Records of proceeding.

Subpart D—Administrative Hearings

1316.41 Scope of Subpart D.
1316.42 Definitions.
1316.43 Information; special instructions.
1316.44 Waiver or modification of rules.
1316.45 Filings; address; hours.
1316.46 Inspection of record.
1316.47 Request for hearing.
1316.48 Notice of appearance.
1316.49 Waiver of hearing.
1316.50 Appearance; representation; authorization.
1316.51 Conduct of hearing and parties; ex parte communications.
1316.52 Presiding officer.
1316.53 Time and place of hearing.
1316.54 Prehearing conference.
1316.55 Prehearing ruling.

Drug Enforcement Administration, Justice

Sec.
1316.56 Burden of proof.
1316.57 Submission of documentary evidence and affidavits and identification of witnesses subsequent to prehearing conference.
1316.58 Summary of testimony; affidavits.
1316.59 Submission and receipt of evidence.
1316.60 Objections; offer of proof.
1316.61 Exceptions to rulings.
1316.62 Appeal from ruling of presiding officer.
1316.63 Official transcript; index; corrections.
1316.64 Proposed findings of fact and conclusions of law.
1316.65 Report and record.
1315.66 Exceptions.
1316.67 Final order.
1316.68 Copies of petitions for judicial review.

Subpart E—Seizure, Forfeiture, and Disposition of Property

1316.71 Definitions.
1316.72 Officers who will make seizures.
1316.73 Custody and other duties.
1316.74 Appraisement.
1316.75 Advertisement.
1316.76 Requirements as to claim and bond.

21 C.F.R. Part 1316

§ 1316.71 Definitions.

As used in this subpart, the following terms shall have the meanings specified:

(a) The term *Act* means the Controlled Substances Act (84 Stat. 1242; 21 U.S.C. 801) and/or the Controlled Substances Import and Export Act (84 Stat. 1285; 21 U.S.C. 951).

(b) The term *custodian* means the officer required under § 1316.72 to take custody of particular property which has been seized pursuant to the Act.

(c) The term *property* means a controlled substance, raw material, product, container, equipment, money or other asset, vessel, vehicle, or aircraft within the scope of the Act.

(d) The terms *seizing officer, officer seizing,* etc., mean any officer, authorized and designated by § 1316.72 to carry out the provisions of the Act, who initially seizes property or adopts a seizure initially made by any other officer or by a private person.

(e) The term *Special Agents-in-Charge* means Drug Enforcement Administration Special Agents-in-Charge or Resident Agents in Charge and Federal Bureau of Investigation Special Agents-in-Charge.

(f) Any term not defined in this section shall have the definition set forth in sections 102 and 1001 of the Act (21 U.S.C. 802 and 951) and in § 1301.02 of this chapter.

[36 FR 7820, Apr. 24, 1971. Redesignated at 38 FR 26609, Sept. 24, 1973, and amended at 45 FR 20096, Mar. 27, 1980; 47 FR 43370, Oct. 1. 1982; 49 FR 28701, July 16, 1984]

§ 1316.72 Officers who will make seizures.

For the purpose of carrying out the provisions of the Act, all special agents of the Drug Enforcement Administration and the Federal Bureau of Investigation are authorized and designated to seize such property as may be subject to seizure.

[47 FR 43370, Oct. 1, 1982]

§ 1316.73 Custody and other duties.

An officer seizing property under the Act shall store the property in a location designated by the custodian, generally in the Judicial district of seizure. The Special Agents-in-Charge are designated as custodians to receive and maintain in storage all property seized pursuant to the Act, are authorized to dispose of any property pursuant to the Act and any other applicable statutes or regulations relative to disposal, and to perform such other duties regarding such seized property as are appropriate, including the impound release of property pursuant to 28 CFR 0.101(c).

[47 FR 43370, Oct. 1, 1982]

(Continued)

§ 1316.74 Appraisement.

The custodian shall appraise the property to determine the domestic value at the time and place of seizure. The domestic value shall be considered the price at which such or similar property is freely offered for sale. If there is no market for the property at the place of seizure, the domestic value shall be considered the value in the principal market nearest the place of seizure.

(Sec. 606, 46 Stat. 754 (19 U.S.C. 1606))

[36 FR 7820, Apr. 24, 1971. Redesignated at 38 FR 26609, Sept. 24, 1973, and amended at 52 FR 41418, Oct. 28, 1987]

§ 1316.75 Advertisement.

(a) If the appraised value does not exceed the monetary amount set forth in title 19, United States Code, Section 1607; the seized merchandise is any monetary instrument within the meaning of section 5312(a)(3) of title 31 of the United States Code; or if a conveyance used to import, export or otherwise transport or store any controlled substance is involved, the custodian or DEA Asset Forfeiture Section shall cause a notice of the seizure and of the intention to forfeit and sell or otherwise dispose of the property to be published once a week for at least 3 successive weeks in a newspaper of general circulation in the judicial district in which the processing for forfeiture is brought.

(b) The notice shall: (1) Describe the property seized and show the motor and serial numbers, if any; (2) state the time. cause. and place of seizure; and (3) state that any person desiring to claim the property may, within 20 days from the date of first publication of the notice, file with the custodian or DEA Asset Forfeiture Section a claim to the property and a bond with satisfactory sureties in the sum of $5.000 or ten percent of the value of the claimed property whichever is lower, but not less than $250.

(Sec. 607, 46 Stat. 754, as amended (19 U.S.C. 1607); Pub. L. 98–473, Pub. L. 98–573)

[36 FR 7820, Apr. 24, 1971. Redesignated at 38 FR 26609, Sept. 24, 1973 and amended at 44 FR 56324, Oct. 1, 1979; 49 FR 1178, Jan. 10, 1984; 49 FR 50643, Dec. 31, 1984; 52 FR 24446, July 1. 1987; 56 FR 8686, Mar. 1, 1991]

§ 1316.76 Requirements as to claim and bond.

(a) The bond shall be rendered to the United States, with sureties to be approved by the custodian or DEA Asset Forfeiture Section, conditioned that in the case of condemnation of the property the obligor shall pay all costs and expenses of the proceedings to obtain such condemnation. When the claim and bond are received by the custodian or DEA Asset Forfeiture Section, he shall, after finding the documents in proper form and the sureties satisfactory, transmit the documents, together with a description of the property and a complete statement of the facts and circumstances surrounding the seizure, to the United States Attorney for the judicial district in which the proceeding for forfeiture is brought. If the documents are not in satisfactory condition when first received, a reasonable time for correction may be allowed. If correction is not made within a reasonable time the documents may be treated as nugatory, and the case shall proceed as though they had not been tendered.

(b) The filing of the claim and the posting of the bond does not entitle the claimant to possession of the property, however, it does stop the administrative forfeiture proceedings. The bond posted to cover costs may be in cash, certified check, or satisfactory sureties. The costs and expenses secured by the bond are such as are incurred after the filing of the bond including storage cost, safeguarding, court fees, marshal's costs, etc.

(Sec. 608, 46 Stat. 755 (19 U.S.C. 1608); Pub. L. 98–473, Pub. L. 98–573)

[36 FR 7820, Apr. 24, 1971, Redesignated at 38 FR 26609, Sept. 24, 1973 and amended at 49 FR 1178, Jan. 10, 1984; 49 FR 50643, Dec. 31, 1984; 56 FR 8686, Mar. 1, 1991]

(Continued)

§ 1316.77 Administrative forfeiture.

(a) For property seized by officers of the Drug Enforcement Administration, if the appraised value does not exceed the jurisdictional limits in § 1316.75(a), and a claim and bond are not filed within the 20 days hereinbefore mentioned, the DEA Special Agent-in-Charge or DEA Asset Forfeiture Section shall declare the property forfeited. The DEA Special Agent-in-Charge or DEA Asset Forfeiture Section shall prepare the Declaration of Forfeiture and forward it to the Administrator of the Administration as notification of the action he has taken. Thereafter, the property shall be retained in the district of the DEA Special Agent-in-Charge or DEA Asset Forfeiture Section or delivered elsewhere for official use, or otherwise disposed of, in accordance with official instructions received by the DEA Special Agent-in-Charge or DEA Asset Forfeiture Section.

(b) For property seized by officers of the Federal Bureau of Investigation, if the appraised value does not exceed the jurisdictional limits in § 1316.75(a), and a claim and bond are not filed within the 20 days hereinbefore mentioned, the FBI Property Management Officer shall declare the property forfeited. The FBI Property Management Officer shall prepare the Declaration of Forfeiture. Thereafter, the property shall be retained in the field office or delivered elsewhere for official use, or otherwise disposed of, in accordance with the official instructions of the FBI Property Management Officer.

(28 U.S.C. 509 and 510; 21 U.S.C. 871 and 881(d); Pub. L. 98–473, Pub. L. 98–573)

[48 FR 35087, Aug. 3, 1983, as amended at 49 FR 1178, Jan. 10, 1984; 49 FR 50643, Dec. 31, 1984; 56 FR 8686, Mar.1, 1991]

§ 1316.78 Judicial forfeiture.

If the appraised value is greater than the jurisdictional limits in § 1316.75(a) or a claim and satisfactory bond have been received for property the jurisdictional limits in § 1316.76, the custodian or DEA Asset Forfeiture Section shall transmit a description of the property and a complete statement of the facts and circumstances surrounding the seizure to the U.S. Attorney for the judicial district in which the proceeding for forfeiture is sought for the purpose of instituting condemnation proceedings. The U.S. Attorney shall also be furnished the newspaper advertisements required by § 1316.75. The Forfeiture Counsel of DEA shall make applications to the U.S. District Courts to place property in official DEA use.

(Sec. 610, 46 Stat. 755 (19 U.S.C. 1610); Pub. L. 98–473, Pub. L. 98–573)

[36 FR 7820, Apr. 24, 1971. Redesignated at 38 FR 26609, Sept. 24, 1973 and amended at 44 FR 56324, Oct. 1, 1979; 49 FR 1178, Jan. 10, 1984; 49 FR 32174, Aug. 13, 1984; 49 FR 50643, Dec. 31, 1984; 56 FR 8686, Mar. 1, 1991]

§ 1316.79 Petitions for remission or mitigation of forfeiture.

(a) Any person interested in any property which has been seized, or forfeited either administratively or by court proceedings, may file a petition for remission or mitigation of the forfeiture. Such petition shall be filed in triplicate with the DEA Asset Forfeiture Section or Special Agent-in-Charge of the DEA or FBI, depending upon which agency seized the property, for the judicial district in which the proceeding for forfeiture is brought. It shall be addressed to the Director of the FBI or the Administrator of the DEA, depending upon which agency seized the property. If the property is subject to administrative forfeiture pursuant to § 1316.77, and addressed to the Attorney General if the property is subject to judicial forfeiture pursuant to § 1316.77. The petition must be executed and sworn to by the person alleging interest in the property.

(b) The petition shall include the following: (1) A complete description of the property, including motor and serial numbers, if any, and the date and place of seizure; (2) the petitioner's interest in the property, which shall be supported by bills of sale, contracts, mortgages. or other satisfactory documentary evidence: and, (3) the facts and circumstances, to be established by satisfactory proof, relied upon by the petitioner to justify remission or mitigation.

(c) Where the petition is for restoration of the proceeds of sale, or for value of the property placed in official use, it must be supported by satisfactory proof that the petitioner did not know of the seizure prior to the declaration of condemnation of forfeiture and was in such circumstances as prevented him from knowing of the same.

(Secs. 613, 618, 46 Stat. 756, 757, as amended (19 U.S.C. 1613, 1618; 28 U.S.C. 509 and 510; 21 U.S.C. 871 and 881(d)); Pub. L. 98–473, Pub. L. 98–573)

[36 FR 7820, Apr. 24, 1971. Redesignated at 38 FR 26609, Sept. 24, 1973, and amended at 48 FR 35088, Aug. 3, 1983; 49 FR 1178, Jan. 10, 1984; 49 FR 50643, Dec. 31, 1984; 56 FR 8686, Mar.1, 1991]

§ 1316.80 Time for filing petitions.

(a) In order to be considered as seasonably filed, a petition for remission or mitigation of forfeiture should be filed within 30 days of the receipt of the notice of seizure. If a petition for remission or mitigation of forfeiture has not been received within 30 days of the notice of seizure, the property will either be placed in official service or sold ss soon as it is forfeited. Once property is placed in official use, or is sold, a petition for remission or mitigation of forfeiture can no longer be accepted.

(b) A petition for restoration of proceeds of sale, or for the value of property placed in official use, must be filed within 90 days of the sale of the property, or within 90 days of the date the property is placed in official use.

(Secs. 613, 618, 46 Stat. 756, 757, as amended (19 U.S.C. 1613, 1618); Pub. L. 98–473, Pub. L. 98–573)

[36 FR 7820, Apr. 24, 1971. Redesignated at 38 FR 26609, Sept. 24, 1973, and amended at 49 FR 50643, Dec. 31, 1984]

§ 1316.81 Handling of petitions.

Upon receipt of a petition, the custodian or DEA Asset Forfeiture System shall request an appropriate investigation. The petition and the report of investigation shall be forwarded to the Director of the FBI or to the Administrator of the DEA, depending upon which agency seized the property. If the petition involves a case which has been referred to the U.S. Attorney for the institution of court proceedings, the custodian or DEA Asset Forfeiture System shall transmit The petition to the U.S. Attorney for the judicial district in which the proceeeding for forfeiture is brought. He shall notify the petitioner of this action.

(Continued)

SEARCH AND SEIZURE AND THE EXCLUSIONARY RULE

Introduction

This section of the appendix gives you some background on search and seizure and the exclusionary rule. It should be of help in understanding the Williamses' problem and other search and seizure materials in this book.

The Fourth Amendment[1]

Searches, seizures, and arrests are vital aspects of law enforcement. Because they involve significant invasions of individual liberties, limits on their use can be found in the constitutions, statutes, and other laws of the states and federal government.

The most important limitation is the fourth amendment to the United States Constitution, which reads:

> The right of the people to be secure in their persons, papers, and effects, against unreasonable searches and seizures, shall not be violated, and no warrants shall issue but upon probable cause, supported by oath or affirmation, and particularly describing the place to be searched and the persons or things to be seized.

Two remedies are available to the defendant whose fourth amendment rights have been violated by the government. First, in a criminal prosecution, the defendant may invoke the exclusionary rule. Second, he or she may have a civil cause of action against the offending officer under a rights statute or for a "constitutional tort."[2]

The concepts of reasonable expectation of privacy and probable cause are important throughout the law of searches, seizures, and arrests. Accordingly, they will be examined first. The Supreme Court has defined a *search* as occurring "when an expectation in privacy that society is prepared to consider reasonable is infringed" and a *seizure* as a "meaningful interference with an individual's possessory interest" in property.[3]

Probable Cause Defined

Probable cause is a phrase describing the minimum amount of evidence necessary before a search, seizure, or arrest is proper. Whether the issue concerns a search and seizure or an arrest, the same quantity of evidence is necessary to establish probable cause.

There is no one universal definition of probable cause. In fact, the definition of probable cause differs depending on the context. In all situations, it is more than mere suspicion and less than the standard required to prove a defendant guilty at trial (beyond a reasonable doubt). As the Supreme court has expressed, probable cause is present when the trustworthy facts within the law enforcement officer's knowledge are sufficient in themselves to justify a "person of reasonable caution" in the belief that seizable property would be found or that the person to be arrested committed the crime in question.[4]

Searches and Seizures

The Warrant Requirement

Depending upon the circumstances, a search may be conducted with or without a warrant. The Supreme Court has expressed a strong preference for the use of warrants, when possible, over warrantless actions.[5] The warrant preference serves an important purpose: it protects citizens from overzealous law enforcement practices.

Exceptions to the Search Warrant Requirement

Although the general rule is that a warrant must be obtained before a search may be undertaken, there are many exceptions. The exceptions to the warrant requirement are sometimes referred to as *exigent circumstances.*

Consent Searches

Voluntary consent to a search obviates the warrant requirement. A person may consent to a search of his or her person or property. The scope of the search is limited by the person consenting. Absent special circumstances, a consent to search may be terminated at any time by the person giving consent.

A person's consent must be voluntary. All of the circumstances surrounding the consent are examined to determine whether the consent was voluntary. There is no requirement that police officers inform a person that he or she may refuse to consent.[6]

Of course, a defendant who is threatened or coerced into consenting has not voluntarily consented. It is not coercion for a person to be told that, if he or she does not consent, a warrant will be obtained authorizing the desired search. It is coercion for officers to tell a person that, if he or she does not consent to a search, a warrant will be obtained and the officers will ransack the person's home.[7]

Motor Vehicles

Automobiles are protected by the fourth amendment. However, the Supreme Court has refused to extend full fourth amendment protection to people in automobiles. The Court's rationale for decreased protection is twofold. First, because of the mobile nature of vehicles they can be moved quickly. Second, they are used on the public roads where they and their occupants are visible to the public; therefore, persons in vehicles have a lesser expectation of privacy.

In *Carroll v. United States,* 267 U.S. 132 (1925), it was announced that a warrantless search of a vehicle stopped on a public road is reasonable, provided that the officer has probable cause to believe that an object subject to seizure will be found in the vehicle. the existence of probable cause is the key to such a search.

The sticky question in this area is: What is the scope of this right to search? Generally, the officer is given the scope that a magistrate would have if a warrant were sought. So, if an officer has probable cause to believe that a shotgun used in a crime will be found in the car, a search of the glove box is improper. The opposite would be true if the item sought was a piece of jewelry, such as a ring.

Officers may also search closed items found in the vehicle, provided that probable cause exists to believe that the item sought may be contained therein. The same rules apply as explained previously. Rifling through a suitcase found in a car, in search of a stolen painting that is larger than the suitcase, is unreasonable and violative of the fourth amendment. Once the sought-after evidence is found, the search must cease.

Stop and Frisk

On October 31, 1963, in Cleveland, Ohio, a police detective observed three men standing on a street corner. Suspicious of the men, the detective positioned himself in order to watch their behavior. After some time, the officer concluded that the men were "casing a job, a stick-up."

The officer approached the men, identified himself, and asked them to identify themselves. After the men "mumbled something," the officer grabbed one of the men and conducted a *frisk,* or a pat-down, of the man's clothing. The officer felt a pistol in the man's coat pocket. He removed the gun from the coat and then patted down the other two men. Another gun was discovered during those frisks.

The officer testified that he conducted the frisks because he believed the men were carrying weapons. The first man frisked was defendant Terry. At trial, he was convicted of carrying a concealed weapon and was subsequently sentenced to one to three years in prison. His appeal made it to the United States Supreme Court.

In *Terry v. Ohio,* 392 U.S. 1 (1968), the Supreme Court was confronted with these issues: Did the officer's behavior amount to a search or seizure under the fourth amendment? If so, was the search and seizure by the officer reasonable?

The Court decided that defendant Terry had been seized under the fourth amendment. "It must be recognized that whenever a police officer accosts and individual and restrains his freedom to walk away, he has 'seized' that person." As to the frisk, the court stated that "it is nothing less than sheer torture of the English language to suggest that a careful exploration of the outer surfaces of a person's clothing all over his or her body in an attempt to find weapons is not a search."

With these statements, the Court made it clear that the police practice of stopping and frisking people is one governed by the fourth amendment. However, the Court then concluded that an exception to the probable cause requirement was justified because the intrusion upon a person's privacy is limited in a stop and frisk, as opposed to an arrest and full search.

Officers are not given carte blanche to stop and frisk. Although probable suspicion is not required, officers must have a "reasonable suspicion" that the person to be stopped has committed, is committing, or is about to commit a crime. The officer's suspicion must be supported by "specific and articulable facts which, taken together with rational inferences from those facts, reasonably warrant that intrusion." *Terry,* 392 U.S. at 21. An officer's intuition alone is not enough suspicion to support a *Terry* seizure.

The stopping of a vehicle does fall within the reach of the fourth amendment. However, the Supreme Court has said that once a person is lawfully pulled over, he or she may be ordered out of the vehicle, even though there is no reason to believe that the driver is a threat.

In addition to requiring reasonable suspicion, the *Terry* court also stated that stops are to "last no longer than is necessary," and the investigative methods employed during the stop should be the "least intrusive means reasonably available to verify or dispel the officer's suspicion in a short period of time." If an officer detains a person longer than necessary, the investigatory detention turns into a full seizure (arrest), and the probable cause requirement of the Fourth Amendment is triggered.

Florida v. Royer, 460 U.S. 491 (1983), provides an example of the distinction between an investigatory detention and an arrest. The defendant, a suspected drug dealer, was questioned in a public area of an airport. After a few minutes, he was taken 40 feet away to a small police office, where he consented to a search of his luggage. The Court concluded that the search was the product of an illegal arrest, as less intrusive methods of investigation were available. As alternatives, the Court mentioned that the officers could have used narcotics dogs to inspect the luggage or could have immediately requested consent to search the defendant's luggage. The act of requiring the defendant to accompany the officers to a small room 40 feet away transformed the detention from a *Terry* stop to an arrest, which was violative of the fourth amendment because it was not supported by probable cause.

The Exclusionary Rule

An important constitutional development was the creation of the *exclusionary rule.* The rule is simple: Evidence that is obtained by an unconstitutional search or seizure is inadmissible at trial.

The rule was first announced by the Supreme Court in 1914.[8] However, at that time the rule had not been incorporated into the due process clause of the fourteenth amendment. As such, the exclusionary rule did not apply to state court proceedings. This was changed in 1961 when the Supreme Court declared that evidence obtained in violation of the Constitution could not be used in state or federal criminal proceedings. The case was *Mapp v. Ohio,* 367 U.S. 643 (1961).

The exclusionary rule has been the subject of intense debate. There is no explicit textual language in the Constitution establishing the rule. For that reason, many contend that the Supreme Court has exceeded its authority by creating it; that it is the responsibility of the legislative branch to make such laws.

On the other side is the argument that without the exclusionary rule the Bill of Rights is ineffective. Why have constitutional standards if there is no method to enforce them. For example, why require that the officers in the *Mapp* case have a search warrant, yet permit them to conduct a warrantless search and use the evidence obtained against the defendant? These questions go to the purpose of the exclusionary rule: it discourages law enforcement personnel from engaging in unconstitutional conduct. The exclusionary rule works to prevent the admission into evidence of any item, confession, or other thing that was obtained by law enforcement officers in an unconstitutional manner.

Most exclusionary rule issues are resolved prior to trial by way of a motion to suppress. In some instances the motion may be made at the moment the prosecutor attempts to introduce such evidence at trial. This is known as a *contemporaneous objection.*

Fruit of the Poisonous Tree

The exclusionary rule applies to *primary evidence,* evidence that is the direct result of an illegal search or seizure. It is possible that such primary evidence may lead the police to other evidence. Suppose that police officers beat a confession out of a bank robber. In that confession the defendant tells the police where he has hidden the stolen money. The confession is the primary evidence and is inadmissible under the exclusionary rule. The money (after it is retrieved by the police) is *secondary,* or *derivative, evidence.* Such evidence is known as *fruit of the poisonous tree* and is also inadmissible evidence. Generally, evidence that is tainted by the prior illegal conduct is inadmissible. The rule does not make all evidence later obtained by law enforcement inadmissible, though. In some instances, evidence may be admissible because the connection between the illegally seized evidence and the subsequently obtained evidence is marginal, or as the Supreme Court put it, "the causal connection . . . may have become so attenuated as to dissipate the taint."[9]

1 Grateful thanks is given to Dr. Daniel Hall who authored this portion of the appendix. Reproduced by permission. *Criminal Law and Procedure* by Daniel Hall, Delmar Publishers, Inc., Albany, New York, Copyright 1992.

2 *Biven v. Six Unknown Named Agents,* 403 U.S. 388 (1971).

3 *United States v. Jacobsen,* 466 U.S. 109, 113 (1984).

4 *Carroll v. United States,* 267 U.S. 132 (1934).

5 *Beck v. Ohio,* 379 U.S. 89 (1964).

6 *Schneckloth v. Bustamonte,* 412 U.S. 218 (1973).

7 *United States v. Kampbell,* 574 F.2d 962 (8th Cir. 1978).

8 The rule, as applied in federal courts, was announced in *Weeks v. United States*, 232 U.S. 383 (1914).

9 *Nardone v. United States,* 308 U.S. ____ (1939).

FLOWCHART FOR LAW OFFICE MEMO ON WILLIAMS BROTHERS

Background: To have a judge determine whether the money should be forfeited, the Williams brothers would first have to follow statutory requirements (file a claim and post a bond). Once the judicial proceeding is filed, the brothers can file a motion to have the money excluded from evidence. They would allege that it should be excluded from evidence because the stop and seizure violated their right against unreasonable search and seizure. If the brothers did not file a claim and post a bond, the government could declare their money forfeited in an administrative proceeding.

The following is a flowchart of the determinations the judge would have to make.

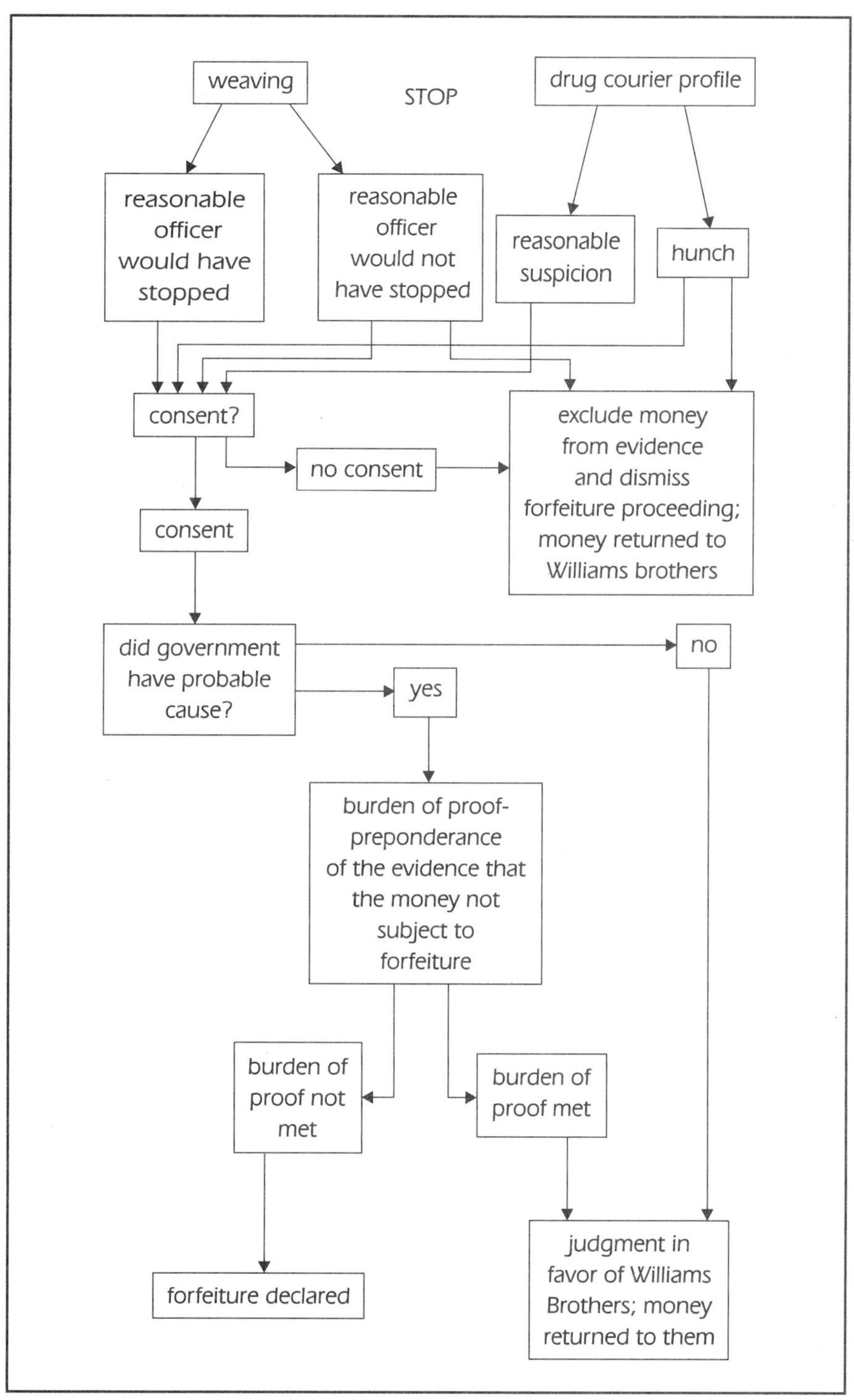

Flowchart for office memo on the Williams case.

SAMPLE OUTLINE FOR LAW OFFICE MEMO

The following is a sample outline for a law office memo concerning the Williams brothers. Read through it and think how it could be expanded and what you would do differently.

The two cases used as authority in the application sections of the outline are *Jimeno* and *Smith. Jimeno* is reprinted in this appendix. The citation for *Smith* is *United States v. Smith,* 799 F.2d 704 (11th Cir. 1986).

To: [professor's name]
From: [writer's name]
Re: Whether the confiscated money will be returned to the Williams brothers.
Date: [date on which research completed or office memo written]

Facts: [state basic facts; be sure to describe in detail the interchange between the officer and the Williams brothers]

Issues:

1. Was the officer's stop of the Williams brothers' car constitutional?
2. Did the officer have consent to search the Williams brothers' car, when the officer said, "You don't mind if I search, do you?" and proceeded with the search without giving the brothers a chance to respond?

Answers:

1a. Because the factors in the drug courier profile, even if taken together, did not support reasonable suspicion of illegal activity, the money should be returned to the Williams brothers unless the officer had probable cause to stop the car for a traffic violation.

1b. Because a reasonable officer would have stopped the Williams brothers' car to investigate for a sleepy or drunk driver, the stop was constitutional.

2. Because the Williams brothers did not consent to the search, the search was unconstitutional and the money should be returned to them.

Reasoning:

I. Thesis paragraph
   A. Drug courier or law-abiding citizen
   B. Use of drug courier profile
   C. Violation of driver's right against search and seizure
II. Law common to issues 1 and 2—fourth amendment to the United States Constitution (quote)
III. Reasoning for issue 1
   A. Law
      1. *Terry v. Ohio*
      2. *United States v. Smith*
   B. Application of law to facts re drug courier profile
      1. Similarities between *Smith* and *Williams*
         a. cars traveling at night
         b. two occupants of cars
         c. out-of-state tags
         d. car driven cautiously
         e. occupants did not look in patrol car's direction
         f. car traveling on I-95, a known drug corridor
      2. Differences between *Smith* and *Williams*
         a. Cocaine found in *Smith;* cash found in *Williams*
         b. *Smith*—occupants around 30; *Williams*—ages unknown
         c. *Williams*—race claimed as a factor; *Smith*—race unknown
   C. Application of law to facts re alleged traffic violation
      1. Similarities between *Smith* and *Williams*
         a. cars were "weaving"
         b. officers did not investigate for drunk driving
      2. Differences between *Smith* and *Williams*
         a. Length of time observed
         b. *Williams*—tire crossed center line before car was followed; *Smith*—tire went over white line

six inches as car was being followed

D. Conclusion for issue 1

1. Because of similarities between *Smith* and *Williams* and because the officer did not have reasonable suspicion as required by *Terry,* the stop made on the drug courier profile was unconstitutional; the money should be excluded as evidence unless the officer had probable cause to stop the car for an alleged traffic violation

2. Because the Williams car swerved before it was followed and checking for a sleepy or drunk driver was a legitimate reason for a traffic stop, the stop was constitutional; the facts contrast with the facts in *Smith,* where Smith did not swerve until he was followed by the patrol car a mile or so

IV. Reasoning for issue 2

A. Law—*Jimeno*

B. Application of law to facts

1. Similarities between *Williams* and *Jimeno*

   a. cars stopped after alleged traffic violation
   b. officer asked to search car
   c. officer found something in car
   d. two passengers in car

2. Differences between *Williams* and *Jimeno*

   a. officer explained to Jimeno that officer suspected drugs in car; officer did not explain object of search to Williams brothers
   b. Jimeno specifically gave consent to the search; Williams brothers remained silent
   c. officer waited until Jimeno consented to the search before beginning search; officer did not give the Williams brothers sufficient time to respond
   d. officer found cocaine in Jimeno's car; the officer found money in the Williams car
   e. Jimeno arrested; Williams brothers not arrested

C. Conclusion for issue 2

Differences between *Jimeno* and *Williams* show that Jimeno clearly consented to the search, whereas the Williams brothers did not; therefore, because the Williams brothers did not consent to the search, it was unconstitutional; the Williams brothers should be successful in having the money excluded from evidence, the case dismissed, and the money returned to them.

APPENDIX B

Citation Rules

This appendix gives you a summary of basic citation rules. For a more detailed explanation of the citation rule for a particular authority, refer back to the chapter in which the authority was discussed.

GENERAL CITATION TIPS

Citation tip: ordinal numbers. In legal citations, the ordinal numbers "second" and "third" are abbreviated to "2d" and "3d." For all other ordinal numbers, use the standard abbreviations.

Citation tip: case names. In a reporter, a case begins with the full name of the case; a portion of the name appears in all capital letters. Unless your reader requires *Bluebook* form for case names, use the portion of the case name that appears in all capitals, with the further modifications explained in this paragraph, as the case name in your citation. You will have a very close approximation of *Bluebook* form without having to master a very complicated *Bluebook* rule. For case names, individuals are referred to only by their surnames. When the United States of America is a party to a case, the citation should show "United States" rather than "United States of America" or "U.S." If a state is a party to the case and the case is being decided by a court of the state, the citation should contain only "State," "Commonwealth," or "People." If a state is a party to the case but the case is being decided by a court other than a court of the state, then the citation should contain only the name of the state (for example, "Minnesota," not "State of Minnesota").

Citation tip: subsequent history. Connect subsequent history to the end of the citation of the lower court decision by explaining what the higher court did, underlining (italicizing) the explanation, and setting it off by commas, "Certiorari denied" should be abbreviated to "*cert. denied,*" "affirmed" should be abbreviated to "*aff'd,*" and "reversed" should be abbreviated to "*rev'd.*" Otherwise the explanation should be written out (for example, "*vacated*").

UNITED STATES SUPREME COURT CASES

The following is an example of a citation for a case found in United States Law Week but which has not yet been published in the reporters:

> *Lee v. International Society for Krishna Consciousness, Inc.*, 60 U.S.L.W. 4761 (U.S. 1992).

If the case has been printed in a reporter, you should give the citation to the reporter rather than to the advance sheets. Although the *Bluebook* does not require you to give parallel citations to United States Supreme Court cases, parallel citations to those cases are often given, for example:

> *Lee v. International Society for Krishna Consciousness, Inc.*, 505 U.S. ___, 112 S. Ct. 2709, 120 L. Ed. 2d 669 (1992).

There is a blank in the citation to United States Reports because the page number of the case in that reporter is not yet known. If you are citing to only one reporter, cite to United States Reports, if the case is contained in it, or to the Supreme Court Reporter.

UNITED STATES CIRCUIT COURTS OF APPEAL

The following example shows the correct format for a citation to a case in a United States circuit court of appeal:

> *United States v. Walker*, 933 F.2d 812 (10th Cir. 1991), *cert. denied*, 112 S. Ct. 1168 (1992).

UNITED STATES DISTRICT COURTS

The following is an example of a citation to a case from the United States District Court for the Northern District of Texas:

> *Sexton v. Gibbs*, 327 F. Supp. 134 (N.D. Tex. 1970), *aff'd*, 446 F.2d 904 (5th Cir. 1971), *cert. denied*, 404 U.S. 1062 (1972).

Notice that "Northern District of Texas" has been abbreviated to "N.D. Tex." You know from this citation that Texas has more than one district. Some of the less populous or smaller states, such as New Jersey, have only one United States district court to cover the whole state. The abbreviation for the United States District Court for the District of New Jersey would be "D.N.J."

CITATIONS FOR CONSTITUTIONS

The clause prohibiting ex post facto laws and section 1 of the fourteenth amendment to the federal Constitution may be cited as follows:

> U.S. Const. art. I, § 9, cl. 3.
> U.S. Const. amend. XIV, § 1.

Give the section number when the Constitution specifically identifies a portion of an article as a section. When a section such as section nine of article I is long and contains a number of paragraphs, you can reference a particular paragraph as a "clause." Some copies of the United States Constitution identify the amendments as "articles" instead of "amendments." This is because the amendments are technically articles in amendment of the Constitution. To avoid confusion, cite the amendments to the Constitution as "amendments" rather than as "articles." State constitutions can be cited using this same citation form or using your state's citation rules.

Capitalize a state constitution only when naming it in full. Capitalize the United States Constitution or any reference to it. Do not capitalize the name of any other portion of a constitution except for the "Bill of Rights."

CITATIONS FOR STATUTES

Subsection (b)(4) of the federal forfeiture statute reprinted in Chapter 2 of this book may be cited as follows:

> 21 U.S.C. § 881(b)(4) (1988).

A citation to the United States Code is preferred because the United States Code is the official code. Because many law libraries do not have the United States Code, you may use the following citations to either United States Code Service or United States Code Annotated:

> 21 U.S.C.S. § 881(b)(4) (Law. Co-op. 1984 & Supp. 1993).
> 21 U.S.C.A. § 881(b)(4) (West 1981 & Supp. 1993).

If you are referring to a portion of the statute rather than to the entire statute, pinpoint the portion by subsection. If you do give the subsection in your citation, be sure the subsection is designated just as it is in the statute, including whether letters are lower or upper case, whether numbers are arabic or roman, and whether numbers and letters are enclosed in parentheses or not. For example, the preceding citation refers to sub-subsection (4) of subsection (b) of section 881 of title 21 of the United States Code.

The parenthetical material at the end of the citation gives an abbreviation of the commercial publisher's name and the location of the statute. In the two preceding citations, "Law. Co-op." is an abbreviation for "Lawyers Cooperative Publishing" and "West" is an abbreviation for "West Publishing Company." At the time this chapter was written, the hardbound volume of United States Code Service containing the statutes was copyrighted "1984" and the pocket part supplement was dated "1993." Similarly, the hardbound volume of United States Code Annotated was copyrighted "1981" and the pocket part supplement was dated "1993." Include as much parenthetical information as needed to locate the statutory language. In these citations, information was given for both the hardbound volume and the pocket part supplement. If the statutory language is found entirely in the hardbound volume, you need only include information on the hardbound volume in the parentheses. Conversely, if the statutory language is found entirely in the pocket part supplement, you need only include information on the pocket part supplement in the parentheses.

CITATIONS FOR COURT RULES

The following are sample citations to the most important types of court rules identified in this book:

Fed. R. Civ. P. 23.	(Rule 23 of the Federal Rules of Civil Procedure)
Fed. R. Crim. P. 1.	(Rule 1 of the Federal Rules of Criminal Procedure)
Fed. R. App. P. 5.	(Rule 5 of the Federal Rules of Appellate Procedure)
Fed. R. Evid. 610.	(Rule 610 of the Federal Rules of Evidence)
Sup. Ct. R. 1.	(Rule 1 of the Rules of the United States Supreme Court)

CITATIONS FOR ADMINISTRATIVE LAW

The following are sample citations to the *Federal Register* and the Code of Federal Regulations:

56 Fed. Reg. 23000 (1992).
21 C.F.R. § 1316.71 (1992).

In the citation for the *Federal Register*, "56" is the volume, "23000" is the page number, and "(1992)" is the year of publication. In the citation for the Code of Federal Regulations, "21" is the title, "1316" is the part, "71" is the section, and "(1992)" is the year of publication.

CITATIONS TO LEGAL ENCYCLOPEDIAS

Although legal encyclopedias are not usually cited in documents submitted to the court or opposing counsel, you will need to cite legal encyclopedias for assignments and more informal documents such as law office memos. See Chapter 13 for an explanation of the purpose and use of law office memos. The following is the citation for section 1 of the American Jurisprudence Forfeitures and Penalties topic.

36 Am. Jur. 2d *Forfeitures and Penalties* § 1 (1968 & Supp. 1993).

The number "36" is the volume in which section 1 is located, "1968" is the copyright year of the volume, and "1993" is the year of the pocket part supplement. The ampersand ("&") indicates that the material you are referring to was found in both the hardbound volume and the pocket part supplement. The citation should be revised to show only "1968" in the parentheses if the material you are referring to was found only in the hardbound volume. Similarly, the parentheses should contain only "Supp. 1993" if the material you are referring to was found only in the pocket part supplement. A citation to Corpus Juris Secundum or a state legal encyclopedia would be in similar form except for substituting the abbreviation for the legal encyclopedia used instead of "Am. Jur. 2d":

> 25 C.J.S. *Damages* § 101 (1966).

CITATIONS TO AMERICAN LAW REPORTS

This citation is to the annotation entitled "Effect of Forfeiture Proceedings under the Uniform Controlled Substances Act or Similar Statute on Lien against Property Subject to Forfeiture" beginning on page 317 of the first volume of American Law Reports Fifth Series, copyright 1992. The title of the annotation is fairly descriptive of the scope of the annotation. The case published in American Law Reports which serves as a springboard for the annotation is *State v. One 1979 Pontiac Trans Am*, 771 P.2d 682 (Utah Ct. App. 1989). The annotation would be cited as:

> Annotation, *Effect of Forfeiture Proceedings under the Uniform Controlled Substances Act or Similar Statute on Lien against Property Subject to Forfeiture*, 1 A.L.R.5th 317 (1992).

A citation to an annotation from American Law Reports Federal would be similar in form except for substituting "A.L.R. Fed." for "A.L.R.5th."

APPENDIX C

Rules for Quotations and Short Form Citations

INTRODUCTION

Many students have a mental block about using quotations and short form citations in their legal writing. They have so convinced themselves that they will never master the rules of quotations and short form citations that they structure their writing to avoid having to deal with quotations and short form citations at all. This appendix is designed to help you through this writer's block. First, it gives you the most basic rules for quotations and short form citations and then it lets you practice applying the rules by working through some exercises. These basic rules should be sufficient for your writing assignments in a legal writing class. If you have questions not covered by the rules, refer to Colum. L. Rev. et al., *The Bluebook: A Uniform System of Citation (15th ed. 1991) (the "Bluebook*").

The *Bluebook* rules for writing and citing law review articles differ in many respects from the rules used in other types of legal writing you will be doing. The rules discussed in this appendix can be used for all types of legal writing other than law review articles. If you have the occasion to write a law review article, you will need to follow *Bluebook* form or the form specified by the journal or publisher for which you are writing.

QUOTATIONS

To Quote or Not to Quote

When your authority is a constitutional or statutory provision it is a good idea to quote the relevant portions of the provision. The reason is that each word in those provisions has been carefully selected and a court interpreting those provisions will use the wording of those provisions as a starting point. Focus your reader's attention by quoting only the relevant portions. You may want to make sure your reader understands a complicated provision you have quoted by following up the quotation with a summary of the provision in your own words. You do not have to quote constitutional or statutory provisions if they are simple and you can put them in your own words.

For example, if you are discussing 21 U.S.C. § 881 and the fourth amendment to the United States Constitution, you would want to quote the relevant portion of the statute.[1] Then, because the statutory language may be difficult for your reader to understand, you might summarize the quoted portion of the statute in your own words. The relevant portion of the fourth amendment could be paraphrased.

> The government claims it had the right to confiscate your money under 21 U.S.C. § 881. The relevant portion of the statute

provides: "The following shall be subject to forfeiture to the United States and no property right shall exist in them: . . . All moneys . . . furnished or intended to be furnished by any person in exchange for a controlled substance . . . [and] all proceeds traceable to such an exchange . . . ." This means that your money can become property of the United States government if the money was proceeds from the sale of illegal drugs or you were purchasing or intended to purchase illegal drugs with the money. However, the fourth amendment to the United States Constitution protects you against the government unreasonably searching you and seizing your money. If we can prove that the search and seizure were "unreasonable," then the government would have to return your money to you.

Quoting from cases is a little different from quoting constitutions or statutes. Your own personal writing style determines, to a great extent, whether you use quotations in your legal writing and how many you use. You do not have to use any quotations at all if you can state everything in your own words. If you like to quote, however, do not use so many quotations that your writing is mostly quotations with very little in between. A reader who is faced with a number of long block quotes may be tempted to skip over them and read only what is between the quotes. Your goal is to keep your reader interested in what you have written. Quotations should be reserved for well-stated passages that you would have trouble stating in your own words. You may want to quote a portion of the issues, the holdings, and the reasoning. Usually you would not quote the facts, the case history, or the results, because you can state those portions of the case better yourself.

Quote Accurately

When you quote, your quote must be accurate down to punctuation and case of letters. (An *upper-case letter* means a capital letter and a *lower-case letter* means a small letter.) If your reader happens to check your quotation against the original source and finds differences, the reader will know you have been sloppy. Then the reader will wonder how far the sloppiness extended; if the writer did not take the time to quote accurately, perhaps the writer did not take the time to research thoroughly. You will quickly lose your credibility and the reader's confidence by not quoting accurately.

Avoid Plagiarism

Be wary of the possibility of plagiarism. *Plagiarism* occurs when you use portions of someone else's writing without indicating that you are quoting. It also occurs when your paraphrasing of portions of a case differs little from the wording of the case except for word order. One way to avoid this is to quote. A second way is to spend enough time with the case so that you know it intimately ("internalize" it) and can write about it as if you were telling someone a story. Test yourself to see whether you understand a case by explaining it out loud to someone else. If you have trouble, go back and read the case again until you understand it.

Types of Quotations

Quotations can appear:

1. as block quotations;
2. as complete sentences within your paragraph; or
3. as phrases within your sentence.

The following sections of this appendix discuss these three types of quotations.

Block Quotations

A *block quotation* is a long quotation which is indented and set off from the rest of the text so that it looks like a "block" on the page. It is set off from the rest of your writing by extra line spacing and is indented on both left and right. Do not use quotation marks around the outside of the block quote. You may use quotation marks inside the block quote if the passage you are quoting in turn quotes something else. If your citation follows the block quote, double-space after your block quote and place your citation back at the left-hand margin. The *Bluebook* tells you to use a block quote if the quotation contains at least 50 words. This is a good rule of thumb which is frequently violated by block-quoting shorter passages. Unless your professor wants you to adhere strictly to this rule, use a block quote when the block quote format makes the quotation easier to understand.

Rules for block quotations

1. Use if quotation is 50 words or more.
2. Indent left and right.
3. Do not enclose in quotation marks.
4. Double-space between block quote and text.
5. Place citation at left-hand margin.

Sample Block Quotation

The following is a sample block quotation from *United States v. Smith,* 799 F.2d 704 (11th Cir. 1986). The superscript numbers, which indicate editing changes, correspond to the numbered rules in Figure C-1, and appear in the example to help you understand the changes from the original text.

> We first consider . . .[1] [whether][2] the stop was a valid investigation of possible drug activity. . . .[1] [A]n[2] officer may conduct a brief investigative stop of a vehicle[3] [but][2] such a stop must be justified by *specific, articulable facts*[4] sufficient to give rise to a reasonable suspicion of criminal conduct.[3] Investigative stops of vehicles are analogous to *Terry*-stops[3] and are invalid if based upon only "unparticularized suspicion or 'hunch.[5]' "[6]

United States v. Smith, 799 F.2d 704, 707 (11th Cir. 1986) (quoting *Terry v. Ohio*, 392 U.S. 1, 27 (1968))[7] (emphasis added)[8] (citations omitted)[8]

Now compare the block quote with the original case text:

> We first consider the district court's determination that the stop was a valid investigation of possible drug activity. Although an officer may conduct a brief investigative stop of a vehicle, *see Delaware v. Prouse*, 440 U.S. 648, 99 S. Ct. 1391, 59 L. Ed. 2d 660 (1979), such a stop must be justified by specific, articulable facts sufficient to give rise to a reasonable suspicion of criminal conduct, *Terry v. Ohio*, 392 U.S. 1, 27, 88 S. Ct. 1868, 1883, 20 L. Ed. 2d 889, 909 (1968); *United States v. Brignoni-Ponce*, 422 U.S. 873, 95 S. Ct. 2574, 45 L. Ed. 2d 607 (1975). Investigative stops of vehicles are analogous to *Terry*-stops and are invalid if based upon only "unparticularized suspicion or 'hunch,' " 392 U.S. at 27, 88 S. Ct. at 1883, 20 L. Ed. 2d at 909.

Show Readers Changes from Original Text

The first sample block quote is much more reader-friendly because it is not clogged with citations and unnecessary words. Omitting citations and unnecessary words allows the reader to focus on what the court was trying to communicate. The rules in Figure C-1 explain how to indicate any editing you have done to quotations by using ellipses (. . .), brackets ([ ]), and explanatory parentheticals (explanations within parentheses). The rules apply to all types of quotations, not just block quotations. Again, the rule numbers coincide with the superscript references in the first sample block quotation.

Quoting Complete Sentences and Quoting Phrases

When the passage you are quoting contains fewer than 50 words and can stand alone as one or more complete sentences, the passage should be part of your paragraph rather than being set apart as a block quote. Capitalize the first letter of the quoted passage and bracket the capital letter if this is a change. When the passage you are quoting is not a complete sentence, use it as a phrase in your sentence without capitalizing the first letter of the quoted phrase, unless it begins your sentence. Don't forget to use the eight quotation rules in Figure C-1 when quoting complete sentences and phrases.

The following example contains both types of quotations—complete sentences and phrases. The superscript numbers correspond to the numbered rules following the sample, and appear in the example to help you understand the changes from the original text.

Basic quotation rules for block quotation and for quoting sentences and phrases

1. **Use of ellipses.** Delete any unnecessary wording. If the wording is in the *middle* of a quoted passage, indicate the deletion by using an ellipsis. Do not use an ellipsis when you are omitting something at the *beginning* of a quoted passage. Whether you use an ellipsis at the *end* of a quoted passage depends on whether you are quoting a complete sentence or a phrase used as part of your sentence. When quoting a complete sentence and omitting something at the end of the sentence, insert an ellipsis before the final punctuation of the sentence. When quoting a *phrase*, do not use an ellipsis at the end of the phrase.

2. **Use of brackets.** Add your own words to make the quotations easier to understand and place your words inside brackets. When you are changing a letter from upper to lower case or from lower to upper case, place the changed letter in brackets.

3. **Omission of citations.** When you omit a citation, you do not need to replace it with an ellipsis if you use an explanatory parenthetical noting the omission. (See rule 8.)

4. **Adding emphasis.** Add emphasis to quoted words by underlining or italicizing them and indicate this change in an explanatory parenthetical. (See rule 8.)

5. **Placement of punctuation and quotation marks.** Place periods and commas *inside* quotation marks and other punctuation *outside* the quotation marks unless the punctuation was part of the original quotation.

6. **Use of quotation marks.** Do not use quotation marks at the beginning or the end of a block quote, but do use quotation marks within block quotes when the passage you are quoting in turn quotes something else. For quotes other than block quotes, precede and follow the quoted language with quotation marks. Quotation marks for quotations within quotations alternate double and single quotation marks, with the outermost quotation marks double.

7. **Placement of the citation to the quoted passage.** The citation for the quoted passage should be fairly close to the passage and may precede or follow it. The citation may appear in a textual sentence or in a citation sentence. A citation following a block quote should be placed back at the left-hand margin and should be separated from the block quote by extra line spacing between the block quote and the citation.

8. **Use of explanatory parentheticals.** When the case you are quoting in turn quotes a second case, identify the second case, including a page reference to the quoted material, by using an explanatory parenthetical. Explain that you have emphasized something or omitted citations by using an explanatory parenthetical.

FIGURE C-1 Basic quotation rules.

In *Florida v. Jimeno*, 111 S. Ct. 1801, 1804 (1991),[1] the United States Supreme Court looked at the "expressed object"[2] of a search to determine "[t]he[3] scope of a search." After the officer told the suspect that the officer thought there were drugs in the suspect's car, the suspect consented to the search.[4] "[I]t[5] was objectively reasonable for the police to conclude that the general consent to search [the suspect's] . . .[6] car included consent to search containers within that car which might bear drugs . . . .[7] The authorization to search in this case therefore, extended beyond the surfaces of the car's interior to the paper bag . . .[8]." *Id.*[9]

1. The citation to two quoted phrases precedes the phrases and gives the page reference to those phrases.
2. The quoted phrases are enclosed in quotation marks. Following basic quotation rule 1 from Figure C-1, no ellipsis is needed to indicate omission of words preceding the phrases: because these are phrases, no ellipsis is needed to indicate omission of words preceding the phrases.
3. The "t" is changed from upper to lower case because the phrase is in the middle of the author's sentence. The change is bracketed to show the change from the original.
4. This sentence does not need quotation marks because it is stated in the author's own words. Even though the sentence is not a direct quote, it does need a page reference because the substance of the sentence is taken from the case. In this paragraph, the two citations at the beginning and the end give the page reference and are close enough to this sentence so that no additional citation is needed. If the sentence were not so near the two citations, a reference to page 1804 should be given.
5. Following basic quotation rule 1 from Figure C-1, no ellipsis is needed to indicate omission of words at the beginning of the quoted complete sentence. The "i" is bracketed to indicate that the letter was changed from lower to upper case.
6. The ellipsis indicates that the word "respondent" was omitted and the brackets indicate that the words "the suspect's" were added. "Suspect" is used instead of "respondent" because this reference makes it easier for the reader to understand who is being identified.
7. Following basic quotation rule 1 from Figure C-1, the ellipsis indicates that wording has been omitted. Here a textual sentence and a citation sentence were omitted.
8. Following basic quotation rule 1 from Figure C-1, the ellipsis indicates that wording was omitted from the end of this quoted sentence and the ellipsis is followed by the final punctuation (a period).
9. Here the citation follows the quoted complete sentences and is placed in a citation sentence.

Now compare the preceding example with the original text:

> The scope of a search is generally defined by its expressed object. *United States v. Ross,* 456 U.S. 798, 102 S. Ct. 2157, 72 L. Ed. 2d 572 (1982). In this case, the terms of the search's authorization were simple. Respondent granted Officer Trujillo permission to search his car, and did not place any explicit limitation on the scope of the search. Trujillo had informed respondent that he believed respondent was carrying narcotics, and that he would be looking for narcotics in the car. We think it was objectively reasonable for the police to conclude that the general consent to search respondent's car included consent to search containers within that car which might bear drugs. A reasonable person may be expected to know that narcotics are generally carried in some form of a container. "Contraband goods rarely are strewn across the trunk or floor of a car." *Id.,* at 820, 102 S. Ct., at 2170. The authorization to search in this case therefore, extended beyond the surfaces of the car's interior to the paper bag lying on the car's floor.

Exercise Using Basic Quotation Rules

Practice the quotation rules you have learned by editing the following passage to indicate changes from the original text. Do not forget to add citations where needed. Refer to the preceding section of this appendix for the original text.

> In deciding the Williams case, the court must first decide whether the stop was a valid investigation of possible drug activity. To be valid, such a stop must be justified by specific, articulable facts sufficient to give rise to a reasonable suspicion of criminal conduct. Investigative stops of vehicles are analogous to *Terry* stops and are invalid if based upon only "unparticularized suspicion or 'hunch.' "
>
> If the stop was valid, the next questions are whether the Williamses consented to the search and, if they did, what was the scope of the consent. The United States Supreme Court discussed the scope of a car search in *Florida v. Jimeno*, 111 S. Ct. 1801, 1804 (1991). The scope of a search is generally defined by its expressed object. In *Jimeno*, the terms of the search's authorization were simple. Respondent granted Officer Trujillo permission to search his car and did not place any explicit limitation on the scope of the search. Trujillo had informed respondent that he believed respondent was carrying narcotics, and that he would be looking for narcotics in the car. It was objectively reasonable for the police to conclude that the general consent to search respondent's car included consent to search containers within that car which might bear drugs. The authorization to search in this case therefore extended beyond the surfaces of the car's interior to the paper bag lying on the car's floor.

SHORT FORM CITATIONS

The first time you refer to a case, you must give its full citation. If you refer to the case again, you should use an abbreviation to the citation rather than giving the full citation. This abbreviated citation is called a *short form citation*. In this section of the appendix, we use the following citations in the examples and exercises:

Florida v. Jimeno, 111 S. Ct. 1801 (1991).
United States v. Smith, 799 F.2d 704 (11th Cir. 1986).
United States v. Sokolow, 490 U.S. 1 (1989).
Sexton v. Gibbs, 327 F. Supp. 134 (N.D. Tex. 1970), *aff'd*, 446 F.2d 904 (5th Cir. 1971), *cert. denied*, 404 U.S. 1062 (1972).

This section of the appendix analyzes some examples of both full and short form citations. In the examples, the citations are all followed by periods, as they would be in citation sentences. If you are using the citations in textual sentences, you would not need a period at the end of a citation unless it is the end of the sentence.

The two types of sentences in legal writing are textual sentences and citation sentences. A *textual sentence* is the type of sentence you have been writing all your life. It is a complete grammatical sentence with a subject and a verb. A *citation sentence* contains only citations. The four sample citations in the text are written as citation sentences. Each is appropriately ended with a period.

Let's say that, in a law office memo, you first give the following string cite to *Sokolow* and *Smith* (a *string cite* is a citation to more than one case, with the cases separated by a semicolon):

> *United States v. Sokolow*, 490 U.S. 1 (1989); *United States v. Smith*, 799 F.2d 704 (11th Cir. 1986).

Then you want to cite to *Sokolow* again, this time to page eight. You might think that you could use *id.* as a short form citation for *Sokolow,* because you just cited it. However, if you used *id.,* you would be referring your reader back to the immediately preceding citation which is your string cite. Unless you want to refer to all the cases in the string cite, you must use another short citation form to cite to *Sokolow*. Any of the following short citation forms for *Sokolow* are acceptable:

> *United States v. Sokolow*, 490 U.S. at 8.
> *Sokolow*, 490 U.S. at 8.
> *490 U.S. at 8.*

When using short form citations, try to use the shortest form possible that is clear and causes no confusion. If you cited *Sokolow* within the last few pages and had not cited any other United States Supreme Court case from volume 490 of United States Reports, you could use the third type of short citation form. If it has been several pages since you last cited *Sokolow*, or if the reader might confuse *Sokolow* with another case in the same volume of the same reporter, use either the first or second version of short form citation. When you are referring to a case by the name of only one of the parties, select a name that easily distinguishes the case from other cases. Because there are thousands of case names that contain "United States" but virtually no others that contain "Sokolow," you would use "Sokolow" rather than "United States."

If you wanted to refer to page eight of *Sokolow* again, use:

> *Id.*

"*Id.*" is always underlined (italicized). It is capitalized when it begins a sentence, but is not when it appears in the middle of a sentence. If you then wanted to refer to page thirteen of *Sokolow*, use:

> *Id.* at 13 (Marshall, J., dissenting).

You must indicate the page number because it is not the same one referred to before. The explanatory parenthetical is needed because you are referring to something other than the majority opinion.

If you want to refer to pages 705 through 706 and 708 of *Smith*, you cannot use *"id."* because *Smith* is not the immediately preceding citation. If you have recently cited *Smith*, use:

> 799 F. 2d at 705–06, 708.

If you have not referred to *Smith* recently, precede this short form citation by either "*United States v. Smith*" or "*Smith*." When the referenced material spans more than one page, give the numbers of the first and last pages, joined by a hyphen or an en dash. Retain only the last two digits of the second number. When material appears on more than one page but does not span pages, separate the page numbers by a comma.

If you want to refer to footnote 5 on page 708 of *Smith*, use:

> *Id.* at 708 n.5.

If you want to refer to *Smith* in general rather than to any specific material from *Smith*, use:

> *Smith.*

When you are using *Smith* as a shorthand abbreviation to refer to the case, "Smith" is underlined (or italicized). "Smith" is not underlined if you are referring to the individual.

If you want to refer to pages 134 (the first page of the case), 136, and 139 of *Sexton* and you have not given the full citation of *Sexton* before, use:

> *Sexton v. Gibbs*, 327 F. Supp. 134, 134, 136, 139 (N.D. Tex. 1970), *aff'd*, 446 F.2d 904 (5th Cir. 1971), *cert. denied*, 404 U.S. 1062 (1972).

Because you wanted to refer to the first page of the case in the full citation, the number "134" must be written twice, with the two numbers separated by a comma.

If you then want to refer to pages 141 through 143 of *Sexton*, use:

> *Id.* at 141–43.

Notice that you do not need subsequent history in the short form citation.

Exercise on Short Form Citations

Using the preceding citations to *Sokolow, Smith, Sexton,* and *Jimeno,* give the correct citations called for by the following descriptions:

1. String cite to *Sokolow*, *Sexton*, and *Jimeno*.
2. Cite to pages 706 and 708 of *Smith.*
3. Cite to pages 711 through 712 of *Smith*.
4. Refer to *Smith* in general terms.
5. Cite to pages 3 through 5 of *Sokolow*.
6. Cite to page 1804 of *Jimeno*.
7. Cite to page 1804 of *Jimeno*.
8. Cite to note 1 on page 14 of *Sokolow.*
9. Cite to pages 9 and 11 of *Sokolow*.
10. Refer to *Jimeno* and *Sokolow* in general terms.

[1] For an explanation of the use of ellipses (. . .) and brackets ([ ]), see the discussion of those terms later in this appendix. For the complete text of the statute and the fourth amendment to the United States Constitution, see Appendix A.

APPENDIX D

Mechanical Errors

INTRODUCTION

Elimination of mechanical errors is the tedious, though necessary, part of writing. You need to do your best to eliminate mechanical errors for two reasons. First, you want your reader to concentrate on your message and not be distracted by mechanical errors. Second, a reader who spots a number of mechanical errors will begin to wonder if the writer is sloppy. If the writer did not take the time to proofread for typographical and spelling errors, perhaps the writer's sloppiness extended to legal research too. You do not want to lose your credibility over a few easily eliminated mechanical errors.

You know your own writing and you probably know from past experience what types of mechanical errors give you problems. Keep in mind the kinds of mechanical errors that have given you problems in the past so you can eliminate them when you get to the editing and proofing stage of your legal writing. If you have trouble spotting them yourself, ask a fellow student to help you by proofing your writing. You can do the same for that student.

This appendix covers nine different mechanical errors. You have certainly been warned about a number of mechanical errors discussed in this appendix. They include incorrect use of apostrophes, sentence fragments, and run-on sentences. Problems with passive voice, parallel construction, and unclear antecedents may be less familiar to you. Two other errors covered in this appendix are using excess words and changing tenses without reason.

Once you have mastered the material in this appendix and you are ready for a challenge, try completing the exercises in the last section of this appendix, which involve a combination of mechanical errors. When you consider yourself an expert, try rewriting the complaint found in Appendix F.

EXCESS WORDS

Don't tire your readers by making them wade through excess words to understand your point. Your message will be easier to understand if you delete anything not necessary. When you get to the editing stage, look at each sentence again. Identify the meaning of the sentence and then see whether you can eliminate any excess words.

The following sentences contain excess words. Look at each sentence and identify any words that can be deleted. Then compare your results with the suggested answers. (The supplied answers are only suggestions; your results may be better.)

1. The United States Constitution provides for protection against unreasonable search and seizure.
2. The similarities among *Smith, Forfeiture,* and *Nelson* are almost identical.
3. The Court found that the factors taken together as they were, amounted to reasonable suspicion.
4. In deciding the *Nelson* case, the court will have the difficult job of balancing Nelson's constitutional right against unreasonable search and seizure and society's interest in controlling drug trafficking on the nation's highways.
5. In regards to investigatory stops there must be a balance between an individual's right to privacy and society's interest in being safe.

Suggested answers

1. The United States Constitution prohibits unreasonable search and seizure.
2. *Smith, Forfeiture,* and *Nelson* are almost identical.
3. The Court found that the factors, taken together, amounted to reasonable suspicion.
4. In deciding *Nelson,* the court will have the difficult job of balancing Nelson's constitutional right against unreasonable search and seizure and society's interest in controlling drug trafficking on the nation's highways.
5. Investigatory stops must balance an individual's right to privacy and society's interest in enforcing the law.

Now rewrite the following sentences to eliminate excess words:

1. On appeal, the issue was whether the profile used by Vogel provided reasonable suspicion to warrant a stop under the United States Supreme Court decision in *Terry.*
2. The *Smith* case is also based on the validity of a stop, and if the patrolman has reasonable suspicion to make such a stop.
3. Reasonable suspicion means that the officer must be able to articulate exactly what was suspicious to make him feel that illegal activity was taking place.
4. The stop was based on a personal drug courier profile Vogel had developed, with the following facts applying:
5. This particular stop was unconstitutional and any evidence seized as a product of this stop is deemed to be regarded as inadmissible in court.
6. When deciding this case the court will have to determine whether this particular stop made by Sheriff Vogel violates Nelson's right against an unreasonable search and seizure as provided under the United States Constitution and the Florida Constitution.
7. The court will apply the exclusionary rule which prohibits the court to use at trial any evidence which was seized through an unconstitutional search and seizure to be used.
8. These three cases involve facts similar to the facts in this case, Nelson.
9. In deciding cases on the issue of search and seizure and the constitutionality of such, the courts will have to look to the fourth amendment.
10. According to the fourth amendment to the United States Constitution, individuals are guaranteed protection against unreasonable search and seizure.
11. Vogel proceeded to confiscate the amount of $6,003.00.
12. In the above facts in the *Sokolow* case, the suspect's behavior was consistent with the DEA's drug courier profile.
13. The stop cannot be upheld on the ground that Vogel did not have reasonable suspicion that the appellants were hauling drugs.
14. The use of a drug courier profile attempts to protect society from crime but the use of it may interfere with an individual's federal and Florida constitutional rights against unreasonable search and seizure.

15. The decision was based on facts that the traffic stop was rejected as pretextual and that the stop was not a valid drug investigation.
16. The Constitutions both have language stating that probable cause is needed to support a warrant.
17. In deciding this case, the court will have to consider and evaluate the essence of the drug courier profile used by police officers as a basis for reasonable suspicion.
18. Another case pertaining to the aspects of a drug courier profile is *United States v. Sokolow,* 490 U.S. 1 (1989).

USE OF APOSTROPHES

Apostrophes have two uses. They tell your reader that something belongs to someone (possessive use) and that letters have been omitted (use in contractions). This section deals primarily with the use of apostrophes in possessives, because contractions are generally too informal to be used in legal writing.

Rewrite the following sentences using the rules in Figure D-1.

1. He decided to make an investigatory stop because the driver matched the troopers drug courier profile.
2. The officers shone their lights on Smith's car but Smith did not look in the officers direction.
3. The judgments of conviction against the defendant's were vacated.
4. All the suspects were stopped because of Vogels' drug courier profile.
5. Trooper Vogels stop of the appellants vehicle was held not to be reasonable under the fourth amendment. [Assume there were three appellants.]
6. Although police officers have a duty to protect the community, sometimes the standards used violate citizens constitutional rights.
7. Public interest is at it's peak when contemplating the next step to combat the drug problem in this country.
8. The Eleventh Circuit reversed the district court's denial of appellants motion to suppress the evidence. [Assume there was one appellant.]
9. The court found Vogels courier profile to be too general and vague.
10. The dog sniffed defendants car and indicated the presence of drugs. [Assume there were two defendants.]
11. Although these stops may be warranted at times, the Court emphasized that the individuals constitutional right against unreasonable search and seizure must be safeguarded.

Rules for use of apostrophes in possessives

1. To make a singular noun possessive, add an apostrophe and an "s." (If your noun already ends in an "s," follow this rule anyway.)

   Examples:

   the car of the officer = the **officer's** car
   the car of Mr. Williams = Mr. **Williams's** car

2. To make a plural noun possessive, add an apostrophe.

   Example:

   the car of the officers = the **officers'** car

3. Do not, under pain of mortal embarrassment, use an apostrophe with a pronoun like "its" to make it possessive. "It's" means "it is."

   Examples:

   the speed of it (when it refers to a car) = **its** speed
   it is a speedy car = **it's** a speedy car.

FIGURE D-1 Rules for use of apostrophes in possessives.

SENTENCE FRAGMENTS

A sentence fragment results when the writer attempts to write a sentence, but the thought is expressed incompletely. There are three common causes of sentence fragments. The first is omission of the verb. Obviously, this can easily be corrected by supplying the verb. A second cause is beginning a sentence with a subordinating conjunction such as "while" or "although," and not following the dependent clause with an independent clause. "While" and "although" tell the reader: "I'm going to tell you something less important before I tell you the really important information." The reader reads what he or she was cued to think was the less important information and is left hanging when the sentence doesn't supply the "important information" promised. This error can be corrected either by deleting the subordinating conjunction or adding the important information. The third cause of sentence fragments is incorrect punctuation. This happens when the writer puts a period where a comma should be and capitalizes the next word in the sentence. Correct this error by putting the comma back in and changing the capital to lower case.

Rewrite the following sentences to correct any sentence fragments.

1. The question is whether the evidence seized from the vehicle be suppressed.
2. The two main similarities between *Smith* and *Sokolow.*
3. While in *Sokolow* it was held that all the factors as a whole were enough for reasonable suspicion.
4. Looking at the two cases cited, it is apparent that the use of the drug courier profile has not been overwhelmingly embraced by the courts. Especially when it is the only reason given for the investigatory stop. As is *Nelson,* which factually is almost indistinguishable from the cases cited.
5. Whereas in *Smith* a traffic violation never occurred.
6. Order denying the motion to suppress reversed, judgments of conviction vacated, cases remanded to district court.
7. Because we are protected by the fourth amendment to the United States Constitution.
8. A *Terry* stop based on an Ohio case which eventually went to the United States Supreme Court.
9. The Court reasoned that the totality of the circumstances must be considered in evaluating the stop and that any one of the factors by itself was not proof of any illegal conduct. But when taken together they amount to a reasonable suspicion.
10. In *United States v. Sokolow,* 490 U.S. 1 (1989). Andrew Sokolow was stopped by DEA agents while trying to leave Honolulu International Airport.

RUN-ON SENTENCES

Run-on sentences are usually caused by trying to pack too much information into a sentence. The solution is to break up the run-on sentence into several sentences. Another cause of run-on sentences is poor wording. The wording of a sentence may make the reader perceive a sentence as a run-on sentence. The solution is to reword and reorganize the sentence so the reader can handle the information as a single sentence.

Analyze the following passages and rewrite them to eliminate run-on sentences.

1. Based solely upon these factors, no traffic violation was alleged, Vogel stopped and detained Nelson.
2. In *Forfeiture* Vogel observed Coleman driving on the interstate and because Coleman and Williams fit Vogel's drug courier profile he pulled them over even they had not broken any law.
3. The exclusionary rule prohibits the trial use of evidence secured through unreasonable search and seizure as applied to the

federal courts in *Weeks v. United States,* 323 U.S. 383 (1914) and applied to the states, incorporated in the due process clause of the fourteenth amendment to the United States Constitution in *Mapp v. Ohio,* 367 U.S. 643 (1961).

4. Using a drug courier profile supported by only an "unparticularized suspicion or hunch" is prohibited by the United States Supreme Court in *Terry* which allows police stops when the officer has a reasonable suspicion.
5. The defendant filed a motion to suppress, motion denied, convicted, appealed. There was not reasonable suspicion therefore the stop is not lawful for reasons of carrying drugs or traffic violations.
6. Vogel did not have reasonable suspicion therefore the stop cannot be upheld on that ground.
7. The facts are too general to be of any value, they could be used for anyone driving on I-95, the same officer was Vogel in all three cases.
8. The motions to suppress were filed and denied, after jury trial both defendants were convicted.
9. Trooper Vogel had developed a reasonable suspicion of illegal activity based on the fact that the suspect, a thirty-year-old man, was driving at 3:00 a.m. on a known drug corridor highway and being very cautious by driving 50 miles per hour and did not look at the marked patrol car as the car went past.
10. In previous cases with similar facts courts have found the drug courier profile to be too general to support reasonable suspicion therefore finding several searches and seizures unjustified and in violation of the individual's rights against unreasonable search and seizure.
11. Because the suspect produced an expired automobile rental contract Vogel called his dispatcher to verify the information given by the suspect, Vogel also requested that a drug dog be brought to the scene.
12. The federal appeals court held that the drug courier profile used in this case was too general and unparticularized to support a *Terry* stop, thus granted the return of the money to the suspects.
13. These are very general factors, there was no traffic ticket written, it was more of a hunch, combined with Vogel's experience that instigated the stop.

PARALLEL CONSTRUCTION

When you write about a series of items or activities, you must use parallel construction. This means that the wording of each item or activity must be similar in grammatical structure. For example, the following sentence discusses three different activities:

> The officers stopped the car, were questioning the occupants, and searched the car trunk.

The sentence is an example of poor parallel construction because the verb tense in the middle of the sentence does not match up with the verb tense at the beginning and at the end of the sentence. "Stopped" and "searched" are simple past tense, whereas "were questioning" is past progressive tense. "Stopped" and "searched" describe two completed actions and "were questioning" describes an action in progress. The parallel construction problem can be corrected by changing the second verb to match the tense of the other two verbs in the sentence:

> The officers stopped the car, questioned the occupants, and searched the car trunk.

Now rewrite the following sentences correcting any errors in parallel construction.

1. The differences consist of the time observed, the location, and the subject was investigated more thoroughly in *Sokolow.*
2. The motions to suppress were reversed, judgments of conviction were vacated, and the cases remanded.

3. The profile consists of a late model car, Florida rental tag, 2 persons about 35 years old, driver-male, car going Northbound on I-95, driving in a cautious manner, and not looking at the trooper while passing.
4. Issue: Did Vogel have reasonable suspicion that suspects were committing, has committed, or is about to commit a crime enough to make a valid stop?
5. Issue: Whether Vogel had reasonable suspicion to believe that the defendants were committing, committed, or was about to commit a crime?
6. In this case the profile consisted of:
    1. traveling at 3:00 a.m.;
    2. traveling at 50 mph;
    3. car occupied by two individuals who were approximately 30 years of age;
    4. out-of-state tags;
    5. driving very cautiously;
    6. did not look in the troopers' direction as he proceeded past them.
7. Both suspects were dressed casually and driving in the early morning.
8. It is not common to spend $2,100 in cash for plane fare and making a long trip only to return 48 hours later.
9. Drug dogs alerted, search warrants obtained, and drugs were found in the luggage.

ANTECEDENTS

To understand the problem with antecedents, look at the following example:

> The DEA agents made an investigative stop of the suspect and his companion because they fit the drug courier profile as well as other information they had obtained.

There are three pronouns in the sentence: "his," "they," and "they." Out of context, the reader would not know what these pronouns refer to. Used in a sentence, the reader will determine who the pronoun refers to by assuming that it refers to the last person or persons identified before the pronoun (the "antecedent"). That means that "his" refers back to "suspect," "they" refers back to "the suspect and his companion," and "they" refers back to "the suspect and his companion." Do you see any problems? The problem is that the second "they" in the sentence should refer back to "the DEA agents" rather than to "the suspect and his companion." The way to correct this is to replace the second "they" with "the agents." Then the sentence would read:

> The DEA agents made an investigative stop of the suspect and his companion because they fit the drug courier profile as well as other information the agents had obtained.

The pronoun must agree in number with its antecedent. Many students have problems with antecedents and the word "court." Even though a number of judges make up a court, *court* is a singular noun. The proper pronoun to use with "court" is "it" rather than "they." Likewise, an agency or organization, when referred to as an entity, is singular: "The DEA acts through its agents."

Rewrite the following sentences, correcting any antecedent problems.

1. In so holding, the Court relied heavily on their earlier decision in *Terry v. Ohio,* 392 U.S. 1 (1968).
2. The DEA agents escorted Sokolow and Norian to their office in the airport.
3. The appellants filed a motion to suppress the cocaine charge on the grounds that the stop of their car was unreasonable.
4. The patrolman stated that Coleman didn't break any laws, but he was stopped because in his experience, people who fit the profile sometimes had drugs.
5. Smith and Swindell filed motions to suppress, but it was denied.
6. In their opinion, the court cited *Terry.*
7. Vogel stopped a driver and passenger because he thought he had reasonable suspicion that he fit a profile of a drug courier.
8. Vogel did not have enough facts to stop him.

9. The court stated that if they let officers stop vehicles based only on a hunch, there would be great potential for abuse.
10. The Court reasoned that they must consider all the factors, "the totality of the circumstances."

ACTIVE VERSUS PASSIVE VOICE

To understand active and passive voice, look at the following sentences:

> The officer returned the money to the driver.
>
> The money was returned to the driver by the officer.

The first sentence is written in active voice. "Officer" is the subject, "returned" is the verb, "money" is the object, and "driver" is the indirect object. The officer is also the person taking the action of returning the money. Sentences written in active voice have the performer as the subject of the sentence, with the subject preceding the verb. The second sentence is written in passive voice. In passive-voice sentences, the object of the action (the thing or person performed on) comes first, then the verb, and then the performer.

Active voice is preferable in legal writing because it makes the sentence more powerful and easier to understand. See whether this is true by reading the two sample sentences again. Which do you prefer? Passive voice is fine for instances when you do not know or do not want to identify the performer. In the example, if you did not know who returned the money, you could write:

> The money was returned to the driver.

When you edit your writing and you find a sentence in passive voice, rewrite it in active voice. Even if the performer is not specifically identified in the sentence, you may be able to identify the performer by the context of the sentence.

Now rewrite the following sentences in active voice.

1. Unlike the other cases, it was held that the agents did have the needed suspicion to make a valid stop.
2. The application to the instant case detailing the similarities and differences will also be noted.
3. The money was ordered returned to the persons from whom it was taken.
4. Based entirely on these factors Nelson was detained by Vogel.
5. The cocaine seized was ordered by the court to be suppressed.
6. It was testified by Vogel that the appellees were stopped because they fit a drug courier profile.
7. Trooper Vogel testified that the vehicle was being driven by Mr. Johnson in an "overly cautious" manner.

CHANGE IN TENSE

Usually sentences and paragraphs are written in the same tense, unless there is a reason for changing tenses. Your reader will be distracted from what you are trying to communicate if you change tenses in midstream without a reason. The following example contains a distracting change in tenses:

> DEA agents arrested Smith and Swindell and charged them with conspiracy to possess cocaine with intent to distribute. Defendants file motions to suppress. The motions were denied.

Why did the writer change from past tense ("arrested" and "charged"), to present tense ("file"), and back to past tense ("were denied")? Your reader may wonder about that error more than the writer's message. Keep your tenses consistent unless you have a reason for changing tenses.

Rewrite the following sentences, keeping the verb tense consistent.

1. The court looked at the totality of the circumstances in deciding this case and decided that any one of the reasons does not by itself support reasonable suspicion, but altogether they do amount to reasonable suspicion.
2. The suspect admitted that his real name is Sokolow.
3. The court held that the drug courier profile was too general and did not establish any more than a hunch which is condemned by the United States Supreme Court in *Terry*.
4. The issue in this case is whether the stop was a reasonable *Terry* stop. The court held that the stop was not supported by reasonable suspicion.
5. In *Smith,* the same officer is on a special operation to intercept drug couriers. He was parked in the median with his car's headlights shining into the northbound lanes.
6. The Court agreed that any one of these factors alone may not qualify as reasonable suspicion, but when combined they provide adequate proof for reasonable suspicion.
7. The court of appeals held that because Vogel did not have reasonable suspicion that the appellants were hauling drugs, the stop cannot be upheld on that ground.
8. On appeal, the stop was ruled unreasonable and any evidence obtained from the stop must be suppressed.
9. The court finds that there was no reasonable suspicion that the individual was committing, had committed, or was going to commit a crime. Therefore the evidence was suppressed.
10. The stop wasn't constitutionally permitted because the drug profile is too general and unparticularized to support a Terry stop.
11. The Fifth District Court of Appeal ruled the lack of reasonable suspicion and reliance upon a hunch, coupled with a drug courier profile too general to support a *Terry* stop, is inconsistent with the Florida Constitution.
12. The trial court denied a motion to suppress the evidence, and thus stipulating that the stop was a legal one.

COMBINATION OF ERRORS

Challenge yourself by rewriting the following sentences, which contain a combination of errors:

1. Trooper stated that he initially stopped the car for a traffic violation, of weaving, to investigate for drunk driving, however, when the vehicle was stopped, no test for alcohol was conducted and a drug dog was called to the scene immediately, which leads to an obvious different scope for the reason of stopping the vehicle, upon which Vogel had no reasonable suspicion.
2. On June 5, 1985 at 3:00 AM, Trooper Robert Vogel and an unmarked DEA agent were stopped in the median of I-95 with the cars headlights shinning into the northbound lane.
3. The Court reasoned that Vogel's profile could not reasonably infer that a vehicle meeting such criteria should be characterized as unusual.
4. Does the fact that driver fits a drug courier profile give the highway trooper reasonable suspicion that the driver was committing, committed or about to commit a crime and justify an investigatory Terry stop?

APPENDIX E

Preparing a Table of Authorities for a Legal Brief

INTRODUCTION

All who work with legal documents are familiar with the *Bluebook,* which is compiled by the editors of the *Columbia Law Review,* the *Harvard Law Review,* the *University of Pennsylvania Law Review,* and *The Yale Law Journal,* and published and distributed by the Harvard Law Review Association. The *Bluebook* tells us about legal citation format, and it is the accepted authority. We do not, however, find therein any clues pertaining to a table of authorities—exactly how to generate one or how it should look. Nor have we found any other source for this information. This appendix suggests guidelines for the preparation of an accurate and visually appealing table of authorities, based primarily upon my own experience and the responses I have received throughout my years as a legal assistant. I have often been given varied answers to the same specific question, precisely because there has been no authority to which to refer. This appendix represents only my judgment and the way our law firm has chosen to treat these matters. It is my sincere hope that it will offer helpful guidance, especially to those who are new to the process of preparing a table of authorities.

APPEARANCE

The table of authorities obviously does not contain the substance of your legal arguments, and it is not going to win or lose the case for you. However, it is one of the very first pages of your brief and its appearance does make an impression on the reader. Also, the table of authorities serves a real function—it is actually used to locate all the references to any cited material. For these reasons, it is important to make it perfectly accurate, comprehensive, and consistent, and to make it "look pretty."

PROCEDURES

1. Begin by making a 3-by-5-inch index card for every authority cited in your brief,

---

Kathie Walvick, who prepared Appendix E, is the Senior Legal Editor at the law firm of Dickstein, Shapiro & Morin in Washington, DC. She has been with the firm for 17 years, primarily in the litigation practice area. Kathie has been responsible for proofreading, cite checking, shepardizing, and preparing tables of contents and tables of authorities for legal briefs filed in courts and agencies all over the country. She has extensively studied the most efficient ways of accomplishing these tasks, with the goal of producing a work product that is accurate, consistent, and visually appealing.

including citations to cases, statutes, regulations, rules, legislative materials, law review articles, books, and magazine and newspaper articles, but not including citations to transcripts, pleadings, or other such records to which you refer in your brief. Experience has taught me that these index cards are the best source of control for the cite-checking and shepardizing phases, as well as for preparing the table of authorities. You may want to use a system for marking on each card when that case has been shepardized. It is a good idea to write the page number(s) of the brief on which a citation appears (I do this in the lower right-hand corner of the index card itself), but do not type the page numbers in the Page column of the table of authorities until the brief is in final form. Having these page numbers at which an authority has been cited on the index card prepared for each authority is useful for locating the case within the brief so you can make corrections and additions that are discovered during the cite-checking phase and so that you can add subsequent history found by shepardizing. It is also helpful in making sure that each case is cited in full form the first time it appears in the brief and in short form thereafter.

2. Make a 3-by-5-inch index card for each category that you will need for the citations in your particular brief, using initial capital letters for all words except articles and prepositions of four or fewer letters, underlining the category heading, and putting a colon at the end (not underlined). For example, create a category divider for each of the following headings: "*Cases:*," "*Statutes:*," "*Federal Rules of Civil Procedure:*," and "*Miscellaneous:*."

3. Arrange your index cards as follows:

a. Put your "*Cases:*" card first and then arrange all the cards you have for cases in alphabetical order behind it.

b. Put your "*Statutues:*" card next, and arrange all the cards you have for statutes behind it, putting federal statutes first, in numerical order by U.S.C. number, and then state stautes in alphabetical order by state name, with all sections of the same state code in numerical order.

c. Continue with your cards for your other categories, with the appropriate cards behind each category divider card—always in alphabetical and then numerical order. See the Format section of this appendix for a suggested order of categories.

4. Have the table of authorities typed up from your pack of index cards, in exactly the same order as you have arranged them.

5. Proofread the table of authorities from your index cards.

6. If any new authority is added after the table of authorities has been prepared, make a card for each additional authority, shepardize each newly added case, and insert each new authority in the appropriate place in the table of authorities. If any authority is completely deleted from the brief, it must be removed from the table of authorities.

7. Only after the brief is in final form can you enter the page numbers in the Page column. Remember to include the short form citations and the *Id.*s in identifying the pages at which citations appear to an authority cited earlier in full citation form. One good way to do the page numbers task is to have one person do it alone first and then use two people for a double-check—one to go through the brief and call out the citations for each page and the other to spread out the table of authorities pages and check off the page numbers as they are called out, adding any that were missed and crossing off any that do not belong.

FORMAT

The usual order for the authorities is as follows:

1. Cases
2. Statutes
3. Regulations
4. United States Constitution
5. State Constitutions

6. Federal Rules
7. Court Rules
8. Legislative Material
9. Other, *e.q.,* Orders, Executive Material, Uniform Commercial Code
10. Miscellaneous. (Some people choose to call this category "Other Authorities." This category includes treatises, books, law review articles, and newspaper and magazine articles.)

For some briefs, you may want to modify this list. For example, you might combine the "Statutes" and "Regulations" categories into a "Statutes and Regulations" category, or combine the "Legislative Material" and "Executive Material" categories into a "Legislative and Executive Materials" category. You might combine the "Federal Rules of Criminal Procedure" and "Federal Rules of Evidence" categories into a "Federal Rules" category and use the format, for example, Fed. R. Crim. P. 42(a) and Fed. R. Evid. 613 for the entries under the "Federal Rules" category. Also, if you have only one citation under the "Legislative Material" or "Executive Material" category, you may want to put it under the "Miscellaneous" category. You should always consult with the attorney in charge about such decisions.

For some briefs, you may want to divide the "Statutes" category into a "Federal Statutes" category and a "State Statutes" category.

The "Miscellaneous" category has room for a great deal of discretion and individual decisions. For example, you may or may not want to include here the articles and other materials that you are attaching as exhibits.

A sample table of authorities in a recommended format appears in Figure E-1.

Following are some recommendations:

1. Put the heading *TABLE OF AUTHORITIES,* centered, at the top of the first page and put the *Page* heading at the right. For every page after the first page, put the heading *TABLE OF AUTHORITIES (Cont'd),* centered, at the top and the *Page* heading at the right.
2. For the page (folio) numbers at the bottom of the pages of the table of authorities, use the format -i-, -ii-, etc., beginning with the page number after the last page of the table of contents. For example, if your table of contents is two pages long, number these pages -i- and -ii- and number the table of authorities beginning with -iii-. Center these page numbers at the bottom in the same place as the page numbers for the text.
3. Include TABLE OF AUTHORITIES as the first entry on your table of contents.
4. Begin the cases at the left margin and indent every carryover line two spaces.
5. Leave one space between the end of the citation and the beginning of the leader dots and one space between the last dot and the first page number in the Page column.
6. Line up the page numbers in the Page column evenly at the right margin, with the numbers backing into the line of leader dots whenever there is more than one page.
7. If you have a citation that has separate sections listed (*see* Restatement (Second) of Contracts (1981) on page 11 of the sample), do not put dots after the top citation line, and include all cited sections in numerical order, indented. *See also* Question 1 in the Questions section of this appendix.
8. Make each case entry appear well balanced. Do not go too far to the right; always have at least two dots between the end of the case citation and the first page number. Do not split up parts of the citation. For example, begin a new line if the volume, reporter, and page do not all fit on the same line or if the parentheses with the court and year do not all fit on the same line. Also, do not split subsequent history phrases such as *cert. denied.*
9. Insert an extra line space between categories.
10. Make the entries in the table of authorities *exactly* match the entries in your brief, but do not include "jump cites" or pinpoint cites in the table, and do not include the

name of the judge (which you may have chosen to include in parentheses after the cite in your brief). Include in the table of authorities all subsequent history and any (per curiam) or (en banc) notations in the case citations in the brief.

11. Be sure that the style you adopt for subsequent history phrases in the table of authorities matches *exactly* the style adopted for these phrases in your brief. For example, be consistent about whether you underline the period and/or the space in *cert. denied.*

LOCAL RULES

Some courts have local rules about tables of authorities, so always check to see if special rules apply. Frequently, the attorney filing the brief in a particular jurisdiction (probably your client's local counsel) will be the first person to contact regarding the existence of special rules for that jurisdiction. You can also call the clerk of the court.

One common example of such a special rule is that some courts require that you put an asterisk (*) before the authorities upon which you have principally relied, in which case you also include a footnote that says something like "Authorities principally relied upon are indicated by an asterisk." The attorneys in charge will decide which cases deserve the asterisks; it is not always simply the ones that are cited more than once.

COMPUTERIZED TABLE OF AUTHORITIES

There are computer products on the market these days that will generate your table of authorities directly from your brief. These are beyond the scope of this appendix, but even if you are using one of these, you will want to inspect the final table of authorities for accuracy and appearance, using the guidelines suggested here.

MOST FREQUENTLY ASKED QUESTIONS

Q1. Should the table of authorities include paragraph numbers, section numbers, and page numbers for books in the Miscellaneous category?

A. Page numbers should not be included, just as jump cites are not included for cases, but section and paragraph numbers may be useful, especially if you are citing more than one for a particular volume. In that case, you could set it up as follows:

4A Charles Alan Wright & Arthur R. Miller, *Federal Practice and Procdure* (2d ed. 1987)

§ 1104 . . . .
§ 1118 . . . .
§ 1164 . . . .

Note that you would make a separate entry for each volume of the same treatise, even if the authors, title, edition, and date are all identical.

Q2. Where does *George Jones Co. v. Morgan* go in the alphabetical list of cases—under "G" or "J"?

A. We put it under "G".

Q3. Where do the *In re* cases go in the alphabetical list of cases—under "I" or under the party's name?

A. Put them under the parties names, for example:

Best Repair Co., In re, 789 F.2d 1080 (4th Cir. 1986) . . . .
Black Ranches, Inc., In re, 362 F.2d 8 (8th Cir.), *cert. denied,* 385 U.S. 990 (1966)
Dean v. Gadsden Times Publishing Corp., 412 U.S. 543 (1973) (per curiam) . . . .
Deep Rock Oil Corp., In re, 113 F.2d 266 (10th Cir. 1940) . . . .
Kungys v. United States, 485 U.S. 759 (1988)
Macomb Trailer Coach, In re, 200 F.2d 611 (6th Cir. 1952), *cert. denied,* 345 U.S. 958 (1953) . . . .

Q4. When should I use *passim?*

A. The general rule is to use *passim* in the Page column if the cited authority appears on five or more pages of your brief. The use of *passim* seems to imply that the authority is cited throughout your brief, so you might consider using hyphenated page spreads if the five or more pages are actually within only certain sections. For example, if your brief is 50 pages long and you rely on the *United States v. Carlton* case on pages 24, 25, 26, 27, 28, 29 and 40, you might use 24–29, 40 in the Page column rather than *passim.*

Q5. Should the words that are abbreviated in the brief be abbreviated in the table of authorities?

A. Yes. The case name in the table of authorities should *exactly* match the style of the citation in the brief. Remember that you *never* abbreviate the first word of a party's name and that you use only the abbreviations listed in the *Bluebook* for other words. Also, if the case name is used in a sentence of text rather than as a citation, you do not use abbreviations except for "&, " "Ass'n," "Bros.," "Co.," "Corp.," "Inc.," "Ltd." and "No." If your brief includes a particular case both as a citation (with abbreviations) and in text (without abbreviations), the table of authorities should use the format without abbreviations.

Q6. When do you use a hyphen instead of a comma to separate the page numbers in the Page column?

A. A hyphen is used when the actual citation in your brief is divided between two pages, and the case is not cited again on the second page. If the case is cited again on the second page, use a comma. Also, you can use a hyphen as discussed in Question 4 above.

Q7. If a case is discussed but not actually named or cited on a page, should that page be included in the Page column?

A. No. Only include pages on which the case is actually mentioned or cited, either by name in full citation format, by name in "short form" (for example, *Rosemount*), or by use of an *Id.* format or a 498 U.S. at 341 format.

Q8. Should the table of authorities include the cases quoted or cited by other decisions? For example, if the brief says "*Rosemount, Inc. v. United States Int'l Trade Comm'n*, 910 F.2d 819, 822 (Fed. Cir. 1990) (quoting *Panduit Corp. v. All States Plastics Mfg. Co.*, 744 F.2d 1564, 1579 (Fed. Cir. 1984))," should the *Panduit Corp.* case be in the table of authorities?

A. Yes; in this example, *Panduit Corp.* should be included in your table of authorities.

Q9. Should the table of authorities include the cases cited in block quotes or regular quotes that appear in the brief? For example, the brief quotes and cites as follows:

> The normal rule of statutory construction is that if Congress intends for legislation to change the interpretation of a judicially created concept, it makes that intent specific. *Edmonds v. Compagnie Generale Transatlantique,* 443 U.S. 256, 266–67 (1979). The Court has followed this rule with particular care in construing the scope of bankruptcy codifications.

Midlantic Nat'l Bank v. New Jersey Dep't of Envtl. Protection, 474 U.S. 494, 501 (1986). Should the *Edmonds* case be in the table of authorities?

A. No; *Edmonds* should not be included in the table of authorities (unless it also appears elsewhere in the brief). Note that if the *Edmonds* case does appear somewhere else and is therefore in your table of authorities, this appearance within the block quote does not count for purposes of entering the page numbers in the Page column.

Q10. Should I include subsections of statutes as separate entries on my table of authorities:

A. Yes, unless the attorney in charge prefers not to include them. An example of a part of your table of authorities for statutes might be:

28 U.S.C. § 502 . . . .
28 U.S.C. § 502(a) . . . .
28 U.S.C. § 502(a)(1) . . . .
28 U.S.C. § 502(a)(5) . . . .
28 U.S.C. § 502(c) . . . .
28 U.S.C. § 502(c)(8) . . . .
28 U.S.C. § 502(c)(8)(i) . . . .

TABLE OF AUTHORITIES

Cases: Page

Adickes v. S.H. Kress & Co., 398 U.S. 144 (1970) . . . 17

Aim Leasing Corp. v. Helicopter Medical Evacuation, Inc., 687 F.2d 354 (11th Cir. 1982) . . . 40, 42

Allenberg Cotton Co. v. Pittman, 419 U.S. 20 (1974) . . . 44

Barclays Discount Bank Ltd. v. Levy, 743 F.2d 722 (9th Cir. 1984) . . . 18

Goldstick v. ICM Realty, 788 F.2d 456 (7th Cir. 1986) . . . 21

Linton & Co. v. Robert Reid Engineers, Inc., 504 F. Supp. 1169 (M.D. Ala.) *aff'd mem.*, 664 F.2d 295 (11th Cir. 1981) . . . 40, 44

Proctor v. Consolidated Freightways Corp., 795 F.2d 1472 (9th Cir. 1986) . . . 23

Water West, Inc. v. Entek Corp., 788 F.2d 627 (9th Cir. 1986) . . . 14, 16, 19, 22

White Dragon Productions, Inc. v. Performance Guarantees, Inc., 196 Cal. App. 3d 163 (1987) . . . *passim*

Statutes:

18 U.S.C. § 2 . . . 33

28 U.S.C. § 1291 . . . 2

28 U.S.C. § 1332 . . . 1

50 U.S.C. § 833 . . . 8

Ala. Code (1975)

§ 35-12-21 . . . 2

§ 35-12-32 . . . 4, 14

§ 35-12-34 . . . 4

Del. Code Ann. tit. 12, §§ 1130–1212 (1987 & Supp. 1990) . . . 3

N.H. Rev. Stat. Ann. § 471-C:1 (Supp. 1990) . . . 3

Regulations:

49 C.F.R. § 1300.14 (1978) . . . 49, 50

44 Fed. Reg. 22,010 (1979) . . . 46

United States Constitution:

Due Process Clause . . . 14

Fifth Amendment . . . *passim*

Sixth Amendment . . . 4, 12

Constitution of Illinois:

Art. I, § 2 . . . 44

Art. I, § 11 . . . 27

Federal Rules of Civil Procedure:

Rule 56 . . . 4, 15

Rule 65(c) 22

FIGURE E-1 Sample table of authorities.

Federal Rules of Evidence: Page
Rule 403 21
Rule 501 . . . . 43, 44
Rule 702 30
Rule 901(a) 36

Legislative Material:
123 Cong. Rec. H5322 (daily ed. June 2, 1977) 23, 24
Hearings on S. 1040, S. 1056 and S. 1081, Before the Senate Comm. on Interior and Insular Affairs, 93d Cong., 1st Sess. (1973) 16
Report of the Commissioner of Corporations on the Transportation of Petroleum, H.R. Rep. No. 812, 59th Cong., 1st Sess. (1906) 15

Executive Material:
Exec. Order No. 12009, 42 Fed. Reg. 46,267 (1977) 30

Miscellaneous:
Jonathan Fuerbringer, *Deficit and Economic News Batter the Treasury Market,* N.Y. Times, Jan. 8, 1993, at D1 30
Grant Gilmore, *The Assignee of Contract Rights and His Precarious Security,* 74 Yale L.J. 217 (1964) *43*
1 Floyd R. Mecham, *A Treatise on the Law of Agency* (2d ed. 1982) 22
Restatement (Second) of Contracts (1981)
§ 5 13
§ 86 16
Harold G. Reuschlein & William A. Gregory, *The Law of Agency and Partnership* (2d ed. 1990) 8

FIGURE E-1 *(Continued)*

APPENDIX F

Complaint Rewrite Exercise

INTRODUCTION

Just because someone is an attorney does not mean that he or she can write well. When you master the material in this book you will be writing better than many attorneys and judges. The following rewrite exercise was taken from an actual complaint filed in federal court. It was selected for this exercise because it contains many mechanical errors, including those discussed in Appendix D. Although certain identifying information has been changed, the text of the complaint appears just as it was filed in federal court. Your assignment is to rewrite the complaint, correcting it for mechanical errors.

IN THE UNITED STATES
DISTRICT COURT
IN AND FOR THE MIDDLE
DISTRICT OF FLORIDA

AUBREY MARCUS DUNCAN
Plaintiff,
CASE: 93-000-CIV-ORL
CIVIL TRIAL DIVISION:

v.

THE VOLUSIA COUNTY SHERIFF'S OFFICE

and

ROBERT VOGEL /

FIRST AMENDED COMPLAINT

COMES NOW, the plaintiff, AUBREY DUNCAN through his undersigned Counsel, NAMELESS ATTORNEY, files the COMPLAINT and allege the following:

1. This honorable Court has jurisdiction pursuant to Title 28 Section 1343 U.S.C.A.

2. This Action is filed pursuant to Title 42 Section 1983 U.S.C.A., which states, "Every person who, under color of any statute, ordinance, regulation, custom, or usage, of any State or Territory or the District of Columbia, subjects, or causes to be subjected, any citizen of the United States or other person within the jurisdiction thereof to the deprivation of any rights, privileges, or immunities secured by the Constitution and laws, shall be liable to the party injured in an action at law, suit in equity, or other proper proceeding for redress. For the purposes of this section, any Act of Congress applicable exclusively to the District of Columbia shall be considered to be a statute of the District of Columbia."

3. AUBREY DUNCAN, the plaintiff, is a citizen of the United States whose residence is 123 Main Street, Maryland and he is sui juris.

4. The Volusia County Sheriff's Office is a law enforcement agency of the State

of Florida located in Volusia County, Florida and is sui juris.

5. On April 25, 1991, the Sheriff of Volusia County was operating what he called a selective enforcement team. The selective enforcement team concentrated on highway seizures along Interstate Highway 95. The selective enforcement team operated or responded to a set of indicators created by Sheriff Vogel of Volusia County, Florida. The indicators were and or the following:

a. Black people driving a car with out of state tags.

b. The car is being driven with an abundance of caution.

c. The car is either being driven to the Miami area or away from the Miami area.

d. The determination to search and detain made when the Deputy asks the driver where he is going and where he came from.

e. If the driver declined to give consent to search to the deputy then the exercising of his constitutional right was determined to give the deuputy reasonable suspicion that something illegal is going on.

6. In particular, on April 25, 1991 Deputy Ray Almodovar stopped Aubrey Duncan herein after referred to as plaintiff, on Interstate Highway 95 for weaving within his lane. The Deputy had followed the Plaintiff approximately a mile and then stopped him. When the Deputy approached the Plaintiff's vehicle he requested the Plaintiff's Drivers license and registration and the items requested were presented. The Deputy then started to ask questions about where the Plaintiff was going and if the vehicle belonged to the Plaintiff. The Deputy then walked to the drivers side of the Plaintiff's vehicle and started to inquire of his passenger. The Deputy asked the passenger where they were headed and she told him to Miami. After questioning both people in the vehicle for 15 minutes the Deputy advised the Plaintiff he was free to go and that he would only issue a warning to let his passenger drive if eh gets tired. As soon as the Plaintiff walks a couple of steps toward his vehicle the Deputy then requested to search the Plaintiff's vehicle. The Plaintiff tells the Deputy, "I would prefer you not do that and for what reason would you want to search my car." The Deputy then asks more questions about weapons, illegal narcotics and contraband. The Plaintiff answers no to the Deputy's additional inquiry and at that time the Deputy tells the Plaintiff was going to detain him until he could call for a drug dog. The Plaintiff waited along side the highway for an additional twenty five minutes waiting for the dog to arrive. When the dog arrived the handler started to walk the dog around the vehicle from the passenger side of the car and the dog did not alert, however it was the second time around to the drivers side of the vehicle when the dog alerts. It is important to note this Deputy was equipped with audio and visual equipment. The audio was turned on and off at the Deputy's convenience yet the visual tape continued to record the events. this is important because you cannot hear what is said to the dog the second time around the vehicle. A person viewing the visual tape will notice the slight turn of the head of the handler and suddenly the dog jumps on the passenger door of the vehicle. While the search was being conducted the Plaintiff was being held in the patrol car. The Plaintiff is not free to leave on two accounts, one he is locked in the patrol car and the other is his car had been seized for purposes of the search. The search revealed $265,000.00 and no illegal narcotics nor anything that was illegal. The money was seized and not returned to the Plaintiff.

On June 23, 1992 Judge William Johnson granted a directed verdict during the forfeiture hearing in favor of the Plaintiff on the basis that the Deputy violated the Plaintiff's rights under the Fourth Amendment of the Constitution of the United States of America and that there was no nexus to anything illegal. The Court went on to comment that the stop violated United States v. Smith, 799 F. 2d 704 (11th Cir. 1986) which held that the same Volusia County Sheriff Robert Vogel could not stop vehicles for one second swerves within the driver's lane of traffic. The Court reduced the ruling to writing on July 31, 1991 and stated the money should be returned forthwith. The Volusia County Sheriff's Office refused to return the money forthwith and instead contacted the Internal Revenue Service to inquire if it could create another lien that would totally consume the money. The sheriff fails at forfeiting the property. In fact, the Plaintiff never saw any of that money again.

During this process the Plaintiff lost his home in Maryland to foreclosure which was valued at $500,000.00 The Plaintiff lost because of seizure of his money was like taking away the tools of his trade, in that he was a professional gambler. The equity in the home was $350,000.00 The Plaintiff also lost his automobile and could not get needed cancer treatment due to the loss of his savings to the forfeiture action wrongfully initiated in Florida.

Count I

7. The Plaintiff adopts and realleges the facts as stated in paragraphs 1 through 6 and state this is an action for violation of the Fourth Amendment of the Constitution of the United States of America in that the detention violated the Constitution of the United States of America.

8. The Deputy allegedly stopped the Plaintiff, AUBREY DUNCAN because he was weaving just a bit within his lane of traffic.

9. The stop was in violation of law and only happened because the Plaintiff fit the profile when the indicators were considered by the Deputy.

10. The Deputy was well aware of *United States v. Smith*, 799 F.2d 704 (11th Cir. 1986) which held a one second swerve within the drivers lane is not cause to stop the vehicle.

11. The Plaintiff demands trial by jury, damages, costs, reasonable attorney's fees and all that which id seemed proper.

COUNT II

12. The Plaintiff adopts and realleges the facts as stated in paragraphs 1 through 6 and states this is an action for wrongful detention in violation of the Fourth Amendment of the Constitution of the United States of America.

13. After the Deputy decided there was no reason to issue a traffic citation, the Plaintiff should have been free to go as he was told by the Deputy.

14. The Deputy instructed the Plaintiff to stay put until he could get the drug sniffing dog to show up.

15. The drug sniffing dog did not show up for more than twenty minutes.

16. The Plaintiff was not free to leave as required by *Berkemer v. McCarty*, 104 S. Ct. 3138 (1984) which held that if an individual is stopped for an ordinary traffic violation he expects to be allowed to continue on his way after the traffic stop is over.

17. The Plaintiff demands trial by jury, damages, costs and reasonable attorney's fees.

COUNT III

18. The Plaintiff adopts and realleges the facts as stated in paragraphs 1 through 6 and states this is an action for an illegal arrest in violation of the Fourth Amendment of the Constitution of the United States of America.

19. The Deputy placed the Plaintiff in his patrol car where the Plaintiff was held for over an hour while the search took place and after.

20. The Deputy had no probable cause to arrest or take the Plaintiff into custody while he searched the Plaintiff's vehicle he in effect arrested the Plaintiff. The Deputy's actions were indeed a violation of the Fourth Amendment but also in violation of *Dunaway v. New York*, 442 U.S. 200 (1979) which held to take one into custody on less than probable cause amounts to an illegal arrest.

22. The Plaintiff demands trial by jury, damages, costs, and reasonable attorney's fees.

COUNT IV

23. The Plaintiff adopts and realleges the facts as stated in paragraphs 1 through 6

and states this is an action for wrongfully seizing his property in violation of the Fourth Amendment of the Constitution of the United States of America.

24. The Deputy seized the Plaintiff's property because he was black and he did not believe a black man could legitimately have $265,000.00.

25. At the time of the seizure the Deputy had no reason, no nexus whatsoever to believe the Plaintiff's property was contraband.

26. There is no law in the United States that require black people to put there money in the bank.

27. The Plaintiff demands trial by jury, damages, pre-judgment interest, costs, and reasonable attorney's fees.

COUNT V

28. The Plaintiff adopts and realleges the facts as stated in paragraphs 1 through 6 and states this is an action against the individual who is the Sheriff of Volusia County Florida, Robert Vogel for intentionally violating the constitutional rights of Black citizens who travel through Volusia County, Florida when he had full knowledge that he was violating the constitutional rights of blacks and hispanics.

29. Robert Vogel, Sheriff of Volusia County, Florida knew his selective enforcement team was stopping automobiles on interstate 95 in violation of *United States v. Smith* 799 F.2d 704 (11th Cir. 1986) which held, in a case that he was involved as a Florida Highway Patrolman, that law enforcement could not stop vehicles for one second swerves within the drivers lane of traffic.

30. Robert Vogel, Sheriff of Volusia County, Florida knew he was stopping and searching blacks and hispanics nearly 80% of the time when he knew there was no lawful reason to interfere with the privacy of those travelers.

31. Robert Vogel, knew and understood his acts violated the Fourth Amendment constitutional rights of blacks and hispanics, yet he showed no regard or respect to Court rulings involving himself nor advice of legal counsel at his disposal.

32. The Plaintiff respectfully requests the Court to award punitive damages against Robert Vogel in the amount of one million dollars for knowingly and intentionally violating his constitutional rights simply for race based reasons.

33. The Plaintiff also requests attorney's fees, cost and damages as this court deems just and proper.

WHEREFORE the Plaintiff demands judgment for the following:

A. $1,000,000.00 for the damages caused him by the wrongful highway stop and seizure.

B. Cost of defending himself against the wrongful forfeiture.

C. Reasonable attorney's fees incurred in the forfeiture.

D. Pre-judgment interest on the $265,000.00.

E. Reasonable attorney's fees and costs.

F. $1,000,000.00 in punitive damages because Robert Vogel knowingly and intentionally, against advice of counsel and the Courts, for violating his Constitutional rights under the United States Constitution.

Respectively Submitted,

____

Nameless attorney, Esq.

APPENDIX G

Problems

The following four problems were designed to give students practice in research and writing. Students can be assigned one or more of the problems to research. Writing assignments on the problems can include:

1. A client opinion letter (written to one of the persons named in a problem).
2. An attorney-client contract (the agreement one of the persons named in the problem signs to retain an attorney).
3. A law office memo to a senior partner concerning one of the problems.
4. A memorandum of law in support of a motion for summary judgment or other litigation motion filed in a lawsuit concerning one of the problems.
5. An appellate brief filed after a judgment is reached in a lawsuit concerning one of the problems.

WAS SWIMMING POOL AN ATTRACTIVE NUISANCE?

John and Mary Cooke own a home in Anytown, Your State, with a private swimming pool in their back yard. Pursuant to local ordinances, their back yard is completely fenced by a five-foot wooden fence and the gate is kept closed with a latch at the top of the fence.

The Cookes live next door to the Andersons, a family with a two-year-old son, Joseph. Joseph loved water and the Andersons had joined the Cookes swimming in the Cookes' pool on numerous occasions. Although not yet "swimming" on his own, Joseph greatly enjoyed splashing in the pool and looked forward to playing with the Cookes' dog Rover. From the moment Joseph woke up in the morning until he went to bed at night, his favorite topics were "pool" and "dog." Rover spent most of his days in the pool enclosure, relaxing on the pool deck or swimming. Joseph would become extremely excited anytime he heard Rover bark from next door.

One Saturday morning, Joseph was playing on the screened-in porch of his home. He seemed quite content playing with his toys while his parents completed some odd jobs around the house. Once when his mother checked on him, he was gazing toward the Cookes' house and listening for Rover's bark. His mother told Joseph that they could go swimming and visit Rover later in the day.

The parents lost track of time, each assuming that the other had been checking on Joseph. All of a sudden the Andersons realized that neither one of them had checked on Joseph for a while. When they went to the screened-in porch, Joseph was nowhere to be found and the outside screen door was slightly ajar. They called to Joseph but he didn't answer, even though he was usually very good about coming when called.

The Andersons immediately started looking outside for Joseph. He was not in the Andersons' yard. At that moment, they noticed that the gate to the Cookes' pool fence was wide open. Fearing the worst, they rushed through the gate calling for Joseph. Initially nothing appeared out of the ordinary, except that Rover was dashing around the outside of the pool and barking as if to attract someone's attention. Then they noticed the pool blanket was slightly pulled back from the side of the pool at the deep end.

The Cookes always kept the pool covered with a pool blanket when the pool was not in use. The blanket kept the water from losing heat during the night and kept debris from falling into the water. The pool blanket was constructed of two layers of blue plastic material with small air pockets between the layers. The blanket, floating on the surface of the water, covered the entire pool surface except for a small area left open so Rover could swim.

When the Cookes heard the Andersons yelling, they rushed out to the pool to find out what was the matter. When they heard that Joseph was missing, the Cookes' first thought was that he might have fallen into the pool while following Rover. John Cooke called for Phil Smith so Phil could help remove the pool blanket. Phil was a 15-year-old neighbor who often came to play with Rover. Phil had been playing with Rover inside the pool fence that morning. Phil did not answer, so the Cookes and the Andersons together started pulling back the pool blanket.

To their horror, they saw two bodies in the deep end of the pool. They all jumped into the pool and pulled out the bodies. The two women tried to revive Joseph and Phil while the two men called the police and fire departments. When they arrived, the police and firefighters joined the Andersons and the Cookes in trying to revive the two boys. The two boys were rushed to the hospital but died a few hours later.

The police report of the incident showed that Mr. Cooke remembered opening the gate early in the morning while he was doing work around the pool. Joseph must have opened the outside screened door to his house and entered the pool enclosure looking for Rover. He may have fallen into the deep end of the pool while chasing Rover. The pool blanket would have parted enough from the side of the pool to allow Joseph to fall into the water. Although not a very good swimmer, Phil apparently jumped in to rescue Joseph at the same place Joseph had fallen in. The police theorized that Phil became disoriented while trying to rescue Joseph and couldn't get out from under the pool blanket.

The Cookes have just been told that their neighbors are planning to file suit against them, holding them responsible for Joseph and Phil's deaths. The Cookes hired your firm to represent them. The senior partner in your firm has asked you to research the law of your state and answer the following questions:

1. Does your state follow the attractive nuisance doctrine and, if so, how does it apply to private swimming pools?
2. Can the Andersons hold the Cookes responsible for Joseph's death?
3. What duty did the Cookes owe Phil and can the Smiths hold the Cookes liable for Phil's death?

DEFAMATION

Tom Harris and Jake Carson had been sports and political leaders and rivals ever since high school. They competed on the same sports teams and were of equal physical ability. In track and swimming races, Tom would come in first in one race, Jake would come in first in the next race, and then they would tie each other for first in a third race. Either Tom or Jake had been class president each of their four years in high school. Jake had been class president of the freshman and senior classes; Tom had been class president of the sophomore and junior classes.

Their friends speculated that the rivalry would continue in college. They both were to attend Collegiate University in nearby University Town. As freshmen they pledged two rival fraternities. Tom pledged Collegiate Alphas and Jake pledged Collegiate Betas. What had been friendly rivalry in high school gradually turned nasty during their years at the University. The Alphas pulled all sorts of pranks on the Betas and tried to discredit the Betas in the university community. The Betas did the same to the Alphas.

In the fall of their senior year at the University, Tom and Jake both decided to run for student body president. There was a lot of mud slinging during the campaign. At one point in the campaign, it was rumored that Jake was gay. The rumors were traced back to the Alphas. Although no one seemed to believe the rumor, Jake and his fraternity brothers were very upset about it.

The night before the election, the candidates participated in skits in the football stadium. Everyone eagerly looked forward to the skits each year, with most of the students and faculty of Collegiate University attending. The skits were usually half serious and half in jest. On skit night, the crowd in the stadium enjoyed the first skits while they speculated about Tom and Jake's skits. Jake's skit was the next-to-the-last and Tom's was the last of the evening. In Jake's skit, Jake neatly poked fun at Tom and emphasized how he, Jake, was the better candidate.

Then came time for Tom's skit. The scene was Jake's doctor's office. Tom played Jake's doctor and one of the Alphas played Jake. In the skit "Jake" walked into the doctor's office and says, "Well, doctor, now that I've completed my executive physical, I feel ready to complete my duties as Collegiate University student body president and lead the University to great achievements. How did my tests come out?" The "doctor" replied, "Well, Jake, you better sit down. I have good news and bad news for you. The good news is that most of your tests came back negative and you should make a fine student body president. The bad news is that you and Magic Johnson have something in common. Both of you tested HIV positive."

Those words were barely out of Tom's mouth when the stadium crowd gasped. A fight immediately broke out between the Alphas and Betas sitting near each other and the police were called in to clear the stands.

Although the student body president race had seemed almost even before the skits, Tom won with two-thirds of the vote. Jake was so outraged by Tom's skit that he hired your law firm to represent him. The senior partner in your firm has asked you to research the law of your state and answer the following questions:

1. Is it actionable per se as slander to announce that a person has tested HIV positive when the statement is not true?
2. Although Tom claims that his statement that Jake was HIV positive was made in jest, would the words give rise to an action for slander?
3. Could Jake be considered a public official or public figure in a slander action brought by him, and, if he is considered a public official or public figure, will it make any difference in the lawsuit?

THE NIGHTMARE PROPERTY

The Longs had purchased two adjoining lots on Nice Street in Anytown, Your State, as investment property. One of the lots was zoned residential and contained a three-bedroom, two-bathroom house which the Longs rented out. The other lot, zoned commercial, was vacant.

In September 1988, the Longs rented the house to a 30-year-old business woman. Barely a month later, the police called the Longs. A neighbor of the business woman had asked the police to investigate the Longs' Nice Street house. The neighbor reported he had heard a lot of yelling at the house and then a gunshot. The police found the front door open and the business woman dead, apparently shot by an intruder.

The Longs next rented the Nice Street house to a family. As soon as the family moved in, they reported that their television set repeatedly turned on and off, often in the middle of the night. The children claimed they had seen the ghost of the dead woman and were too terrified to sleep in their rooms. The neighborhood children started calling the Nice Street house the "haunted house" and refused to play with the children of the family renting the house. A few months later, the family moved out, complaining that they did not want to live with a ghost.

After that, the Longs tried without success to rent the Nice Street house. At the same time, the Longs posted a "For Sale" sign on the two lots. The Longs wanted to sell them for $250,000, the price at which the Longs had purchased them 10 years earlier. The Longs received no offers until almost a year later. A retired couple, the Browns, called the Longs to ask the sale price on the two lots. The couple was looking to move to a warmer climate and open a small toy store. When the Browns heard the asking price of $250,000, they said they might be interested in purchasing the lots.

The Longs met the Browns at the lots and gave them a tour of the house. The Browns explained to the Longs that they wanted to build a small toy store on the vacant commercial property and live next door in the house. They said that they were attracted to the lots because of their location and because the asking price seemed reasonable. The Longs told the Browns that the only reason they had put such a low price on the property was because it had been on the market for a while. The Longs needed to sell the property quickly because they were in need of cash to pay for unexpected expenses.

The sale went through 60 days later and the Browns immediately started construction on the vacant lot. They hoped to have the construction finished by the time they moved to Anytown. Six months later, the Browns moved into the Nice Street house and opened the then-completed toy store. Business at the toy store seemed very slow. The Browns noticed that none of the children from the neighborhood came into the store, although they did get some business from people vacationing in Anytown.

A week after the Browns moved into the house, their television turned on in the middle of the night. They didn't think anything of it until it happened the next two nights in a row. When Mr. Brown got up to turn off the television, he thought he saw something white and filmy at the other end of the room. Then the same thing started happening to the small television in the toy store. The Browns made sure they had turned off the television before locking the store for the evening, but they found the television turned on when they opened the store the next morning. Before they turned on the store lights in the morning, the Browns thought they glimpsed something white moving at the other end of the store. They didn't see anything out of the ordinary when they turned the lights on.

A few days later, Mr. Brown struck up a conversation with the teenage clerk at the local grocery store. The clerk asked Mr. Brown whether he had just moved to town. When Mr. Brown told him he owned the new toy store and lived next door, the clerk said, "I didn't think the Longs would ever sell the haunted house." Mr. Brown said, "What do you mean?" The clerk said, "Everybody around here knows the house is haunted. Why do you think you paid such a low price for it?"

Understandably shaken, Mr. Brown went home and told his wife the news. They immediately called the Longs and accused them of tricking the retired couple. The Browns demanded their money back and demanded to be reimbursed for the cost of construction of the toy store. When the Longs refused, the Browns hired your law firm to represent them. The senior partner in your firm has asked you to research the law of your state and answer the following questions:

1. Did the Longs have a duty to disclose that the two lots were "haunted"?
2. What are the elements of fraud concerning the sale of real property?
3. Are there enough facts for the Browns to win if they sue the Longs for fraud?

I WONDER WHAT IS IN THE PACKAGE

Margie and Floyd Walker had been happily married for 45 years. Even though he was past retirement age, Floyd continued to work for the railroad as a porter on its passenger trains. Margie was worried about Floyd's health and had been trying to get him to stop working for some time. She was concerned that the porter's job was too physically taxing for someone of Floyd's age.

One Monday morning, as Floyd was getting ready for work, Margie had the uncomfortable feeling that something would happen to Floyd at work. Margie pleaded with Floyd to call in sick. Floyd said, "I feel fine. Why should I call in sick if I feel fine?" Floyd reported for work as usual. Margie tried to convince herself that she was worrying for nothing, but to no avail. She wandered through the house all day, not able to get anything done except worry.

At three o'clock in the afternoon the telephone rang. Margie was so frightened that her hand shook as she answered the telephone. Floyd's supervisor at the railroad said, "Margie, I think you better sit down. I have bad news for you. Floyd fell from the train as it was going full speed and was killed. It appears he became disoriented, opened the outside door of the train, and was pulled off the train step by a sudden gust of wind. Floyd's body is at the Near Town Funeral Home. I'll make arrangements, if you like, to have the body transferred to a funeral home in Anytown." Margie felt like she had been hit by a truck. She was glad that she was sitting down or she very likely would have fainted. She responded, "Please make the arrangements with Webury Funeral Home."

Margie's worst fear had come true. Somehow she made it through the funeral. She kept feeling that it must all be a bad dream. She kept imagining that she would wake up one morning with Floyd still alive. She did remember having to call the Near Town Funeral Home several times to have Floyd's personal effects forwarded to Webury. Webury delivered the personal effects to her the day after the funeral.

It was not until almost a week after Floyd's death that Margie went through Floyd's personal effects. To her horror, in a plastic bag labeled "personal effects" she found a kidney, teeth, and fingers. At the sight of her dead husband's body parts, she fainted. A neighbor lady friend found Margie an hour later, collapsed on the floor. Margie was hospitalized for extreme exhaustion for two days and her doctor put her on antidepressant medication.

When she had recovered sufficiently, she called Webury to complain. Webury's owner disclaimed all responsibility. The owner said that Webury had simply forwarded the plastic bag, at Margie's insistence, from the Near Town Funeral Home. The owner added that the Webury employees had no reason to check what was in the bag.

Margie still suffers from depression and has not had a good night's sleep since she opened the plastic bag. She keeps having nightmares about the employees of Near Town Funeral Home placing Floyd's body parts in the plastic bag and imagines them laughing as they label the bag "personal effects." It also makes her angry that Webury seemed so unconcerned and did not even offer an apology. Margie has hired your law firm to represent her in a possible lawsuit against the funeral home. The senior partner in your firm has asked you to research the law of your state and answer the following questions:

1. What would Margie Walker have to prove to recover damages for the tort of interference with a dead body?
2. What are the elements of the tort of intentional infliction of emotional distress, sometimes called the "tort of outrage"?
3. Will Margie Walker be able to hold Near Town Funeral Home and Webury Funeral Home liable for the torts of interference with a dead body and intentional infliction of emotional distress?

GLOSSARY

act A statute; a bill that has been enacted by the legislature.

act of God An unusual, extraordinary, and unexpected act caused solely by the forces of nature. A person cannot be held liable for an act of God.

addendum An appendix or addition to a document.

advance sheets Printed copies of judicial opinions published in looseleaf form shortly after the opinions are issued. These published opinions are later collected and published in bound form with the other reported cases which are issued over a longer period of time.

affirm In the case of an appellate court, to uphold the decision or judgment of the lower court after an appeal.

affirmative defense A defense that amounts to more than simply a denial of the allegations of the plaintiff's complaint. It sets up new matter which, if proven, could result in a judgment against the plaintiff even if all the allegations of the complaint are true.

amicus curiae (*Latin*) "Friend of the court." A person who is interested in the outcome of the case, but who is not a party, whom the court permits to file a brief for the purpose of providing the court with a position or a point of view which it might not otherwise have. An *amicus curiae* is often referred to simply as an *amicus*.

annotation 1. A notation, appended to any written work, which explains or comments upon its meaning. 2. A commentary that appears immediately following a printed statute and describes the application of the statute in actual cases. Such annotations, with the statutes on which they comment, are published in volumes known as *annotated statutes* or *annotated codes*. 3. A notation that follows an opinion of court printed in a court report, explaining the court's action in detail.

answer A pleading in response to a complaint. An answer may deny the allegations of the complaint, demur to them, agree with them, or introduce affirmative defenses intended to defeat the plaintiff's lawsuit or delay it.

appellant A party who appeals from a lower court to a higher court.

appellee A party against whom a case is appealed from a lower court to a higher court.

assignment 1. A transfer of property, or a right in property, from one person to another. 2. A designation or appointment.

attorney fees Compensation to which an attorney is entitled for his or her services.

bench trial A trial before a judge without a jury; a nonjury trial.

Bill of Rights The first 10 amendments to the United States Constitution. The Bill of Rights is the portion of the Constitution that sets forth the rights which are the fundamental principles of the United States and the foundation of American citizenship.

binding (mandatory) authority Previous decisions of a higher court or statutes that a judge must follow in reaching a decision in a case.

boilerplate language Language common to all legal documents of the same type. Attorneys maintain files of such standardized language for use where appropriate.

brief 1. A written statement submitted to a court for the purpose of persuading [the court] of the correctness of one's position. A brief argues the facts of the case and the applicable law, supported by citations of authority. 2. A text that an attorney prepares to guide him or her in the trial of a case. Called a *trial brief*, it can include lists of questions to be asked of various witnesses, points to be covered, and arguments to be made. 3. An outline of the published opinion in a case, made by an attorney or a paralegal for the purpose of understanding the case.

caption A heading. As applied in legal practice, when "caption" is used to mean "heading," it generally refers to the heading of a court paper.

case law The law as laid down in the decisions of the courts in similar cases that have previously been decided.

certificate A formal or official written declaration intended as an authentication of the fact or facts set forth therein.

citation Reference to authority (a case, article, or other text) on a point of law, by name, volume, and page or section of the court report or other book in which it appears.

common law Law found in the decisions of the courts rather than in statutes; judge-made law.

complaint The initial pleading in a civil action, in which the plaintiff alleges a cause of action and asks that the wrong done him or her be remedied by the court.

concurring opinion An opinion issued by one or more judges which agrees with the result reached by the majority opinion rendered by the court, but reaches that result for different reasons.

consequential damages Indirect losses; damages that do not result from the wrongful act itself, but from the result or the aftermath of the wrongful act.

consideration The reason a person enters into a contract; that which is given in exchange for performance or the promise to perform; the price bargained and paid; the inducement. Consideration is an essential element of a valid and enforceable contract. A promise to *refrain* from doing something one is entitled to do also constitutes consideration.

contract An agreement entered into, for adequate consideration, to do, or refrain from doing, a particular thing. The Uniform Commercial Code defines a contract as the total legal obligation resulting from the parties' agreement. In addition to adequate consideration, the transaction must involve an undertaking that is legal to perform, and there must be mutuality of agreement and obligation between at least two competent parties.

counterclaim A cause of action on which a defendant in a lawsuit might have sued the plaintiff in a separate action. Such a cause of action, stated in a separate division of a defendant's answer, is a counterclaim.

court of last resort (highest court) The highest court of a state; the Supreme Court of the United States; a court whose decisions are not subject to review by a higher court.

court of limited jurisdiction A court whose jurisdiction is limited to civil cases of a certain type or which involve a limited amount of money, or whose jurisdiction in criminal cases is confined to petty offenses and preliminary hearings. A court of limited jurisdiction is sometimes called a *court of special jurisdiction.*

damages The sum of money that may be recovered in the courts as financial reparation for an injury or wrong suffered as a result of breach of contract or a tortious act.

deed A document by which real property, or an interest in real property, is conveyed from one person to another.

defendant The person against whom an action is brought.

dissenting opinion A written opinion filed by a judge of an appellate court who disagrees with the decision of the majority of judges in a case, giving the reasons for his or her differing view. Often a dissenting opinion is written by one judge on behalf of one or more other dissenting judges.

distinguish To explain why a particular case is not precedent or authority with respect to the matter in controversy.

en banc Means "on the bench." A court, particularly an appellate court, with all the judges sitting together (*sitting en banc*) in a case.

enumerated powers Powers specifically granted by the Constitution to one of the three branches of government. Another term for enumerated powers is *express powers.*

executive branch 1. With the legislative branch and the judicial branch, one of the three divisions into which the Constitution separates the government of the United States. . . . The executive branch is primarily responsible for enforcing the laws. 2. A similar division in state government.

ex post facto law A law making a person criminally liable for an act that was not criminal at the time it was committed. The Constitution prohibits both Congress and the states from enacting such laws.

form A printed instrument with blank spaces for the insertion of such details as may be required to make it a complete document.

fruit of the poisonous tree doctrine The constitutional law doctrine that evidence, including derivative evidence, obtained as the result of an illegal search is inadmissible.

headnote A summary statement that appears at the beginning of a reported case to indicate the points decided by the case.

holding The proposition of law for which a case stands; the "bottom line" of a judicial decision.

injunction A court order that commands or prohibits some act or course of conduct. It is preventive in nature and designed to protect a plaintiff from irreparable injury to his or her property or property rights by prohibiting or commanding the doing of certain acts. An injunction is a form of equitable relief.

judicial branch 1. With the legislative branch and the executive branch, one of the three divisions into which the Constitution separates the government of the United States. . . . The judicial branch is primarily responsible for interpreting the laws. 2. A similar division in state government.

jury trial A trial in which the jurors are the judges of the facts and the court is the judge of the law. Trial by jury is guaranteed in all criminal cases by the Sixth Amendment, and in most civil cases by the Seventh Amendment.

landmark case (leading case) A court decision of great significance in establishing an important legal precedent.

law review A publication containing articles by law professors and other authorities, with respect to legal issues of current interest, and summaries of significant recent cases, written by law students. Another name for a law review is *law journal* or *legal periodical.*

legalese The use by lawyers of specialized words and phrases, rather than plain talk, when it serves no purpose; legal jargon.

legislative branch 1. With the judicial branch and the executive branch, one of the three divisions into which the Constitution separates the government of the United States. These branches of government are also referred to as *departments of government.* The legislative branch is primarily responsible for enacting the laws. 2. A similar division in state government.

legislative history Recorded events that provide a basis for determining the legislative intent underlying a statute enacted by a legislature. The records of legislative committee hearings and of debates on the floor of the legislature are among the sources for legislative history.

limit To restrain; to restrict; to impose a limitation.

liquidated damages A sum agreed upon by the parties at the time of entering into a contract as being payable by way of compensation for loss suffered in the event of a breach of contract; a sum similarly determined by a court in a lawsuit resulting from breach of contract.

majority opinion An opinion issued by an appellate court that represents the view of a majority of the members of the court.

memorandum of law A written statement submitted to a court for the purpose of persuading [the court] of the correctness of one's position. It is similar to a brief, although usually not as extensive.

notice 1. As defined by judicial decision, "information concerning a fact, actually communicated to a person by an authorized person, or actually derived by him from a proper source." . . . 3. Information; intelligence; knowledge.

on point Refers to a judicial opinion that, with respect to the facts involved and the applicable law, is similar to but not on all fours with another case.

overrule To disallow; to override; to reverse; to veto; to annul; to nullify. The overruling of precedent is the nullification of a prior decision as precedent; it occurs when the same court, or a higher court in a later case, establishes a different rule on the same point of law involved in the earlier case. When a decision is overruled, it is said to be "reversed."

parallel citation A citation to a court opinion or decision that is printed in two or more reporters.

penumbra doctrine The doctrine of constitutional law that the rights specifically guaranteed in the Bill of Rights have "penumbras" creating other rights that are not specifically enumerated.

per curiam opinion An opinion, usually of an appellate court, in which the judges are all of one view and the legal question is sufficiently clear that a full written opinion is not required and a one- or two-paragraph opinion suffices.

persuasive authority Authority that is neither binding authority nor precedent, but which a court may use to support its decision if it chooses.

plagiarism Stealing a person's ideas or copying or adapting his or her creative composition . . . and passing it off as one's own.

plaintiff A person who brings a lawsuit.

pleadings Formal statements by the parties to an action setting forth their claims or defenses. . . . The various kinds of pleadings, and the rules governing them, are set forth in detail in the Federal Rules of Civil Procedure and, with respect to pleading in state courts, by the rules of civil procedure of the several states. These rules of procedure abolished common law pleading.

plurality opinion An appellate court opinion joined in by less than a majority of the justices, but by more justices than the number joining any other concurring opinion.

prayer Portion of a bill in equity or a petition that asks for equitable relief and specifies the relief sought.

preamble A paragraph or clause at the beginning of a constitution, statute, or ordinance explaining the reasons for its enactment and the object or objects it seeks to accomplish.

precedent Prior decisions of the same court, or a higher court, which a judge must follow in deciding a subsequent case presenting similar facts and the same legal problem, even though different parties are involved and many years have elapsed.

quitclaim deed A deed that conveys whatever interest the grantor has in a piece of real property, as distinguished from the more usual deed which conveys a fee and contains various covenants, particularly title covenants. A quitclaim deed is often referred to simply as a "quitclaim."

recuse To disqualify oneself from sitting as a judge in a case, either on the motion of a party or on the judge's own motion, usually because of bias or some interest in the outcome of the litigation.

remand To return or send back. . . . The return of a case by an appellate court to the trial court for further proceedings, for new trial, or for entry of judgment in accordance with an order of the appellate court.

reporters Court reports, as well as official, published reports of cases decided by administrative agencies.

Restatement of the Law A series of volumes published by the American Law Institute, written by legal scholars, each volume or set of volumes covering a major field of the law. Each of the Restatements is, among other things, a statement of the law as it is generally interpreted and applied by the courts with respect to particular legal principles.

reverse To turn around or in an opposite direction. . . . A term used in appellate court opinions to indicate that the court has set aside the judgment of the trial court.

session laws The collected statutes enacted during a session of a legislature.

shepardizing Using a citator.

slip opinion A single judicial decision published shortly after it has been issued by the court and well before it is incorporated into a reporter.

specific performance The equitable remedy of compelling performance of a contract, as distinguished from an action at law for damages for breach of contract due to nonperformance. Specific performance may be ordered in circumstances where damages are an inadequate remedy.

stare decisis Means "standing by the decision." *Stare decisis* is the doctrine that judicial decisions stand as precedents for cases arising in the future. It is a fundamental policy of our law that, except in unusual circumstances, a court's determination on a point of law will be followed by courts of the same or lower rank in later cases presenting the same legal issue, even though different parties are involved and many years have elapsed.

statute A law enacted by a legislature; an act.

Statute of Frauds A statute, existing in one or another form in every state, that requires certain classes of contracts to be in writing and signed by the parties. Its purpose is to prevent fraud or reduce the opportunities for fraud. A contract to guarantee the debt of another is an example of an agreement that the statute of frauds requires to be in writing.

Statutes at Large An official publication of the federal government, issued after each session of Congress, which includes all statutes enacted by the Congress and all congressional resolutions and treaties, as well as presidential proclamations and proposed or ratified amendments to the Constitution.

style Caption or heading; the caption of a case.

subject matter jurisdiction The jurisdiction of a court to hear and determine the type of case before it.

supremacy clause The provision in Article VI of the Constitution that "this Constitution and the laws of the United States . . . shall be the supreme law of the land, and the judges in every state shall be bound thereby."

syllabus 1. The headnote of a reported case. 2. A summary outline of a course of study.

treatise A book that discusses, in depth, important principles in some area of human activity or interest, [such as] law or medicine.

Uniform Commercial Code One of the Uniform Laws, which has been adopted in much the same form in every state. It governs most aspects of commercial transactions, including sales, leases, negotiable instruments, deposits and collections, letters of credit, bulk sales, warehouse receipts, bills of lading and other documents of title, investment securities, and secured transactions.

verification A sworn statement certifying the truth of the facts recited in an instrument or document. Thus,. . ., a verified complaint is a pleading accompanied by an affidavit stating that the facts set forth in the complaint are true.

warranty deed A deed that contains title covenants.

will An instrument by which a person (the *testator*) makes a disposition of his or her property, to take effect after his or her death.

INDEX

Note: Entries designated "(m)" refer to material in sidebars in the margin. Those designated "(f)" refer to materials in figures or illustrations. Entries designated "(d)" refer to definitions in the margin.

A

B

C

D

E

F

M

N

U

V

W